Library of
Davidson College

THE DISOBEDIENT SPIRITS
AND
CHRISTIAN BAPTISM

AMS PRESS
NEW YORK

ACTA SEMINARII NEOTESTAMENTICI UPSALIENSIS
EDENDA CURAVIT A. FRIDRICHSEN
XIII.

THE DISOBEDIENT SPIRITS
AND
CHRISTIAN BAPTISM

A STUDY OF 1 PET. III. 19
AND ITS CONTEXT

BY

BO REICKE

EJNAR MUNKSGAARD, KØBENHAVN
1946

Library of Congress Cataloging in Publication Data

Reicke, Bo Ivar, 1914-
  The disobedient spirits and Christian baptism.

  Reprint of thesis—Uppsala. Originally
published: Kobenhaven: E. Munksgaard, 1946. (Acta
Seminarii Noetestamentici Upsaliensis; 13)
  Bibliography: p.
  Includes index.
  1. Bible. N. T. Peter, 1st III, 17-22—Criticism,
interpretation, etc. 2. Jesus Christ—Descent into hell.
I. Title. II. Series: Acta Seminarii Neotestamentici
Upsaliensis; 13.
BS2795.R45   1984   227'.9206   79-8117
ISBN 0-404-18430-8

AMS PRESS, INC.
56 East 13th Street, New York, N.Y. 10003

Reprinted from an original in the collections of the University of Chicago Library, edition of 1946, Copenhagen. Trim size and text area have been slightly altered. Original trim: 14.3 × 23.5 cm.; text: 10.8 × 17.7 cm.

MANUFACTURED IN THE
UNITED STATES OF AMERICA

v

CONTENTS

CONTENTS	v
NOTICE	viii
INTRODUCTION	1
Ch. i. EARLIER INTERPRETATIONS OF VERSE 19	7
Introductory Remarks	7
Fundamental Principles determining the Historical Development of the Problem	11
Scarcity of Records in the First Two Centuries	14
An Interesting Passage from Hippolytus' Writings	23
The Alexandrian School's Theory of Universal Salvation	27
The Greek Church of the Middle Ages	32
The Assyrian Church	34
Different Impulses in the Early Roman Church	36
The Evasive Interpretation of Augustine	37
The Augustinian Line in the Roman Church of the Middle Ages	39
The Augustinian Line and Certain Special Forms of its Development in Protestantism	40
The Later Roman Catholic Interpretation characterized by the Vulgate and by Cardinal Bellarmine	42
The Orthodox Lutheran Theory of a Triumphant and Judicial Sermon, and a New Form of it	44
The Theory of a Hopeful Gospel to Unbelievers generally accepted by Later Protestant Writers	47
The Interpolation Theory	49
Summary	50

Ch. ii. WHO ARE »THE SPIRITS» IN VERSE 19?	52
Connection with the Story of the Flood in Genesis	52
Possible to Think both of Fallen Angels and Souls of Men	52
Relations to the Book of Enoch	59
What can be learned from the Ideas of the Flood Beings in the Book of Enoch and Related Writings	70
Conclusion	90
Ch. iii. OTHER PRELIMINARY QUESTIONS IN VERSE 19	93
Who should be considered to have preached in iii. 19?	93
Christ as the New Enoch	100
What does ἐν ᾧ mean?	103
When and Where was the Kerygma performed?	115
The Content and the Effect of the Preaching	118
Ch. iv. COMPREHENSIVE STUDY OF VERSE 19	126
We must seek for the Author's Purpose with Verse 19	126
A Glance at the Context: Especially Verse 18 and the Parenesis in 13-16	127
The Solution of our Most Important Problem	130
The Beings from the Flood and the Pagan World	131
The Conversion of the Heathen	132
The Spirits of the Flood and the Earthly Powers	133
The Logical Connection with the Text	135
Ch. v. INVESTIGATION OF VERSES 20 AND 21 A	137
Verse 20	137
The First Part of Verse 21	143
Ch. vi. AN APPOSITIONAL ANTECEDENT INCORPORATED IN A RELATIVE CLAUSE	149
Relative Incorporation in General	149
Incorporation of an Apposition	150
Homer	152
The Great Dramatists	155
The Attic Prosaists	159
Examples from Earlier Hellenistic Writers	161

vii

The New Testament	165
Examples from Later Greek Texts	169
Concluding Remarks	172
Ch. vii. HOW BAPTISM IS CHARACTERIZED IN 21 B—22	173
Two Appositions to the Word βάπτισμα	173
The Special Meaning of συνείδησις ἀγαθή	174
What then is ἐπερώτημα?	182
Where does εἰς θεόν belong?	186
Purpose of the Negative Remarks about Physical Uncleanness	187
Comparison of Some Important Baptismal Texts of the Early Church	191
The Aim of the Christological Formulæ in Verses 21c—22	198
Ch. viii. COMPARATIVE EXAMINATION OF IV. 1—6	202
Verses 1—5	202
The Difficult Verse iv. 6	204
Conclusion	210
Ch. ix. BACKWARD GLANCE AT III. 17—18	211
The Special Import of the Thesis in Verse 17	211
What is the Tertium Comparationis in Verse 18?	213
Ch. x. PARALLELS TO THE WHOLE PERICOPE	220
The Close Parallel in 1 Pet. ii. 19—25	220
An Analogy Perhaps Still More Striking in Tit. iii	222
Other Points of Comparison in Titus	225
Conclusion	227
Ch. xi. PARALLELS TO THE APPEARANCE BEFORE »THE SPIRITS»	231
The Descent a Constituent Part of the Messianic Drama	231
A Preaching by the Saviour at His Death	234
The Transgressors from the Flood	235
The Transition from Verse 18 to 19 f. and thence to 21 f.	245
BIBLIOGRAPHY	249
INDEX OF SUBJECTS	270
INDEX OF BIBLICAL QUOTATIONS	272

NOTICE

We have tried to avoid using other abbreviations than such as can be understood without explanations, in order to make the reading of the book as easy as possible. One must only notice the following details:

P.G. = *Patrologiæ cursus completus*, Series Græca, ed. J. P. MIGNE.

P.L. = *op. cit.*, Patres ... Ecclesiæ Latinæ.

For Biblical or Jewish writings, works of Classical authors &c. we have used common names and abbreviations readily understood by everyone who has some knowledge of this literature. In doubtful cases see *e.g.* the well-known dictionaries of W. BAUER or H. G. LIDDELL, R. SCOTT & H. S. JONES, and G. KITTEL's *Theologisches Wörterbuch* (*cf.* the Bibliography below).

INTRODUCTION.

»Das ist eyn wunderlicher text unb eyn finsterer spruch, als freylich eyner ym newen Testament ist, das ich noch nicht gewiß weyß, was S. Peter meynet.»
M. LUTHER, *Epistel S. Petri gepredigt und erklärt*, erste Bearbeitung, 1523.[1]

The subject of this investigation is the passage in 1 Pet., iii. 17—22, which is so difficult to interpret and so much discussed: (17) κρεῖττον γὰρ ἀγαθοποιοῦντας, εἰ θέλοι τὸ θέλημα τοῦ θεοῦ, πάσχειν ἢ κακοποιοῦντας. (18) ὅτι καὶ Χριστὸς ἅπαξ περὶ ἁμαρτιῶν ὑπὲρ ἡμῶν ἀπέθανεν, δίκαιος ὑπὲρ ἀδίκων, ἵνα ἡμᾶς προσαγάγῃ τῷ θεῷ, θανατωθεὶς μὲν σαρκὶ ζωοποιηθεὶς δὲ πνεύματι· (19) ἐν ᾧ καὶ τοῖς ἐν φυλακῇ πνεύμασιν πορευθεὶς ἐκήρυξεν (20) ἀπειθήσασίν ποτε ὅτε ἀπεξεδέχετο ἡ τοῦ θεοῦ μακροθυμία ἐν ἡμέραις Νῶε, κατασκευαζομένης κιβωτοῦ, εἰς ἣν ὀλίγοι, τοῦτ' ἔστιν ὀκτὼ ψυχαί, διεσώθησαν δι' ὕδατος· (21) ὃ καὶ ὑμᾶς ἀντίτυπον νῦν σῴζει βάπτισμα, οὐ σαρκὸς ἀπόθεσις ῥύπου ἀλλὰ συνειδήσεως ἀγαθῆς ἐπερώτημα εἰς θεόν, δι' ἀναστάσεως Ἰησοῦ Χριστοῦ, (22) ὅς ἐστιν ἐν δεξιᾷ θεοῦ, πορευθεὶς εἰς οὐρανόν, ὑποταγέντων αὐτῷ ἀγγέλων καὶ ἐξουσιῶν καὶ δυνάμεων.

This famous passage, as is well known, presents great exegetic difficulties especially because of the curious indication in verse 19 of an address, a »preaching», to »the spirits in prison»:

ἐν ᾧ καὶ τοῖς ἐν φυλακῇ πνεύμασιν πορευθεὶς ἐκήρυξεν,

i.e. one of those passages in the Bible generally put forward as scriptural proof of the doctrine of Christ's so-called *descensus ad inferos*, Descent into Hell, which also is one item in the Apostles' Creed. This verse has also often been called a real *crux interpretum*, as

---
[1] »Weimar-Ausgabe», xii, 1891, p. 367.

in Cardinal BELLARMINE's words: *locus, qui semper obscurissimus habitus est*,[1] or SUAREZ': *Verba autem Divi Petri, quæ obscurissima sunt*,[2] or in the statement by H. HOLTZMANN: »(die) Stelle 3, 19, die freilich zugleich als locus vexatissimus eine Leidensgeschichte durchzumachen hatte, wie kaum ein anderer Vers in der Bibel ...»[3]

It is probable that every reader of 1 Pet. has the impression that verses 17—22, or at least 19—22, interrupt the admonitions and comforting words of the context and draw his thought to quite other, apparently completely irrelevant, ideas. One comes upon several Christological, mythical and other notions which seem to arise quite at random, by free association of ideas. And these notions do not seem to agree, even approximately, either with the general theology of 1 Pet. or, on the whole, with the sphere of ideas in the N.T. Even in the literature of the Ancient Church the writers do not seem always to have been familiar with the peculiar notions in 1 Pet. iii. 19 ff.

Certain interpreters have found this passage so alien to its context that they deny its authenticity and term it an interpolation.

But even among those who are not so radical great uncertainty has always prevailed as to the correct explanation of the passage, in spite of the fact that it has been so closely studied. The most learned of modern commentators of 1 Pet., URBAN HOLZMEISTER, *Commentarius in epistulas SS. Petri et Judæ apostolorum*, i, 1937, in a special bibliography,[4] gives 53 works from modern times on 1 Pet. iii. 19 without even then having exhausted the number. Yet no certain positive results, no indication of norms, can be discerned in theological research, and on most of the questions the disagreement is rather wide.

The commentators have always differed greatly as to the actual

---

[1] R. BELLARMINUS, *Disputationes de controversiis*, i. 2 (*De Christo*). 4 (*De anima Christi*). 13, ed. 1586, col. 545.

[2] FR. SVAREZ, *Commentariorum ac disputationum in tert. part. D. Thomæ* tomus ii, *qu*. xliii. 3, ed. 1598, p. 483.

[3] H. HOLTZMANN, *Höllenfahrt im Neuen Testament*, *Arch. f. Rel.-wiss.* xi, 1908, p. 290.

[4] P. 307 ff.

INTRODUCTION 3

purport of verses 19—22. In one commentary is to be found one opinion, in another, a different one, and the views of Catholics, Protestants, and others vary in the highest degree. Often a writer has to confess that his attempt at explanation is only a temporary expedient put forward for lack of a better and more certain one. It also seems extremely difficult to understand the connection of the passage with its context. If unwilling to avoid difficulties radically by some hypothesis of interpolation, one readily speaks of a digression, an excursus, or something similar. In short, disagreement and uncertainty are quite great among the commentators.

Of course, there are also some writers who appear to be very confident in their statements regarding this passage, but often it is easy to discover that they have not analysed the problem with due scientific scepticism and historical method but mostly put forward conventional doctrines. Nevertheless the best support for a more detailed comprehension of our passage is to be found just in the most intelligent commentaries. But it is not always easy to choose out the best theory in every case from among all the varying propositions! And no commentary can be so profound as to give more than general statements. This is true also of one or two great commentaries on 1 Pet. recently published.

One very commendable modern work is the *Commentarius in epistulas SS. Petri et Judæ* by U. HOLZMEISTER, which has already been mentioned. This gives in a concentrated form a wonderfully rich and logically arranged collection of quotations from the earlier interpretations of iii. 19. It also contains some valuable observations in the very analysis of this passage. But the analytical presentation had naturally to be very short on many points and many enigmas are left unsolved.

Another great commentary on 1 Pet. has appeared during the writing of this presentation: E. G. SELWYN, *The First Epistle of St. Peter*, 1946. This is perhaps the most sensible explanation of the Epistle ever published. We are very glad that in many respects our conception agrees with Selwyn's wise views. Above all we appreciate his successful efforts to find the logical connections in the whole context. But there are also several differences of opinion. We think it is possible to go even still more deeply into the main question, viz. the purpose of verse 19 seen against the background of the context. Besides this there are details and especially many linguistic problems that need a more profound exploration than can be given in a commentatory presentation, however exhaustive.

It might perhaps be expected that in special treatises on our subject more certain results and more profound observations should be found, than in the commentaries. Actually however, not much material of that kind is accessible. Many presentations have been devoted to the Descent dogma in general, but their authors have naturally not been so interested in our text itself that they could treat its many detailed problems with sufficient thoroughness. And even the few more profound investigations of this passage in 1 Pet. give an impression of insufficiency.

We can, for example, mention two such solid and admirably learned works as J. A. MacCulloch, *The Harrowing of Hell*, 1930, and Joseph Kroll, *Gott und Hölle*, 1932. It is an obvious deficiency in these works as regards our present subject that though they deal very thoroughly with Descent *motifs* in general in Christianity and in other religions, they have not applied so deep and penetrating an analysis to 1 Pet. iii. 17—22 as was needed. Thus even these specialist treatises give the impression of uncertainty on the subject we shall study here. Further, they are not quite agreed in their actual, main province, either as to method or result.[1]

There are only two really important modern works which analyse with greater thoroughness the language and theology of this passage. They are P. Johs. Jensen, *Læren om Kristi Nedfart till de döde*, 1903, and Karl Gschwind, *Die Niederfahrt Christi in die Unterwelt*, 1911. These works, highly commendable as to method, penetrating and also very learned, are based on several exegetic principles which in the present writer's view are especially reasonable and estimable, above all in their efforts to pay attention to the connected text and observe the logical relationship with the context. However, neither Jensen's nor Gschwind's book has had very much effect on subsequent scientific literature. In the case of the former this is evidently due to language difficulties, for his book is in Danish, but in the case of Gschwind, probably to the fact that many scholars have felt obliged to dissociate themselves from the relatively unique results to which he had come just in the exposition of 1 Pet. iii. 19 and the adjoining verses. This explanation could have been equally applied to Jensen's book if its language had not condemned it to a regrettable isolation: for Jensen has, curiously enough, interpreted this passage in a way which very much

---

[1] Curiously enough these books seem to have been written quite independently of one another. Kroll, for instance, does not mention MacCulloch's book, which was published a few years earlier. — On the other hand Kroll had clearly been thoroughly occupied with his subject for many years, as appears, for example, from his *Beiträge zum Descensus ad Inferos*, Vorles. Braunsb., 1922, p. 2.

INTRODUCTION 5

reminds one of Gschwind although there is no interpendence, as Gschwind states that he could not make use of Jensen's book.[1] As regards the exposition of 1 Pet. iii. 17—22, there is also much in these two books that we feel compelled to take in a rather different way from these two authors. This is true also of many essential points. It seems that the results of the textual interpretation ought to be somewhat different, based on even more profound studies of the religious background and of the linguistic problems, and even more conformable to the context in 1 Pet.

A Polish dissertation by SEWERYN KOWALSKI, Zstąpienie do piekieł Chrystuza Pana wedle nauki św Piotra Apostoła (Razbiór krytyczny Dz. II, 27, 31 i 1 Piotr. III, 19, 20; IV, 6), 1938, has not been available to us on account of well-known external circumstances. Nor is it, probably, available to the international public except through some reviews in scientific publications. A detailed review by F. KTONIECKI in *Biblica* xxi, 1940,[2] appears to give a very good idea of the contents. From this it seems that Kowalski keeps rather faithfully to the traditional Catholic lines.

There is a short but suggestive and independently purposeful analysis of 1 Pet. iii. 19—22 in a recently published dissertation by a Swedish investigator, P. LUNDBERG, *La typologie baptismale dans l'ancienne Église*, 1942.[3] It was this book which drew the present writer's attention to the interesting problems of this passage. Lundberg stressed the importance of studying the »typological» combinations in these verses. But he, too, had no room for a more profound exposition, especially as what he does say mainly purports to support his fundamental thesis of the »baptism for death», and therefore many problems remain unsolved.

Thus although there are several modern works, some quite large and learned, which deal with 1 Pet. iii. 17—22, none of them gives a really logical and historically satisfying explanation of all the many obscure problems in these verses. So we need such an explanation, firstly for exegetic and dogmatic reasons — among other things it is important to try to understand the writer's purpose with his peculiar observation about the »preaching», and to understand the logical connections in the whole context — but secondly also for linguistic reasons, for there are many expressions

---

[1] K. GSCHWIND, *Die Niederfahrt Christi*, p. xv. — This must really be regretted, as otherwise JENSEN's book could have been extraordinarily useful just for Gschwind, as also for all later researchers who have studied this subject but have been restrained from reading Jensen's erudite and acute work.
[2] Pp. 96—99.
[3] Pp. 98—116.

6   INTRODUCTION

in these verses (particularly in verse 21) that have not yet been explained in a linguistically satisfactory way.

For these reasons we may perhaps be allowed to make a new attempt to shed light upon this much discussed subject.

*

In attempting to solve the different problems in 1 Pet. iii. 17—22 it is well to begin with iii. 19, for this verse contains the real, main difficulty in this passage. On the one hand, verses 17f. cannot be said to present so many difficult and outstanding problems, at least not on a first consideration: and on the other, verses 20—22 are logically and intimately connected with verse 19 so that they must to a great extent be explained from that starting-point, and in spite of all peculiar difficulties they contain problems of a rather subordinate character in relation to the curious statement about preaching to the »spirits» in verse 19.

CHAPTER I.

EARLIER INTERPRETATIONS OF VERSE 19.

INTRODUCTORY REMARKS.

This review is to form a background of our investigation. Its real object is not to draw conclusions from early tradition as to how the original meaning of 1 Pet. iii. 19 should be interpreted. Tradition has a rather limited value in this connection for, as the reader will find, we have none direct from early Christian times on which to base our reasoning, and the history of later interpretations shows so many opposed ideas that it is impossible only on the ground of frequency or the high authority of their authors to designate a certain attitude as most legitimate or most reliable. Our purpose in giving this review is to contribute some illumination to the history of Christian ideas in a certain connection. This passage is of great interest for all who study the development of Christian dogmata, because so often in the history of theology it has been connected with the dogma of Christ's descent to the underworld, and for this reason has also been important in discussions on the Apostles' Creed.

We cannot go more deeply into the general history of the Descent ideas — although it has perhaps many parts which deserve to be investigated more closely than has been done in the literature available on the subject.[1] But we must make a few short remarks

---
[1] Selected literature on the history of the *descensus* dogma: J. A. DIETEL-MAIER, *Historia dogmatis de descensu Christi ad inferos*, 1762; J. L. KÖNIG, *Die Lehre von Christi Höllenfahrt*, 1842; E. GÜDER, *Die Lehre von der Erscheinung Jesu Christi unter den Todten*, 1853; FRED. HUIDEKOPER, *The Belief of the First Three Centuries concerning Christ's Mission to the Under-*

in order to illuminate our outlook on this *motif* in general and its relations to 1 Pet. iii. 19. The Descent dogma of the Christian Church has wide and intricate connections. Going through it in the literature of the Ancient Church,

---

world, 1854, 7th ed. 1887; C. H. G. DE ZEZSCHWITZ, *Petri Apostoli de Christi ad inferos descensu sententia ex loco nobilissimo I Ep. III, 19 eruta, exacta ad epistolæ argumentum*, 1857; J. KÖRBER, *Die katholische Lehre von der Höllenfahrt Jesu Christi*, 1860; ALEX. SCHWEIZER, *Hinabgefahren zur Hölle, als Mythus ohne biblische Begründung durch Auslegung der Stelle 1 P. 3, 17—22 nachgewiesen*, 1868; E. H. PLUMPTRE, *The Spirits in Prison*, 1884; JOH. MARTIN USTERI, *Hinabgefahren zur Hölle*, 1886; FR. SPITTA, *Christi Predigt an die Geister (1 Petr. 3, 19ff.)*, 1890; C. BRUSTON, *La descente du Christ aux enfers, d'après les Apôtres et d'après l'Eglise*, 1897; C. CLEMEN, *»Niedergefahren zu den Toten«*, 1900; M. LAUTERBURG, Höllenfahrt Christi, *Realencycl. f. prot. Theol.* viii, 1900; W. KELLY, *The Preaching to the Spirits in Prison*, 1900; P. J. JENSEN, *Læren om Kristi Nedfart til de döde*, 1903; J. TURMEL, *La descente du Christ aux enfers*, 1903; J. MONNIER, *La descente aux enfers*, 1904; W. BAUER, *Das Leben Jesu im Zeitalter der Apokryphen*, 1909, pp. 246ff., M. LANDAU, *Hölle und Fegfeuer*, 1909; K. GSCHWIND, *Die Niederfahrt Christi*, 1911; H. QUILLIET, Descente de Jésus aux enfers, *Dict. de théol. cath.*, 1911; C. NORDBLAD, *Föreställningen om Kristi hadesfärd*, 1912; K. W. CH. SCHMIDT, *Die Darstellung von Christi Höllenfahrt*, 1915; C. SCHMIDT, Der Descensus ad inferos in der alten Kirche, *Texte und Untersuchungen* xliii, 1919; W. BOUSSET, Zur Hadesfahrt Christi, *Zeitschr. f. d. neut. Wiss.* xix, 1919/20, pp. 50ff.; GANSCHINIETZ, Katabasis, *Pauly's Real-Encyclopädie*, 1919; F. CABROL, Descente du Christ aux enfers d'après la liturgie, *Dict. d'arch. chrét. et de lit.*, 1920; cols. 682—693; A. DE MEESTER, Descente du Christ aux enfers dans les liturgies orientales, *ibid.*, cols. 693 —696; J. A. MACCULLOCH, *The Harrowing of Hell*, 1930; J. KROLL, *Gott und Hölle*, 1932; J. CHAINE, Descente du Christ aux enfers, *Dict. de la Bible*, Suppl., ii, 1934; K. PRÜMM, *Der christliche Glaube und die altheidnische Welt*, ii, 1935, pp. 15ff.; U. HOLZMEISTER, *Commentarius*, 1937; E. VOGELSANG, Weltbild und Kreuzestheologie in den Höllenfahrtsstreitigkeiten der Reformationszeit, *Arch. f. Reformationsgesch.* xxxviii, 1941, pp. 91ff.; E. G. SELWYN, *The First Epistle*, 1946. — We regret that many of these older books have not been available to us. This lack could, however, to a certain extent be compensated by the circumstance that the solid works of later date by CLEMEN, JENSEN, MONNIER, QUILLIET, GSCHWIND, MAC CULLOCH, HOLZMEISTER &c. may contain practically all the materials collected by earlier scholars, besides a great amount of new material. For the partial assertion of older scholars that the Early Fathers in general thought of a descent with salvation of all the dead, see JENSEN, *op. cit.*, pp. 11ff., GSCHWIND, *op. cit.*, pp. xivf.

as well as of later times, gives us the general impression that in so far as this dogma presupposes a certain activity in the underworld, and not merely a passive sojourn there, as in Jonah's case, three main types can be distinguished: (1) that Christ subdues Hell by violence, which is often described as a veritable *Höllenstürmung*, (2) that He sets free the dead or some of the dead from the power of Hell,[1] and (3) that He proclaims a message for the dead in general, or for certain dead people.[2] These various notions are often separate but can also occur intermingled. The most usual combination is of the first and second.

If verse 19 is at all to be associated with the Descent, it should primarily be regarded as a special form of the third type. This type, however, contains much more than can be applied to verse 19. We have here to include the whole important complex of ideas which treats of Christ's appearance to the righteous of the O.T.,[3] and these ideas evidently imply something quite different from 1 Pet. iii. 19 with its disobedient »spirits» from the days of Noah. It is therefore clear that this verse represents, at the most, a small, distinctive part of the whole widely ramifying Descent dogma.[4] Similarly it is clear that whether or not there was originally any connection between the verse and the dogma, the idea

---

[1] It is chiefly in these two *motifs*, conceived as one, that J. KROLL is interested in *Gott und Hölle*, 1932. Here also we have a gigantic amount of material for illuminating them. Formerly these two ideas, which are connected with much imaginative mythology, specially interested R. REITZENSTEIN in several of his works, which need not be listed here (see J. Kroll, op. cit. p. 2 note 3, p. 3 note 3), and W. BOUSSET in *Kyrios Christos*, 1913, 2. Aufl. 1921, pp. 26ff., and in Zur Hadesfahrt Christi, *Zeitschr. f. d. neut. Wiss.* xix, 1919/20, pp. 50ff.

[2] C. SCHMIDT, Der Descensus ad inferos in der alten Kirche, in P. LACAU, C. SCHMIDT & I. WAJNBERG, *Gespräche Jesu mit seinen Jüngern nach der Auferstehung*, 1919, Exkurs ii, p. 453ff., is directed to the study of such notions of the Descent.

[3] A closer examination shows that it is only this special formulation of the idea that interested C. SCHMIDT in his Der Descensus ad inferos in der alten Kirche, mentioned above.

[4] Many researchers agree on this. See, for example, C. SCHMIDT, Der Descensus ad inferos, p. 464, note 2, J. A. MACCULLOCH, *The Harrowing of Hell*, ch. xv, pp. 240ff.

10   EARLIER INTERPRETATIONS OF VERSE 19   [CH.

of Christ's descent occurs usually in the Church's teaching also in association with several other places in the O.T. and N.T.: places which often play a far more important role there, *e.g.* Ps. xv (xvi). 10, Matt. xii. 40, Acts ii.23ff., Rom. x. 7, Eph. iv. 8ff.[1] The verse on which we are concentrating is really not always so important in the Descent dogma of the Ancient Church. When the Fathers of the Church do touch upon the Descent it generally seems that they quote 1 Pet. iii. 19 more in passing and are actually depending on a more general Descent conception. It can thus be stated that the theory of Descent could have existed to a great extent independently of iii. 19,[2] and that this verse plays no necessary or essential part in its history.

On the other hand there is no denying that our verse really often occurs in connection with the Descent in ecclesiastical literature, and has contributed greatly to the later framing of the dogma by different theologians at different times. It is this procedure, the secondary effect of 1 Pet. iii. 19 on the Descent dogma, that we hope to illuminate through the following review of its different interpretations.

We hope to do this not in a more exhaustive but in a more explanatory way than earlier writers, just by concentrating upon this verse without including the other intricate connections of the dogma, and by striving to draw into prominence the characteristic historical lines and the driving logical forces in the process, so that it will not be merely a loose accumulation of different opinions.[3] In abundance of details our review will in no way

---

[1] One indisputable result of P. J. JENSEN, *Læren om Kristi Nedfart*, 1903, pp. 233ff., and K. GSCHWIND, *Die Niederfahrt Christi*, 1911, pp. 145ff.; yet these two authors are not quite in agreement as to which passages are to be considered.

[2] C. CLEMEN, »Niedergefahren zu den Toten», 1900, does not pay due regard to this. This book is also rightly opposed by the authors mentioned above, JENSEN and GSCHWIND. See also *e.g.* W. BOUSSET, *Kyrios Christos*, 2. Aufl. 1921, p. 27, note 6.

[3] In spite of the great learning in all the available modern works on the history of the Descent dogma, it is hard to find real interest and ability to show any system in its chequered history. We need a survey with more clear

compete with certain earlier specialist presentations. The chief emphasis will be laid on observing factors of principle and on descriptions of early times.

FUNDAMENTAL PRINCIPLES DETERMINING THE HISTORICAL DEVELOPMENT OF THE PROBLEM.

Where do we find the earliest interpretation of 1 Pet. iii. 19? Well, actually the history of this problem's interpretation can be said to begin within 1 Pet., viz. in a few verses farther on in the same Epistle, that is in iv. 6, also a much discussed verse: εἰς τοῦτο γὰρ καὶ νεκροῖς εὐηγγελίσθη, ἵνα κριθῶσι μὲν κατὰ ἀνθρώπους σαρκί, ζῶσι δὲ κατὰ θεὸν πνεύματι. It seems at first sight that these words must be interpreted as referring to Christ's *descensus ad inferos*; at least that is the reader's first impression, if he knows anything at all about this dogma. Further, at first sight there seems very good reason to presume that the writer of the Epistle here recalls the recently mentioned preaching to the »spirits in prison» in iii. 19. If this is so, and iv. 6 really refers to a descent of Christ into the Realm of Death as the first conception of the passage must be, the writer has himself in this verse commented on iii. 19 and thereby made it clear that the latter must be taken as referring to a descent when Christ preached the Gospel to certain dead people. We shall later on[1] try to examine the real relation between

---
lines. It is only E. GÜDER, *Die Lehre von der Erscheinung Jesu Christi unter den Todten*, 1853, to some extent, and above all P. J. JENSEN, *Læren om Kristi Nedfart*, 1903, which seem to rise above the purely listing style. But these books cannot give such a lucid report just of 1 Pet. iii. 19.

U. HOLZMEISTER's *Commentarius* is very meritorious for a meticulous account of different interpretations of 1 Pet. iii. 19 from a systematically logical aspect, but it gives no conception of the lines in the history of ideas. When Holzmeister says, declaring that he has purposely refrained from so doing: *Omisimus inquirere, utrum et quomodo auctores inter se connectantur seu dependentia ut aiunt litteraria tractare. Arduus enim labor et, ut in tali re, sterilis esset* (p. 317), it is an act of resignation which would have béen unnecessary had he only known, for example, Jensen's fine effort to discern certain historical lines.

[1] Below, ch. viii.

these two passages. Here, however, it may at once be stated that, of course, 1 Pet. iv. 6 must have affected all interpreters of iii. 19, whether ancient or modern, chiefly in the direction of a Descent theory, for this must be the spontaneous, unreflecting conception of this passage — and there are perhaps also certain scientific reasons for such an interpretation.

It must also be conceded that this conception has lately shown itself to be by far the most usual both in commentaries and other scientific or popular presentations.

Such a theory, however, has not always dominated the interpretation of iii. 19. In some quarters there was decided unwillingness to consider any *descensus*. And even among those who accepted this verse as evidence of Christ's descent, there has often been great divergence of opinion as to what this descent and the preaching connected with it implies, for the theory of a gospel of hope for unbelievers in Hell has certainly not been generally accepted in earlier epochs.[1] It must be assumed there has been a wide range of different theories at different times and in different environments.

Let us state at once what is in our own opinion the basic reason for the many divergences in the interpretation of verse 19. Certain dogmatic and practical difficulties easily arise, if these words are allowed to indicate that the hardened sinners from the time of Noah received forgiveness at Christ's descent and were even saved from Hell. That opens a way for repentance and salvation after death to any kind of sinners, and in this way, of course, all responsibility for behaviour in the earthly life is removed. One is then easily faced with just such question as MARTIN LUTHER formulates in his interesting *Sendbrief über die Frage, ob auch jemand, ohne Glauben verstorben, selig werden möge* (to Hans v. Rechenberg), 1522, in the following words: »Das were wol eyn ander frag, ob Got etlichen ym sterben oder nach dem sterben den glawben kont

---

[1] As pointed out by P. J. JENSEN and K. GSCHWIND (*cf.* above, pp. 7 f., note 1), the above-mentioned works by J. A. DIETELMAIER, J. L. KÖNIG, E. GÜDER, J. KÖRBER &c. were influenced by a too great trust in the historical importance of this conception, especially during the first centuries.

EARLIER INTERPRETATIONS OF VERSE 19

geben und also durch den glawben kont selig machen. Wer wollt daran zweyffeln, das er das thun kunne. Aber das ers thue, kan man nicht beweyssen. Denn wyr wol lesen, das er todten zuvor widder auff erweckt hatt und also den glawben geben, Er thue nu hierynn, was er thue, Er gebe glawben aber [= oder] nicht, so ists unmüglich, das on glawb yemand selig werde, sonst wer alle predig und Euangelij und glawben vergeblich, falsch und verfurlich, syntemal das gantz Euangelion den glawben nöttig macht.»[1] To such or similar reflections one is driven if iii. 19 is interpreted as indicating Christ preaching salvation to the inveterate sinners from the days of the Flood.

Therefore the interpreter has two alternatives: (a) If he wishes to retain the theory of Descent and a preaching of a gospel of hope to the unbelievers in Hell, which is the first impression received on reading, especially because of iv. 6, he must neglect the dogmatic and practical doubts which follow from this theory; (b) but if he cannot overcome the doubts indicated, he must either deny that a descent to the dead is mentioned here, or at least try to apprehend the preaching then in a less generously positive way, e.g. by considering it as a pronouncement of judgement or as a manifestation of power, or by assuming that the »spirits« were such as had managed to improve in some way, or that it refers to young people or other rather innocent ones among the antidiluvian generation.

Nearly all the interpretations of this verse 19, from ancient times to our own days, are confined to these alternatives. The varying theories are mainly due to the need to take up a position with regard to the dogmatic and practical doubts now mentioned. It is in these varied positions that we find the most significant explanation of the different interpretations. The various renderings of the verse are predominantly based on dogmatic and practical, not purely exegetic considerations.

It must be observed, however, that the views are also to some extent bound by tradition, in that a preference for a certain alternative may prove to be characteristic of a certain epoch and a certain

---

[1] »Weimar-Ausgabe» x. 2, 1907, p. 325.

environment, even although there are, of course, exceptions and differences. Thus it can be stated already here that the direct theory of a preaching of the Gospel to the unbelievers in Hell was chiefly accepted by the ancient Alexandrian School of theology and by the Protestant exegetists of the nineteenth century, that the commentators of the Middle Ages would not see in this verse any mention of the *descensus ad inferos*, and that modern Catholic theology mostly tends to regard those who heard Jesus preaching in the »prison» as sinners already converted.

SCARCITY OF RECORDS IN THE FIRST TWO CENTURIES.

Curiously enough it seems that illuminating quotations, interpretations or reflections of 1 Pet. iii. 19 are lacking in the oldest literature of the Church.[1] No writer before Hippolytus, Clement of Alexandria and Origenes[2] seems to have touched upon this verse.[3]

Now these three authorities mention iii. 19 in clear connection with the Descent. As this dogma was certainly not new in their

---

[1] It is thus misleading to say, as so many do, and even F. KTONIECKI in *Biblica* xxi, 1904, p. 97, clearly with the support of the work by S. KOWALSKI mentioned above (p. 5), that the first four centuries are practically united in interpreting 1 Pet. iii. 19—iv. 6 as to the *descensus ad inferos*. We know too little about the earlier times, and an opposition to such an understanding is also possible. The quoted statement is probably due to a faulty traditional conception, generally inherited through these fundamental older works, of which the one-sided and tendentious character was revealed, as we have just mentioned, by P. J. JENSEN and K. GSCHWIND (p. 12, note 1).

[2] See below, pp. 23ff., 27ff.

[3] *Cf.* P. J. JENSEN, *Læren om Kristi Nedfart*, p. 33, where the writer does not know the Hippolytus text which we shall study later and therefore only mentions the Alexandrians. Curiously enough GSCHWIND also mentions only the Alexandrian theologians as the first who showed that they had used 1 Pet. iii, 19, although Gschwind had himself drawn attention to the Hippolytus text mentioned, *Die Niederfart Christi*, p. 17. — It is remarkable that C. CLEMEN who, in his comprehensive book »*Niedergefahren zu den Toten*», 1900, tries to show that from the first 1 Pet. iii. 19 had had an intimate connection with the Descent item in the Creed, did not deal more in detail with the difficulty which these above-mentioned circumstances ought to have caused him: but because of the prevailing vagueness on this point in general theological literature he very likely did not think of it.

EARLIER INTERPRETATIONS OF VERSE 19

time — for it was clearly developed already in the writings of the Apostolic Fathers, as we shall see below — can we not think that older theologians were also able to use this verse in their Descent doctrine, although we have no direct traces of this fact? Primarily this question must be answered in the negative. Some of the theologians of the Early Church have put forward lines of thought in connection with the Descent theory which not only differ, at least from those of Clement and Origenes, which are more specialised, but also make it *a priori* rather difficult to consider our passage as a suitable link in the theory of these ancient writers. We here refer to the old opinions, fairly well represented in the Christian literature of the second century, that at this Descent there took place a preaching of the Gospel to the righteous of the O.T., or their release — the righteous who are thought to long for the Messiah and His appearing.[1] As an example of this may be mentioned *Ign. Ad Magn.* ix. 2: πῶς ἡμεῖς δυνησόμεθα ζῆσαι χωρὶς αὐτοῦ, οὗ καὶ οἱ προφῆται μαθηταὶ ὄντες τῷ πνεύματι ὡς διδάσκαλον αὐτὸν προσεδόκουν; καὶ διὰ τοῦτο, ὃν δικαίως ἀνέμενον, παρὼν ἤγειρεν αὐτοὺς ἐκ νεκρῶν (*cf. Ad Philad.* ix. 1: αὐτὸς ὢν θύρα τοῦ πατρός, δι' ἧς εἰσέρχονται Ἀβραὰμ καὶ Ἰσαὰκ καὶ Ἰακὼβ καὶ οἱ προφῆται καὶ οἱ ἀπόστολοι καὶ ἡ ἐκκλησία, πάντα ταῦτα εἰς ἑνότητα θεοῦ),[2] and the well-known passage of the Apostles' descent and preaching to the righteous of the O.T. in *Herm. Sim.* ix. 16, compare *Iren. Contra hær.* iv. 27. 2: ... *descendisse, evangelizantem et illis adventum*

---

[1] C. SCHMIDT, in his *Der Descensus ad inferos*, desired to show that this reference to the just of the Old Covenant was the primary Christian *descensus* idea; see especially p. 546 f. J. A. MACCULLOCH similarly has declared that the revelation to these just was the first answer to the question of what Christ did in Hades, *The Harrowing of Hell*, p. 315 ff.

[2] *Ign. Trall.* ix. 1, who is often referred to in this connection (*e.g.* in J. MONNIER, *La Descente*, 1904, p. 69 f.; K. GSCHWIND, *Die Niederfahrt Christi*, p. 223; J. A. MACCULLOCH, *The Harrowing of Hell*, p. 84), does not belong here, because the purpose behind the words βλεπόντων τῶν ἐπουρανίων καὶ ἐπιγείων καὶ ὑποχθονίων in connection with Jesus' death is not at all to show that He moved to these different places, but simply that His death was a generally testified fact (*cf.* also ἀληθῶς in the preceding), not an apparent death, as the Gnostics said.

suum, remissione peccatorum exsistente his qui credunt in eum. Crediderunt autem in eum omnes qui sperabant in eum, id est ... iusti et prophetæ et patriarchæ ...,[1] and Tert. De anima 55: descendit in inferiora terrarum, ut illic Patriarchas et Prophetas compotes sui faceret.[2] Where this idea of the Descent predominates we cannot expect at once to find 1 Pet. iii. 19 with its disobedient »spirits» in the same connection. It might even be assumed that these authors deliberately avoided this passage in connection with the Descent theory, because it was difficult to harmonize it with their general teaching about the Descent and the Salvation: i.e. that the dogmatic and practical doubts already mentioned had brought about restriction on this point.

However, we have some pieces of evidence which can indirectly indicate that at least 1 Pet. iv. 6 had already earlier been conceived as having Christ's descent in view. It is a complex of ideas which can be connected with an apocryphal so-called »Jeremiah-*logion*» quoted in several places by Justin the Martyr and Irenæus. The former in his dialogue with Trypho reproaches the Jews for having removed several passages in the O.T. which point to Christ, and then gives the following words as removed by them from the Book of the prophet Jeremiah: ἐμνήσθη δὲ Κύριος ὁ Θεὸς ἀπὸ Ἰσραὴλ τῶν νεκρῶν αὐτοῦ, τῶν κεκοιμημένων εἰς γῆν χώματος, καὶ κατέβη πρὸς αὐτοὺς ἀναγγελίσασθαι αὐτοῖς τὸ σωτήριον αὐτοῦ, *Just. Dial.*, ch. 72.[3] Irenæus quotes the same words, in somewhat different forms, in *Contra hær.* iii. 20. 4, iv. 22. 1, iv. 33. 1, iv. 33. 12, v. 31. 1,[4] and in *Epid.*, ch. 78, now attributing the words to Jeremiah, now to Isaiah, now to undetermined sources.[5] In *Epid.*, ch. 78, Irenæus

---

[1] *P.G.* vii, col. 1058 B.
[2] *P.L.* ii, cols. 742 f.
[3] *P.G.* vi, col. 645 A—B.
[4] *P.G.* vii, col. 945, &c.
[5] Regarding this so-called Jeremiah-*logion* or -*apocryphon*, see *i.a.* L. ATZBERGER, *Die christliche Eschatologie*, 1890, p. 139, A. RESCH, *Agrapha*, 2. Aufl. 1906, pp. 320 ff.; J. MONNIER, *La première Épître de l'apôtre Pierre*, 1900, p. 206 note 1; C. CLEMEN, »*Niedergefahren zu den Toten*», 1900, p. 142;

expresses himself as follows: »And by Jeremiah He so makes known His death and His descent to Hades saying: 'The Lord, the Holy One of Israel, remembered His dead, those who had formerly slept in the dust of the earth, and descended to them to preach His glad tidings and to deliver them.' Here the reasons of His death are made evident, for His descent to Hades was salvation to the dead.»[1] In the *Gospel of Peter* there seems to be a reflection of these words of Jeremiah, or at least an example of the same notion, in the scene where two men come up from Jesus' grave supporting a third, *i.e.* the risen Saviour, and accompanied by the Cross. A voice is then heard from Heaven which says: ἐκήρυξας τοῖς κοιμωμένοις; and the reply is heard from the Cross: ναί, the *Gospel of Peter*, 35ff.[2] The resemblance to the Jeremiah-*logion* is quite clear. Certain associations with the *Gospel of Nicodemus* can also be made with the *Gospel of Peter* as a connecting link, for in the former the Cross plays a similarly important part in Christ's descent, just as in the scene quoted from the latter, *e.g.* in the Saviour's preaching to Adam and all his descendants: Δεῦρο μετ' ἐμοῦ πάντες ὅσοι διὰ τοῦ ξύλου οὗ ἥψατο οὗτος ἐθανατώθητε· πάλιν γὰρ ὑμᾶς διὰ ξύλου τοῦ σταυροῦ πάντας ἐγὼ ἰδοὺ ἀνιστῶν, *Ev. Nicod.* II, ch. viii (xxiv). Further Matt. xxvii. 52 can be taken in this

---

J. H. A. HART, *The Exp.*, vii. 3, 1907, p. 68; A. HARNACK, *Texte und Unters.* xxxi. 1, 1907, p. 63; K. GSCHWIND, *Die Niederfahrt Christi*, 1911, pp. 199ff.; E. PREUSCHEN, Die Echtheit von Justins Dialog gegen Trypho, *Zeitschr. f. d. neut. Wiss.* xix, 1919—1920, pp. 124f.; C. SCHMIDT, Der Descensus ad inferos, pp. 467ff.; J. A. MACCULLOCH, *The Harrowing of Hell*, 1930, pp. 84f., 88ff.

[1] Irenæus, *Schrift zum Erweise der apostolischen Verkündigung*, übers. von KARAPET TER-MĚKĚRTTSCHIAN & ERWAND TER-MINASSIANTZ, Texte u. Unt. xxxi. 1, 1907, p. 42; or *S. Irenæus*, Εἰς ἐπίδειξιν τοῦ ἀποστολικοῦ κηρύγματος, ed. and transl. by KARAPET TER MĚKĚRTTSCHIAN, S. G. WILSON & MAXE OF SAXONY, Patr. Or. xii, 1919, p. 717.

[2] The literature on the *Gospel of Peter* in E. HENNECKE, *Handbuch zu den neutestamentlichen Apokryphen*. 1904, pp. 72ff.; *id., Neutestamentliche Apokryphen*, 2nd ed. 1924, p. 59; *Lexikon für Theologie und Kirche, s.v.* »Evangelien». — The reading κοιμωμένοις seems to be embraced by all the investigators of this field, except A. HILGENFELD, who prefers to follow the curious κοινωμενοις of the MS; HENNECKE, *Handbuch*, p. 85; C. SCHMIDT, *op. cit.*, p. 467.

connection, where it is stated that at Christ's death, the graves were opened and many bodies of the »saints» arose. For in part this is quite clearly alluded to in the words of the *Gospel of Nicodemus* II, ch. i (xvii), i.e. in the beginning of this part which treats of the *descensus Christi ad inferos*, and in part the words τῶν κεκοιμημένων in the different examples of the Jeremiah-*logion* &c. direct the thought very easily to the words πολλὰ σώματα τῶν κεκοιμημένων ἁγίων in the same passage. Associations can also be multiplied by remembering the words τοῖς προκεκοιμημένοις in the description of the Apostles' preaching at their descent into the underworld in *Herm. Sim.* ix. 16. 6, and the Latin text in Ecclus. xxiv. 45, *Penetrabo omnes inferiores partes terræ, et inspiciam omnes dormientes, et illuminabo omnes sperantes in Domino*.

Thus we find in these texts, more or less historically associated, a whole complex of opinions orientated around Christ's *descensus ad inferos*, and linked in different ways with the so-called Jeremiah-*logion*. In all these cases — except perhaps the *Gospel of Nicodemus* — the question is chiefly one of a gospel of hope to the just of the O.T. It is, however, quite clear that both the Jeremiah-*logion* and several of the other passages mentioned could easily be connected with 1 Pet. iv. 6, for there is mention in both places of a preaching of the Gospel to the dead. Perhaps the connection is specially clear in *Herm. Sim.* ix. 16 with its concrete description of the apostles going down to the righteous already dead so that they should be allowed to live in the Kingdom of God (ix. 16. 7 and 2). Whatever the origin of the Jeremiah-*logion* and the related opinions may have been,[1] we may probably say that there is good reason to assume that the complex here mentioned has had an intimate relation to 1 Pet. iv. 6 in some way.

We can imagine the following possibilities as regards this relation: (*a*) either that the *logion*, if it was pre-Christian, as Justin affirmed, to some extent affected 1 Pet. iv. 6, or even inspired the writer

---

[1] P. J. JENSEN considers that the Jeremia-*logion* has originated from the influence both of Matt. xxvii. 52f. and 1 Pet. iv. 6, *Læren om Kristi Nedfart*, p. 35f. It can, of course, also be the contrary.

of this Epistle to the thought, in which case this verse originally referred to the *descensus ad inferos*, (*b*) or that the prophetical passage, if it is a creation within Christianity, was affected by 1 Pet. iv. 6 in its origin, interpreted as treating of the *descensus ad inferos*. Well, even if the relation is not so primary, we must in any case point out that they who in this way quoted the Jeremiah-*logion*, Justin and Irænus, as possibly Hermas and later the authors of the *Gospels of Peter* and *Nicodemus*, must have conceived iv. 6 as an expression of the Descent and influenced their readers in the same direction.

Thus we find that at least this passage iv. 6 actually seems to have been interpreted as treating of the Descent by leading Christian writers about the middle of the second century.

This would indirectly make it probable that iii. 19 was at that time also associated with Christ's descent and a preaching of the Gospel in its connection. But the preaching mentioned in this passage refers to quite special people who in any case are not directly identical with the just of the O.T. who it seems must be referred to in the Jeremiah-*logion* &c. Strictly speaking it is rather difficult to reconcile iii. 19, if this is to be regarded as a descent to the sinners from the days of the Flood, with the Jeremiah-*logion* and the other passages referred to which rather seem to point to the just of the O.T. Nor are there any special circumstances in the earliest Christian times which justify the assumption that such a meaning was read into iii. 19, that the sinners from the days of the Flood should be regarded in the same way as the righteous of the O.T. But it is in any case possible that already then an explanation of the »spirits» in 1 Pet. iii. 19 as already converted souls was used: this, as we shall see, was quite often done later. In such case these two passages can be combined. Yet it cannot therefore be said that in the Jeremiah-*logion* and the other relative material we have any certain indication as to how iii. 19 was conceived at that time and to what extent the passage was used in the Descent dogma.

On the other hand, wherever such expressions of Christ's descent are found as imply that Christ in so doing subdued the power of Hell and released all the dead,[1] it can apparently on good grounds be assumed that the authors ought to have interpreted iii. 19 as referring to the Descent connected with a preaching of general release from the Realm of the Dead. If this is the case, it is easy to think that this passage was interpreted in a generously positive direction even if there are no direct traces or reflexes of this passage in the same connection.

This kind of Descent ideas is also very ancient. It is probably already indicated in the Bible, *e.g.* in Hos. xiii. 14, Matt. xii. 29 with its parallels, xxvii. 51ff., 1 Cor. xv. 54, Rev. i. 18.[2] In any case they appear quite early in the Christian literature. Melito seems to be the first who can be cited in this connection, from the following words in his *Homily on the Passion* §§ 102f.: ἐγὼ ὁ καταλύσας τὸν θάνατον ... καὶ καταπατήσας τὸν ᾅδην καὶ δήσας τὸν ἰσχυρὸν καὶ καθορμίσας τὸν ἄνθρωπον εἰς τὰ ὕψη ...[3] Here it is considered that everybody will be delivered from Hell without any express reservation. Marcion is another early — though extreme — representative of this thesis of a general forgiveness of sins at the Descent. He wishes even to have the Sodomites and Egyptians saved at that time, though of course not Abel, Enoch or Noah, according to quotations of Iræneus and Epiphanius.[4] The sinners from the Flood could, of course, very well have been mentioned among those saved, as well as the Sodomites &c. In the later Church literature we find many who express them-

---

[1] That is such ideas of the Descent as J. KROLL collected and studied in his great book *Gott und Hölle*, 1932. *Cf.* above, p. 9.

[2] J. KROLL, *op. cit.*, pp. 5ff.

[3] Ed. by C. BONNER, 1940, p. 163. *Cf.* Melito's *Fragm.* xiii, I. C. TH. OTTO, *Corpus apologetarum*, ix, 1872, pp. 419, 497.

[4] *Iren. Contra hær.* i. 27. 3: *Cain, et eos qui similes sunt ei, et Sodomitas, et Ægyptios, et similes eis, et omnes omnino gentes, quæ in omni permistione malignitatis ambulaverunt, salvatos esse a Domino, cum descendisset ad inferos, et accucurrissent ei, et in suum assumpsisse regnum; Abel autem, et Enoch, et Noe ... non participasse salutem (P.G. vii, col. 689A); Epiph. Adv. hær. i. 3, 42. 4: Καὶ ἄχρι ᾅδου καταβεβηκέναι τὸν Κύριον, ἵνα σώσῃ τοὺς περὶ Κάϊν καὶ Κορὲ &c., τοὺς δὲ περὶ Ἄβελ καὶ Ἐνὼχ &c. ἐκεῖ καταλελοιπέναι ... (P.G. xli, col. 700C—D).*

selves much in the same way as Melito, and point out that Hell was despoiled and all its prisoners set free at Christ's descent, without at the same time making any special reservation. For example, we find such expressions in the *Gospel of Nicodemus* II, ch. viii (xxiv), previously quoted,[1] and in Cyril of Alexandria, *Hom. pasch.* vii,[2] »Ambrosiaster», *Comm. in Ep. ad Rom.* v. 15,[3] and Hieronymus, *Comm. in Os.* xiii. 14.[4] At the same time, of course, certain more doubtful expressions, or even quite contrary ones, are often put forward by the same persons, *e.g.* Cyril, *Fragm. in Ep. I B. Pet.* iii. 19 *ss.* (*bis*);[5] compare Gregory of Nazianzen, *Orat.* xlv. 24.[6]

As soon as we find the forms of Descent ideas here indicated, it is probable that we could agree that 1 Pet. iii. 19 could have been interpreted by the authorities in question in the generously positive way. As we now, through Melito and Marcion, have a few quotations of such an idea from the second century, it can be stated that at that time it was possible to interpret our passage as indicating a gospel of hope for release even for the sinners from the Flood.

Such conclusions are supported by texts in which there is a clear connection between a powerful descent coupled with *Höllenstürmung* and release of all dead on the one side and iii. 19 on the other. From such texts we have noted the following:

A fragment, preserved in Syriac, by Hippolytus about Easter, which we shall later on study more closely.[7]

Ephræm, *Carm. Nisib.* xxxv. 75—90: Sheol says: »I must restrain my greed. After this there will be a famine. It was He who triumphed at the wedding. As He turned the water into wine, now He turns the dead people's garments into life. Certainly God caused a flood

---

[1] *Cf.* above, p. 17.
[2] *P.G.* lxxvii, col. 552 A.
[3] *P.L.* xvii, col. 97 B.
[4] *P.L.* xxv, col. 937 B.
[5] *P.G.* lxxiv, cols. 1014 C—D, 1016 A.
[6] *P.G.* xxxvi, col. 657 A.
[7] Below, pp. 23 ff.

and washed the earth and consumed away its debts. Fire and sulphur also He allowed to come over' it to wash the spots white. By means of fire He gave me the Sodomites and, by means of the Flood, the Giants (ܓܢܒܪܐ). He shut the mouth of Sennacherib's house and opened that of Sheol. This and similar things I liked. Instead of the death pains of Justice, however, He has now, by means of His Son, brought about the resurrection of the dead, by Grace.»[1] Here it seems that even the »Giants», that is, the sinners from the time of the Flood, are thought to be saved at Christ's descent. Consequently it seems that Ephræm, at least in some connections, has been able to interpret 1 Pet. iii. 19 as referring to a descent with a gospel of hope regarding the salvation of the »spirits».

A letter, important for the history of dogma, written by Bishop Euodius to Augustine regarding Christ's descent which we shall also study more closely later.[2] From this it is quite clear that there seems to have been in Augustine's time a fairly general conception that Christ at the Descent set free from Hell all the dead, even the »spirits» from the Flood.

Cyril of Alexandria, *Comm. in Joh. ev.*, lib. xi. 2; *Comm. in Luc.* iv. 18 ff., to which we shall also return later.[3]

Eulogius, *Hom. in ramos* viii: ὁ ἄδης ἐσκυλεύθη τῆς ἐνθέου ψυχῆς ἐκεῖ κατελθούσης. πορευθεὶς γὰρ ἐκήρυξε καὶ τοῖς ἐν ἄδῃ πνεύμασιν.[4]

We have thus found two general opinions as to the Descent which in principle seem contradictory. The preaching only for the just and the release of all the dead, both possibly to be found during the first century, of which the one primarily contradicts the possibility of an interpretation of 1 Pet. iii. 19 as the general preaching of the Gospel, in so far as the conversion of those »spirits»

---

[1] *S. Ephræm Syri Carmina Nisibena*, ed. G. BICKELL, 1866, Syriac text p. 57.
[2] Pp. 37 ff.
[3] P. 32.
[4] *P.G.* lxxxvi, col. 2925 B. S. L. EPIFANOVIČ declares this text is not genuine, according to B. ALTANER, *Patrologie*, 1938, p. 331, who states that it has been ascribed to Sophronius of Jerusalem.

before Christ's appearance to them is not assumed, while the other directly supports this possibility without any reservation. (1) On the one hand the type of Descent presentation mentioned above and implying an appeal of the Saviour to the godly of the O.T. is to some extent contrary to the possibility that it was desired to use 1 Pet. iii. 19 in this connection. It may be even that the passage already at this time, as so often later, was in certain theological situations interpreted as referring to a preaching of the Gospel at the Descent to sinners already converted, so that this passage could be reconciled with the relation between this type of Descent and 1 Pet. iv. 6, which we have considered was to be found in certain quarters during the first century: and by means of such a reservation it is possible to attain a certain harmony. That such an interpretation actually occurred during that time is certainly only a loose assumption, without any apparent support. (2) On the other hand the idea of a descent coupled with the release of all dead must naturally favour an interpretation of 1 Pet. iii. 19 in a frankly positive direction, so that it seems possible to interpret the passage at that time in certain theological situations as implying a preaching of the gospel at the Descent, which contained a promise of freedom from Hell for the sinners from the days of Noah without any special reserve. The occurrence of this interpretation already in the first century can perhaps be somewhat more certainly assumed with reference to the important, very early idea of a descent with a general release from the bonds of Hell.

Thus we have found certain indications of a few interpretations of our passage which later come to play an important part in the history of the problem. In most cases they are contradictory — but sometimes they can even be found in agreement.

AN INTERESTING PASSAGE FROM HIPPOLYTUS' WRITINGS.

In a preserved Syriac fragment of an Easter Homily which, judging from the MS, was composed by Bishop Hippolytus (of

Rome) — and this is certainly correct[1] — we find an interpretation of the Descent connected with 1 Pet. iii. 19 which is extremely interesting and peculiarly significant on account of its great age. Its importance in this question seems not to have been generally observed. It was certainly referred to by K. GSCHWIND, who pointed out its value for the textual history of our Epistle, namely through the reflex of iii. 19 which it contains.[2] But as regards the contents, he has not communicated any of the interesting observations which can be made. And none of the later writers on our subject have on the whole concerned themselves with this text.[3] Here, however, we can only make a few remarks on this comprehensive little fragment, which ought to be treated in full detail in regard to the whole history of the Descent dogma — but we must restrict ourselves to 1 Pet. iii. 19 and not go too deeply into Hippolytus and the theology of his time.

To get a basis for some observations we present this text which runs as follows:[4]

---
[1] The following is likely to support the genuineness of the writing. The MS with this text, *Mus. Brit. Syr.* 729 (*Add.* 12156), *fol.* 76 *v.*—77 *r.*, is as old as the vith century (*Hippolytus' kleinere exegetische und homiletische Schriften*, hrsg. von H. ACHELIS, p. 268), which is extremely old for a Syriac MS. The indication on the MS, ܪܐܘܒܩܘܦܐ ܘܐܠܦܐܩܣܪ.ܐ, »by Bishop Hippolytus», is valuably supported by corresponding information in a Greek parallel text to the Syriac fragment, preserved for us in Nicetas Diaconus; the title of this is Ἱππολύτου ἐπισκόπου Ῥώμης καὶ μάρτυρος (*op. cit., ibid.*). Its contents also agree well with what otherwise is known of Hippolytus' theology and the attitude he took up towards different contemporary heresies, such as Monarchianism, Sabellianism, in Christological questions. See also O. BARDENHEWER, *Geschichte der altkirchlichen Literatur*, ii, 1903, p. 544, with references.

[2] K. GSCHWIND, *Die Niederfahrt Christi*, p. 45f.

[3] C. SCHMIDT polemizes against GSCHWIND and asserts that he cannot discover any »Benutzung der Petrusstelle», Der Descensus ad inferos, p. 509 note 2; J. A. MACCULLOCH gives a brief summary of the Hippolytus text without saying anything about the peculiarity of the text's content, or its significance in the history of the Descensus doctrine, *The Harrowing of Hell*, p. 95f.; and U. HOLZMEISTER speaks of the existence of the text, but reserves himself as to its content, *Commentarius*, p. 323; this, however, is no proof that the text received due attention.

[4] The Syriac text is to be found in P. DE LAGARDE, *Analecta syriaca*, 1858, p. 88f., and in J. B. card. PITRA, *Analecta sacra*, iv, 1883, p. 55; the Greek text is to be found in *Hippolytus' kleinere exegetische und homiletische Schriften*, hrsg. von H. ACHELIS, 1897, pp. 268f., where older literature is quoted.

»Oh, Thou Divine Miracle in everything and every place! Oh, Crucifixion, which has been spread (ܕܗܘ ܦܪܝܣ) everywhere! Oh, Thou only-begotten Son among only-begotten sons, and All in all! Seeing that the multitude of Holy Souls was deep down and had been deprived of a Divine visit long enough, the Holy Spirit had previously said that they should be the object of a meeting with the Divine Soul, saying: 'His form we have not seen, but His voice we have heard.'

ܕܝܢ ܗܘܐ ܥܠܘܗܝ	For it behoved Him to go and preach
ܕܢܐܙܠ ܢܟܪܙ ܐܦ	also to those who were in Hell,
ܠܗܢܘܢ ܕܒܫܝܘܠ	namely those who had once[1] been
ܐܝܬܝܗܘܢ ܒܚܕ ܙܒܢ	disobedient.»

For the sake of simplicity the Syriac text of the middle part will be replaced by the Greek text of Niceta, which is parallel with it the whole time except for one sentence, which is lacking in the Greek text:

διὰ τοῦτο »πυλωροὶ ᾅδου ἰδόντες σε ἔπτηξαν», καὶ συνετρίβησαν πύλαι χαλκαῖ, καὶ μοχλοὶ σιδηροῖ συνεκλάσθησαν· καὶ ἰδοὺ ὁ μονογενὴς εἰσῆλθεν ὡς ψυχὴ μετὰ ψυχῶν, θεὸς λόγος ἔμψυχος (the Incarnate Word)[2]· τὸ γὰρ σῶμα ἔκειτο ἐν μνημείῳ, οὐχὶ κενωθὲν τῆς θεότητος, ἀλλ'

— here the Syriac text has the following words, omitted in the Greek:

»(but) while with His Flesh holding fast to the world He despoiled Hell with His Soul, for» —

then the Greek text continues:

ὥσπερ ἐν τῷ ᾅδῃ ὢν τῇ οὐσίᾳ ἦν πρὸς τὸν πατέρα, οὕτως ἦν καὶ ἐν τῷ σώματι καὶ ἐν τῷ ᾅδῃ (that is to say, just as completely as Christ, even in Hell, was in essence with His Father, He was also still in His Body — which lay in the grave — when He as Soul was in the underworld on His journey to Hell). ἀχώρητος γάρ ἐστι καὶ ὁ υἱὸς ὡς ὁ πατήρ, καὶ πάντα περιέχει· ἀλλὰ θέλων ἐχωρήθη ἐν σώματι ἐμψύχῳ, ἵνα μετὰ τῆς ἰδίας ψυχῆς πορευθῇ εἰς τὸν ᾅδην

---

[1] ܒܚܕ here means, of course, »once», ποτέ, *semel* (C. Brockelmann, *Lexicon Syriacum*, 1928, *s.v.*); the translation »in der Zeitlichkeit» in Achelis' edition is misleading (as K. Gschwind also states in *Die Niederfahrt Christi*, p. 46).

[2] Also the Syriac ܡܠܬܐ ܡܢܦܫܐ should be rendered in similar words, not by »das seelische Wort», as in Achelis.

— the reason for the Saviour's *kenosis* at His descent into Hell is given quite clearly later in the Syriac text (the Greek concludes with the words καὶ [*scil.* ἵνα] μὴ γυμνῇ τῇ θεότητι which do really not say so much in this connection) —:

»in order that when He came in His Divinity, the lower parts of the earth should not dissolve by confusion, nay, as a Soul among souls (He appeared to them) without it being forgotten even there that He is God. Moreover in the world also He loosed the fetters of the Dead, using His kingly power as, for example, in the case of Lazarus, (when He said) »Lazarus, come forth», or (to the maid) *Ṭelītā qūm*ⁱ that it should be noted that it was a command with authority.»

In this text we find an undeniable allusion to 1 Pet. iii. 19f. in the sentence, »For it behoved Him to go and preach to those who were in Hell, namely those who had once been disobedient.»[1] We recognise both πορευθείς — notice that the Syriac too has the participial construction —, ἐκήρυξεν, ποτέ[2] and ἀπειθήσασιν — the last word being in the Syriac a form of the verb ܥܨܐ, which is, of course, a loan-word from the Greek πεῖσαι. Not only these isolated words but even the whole of the main thought of the sentence harmonizes with iii. 19f. That the »prison», ἡ φυλακή, here corresponds to ܫܝܘܠ, »Sheol», is quite natural to anyone who has seen that φυλακή in 1 Pet. iii. 19 in the later patristic literature is quite often given with ᾅδης or corresponding words, as we notice also in some texts in this presentation.[3] It is clear from this equivalence that Hippolytus thought this passage referred to a preaching at Christ's descent into the underworld.

What are the ideas of the Descent for which Hippolytus now brings up our passage? We see from the words which follow the allusion to it, here given in Greek, that Hippolytus is clearly thinking of a violent descent with a *Höllenstürmung*. This *motif* also appears later, in saying that the underworld would be destroyed by terror. At the same time the text at the beginning is connected with another Descent idea, namely the appearance of Christ to the »Holy Souls»

---

[1] K. GSCHWIND, *Die Niederfahrt Christi*, p. 45f. How C. SCHMIDT could deny this, as we have mentioned above (p. 24, note 3), is incomprehensible.

[2] *Cf.* above, p. 25, note 1.

[3] See texts quoted above on p. 22, below on p. 32. *Cf.* K. GSCHWIND, *loc. cit.*

who sigh after Him, who must be chiefly those of the people of God who have died, longing for the Messiah and redemption. This notion — as we have stated before — is in principle to be differentiated from that of *Höllenstürmung* which instead is often combined with the notion of a release of all dead. But this is, of course, not to say that the revelation to the just of the O.T. cannot sometimes be connected with the *Höllenstürmung*; here in any case we have an example of this combination. On the other hand the idea of the release of all dead can scarcely be considered to occur in our text.

From these circumstances the conclusion must be drawn that Hippolytus could not include this passage iii. 19 in his reasoning without also considering those who had been disobedient in the days of Noah as already converted before the coming of Christ. Otherwise a troublesome disharmony would arise between the sentence which alludes to the passage in 1 Pet. and the previously pronounced indication of a revelation to the »Holy Souls».

Thus it seems that Hippolytus had conceived our passage in a way that can be observed later in many places, namely so that the »spirits» were such as had been converted before the coming of Christ into the underworld. This may also be said to agree with what we already know of the somewhat rigorous and at the same time careful attitude of Hippolytus to the question of the everlasting punishments of Hell. Further it seems here that the expression ποτέ in the Bible text has been taken to mean »previously». We shall also find this conception in later texts, e.g. in the Peshito, but above all in the Latin translation of the Bible, the Vulgate, and the interpretations based upon it which are most usual in the Roman Church in modern times.[1]

THE ALEXANDRIAN SCHOOL'S THEORY OF UNIVERSAL SALVATION.

It is first with the Alexandrian School that the earliest direct and immediately clear Greek quotation and interpretation of 1 Pet. iii. 19 arises in connection with Christ's descent. For theolog-

---

[1] *Cf.* below, pp. 36, 42 ff.

ians of this school the passage was, of course, rather a grateful one to interpret and use as an argument for their theory of universal salvation. The tendency to a symbolical, allegorical conception of Hell which can sometimes be observed in this quarter made it naturally easier to interpret this passage in a generously positive direction. Thus Clement of Alexandria writes in *Strom*. vi. 6. 37—39 (44. 4): Τί δέ; οὐχὶ δηλοῦσιν εὐηγγελίσθαι τὸν Κύριον τοῖς τε ἀπολωλόσιν ἐν τῷ κατακλυσμῷ, μᾶλλον δὲ πεπεδημένοις, καὶ τοῖς ἐν »φυλακῇ» τε καὶ »φρουρᾷ» συνεχομένοις;[1] Here is a clear quotation of 1 Pet. iii. 19. That Clement refers to a *descensus ad inferos* appears from the following sentences, where he advances the preaching of the Apostles in the underworld in *Herm. Sim.* ix. 16 as an argument for the same thing, 6. 40, also 45 ff. See also *Strom.* ii. 9. 77 (44. 1). An interpretation of our text is found in Clement's *Adumbrationes* to 1 Pet.: »*Christus enim*», inquit, »*semel pro peccatis nostris mortuus est, justus pro injustis, ut nos oferret Deo, mortificatus quidem carne, vivificatus autem spiritu*» (1 Pet. iii. 18). *Hæc ad fidem eorum redigens dicit. Hoc est: in nostris vivificatus est spiritibus.* »*Adveniens*», inquit, »*prædicavit eis, qui quondam erant increduli*» (19 f.). *Speciem quidem eius non viderunt, sonitum vero vocis audierunt.*[2] On the basis of the last sentence, formulated in accordance with Job xxviii. 22:[3] »Destruction and Death say: We have heard a rumour thereof with our ears», in combination with Deut. iv. 13 and which also elsewhere — by Clement in *Strom.* vi. 6. 37, and Hippolytus in *Refut.* v. 8. 14 (concerning pagan mysteries) as well as in the above-mentioned Syriac fragment from his Easter Homily — is quoted in connection with Christ's descent, it is probable that Clement is here thinking of a going down into Hell.[4]

---

[1] *P.G.* ix, col. 268 A.
[2] *P.G.* ix, col. 731 B.
[3] Probably; but O. STÄHLIN, *Clemens und die LXX*, 1901, p. 44, is not quite sure of it.
[4] K. GSCHWIND, *Die Niederfahrt Christi*, p. 43; W. BOUSSET, Zur Hadesfahrt Christi, *Zeitschr. f. d. neut. Wiss.* xix, 1919/20, p. 65 note 1; J. A. MACCULLOCH, *The Harrowing of Hell*, p. 99, *cf.* 96; J. KROLL, *Gott und Hölle*, 1932, p. 39 with notes 2, 3; *cf.* pp. 77, 353.

EARLIER INTERPRETATIONS OF VERSE 19

On the other hand it can be noticed that just in this explanation Clement reveals an allegorical reasoning (cf. his remarks on iv. 6[1]). Yet the passage first quoted, Clement's *Strom.* vi. 6. 37—39, undoubtedly deals with the Descent. This passage, with Hippolytus' Easter Homily, may therefore be taken as the first places in the literature of the Church where we find 1 Pet. iii. 19 clearly explained with a tendency towards a going down into Hell.[2] Now Clement's passage seems to show the idea of the Descent primarily as Christ preaching the Gospel for the unbelievers also, without any reservation. Further on in the same connection it is true that Clement says it was those who believed who were saved, 6. 42 (46. 3). This modification probably in no way alters the fact that Clement, in agreement with his conception of a relatively universal salvation, would be willing to allow all the lost to hear the Gospel at the Descent. When he speaks of the »believers», or more correctly »those who came to believe», οἱ πιστεύσαντες, he means that they were brought to believe just when Christ came, not that they had any belief before: this is clear from 6. 71 (46. 1), where they are mentioned as those »who on the basis of the Saviour's preaching had decided to believe (πιστεῦσαι, aorist) in Him», but the same thing is also clear from Clement's eagerness to include at any cost even the heathen among those who were the object of the Saviour's descent, 6. 43ff. (46. 4f.). It cannot therefore be considered that Clement is necessarily thinking of any conversion for these dead people already in this life.[3] On the other hand it is certainly clear that he was primarily thinking of those who had lived an exemplary life (προηγουμένως), 6. 40 (45. 5). Thus we must concede that an absolutely complete tolerance does not distinguish Clement's theory on this passage.[4]

---

[1] TH. ZAHN, *Forschungen zur Geschichte des neutest. Kanons*, iii, 1884, p. 95; P. J. JENSEN, *Læren om Kristi Nedfart*, p. 43 note 1.

[2] P. J. JENSEN, *loc. cit.*, K. GSCHWIND, *op. cit.*, p. 17, mention only Clemens, as already stated. *Cf.* above, p. 14, note 3.

[3] As stated by U. HOLZMEISTER, *Commentarius*, i, pp. 339f., but in this we cannot say he is quite correct.

[4] But it is just to the credit of HOLZMEISTER that he put forward the

Origenes touches upon 1 Pet. iii. 19 in *De princ.* ii. 5, 3. He says there, in a polemic context: *Non legunt (adversarii), quid scriptum est de spe illorum, qui in diluvio perempti sunt, de qua spe Petrus ipse in prima Epistola sua ita ait* ... after which he quotes 1 Pet. iii. 18—21.[1] From the next part, which deals with Sodom and Gomorrah, it is possible that Origenes does not mean by »hope» any active and conscious anticipatory hope but really thinks of an objective future development. It seems that he took the passage as referring to the generation which suffered the Flood and their general and unconditional salvation through Christ, and this agrees very well with his theory of universal salvation.[2] On the other hand he made a reservation against Celsus when the latter pointed out that Christ was indeed driven to begin preaching the Gospel in Hell simply to make good His failure on earth, and stated that He in Hell, as well as on earth, converted those souls who themselves wished it or whom He saw were most suitable: γυμνὴ σώματος γενόμενος ψυχὴ ταῖς γυμναῖς σωμάτων ὡμίλει ψυχαῖς, ἐπιστρέφων κἀκείνων τὰς βουλομένας πρὸς αὐτὸν ἢ ἃς ἑώρα δι᾽ οὓς ᾔδει αὐτὸς λόγους ἐπιτηδειοτέρας, *Contra Cels.* ii. 43.[3] Thus a certain carefulness in granting salvation to anybody and everybody also distinguishes Origenes. He follows very nearly the line of Clement.[4] Compare *Comm. in Matth.* 132: *Ipse autem Filium Dei se deridentibus quidem non ostendebat, ostendit autem credentibus sibi, postquam dispensavit quæ oportebat eum dispensare in tribus illis diebus, postquam descendens ad inferos »mortificatus corpore, vivificatus autem in spiritu spiritibus qui erant in carcere prædicavit* ...»[5]

---

necessary reservations regarding the older literature's one-sided characteristic of Clement's view on this point as being unrestrictedly soteriological.

[1] *P.G.* xi, col. 206C.

[2] MacCulloch in *The Harrowing of Hell* p. 103, also states that Origenes liked to take up the notion of the Descent in his doctrine because it was in harmony with his hopeful eschatological scheme.

[3] *P.G.* xi, cols. 864f.

[4] P. J. Jensen, *Læren om Kristi Nedfart*, p. 44; C. Schmidt, Der Descensus ad inferos, p. 526.

[5] *P.G.* xiii, col. 1780D.

That these people »believed», here seems to infer that they showed belief in the presence of Christ when He came.

For the rest we find 1 Pet. iii. 19 and Christ's descent into the underworld mentioned quite generally by Origenes in his *Comm. in Joann.*, fragm. lxxix, in connection with Thomas's question in John xi. 16: καταβὰς εἰς τὸ χωρίον αὐτῶν, ἵνα τοῖς ἐν φυλακῇ πνεύμασι κηρύξῃ, πορευθεὶς πρὸς αὐτά, ἀπειθήσασί ποτε ...[1] In the same way Origenes includes the idea of *Catabasis* and a quotation of iii. 19 in his peculiar interpretation of the words of John the Baptist, Mark i. 7, of his unworthiness to loosen the sandals on Jesus' feet, *Comm. in Joann.* vi. 18, where he lets the one sandal signify the Incarnation, the other sandal partly the descent into Hell and partly the going away, ἡ πορεία, to the prison μετὰ τοῦ πνεύματος. For the first aspect of the Descent, Ps. xv (xvi). 10 (οὐκ ἐγκαταλείψεις τὴν ψυχήν μου εἰς τὸν ᾅδην) is put forward as scriptural proof, for the latter aspect 1 Pet. iii. 18—20.[2]

Later Athanasius in his *Epist. ad Epictet.* § 5 (29f.) also makes a clear combination of 1 Pet. iii. 19 with Hell: τοῦτο [τὸ σῶμα] ἦν τὸ ἐν μνημείῳ τεθέν, ὅτε αὐτὸς ἐπορεύθη, μὴ χωρισθεὶς αὐτοῦ, κηρύξαι καὶ τοῖς ἐν φυλακῇ πνεύμασιν, ὡς εἶπεν ὁ Πέτρος ...[3] Compare also what follows, where Athanasius points out that the consequence of the heretics' theory regarding the Logos being changed into flesh and blood must be that Christ would not have required any grave at all, seeing that His Body would then have gone to κηρύξαι τοῖς ἐν τῷ ᾅδῃ πνεύμασιν, *ibid.* § 6 (30).[4] Here the Descent is connected with 1 Pet. iii. 19 primarily because such an interpretation gives Athanasius a good argument against the heretics in a question of the Logos and Incarnation, but he does not here draw any more precise inference from the passage. On the other hand it must be admitted that his reasoning at the same time reveals indirectly to some extent that it must have been general and considered natural at his time and in his theological environment to conceive of this verse as referring to Christ's descent in connection with His death and burial. This is perhaps due to a certain extent to the influence of the Alexandrian School. But it must also be

---

[1] Preuschen's edition fragm. lxxix, p. 546.
[2] *P.G.* xiv, col. 260 B. Preuschen's edition vi. 35. — *Cf.* C. Schmidt, *op. cit.*, pp. 545f.
[3] *P.G.* xxvi. 2, col. 1060 A.
[4] *P.G.*, *ibid.*, col. 1060 B.

observed that the Descent theory in general was an important factor in the theological controversies of Athanasius' time, as it clearly had been at the time and in the environment of Hippolytus (see above). We find also a Latin theologian like Ambrosius polemizing with the Arians on the foundation of this theory in his work *De fide*, iii. 4. 27ff.[1] The Arians and the Apollinarists purposely resorted to just the same theory as the Orthodox, that the Kingdom of the Dead trembled with terror and fear at Christ's descent. By this the heretics thought that their presentation of the Logos' dominating role in Christ as an earthly being was supported, for the trembling of the Kingdom of the Dead was more easily explained if it was the Logos Himself who went down into the underworld. In this way it can be understood that it was just the Arians who arranged for the addition to the Symbol of Christ's *descensus ad inferos* at the synods in Sirmium, Nice and Constantinople, about 359 A.D.[2]

Cyril of Alexandria continues with boldness this relatively generous line within the Eastern Church followed by the great Alexandrian Fathers of the third century. In his *Comm. in Joann.*, *lib.* xi. 2, he says of Christ: τριήμερος ἀνεβίω, κηρύξας καὶ τοῖς ἐν φυλακῇ πνεύμασιν· πληρεστάτη γὰρ οὕτως ἡ τῆς φιλανθρωπίας ἐπίδειξις ἦν, τῷ μὴ μόνον ἀνασῶσαί φημι τοὺς ἔτι ζῶντας ἐπὶ τῆς γῆς, ἀλλὰ καὶ τοῖς ἤδη κατοιχομένοις καὶ ἐν τοῖς τῆς ἀβύσσου μύχοις καθημένοις ἐν σκότῳ κατὰ τὸ γεραμμένον διακηρύξαι τὴν ἄφεσιν,[3] and in *Comm. in Luc.* iv. 18ff. it is said: καὶ τοῖς ἐν ᾅδου πνεύμασιν πορευθεὶς ἐκήρυξε, καὶ τοῖς καθειργμένοις ἐν οἴκῳ φυλακῆς ἐπεφάνη, καὶ πάντας ἀνῆκε δεσμῶν καὶ ἀνάγκης.[4]

THE GREEK CHURCH OF THE MIDDLE AGES.

At the beginning of the Middle Ages we find an extremely interesting interpretation of the Descent indicated by John of Damascus in *De fide orthod.* iv. 29, *De descensu ad inferos:*

[1] *P.L.* xvi, cols. 595f.
[2] HAHN, *Bibliothek der Symbole*, 3. Aufl. 1897, §§ 163—167. — P. J. JENSEN, *Læren om Kristi Nedfart*, pp. 58ff., with references from older literature.
[3] *P.G.* lxxiv, col. 456A. — Allusion to Isa. lxi. 1 &c.
[4] *P.G.* lxxii, col. 537 D.

i.] EARLIER INTERPRETATIONS OF VERSE 19 33

Κάτεισιν (ὁ Κύριος) εἰς ᾅδην ψυχὴ τεθεωμένη, ἵνα ὥσπερ τοῖς ἐν γῇ ὁ τῆς δικαιοσύνης ἀνέτειλεν ἥλιος, οὕτω καὶ τοῖς ὑπὸ γῆν ἐν σκότει καὶ σκιᾷ θανάτου καθημένοις ἐπιλάμψῃ τὸ φῶς· ἵν', ὥσπερ τοῖς ἐν γῇ εὐηγγελίσατο εἰρήνην, αἰχμαλώτοις ἄφεσιν, καὶ τυφλοῖς ἀνάβλεψιν, καὶ τοῖς μὲν πιστεύσασι γέγονεν αἴτιος σωτηρίας αἰωνίου, τοῖς δὲ ἀπειθήσασιν ἀπιστίας ἔλεγχος, οὕτω καὶ τοῖς ἐν ᾅδου· »ἵνα αὐτῷ πᾶν γόνυ κάμψῃ ἐπουρανίων καὶ ἐπιγείων καὶ καταχθονίων», καὶ οὕτω τοὺς ἀπ' αἰώνων λύσας πεπεδημένους, αὖθις ἐκ νεκρῶν ἀνεφοίτησεν, ὁδοιποιήσας ἡμῖν τὴν ἀνάστασιν.[1] Here we find — besides a series of interesting allusions to O.T. passages and a quotation from Phil. ii. 10 — in the words τοὺς ἀπ' αἰώνων λύσας πεπεδημένους, a likely reference to the spirits of Noah's time in 1 Pet. iii. 19f.; but this connection is also indubitably revealed just by the expression πεπεδημένους which was earlier used, as we have seen, by Clement of Alexandria about the spirits from the days of the Flood. Thus it seems that John of Damascus here thought all those in the underworld who came to belief in connection with Christ's preaching were saved.

The Greek Church of the Middle Ages also seems generally to have preserved the tradition from the Alexandrian School that our passage treats of the Descent. Here two different types of interpretation can be found as regards the question of who they were who were saved at Christ's preaching in Hell. The one type, represented by Maximus Confessor, Quæst. ad Thal. vii[2] (regarding 1 Pet. iv. 6), John of Damascus, loc. cit., and Joannes Zonaras, Epist. x,[3] states that those in Hell who were seized by belief in Christ were saved. This idea Clement already had, as we have seen. The other type, represented by »Œcumenius», Comment. in Epist. I S. Petri, ch. v, to 1 Pet. iv. 6,[4] Theophylactus, Expos. in Epist. I S. Petri, to 1 Pet. iii. 19,[5] Nicephorus Callistus, Eccl. hist. i. 31,[6]

[1] P.G. xciv, col. 1101A.
[2] P.G. xc, col. 284C.
[3] P.G. lxxvi, col. 1124A—C.
[4] P.G. cxix, cols. 561f. — Œcumenius here links up with iii. 19. He assumes that in both cases it is a question of a preaching in Hades.
[5] P.G. cxxv, col. 1232.
[6] P.G. cxlv, cols. 724f.

3

is of the opinion that the criterion is rather the attitude those people had during their life in the world. We have already considered that we found this theory in Hippolytus. The later conception seems gradually to have penetrated the Greek Church.[1] Thus, for example, Metrophanes Critopulus in *Confess.* iii says that Christ taught and gave release τοῖς εἰς αὐτὸν ἤδη πιστεύσασιν.[2]

THE ASSYRIAN CHURCH.

As regards the interpretation of 1 Pet. iii. 19 by the provincial Assyrian Church, which cannot be said to have any great importance from the viewpoint of the central history of erudition, two characteristics only may be put forward here.

(1) The translation of this passage in the Peshito must of course have formed an important basis for the idea of this passage held by all later Syriac writers. The verses 19—20a, run as follows in this translation

ܘܐܟܪܙ ܠܢܦܫܬܐ ܐܝܠܝܢ »And He preached (there) to the
ܕܐܚܝܕܢ ܗܘܝ ܒܫܝܘܠ souls who were shut up in Sheol,
ܗܠܝܢ ܕܡܢ ܩܕܝܡ ܠܐ those who had before been dis-
ܐܬܛܦܝܣ ܗܘܝ ܒܝܘܡܬܗ obedient in the days of Noah.»
ܕܢܘܚ

Here one can first notice that ἐν ᾧ has not been translated in the usual way, *i.e.* as referring to πνεύματι in verse 18, but either it has been left untranslated, or can be considered as included in the conjunction ܘ, which in that case means about the same as »whereat», »in doing which», a meaning which ἐν ᾧ can also have.[3]

---

[1] P. J. JENSEN, *Læren om Kristi Nedfart*, pp. 76, 117.
[2] *Op. cit.*, p. 117. — As regards the Descent theory in the Greek Church reference may be made to J. KARMIRIS, Ἡ εἰς ῞Αδου κάθοδος τοῦ Χριστοῦ ἐξ ἐπόψεως ὀρθοδόξου, Athens 1939, a work which has not been available to us; *cf.* review by J. LEBON in *Revue d'histoire ecclésiastique* xxxv, 1939, pp. 929f.
[3] *Cf.* below, p. 103ff.

i.] EARLIER INTERPRETATIONS OF VERSE 19 35

Further it may be observed that πνεύματα is translated by ܪܘܚܐ, »souls», which makes it probable that in the translator's opinion dead people here are primarily meant, not some kind of »Angels». And then it is clear that he has identified »the prison» with Sheol, seeing that he has translated ἡ φυλακή by this expression. Finally it is an illuminating detail that ποτέ is clearly meant by this translator to have the significance »before», as he writes ܡܢ ܩܕܝܡ. Thus the spirits are believed to have been converted before Christ came with His revelation. Consequently, we here find the same interpretation which we previously believed we had found in Hippolytus and certain other writers.

In passing it may be remarked that the choice of words in the Peshito in these verses agrees very much with the passage in the Syriac text of Hippolytus which, as we stated above, we believe is an allusion to 1 Pet. iii. 19. This supports our theory regarding the Hippolytus text.

(2) If we turn to the writings of the older Syriac Fathers we find that the Descent, a quite usual *motif* in Ephræm, Aphraates &c., very often — as generally in the literature of the Eastern Church, specially in the more imaginative »apocryphal» writings — has the character of a *Höllenstürmung* and of a conquest of Death, as well as a release of all the dead. The following are examples of this: Ephræm's *Carm. Nisib.* xxxvi, xxxviii, xxxix, xli, and certain places in Aphraates' Homilies xiv and xxii.[1] The *Odes of Solomon* also belong to this literature; several of them mention just this type of Descent.[2] *Cf.* the Apostle Thaddeus' sermon in the *Doctrina Addai*. As in such texts the allusion is to the storming of the Kingdom of Death, the annihilation of Death and the general release of the dead, 1 Pet. iii. 19 can possibly in this environment have been interpreted as alluding to a release of »the spirits» without any special reservations.

---

[1] Regarding Aphraates see D. PLOOIJ, Der Descensus ad inferos in Aphrahat und den Oden Salomos, *Zeitschr. f. d. neut. Wiss.* xiv, 1913, pp. 222ff.
[2] W. R. NEWBOLD, The Descent of Christ in the Odes of Solomon, *Journ. of Bibl. Lit.* xxxi, 1912, pp. 168ff.; D. PLOOIJ, *op. cit.*

DIFFERENT IMPULSES IN THE EARLY ROMAN CHURCH.

The reasoning discussed in connection with Hippolytus and some later Greek theologians and lastly with the Peshito, that »the spirits in prison» are such as were converted before Christ came there, has an analogy in a kind of conception which appears sporadically in the Roman Church of early times and of the Middle Ages, but later became of current importance, through the Vulgate translation of 1 Pet. iii. 19. In the Vulgate it states that Christ preached to the spirits, *qui increduli fuerant aliquando*, thus in the pluperfect tense. This manner of expression easily causes one to think that they were the spirits from the time before the Flood who had been faithless but had really managed to change and become believers before they met Christ face to face in the underworld. The passage has also been similarly interpreted *e.g.* by Hilarius in *Tract. in cxviii psalmum*, verse 82, where he, in connection with the words of the psalm: *Defecerunt oculi mei in eloquium tuum, dicentes: Quando exhortaberis me?*, directs the thought to Christ's *descensus ad inferos* and there quotes 1 Pet. iii. 19f.[1] According to this interpretation the »spirits» imprisoned in Hell themselves longed for Christ and had therefore been converted earlier. This reasoning can probably be found here and there also later in the Roman Church. To a certain extent it has also influenced MARTIN LUTHER in his *Epistel S. Petri gepredigt und ausgelegt*, erste Bearbeitung, 1523, where the interpretation of iii. 19 issues in the following proposed solution: »Christus ist gen hymel gefaren und hatt den geystern gepredigt, das ist, menschen seelen, unter wilchen menschen seelen unglewbige sind gewest zun zeyten Noe.»[2] Later we speak of the extraordinarily great part played by the interpretation based on the Vulgate in the modern Roman Church.[3]

---

[1] *P.L.* ix, col. 572 f.; a better text is in *Corp. scr. eccl.* xxii, p. 452 (*fuerant* instead of *fuerunt*). — Our observations regarding Hilarius are based upon remarks by P. J. JENSEN, who, in opposition to earlier investigators, puts forward a new conception of this passage, *Læren om Kristi Nedfart*, p. 23.

[2] »Weimar-Ausgabe» xii, 1891, p. 369.

[3] *Cf.* below, pp. 42 ff.

EARLIER INTERPRETATIONS OF VERSE 19

The early and mediæval Roman Church, however, was in general to proceed in quite a different way. The intellectual and moralizing features which distinguished certain Latin theologians made it very difficult, of course, for them generally to accept 1 Pet. iii. 19, especially in the optimistically generous interpretation which was chiefly used by the Alexandrian School. It can also be said that the theologians of Western Christendom in earlier centuries readily avoided verse 19. As we shall soon see, however, Augustine had found himself compelled to combat certain current ideas of the Descent in connection with this verse. It appears, indeed, from this that it was general in Augustine's environment to use it in the Descent teaching, which was perhaps to a great extent a consequence of the influence from the Greek Fathers and the controversy with Arianism &c. which we have already touched upon. Augustine himself, however, was not of this opinion; he denied wholly a connection between this verse and the Descent dogma. And his attitude was of decisive influence after his time.

THE EVASIVE INTERPRETATION OF AUGUSTINE.

Augustine maintained that 1 Pet. iii. 19 did not refer to Christ's *descensus ad inferos*. He wrote an answer to Bishop Euodius, who, probably in agreement with a conception quite common at the time, presumed that Hades had become empty after Christ's descent, in which he stated that St. Peter speaks of Christ preaching in a pre-existing form to the contemporaries of Noah during their lifetime.

Euodius wrote to Augustine: *Quartam interrogo: qui sunt illi spiritus, de quibus in Epistula sua ponit Petrus testimonium de Domino, dicens* ... (1 Pet. iii. 18, 19); *hoc inserens quod in inferno fuerunt, et descendens Christus omnibus evangelizavit, omnesque a tenebris et poenis per gratiam liberavit, ut a tempore resurrectionis Domini judicium expectetur exinanitis inferis.*[1]

To this Augustine replied that he knew quite well what difficulties

---

[1] Euodius' letter is published among the letters of Augustine as number clxiii, *P.L.* xxxiii, col. 708.

were caused by verse 19. It must be asked why just these beings from the time of Noah are mentioned as the objects of Christ's preaching, while an innumerable host of righteous people from the time of the O.T., among them prophets and patriarchs, Jacob, Job, and so on, are not mentioned. That Christ went down into the Realm of the Dead is, however, quite certain (*satis constat*), considering for example Ps. xv. 10, Acts ii. 24, 26;[1] also that Adam was saved, according to Wisd. x. 1 f.: *Hæc illum, qui primus factus est, patrem orbis terrarum, cum solus esset creatus, custodivit, et eduxit illum a delicto suo, et dedit ei virtutem continendi omnia.* Some people also consider that Abel, Seth, Noah, Abraham and other patriarchs and prophets were released from torment. But Abraham had received Lazarus into his bosom, and there was »between us and you a great gulf fixed», as it says in Luke xvi. 26, so that Abraham's bosom cannot really be any part of Hell. If Christ at his descent released all or only some was thus not clear for Augustine. The problem in verse 19, however, he wished to solve by the following interpretation: »*vivificatus autem spiritu, in quo spiritu adveniens prædicavit et illis spiritibus qui increduli fuerant aliquando in diebus Noe*»: *quoniam prius quam veniret in carne pro nobis moriturus, quod semel fecit,*[2] *sæpe antea veniebat in spiritu ad quos volebat, visis eos admonens sicut volebat, utique in spiritu quo spiritu et vivificatus est, cum in passione esset carne mortificatus.*[3] Thus Augustine thinks that the Descent is certainly otherwise a factor to be considered, although it is difficult to determine the circumstances more closely, but that it forms no assumption for verse 19; what is mentioned there is only a revelation, performed in the Spirit by the pre-existing Christ long before the actual Incarnation to the people of Noah's time. Regarding 1 Pet. iv. 6 Augustine considered here also that it is not a question of appearing to the physically dead in Hades but to the spiritually

---

[1] See also such passages in Augustine as *De civit. Dei* xx. 15; *cf. De genes. ad lit.* xii. 32.
[2] *Cf.* ἅπαξ, 1 Pet. iii. 18!
[3] *August. Epist.* clxiv, *P.L.* xxxiii, cols. 709 ff.

dead on earth. Thus he represents a strongly allegorical and spiritualizing interpretation.

A somewhat similar conception of verse 19 to that of Augustine was put forward about the same time or even some years earlier in quite a short form by Hieronymus, in his *Comm. in Isaiam*, liv. 9 s.[1] Cf. also Hilarius, *Tractatus in cxli psalmum*, verse 7.[2] (As far as we understand here *etiam ante Noe tempore* is to be adverbial to *prædicavit*.)

THE AUGUSTINIAN LINE IN THE ROMAN CHURCH OF THE MIDDLE AGES.

Most of the western theologians of the Middle Ages, evidently much for the sake of Augustine, did not direct attention to 1 Pet. iii. 19 when they spoke of Christ's descent. Augustine's interpretation was noticed and followed by several leading European theologians of the Middle Ages. Thus the following theologians are subservient to Augustine in the passages quoted: Beda Venerabilis, *Expos. in Prim. epist. Petri*, iii. 19,[3] Walafrid Strabo, *Glossa ordinaria*, to 1 Pet. iii. 19,[4] Martinus Legionensis, *Expos. in Epist. I B. Petri, ad loc.*[5] Thomas Aquinas, *Summa theol.* iii, qu. 52, art. 2 (ad iii): *Augustinus tamen melius exponit in Epistola ad Evodium, ut referatur non ad descensum Christi ad inferos, sed ad operationem divinitatis ejus, quam exercuit a principio mundi: ut sit sensus, quod »his qui in carcere conclusi erant» viventes scilicet in corpore mortali, quod est quasi quidem carcer animæ »spiritu suæ divinitatis veniens prædicavit», per internas inspirationes, et etiam exteriores admonitiones per ora justorum ...*[6]

Important changes in the text of 1 Pet. iii. 19 can also be noticed in the traditional Latin text of the Middle Ages Bible, which implies

[1] *P.L.* xxiv, col. 521 A.
[2] *P.L.* ix, col. 836 B. — Cf. above, p. 36, regarding Ps. cxviii. 82.
[3] *P.L.* xciii, cols. 58 f.
[4] *P.L.* cxiv, col. 686 A.
[5] *P.L.* ccix, col. 235 B.
[6] *Divi Thomæ Aquinatis Summa Theologica*, Romæ 1886—87, vol. iv, p. 440 f.

a distinct attempt to find an evasive and paraphrasing form for this passage. This is probably due to the influence of Augustine.[1]

THE AUGUSTINIAN LINE AND CERTAIN SPECIAL FORMS OF ITS DEVELOPMENT IN PROTESTANTISM.

In modern times the Augustinian interpretation, which is supported by Thomas Aquinas himself, has mostly been taken up, not by Catholicism but by Protestantism.

Here it is in the first place not only a question of the detail that the preaching to the spirits in prison is assigned to the time before the Flood. In the Protestant communion there are also many other interpretations. During the Reformation there prevailed in general a very great uncertainty regarding 1 Pet. iii. 19. It did not know what to do with this troublesome passage, which is so dangerous and can be so difficult to harmonize with the proclamation of man's responsibility before the threat of the Law and the Gospel's demand for belief. We need only remember our quotation from Martin Luther on page 1. And many different proposals are found both in Luther and his followers. Luther, Calvin, and Zwingli, however, all interpret the passage for the most part in one or other paraphrasing or spiritualizing way in order to avoid the Descent,[2] and in this they are followed by many later Protestant theologians.[3] BEZA, for example, attempts systematically to explain away all the Bible passages which seem to speak of the Descent, and he does this also with 1 Pet. iii. 19.[4] And this evasive, paraphrasing, allegorical interpretation is characteristic of Augustine's rendering of our passage.

---

[1] K. GSCHWIND, *Die Niederfahrt Christi*, pp. 41f., 49, has many examples of the variants of this text.
[2] E. VOGELSANG, Weltbild und Kreuzestheologie in den Höllenfahrtsstreitigkeiten der Reformationszeit pp. 96ff.
[3] Examples in P. J. JENSEN, *Læren om Kristi Nedfart*, pp. 95ff., 110ff. In this book, also, one can generally read of the interesting debates on the Descent doctrine during the Reformation period.
[4] JENSEN, *op. cit.*, pp. 113f.

EARLIER INTERPRETATIONS OF VERSE 19

The special Augustinian motif, that the preaching in question can be thought to have taken place in Noah's time, has also been taken up specially often by just the Protestant theologians. It will be enough to mention some names only in this connection: JOH. WINCKELMANN,[1] JOH. GERHARD,[2] ROB. LEIGHTON,[3] F. W. BESSER,[4] J. CHR. K. HOFMANN,[5] A. OPPENRIEDER,[6] W. KELLY,[7] TH. ZAHN,[8] G. WOHLENBERG.[9]

We have decided to consider as a special development of the Augustinian theory of a preaching in Noah's time by Christ in a pre-existing form, the teaching that it is actually Enoch who preached to the spirits in prison in accordance with the accounts in the Book that bears his name, ch. vi—xxxvi.

This theory appears either in the form that the words of the text ἐν ᾧ καὶ ... ἐκήρυξεν in verse 19 ought to be changed to 'Ενὼχ (καὶ) or ἐν ᾧ καὶ 'Ενὼχ ... ἐκήρυξεν, as earlier students suggested according to W. BOWYER, 1763.[10] This possibility is later indicated by GRIESBACH, KNAPP,[11] and in the polyglot of STIER & THEILE;[12] the change of text has in later times been recommended by J.

---

[1] J. WINCKELMANN, *Commentarius in Epistolas Petrinas*, ed. H. FEUSTKINGIUS, p. 1036. Here he says, in accordance with the doctrine of Christ's omnipresence: *Filius Dei, qui semper adfuit hominum generi, olim etiam ante diluvium per ministerium Noe, præconis Justitiæ ... prædicavit ... animabus hominum ...*
[2] *Commentarius super Priorem D. Petri epistolam*, 1641, p. 466.
[3] *A Practical Commentary*, pp. 217 ff.
[4] *Die Briefe St. Petri*, Bibelstunden, viii, 1854, pp. 216 ff.
[5] *Die heilige Schrift des N.T.*, vii. 1, 1875, pp. 130 ff.; *Der Schriftbeweis*, ii. 1, 2nd ed. 1859, pp. 477 f.; *Theologische Briefe der Professoren* DELITZSCH und VON HOFMANN, hrsg. von W. VOLCK, 1891, pp. 168 f., 227 f.
[6] 1 Petr. 3, 19, *Der Beweis des Glaubens* xxix, 1893, pp. 235 ff.
[7] *The Preaching to the Spirits in Prison*, 1900, p. 21 f.
[8] *Einleitung in das N.T.*, 3. Aufl., ii, 1907, p. 109.
[9] *Der erste und zweite Petrusbrief und der Judasbrief*, 1915, p. 112 ff.
[10] *Novum Testamentum Græcum*, suppl., *Emendationes conjecturales*, 1763. *Cf.* BOWYER, *Critical Conjectures*, 3rd ed. by J. NICHOLS, 1782.
[11] According to G. WOHLENBERG, *Der erste und zweite Petrusbrief und der Judasbrief*, 1915, p. 107 note 59.
[12] *Polyglotten-Bibel*, iv, 2. Aufl. 1849, p. 940.

CRAMER,[1] R. HARRIS,[2] M. R. JAMES,[3] J. MOFFATT,[4] E. GOODSPEED.[5] Or also, this theory takes the form that in verse 19 Christ is said to have gone to the Angels in Noah's time as incarnated in Enoch. This is F. SPITTA's thesis.[6] He was followed by W. BALDENSPERGER.[7]

THE LATER ROMAN CATHOLIC INTERPRETATION CHARACTERIZED BY THE VULGATE AND BY CARDINAL BELLARMINE.

Since the Reformation the theologians of the Roman Catholic Church have in general broken with the interpretation of 1 Pet. iii. 19 which prevailed during the Middle Ages, going back to Augustine. In this position they have usually considered that they ought to keep firmly to the thought that the discussed passage refers to a real *descensus ad inferos*. This probably is greatly due to a wish to support with this passage the theory of the Limbo and Purgatory, as against the Protestant critics of it. Yet the dogmatic difficulties here met, namely to imagine how Christ could preach the glad tidings of the resurrection, or whatever it was, also to the notorious sinners of the time before the Flood, are usually solved in the way mentioned before in considering Hippolytus and Hilarius &c.; *i.e.* it is assumed, mostly with the support of the Vulgate expression — just mentioned above — that the hearers of Christ's preaching were such spirits from the time

---

[1] Exegetica et critica, ii, Het glossematisch karakter van 1. Petr. 3, 19—21 en 4, 6, *Nieuwe Bijdragen* vii, 1891, pp. 73 ff.
[2] A Further Note on the Use of Enoch in 1. Peter, *The Exp.* vi. 4, 1901, pp. 347 ff.
[3] According to R. HARRIS, On a Recent Emendation, *The Exp.* vi. 5, 1902, pp. 317 f.
[4] *The N.T.*, 1913; *A New Transl. of the Bible*, [1925] 1928, p. 305.
[5] *Problems of New Testament Translation*, 1945, pp. 195 ff.
[6] *Christi Predigt an die Geister*, 1890, p. 34 ff.
[7] *Die messianisch-apokalyptischen Hoffnungen des Judentums*, 3. Aufl. 1903, p. 18.

before the Flood who managed to be converted in some way before Christ came to them during the *triduum mortis*.

The first that should be mentioned in this connection seems to be Cardinal CAJETANUS[1] (Thomas de Vio); later A. SALMERON,[2] E. SA[3] can be quoted. These theologians consider that the spirits who heard Christ's preaching had already managed to be converted.

However, he who clearly was of most importance in the spread of this interpretation was Cardinal ROBERT BELLARMINE.[4] In his *Disputationes de controversiis*, ii, *De Christo*, iv, *De anima Christi*, ch. xii—xvi,[5] he treats the whole problem in opposition to Augustine, Beza and Calvin. Bellarmine considers himself justified in stating that St. Peter in his Epistle says *etiam ex illis incredulis fuisse aliquos, qui etiam in fine vitæ pœnitentiam egerint, et licet quantum ad corpus perierint, tamen quantum ad animam salvi fuerint*, ch. xiii.[6] It was to such people that Christ directed His preaching. Thereby Bellarmine assumes that the prison is connected with the underworld, *ibid.*[7] He must then naturally have thought of Purgatory.[8]

This theory penetrated the Roman Catholic Church in general. Only a few of the many supporters of Bellarmine's concept, which was absolutely dominant within the Roman Catholic Church, can be listed: FR. SUAREZ,[9] ESTIUS,[10] BENEDICTUS XIV[11] among earlier theologians and among modern researchers CHR. PESCH,[12] BISPING,[13]

---

[1] According to U. HOLZMEISTER, *Commentarius*, p. 314.
[2] *Disputationes in epistolas canonicas*, 1604, iv, p. 84 col. 2.
[3] *Notationes in totam Scripturam Sacram*, 1598, p. 447.
[4] K. GSCHWIND, *Die Niederfahrt Christi*, pp. 19f., 53; HOLZMEISTER, *op. cit.*, p. 314.
[5] *Disputationes*, Ingolstadii 1586—93, i, cols. 541ff.
[6] *Op. cit.*, col. 547.
[7] *Op. cit.*, cols. 549f.
[8] P. J. JENSEN, *Læren om Kristi Nedfart*, p. 116.
[9] *Commentariorum ac disputationum in tert. part. D. Thomæ* tomus ii, qu. xliii. 3, ed. 1598, p. 483.
[10] *Commentarius in omnes ... epistolas ...*, 1616.
[11] *De festis Domini N. J. Chr.* i. 8. 5 (HOLZMEISTER, *op. cit.*, p. 315).
[12] *Prælectiones dogmaticæ*, iv, 1900.
[13] *Erklärung der sieben Katholischen Briefe*, 1871.

L. GONTARD,[1] L. JANSSENS,[2] W. VREDE,[3] J. FELTEN,[4] U. HOLZMEISTER,[5] S. KOWALSKI.[6]

THE ORTHODOX LUTHERAN THEORY OF A TRIUMPHANT AND JUDICIAL SERMON AND A NEW FORM OF IT.

At beginning of the seventeenth century a few important orthodox Lutheran specialist theses on the Descent opposed with great power the older Protestantism's quite usual allegorization of this point in the teaching, and demanded a literal conception of it as well as of other factors in the Apostles' Creed. They were DAN. CRAMER, *De descensu Jesu Christi ad inferos*, 1615, and HENR. ECKHARD, *Tractatus de descensu Christi ad inferos*, 1623.[7] At the same time they opposed the Catholic theory of an intermediate state after death, that is the theory regarding Purgatory, so important for Catholicism. According to these authors Christ really descended into Hell itself. Those there who heard His preaching could not have been already converted, no, they were sinners for ever lost. But that the preaching should contain a consoling message of salvation for the unbelievers and the lost, this was of course impossible for these orthodox theologians to accept. So their solution was that Christ *ad sedes Tartareas redivivus descendit ... ut ... suum ibi triumphum ageret et sicut paulo post terræ coelique incolis ita tunc quidem ipsis etiam inferis et damnatis in inferno victoriam suam manifestaret* — as ECKHART expressed it. These writers, there-

---

[1] *Essai critique et historique sur la première Épître de Saint Pierre*, 1905, pp. 85 ff.
[2] *Summa theologica*, v, 1902, p. 883.
[3] Judas-, Petrus- und Johannesbriefe, *Die Heilige Schrift des N.T:s*, iv, 1915, pp. 136 ff.
[4] Zur Predigt Jesu an »die Geister im Gefängnis», 1. Petr. 3, 19 f. und 4, 6, *Festschrift der Vereinigung katholischer Theologen »Aurelia»*, 1926, and *Die zwei Briefe des heiligen Petrus*, 1929, p. 110.
[5] *Commentarius*, i, 1937, pp. 346 ff.
[6] *Ztąpienie do piekieł Chrystusa Pana wedle nauki św Pietro Apostoła*, 1938 (cf. above, p. 5).
[7] The importance of these treatises is emphasized by P. J. JENSEN in *Læren om Kristi Nedfart*, pp. 118 ff. — See especially ECKHARD, p. 16.

fore, think of a triumph by Christ over the »spirits» and a terrifying manifestation of His power over them by means of a *prædicatio magis realis quam verbalis*. Fundamentally this was the prevailing theory during the whole time of Lutheran orthodoxy and is found especially in the leading dogmatic system constructors, but also in certain pietists. As an example of this ABRAHAM CALOV,[1] J. A. QUENSTEDT,[2] PH. JAC. SPENER[3] may be mentioned. During the nineteenth century, too, we find several Protestant theologians who tried to solve the problem with this theory, for example C. H. G. VON ZEZSCHWITZ.[4] Similar views have been put forward sporadically also by Roman Catholic theologians, both old and young. J. FRINGS[5] (1925) has an example of this in an essay.

This theory has appeared in a specialist form in two of the most important modern works in this sphere, namely P. J. JENSEN, *Læren om Kristi Nedfart*, 1903, and K. GSCHWIND, *Die Niederfahrt Christi*, 1911. These writers have, independently of one another, come to the result that 1 Pet. iii. 19 does not treat of a descent into the Realm of the Dead but of a revelation to spirits in higher regions, implying a manifestation of Christ's victory and triumph. In this Gschwind thinks of the Ascension and compares our passage *i.a.* with Eph. iv. 10 and 1 Tim. iii. 16.[6] JENSEN also seems to have thought, in the first place, of the Ascension, although he only quite indifferently says that Christ went away to the »transcendental sphere of the spirits».[7] These writers also deny that 1 Pet. iv. 6 has any connection with the Descent.[8]

---

[1] *Biblia Novi Testamenti illustrata*, ii, 1676, pp. 1505 ff.
[2] *Theologia didactico-polemica*, i, 1685, p. 512. (*Descensus*, but *per Noachum!*)
[3] *Einfache Erklärung*, 1677 (new ed. 1833, p. 257).
[4] *Petri Apostoli de Christi ad inferos descensu sententia* ..., 1857.
[5] Zu 1 Petr. 3, 19 und 4, 6, *Bibl. Zeitschr.* xvii, 1925/26, p. 86.
[6] GSCHWIND, *op. cit.*, pp. 119 ff., 144.
[7] JENSEN, *op. cit.*, p. 181.
[8] JENSEN, *op. cit.*, pp. 209 ff., 230; GSCHWIND, *op. cit.*, pp. 37 ff.

It is not possible to decide here to what extent the views of these two important researchers on the main dogmatic question of the kind and the circumstances of the preaching mentioned in iii. 19 was worth more attention and imitation.[1] The fact is however that scarcely any scholars of importance took up Gschwind's theory in its entirety with the central thesis of a preaching during the Ascension — Jensen is unknown in any case because of his language. On the contrary Gschwind's theory is repudiated in several representative publications in this sphere: it is for example quite neglected in the following comprehensive works on the history of the Descent dogma: C. SCHMIDT, Der Descensus ad inferos, 1919,[2] J. A. MACCULLOCH, *The Harrowing of Hell*, 1930, J. KROLL, *Gott und Hölle*, 1932.[3]

It is likely that this small success for Jensen and Gschwind is

---

[1] Quite apart from these special attempts at a solution of one of the main questions in our text, JENSEN and GSCHWIND have separately, and each in his own way, contributed to the understanding of 1 Pet. iii. 18—22 by certain general tendencies which must at once be considered very praiseworthy. They have both striven to show a connection between 1 Pet. iii. 18—22 and the context, and to explain the logical reason for the appearance of such a peculiar motif as the spirits of the Flood. In this way they definitely associate themselves with the thought (this thought is, however, not so generally recognized, as Jensen seems to state on p. 172) that verses 18—22 are all through an illustration of the rule in verse 17, that it is better to suffer in doing good than evil (JENSEN, pp. 172ff.; GSCHWIND, p. 109) and draw attention on the other hand to the position of the spirits of the Flood as a type of the present day unbelieving heathen world (JENSEN, p. 185, GSCHWIND, pp. 129ff.). These remarks must be considered as valuable suggestions.

[2] See above, note on pp. 7f.

[3] The following commentators, H. GUNKEL in *Die heilige Schrift des N.T:s*, ii, 2. Aufl. 1908, pp. 561f., R. KNOPF, *Die Briefe Petri und Judä*, 1912, pp. 147ff., F. HAUCK in *Das Neue Testament deutsch, in loc.*, think, like GSCHWIND, in the first place of the fallen Angels according to Gen. 6, but yet maintain firmly the Descent and the preaching of the Gospel. They, therefore, do not follow Gschwind in his main thesis. The description in U. HOLZMEISTER's *Commentary*, p. 316, is thus somewhat misleading, as Gschwind's theory is here first presented as a special type in research and then is stated to have been copied by Knopf, Gunkel and Hauck. (And Gunkel wrote his commentary before Gschwind's book was published.)

not only due to a certain inner improbability in their hypothesis, which we have already touched upon shortly, but can to a great extent be explained by the fact that the theologians of their time were so much and so generally dominated by the theories of a descent with a preaching of the Gospel that Jensen's and Gschwind's solitary voices were scarcely able to arouse any great attention, although both of them put forward specially powerful criticism just of the popular conception of this subject. At that time indeed, as also to-day, BELLARMINE's thesis regarding a conversion experienced in time, of which we have just spoken, still played a completely dominating role in Catholic quarters, and among the Protestants the constantly reappearing, but earlier mostly rejected, generous theory of a preaching of the Gospel to the unbelievers in Hell had won general approval for a long time past.

THE THEORY OF A HOPEFUL GOSPEL TO UNBELIEVERS GENERALLY ACCEPTED BY LATER PROTESTANT WRITERS.

During recent centuries a general boldness has appeared among the Protestants in accepting the hopeful preaching for the unconverted in Hades, as 1 Pet. iii. 19 at first sight and especially by iv. 6 seems to presume. After certain suggestions about this by some »rationalistic» dogmatists and exegetists in the latter half of the eighteenth century this teaching was strengthened by J. POTT,[1] W. M. L. DE WETTE,[2] and partly W. STEIGER, who published a fundamental commentary to 1 Pet. in 1832.[3] Also after the reaction against rationalism had become strong in the second quarter of the nineteenth century this bold conception was retained in the main, and in many quarters 1 Pet. iii. 19 was uncritically designated as the chief passage for the dogma of the Descent.[4]

---
[1] *Epist. cath.*, ii, 1790.
[2] *Lehrbuch der christl. Dogmatik*, i, 1813, pp. 272f.
[3] *Der erste Brief Petri*, 1832, p. 358ff.
[4] More detailed descriptions of this development are given by C. CLEMEN in »*Niedergefahren zu den Toten*», 1900, pp. 212ff., and P. J. JENSEN in *Læren om Kristi Nedfart*, pp. 142ff.

As examples from modern times the following names may be given: E. H. PLUMPTRE,[1] F. W. FARRAR,[2] CH. BIGG,[3] in England; I. DOEDOES[4] in Holland; J. L. KÖNIG,[5] E. GÜDER,[6] OERTEL,[7] G. F. C. FRONMÜLLER,[8] B. WEISS,[9] BEYSCHLAG,[10] C. CLEMEN,[11] J. T. BECK,[12] E. HUTHER,[13] H. CREMER,[14] H. JOSEPHSON,[15] E. KÜHL,[16] H. v. SODEN,[17] F. DELITZSCH[18] in Germany; J. MONNIER[19] in France.

In North America this teaching, which thus presumed a possibility of a further development after death also for the greatest sinners, has played an important part in learned and even unpopular discussions, some under the title of »Dornerism», after the German dogmatist DORNER, whose *Glaubenslehre*[20] was published in English in 1881—82.[21]

In Sweden, too, this teaching of a descent with general salvation has had defenders, among others the important cultural philosopher and poet VIKTOR RYDBERG who eloquently developed his thoughts

---

[1] *The Spirits in Prison*, 1884.
[2] *Mercy and Judgment*, 1882, p. 79.
[3] *Commentary on the Epistles of St. Peter*, 1901.
[4] *Jaarboeken voor wetensch. theol.* 1848.
[5] *Die Lehre von Christi Höllenfahrt*, 1842.
[6] *Die Lehre von der Erscheinung Jesu Christi unter den Todten*, 1853.
[7] *Hades*, 1863.
[8] *Die Briefe Petri und der Brief Judä*, 1862, p. 45.
[9] *Der Petrinische Lehrbegriff*, 1855, pp. 227ff.; *Lehrbuch der Biblischen Theologie*, 6. Aufl. 1895, § 48, pp. 167ff.
[10] *Neutest. Theol.*, i, pp. 420f.
[11] *»Niedergefahren zu den Toten»*, 1900, pp. 115ff.
[12] *Erklärung der Briefe Petri* (Vorles. 1837—78), hrsg. 1896, pp. 190 ff.
[13] *Kritisch exegetisches Handbuch über den 1. Brief des Petrus ...*, 1877 p. 182.
[14] *Über den Zustand nach dem Tode*, 1883, pp. 59f.
[15] Niedergefahren zur Hölle, *Beweis des Glaubens* xxxiii, 1897, pp. 414f.
[16] *Die Briefe Petri und Judæ*, 6. Aufl. 1897, pp. 219, 224.
[17] Hebräerbrief, Briefe des Petrus ..., *Hand-Commentar Zum N. T.*, iii. 2, 1890, p. 132.
[18] *Theologische Briefe der Professoren Delitzsch und v. Hofman*, pp. 150ff.
[19] *La première Epître de l'apôtre Pierre*, 1900, p. 177f.
[20] J. A. DORNER, *System der christlichen Glaubenslehre*, ii, 1881, pp. 662ff.
[21] See the report in C. CLEMEN, *»Niedergefahren zur Hölle»*, pp. 219f.

EARLIER INTERPRETATIONS OF VERSE 19

of this in »Till läran om de yttersta tingen», *Bibelns lära om Kristus*, 4th ed., 1880.[1] From other Scandinavian countries a sound essay by the Norwegian S. ODLAND, 1901, may be noted, who with several of his contemporary interpreters considered it most probable that iii. 19 speaks of a proclamation to the unbelievers in the Realm of the Dead, offering them salvation.[2] Earlier, in the 1840's, a violent clash of opinions had arisen in Norway in regard to such a preaching to the unbelievers. It was the »Haugians» who opposed an addition to E. PONTOPPIDAN's catechism, introduced in 1843 and containing the statement that Christ preached the Gospel to the spirits in prison. These people said that this teaching made the road to Heaven broad.[3] Thus it was the same doubts that arose here as so often in other places.

It can of course be considered that the light-hearted acceptance of this generous theory in iii. 19 and iv. 6 did not come to distinguish the modern Protestant world by chance. We have in this environment to consider partly a less strict insistence on the religious significance of the words in the Bible in every single passage, and partly a universal attitude conditioned both by the modern humanistic conception of mankind and of cultural views and by the thought of a world-wide mission. And this of course easily favoured the rejection of the doubts mentioned in the beginning of this chapter.

THE INTERPOLATION THEORY.

A convenient way to avoid the difficulties in 1 Pet. iii. 19 and the following verses is to explain that they are »not genuine» and assume an interpolation or a »marginal note by a reader». This theory was specially noticeable in Protestant circles at the end of the nineteenth and beginning of the twentieth centuries. The first

---

[1] Pp. 378, 381ff.
[2] S. ODLAND, Kristi prædiken for »aanderne i forvaring» (1 Petr. 3, 19), *Norsk Theol. Tidsskr.* ii, 1901, p. 216.
[3] W. A. WEXELS, *Aaben Erklæring*, 1845, *cf. Theol. Stud. u. Krit.* 1849, pp. 743ff.

who is usually mentioned in this connection is J. CRAMER;[1] further, A. MEYER,[2] W. SOLTAU,[3] D. VÖLTER,[4] P. SCHMIDT,[5] can be noted. It is perfectly clear that this »attempt at solution», psychologically regarded, has its root in a desire to avoid a troublesome association of ideas and liberate the Epistle from a passage considered as primitively »mythological». To what the interest is really due can also be seen from the following reasoning by the above-mentioned student A. MEYER: »Der erste Petrus-Brief ist vielleicht das liebenswürdigste Buch des Neuen Testaments: auch Luther hat ihn dem paulinischen an die Seite gestellt ... Mir unterliegt es übrigens keinem Zweifel, dass die berühmten Stellen von der Höllenfart Christi, die hier ganz fremdartig wirken, eingeschoben sind, wie auch das Satzgefüge zeigt.»[6]

SUMMARY.

It ought to be clear from this review of earlier interpretations of 1 Pet. iii. 19 that several different theories have appeared

[1] J. CRAMER, Exegetica et critica, II, Het glossematisch karakter van I. Petr. 3, 19—21 en 4, 6, *Nieuwe Bijdragen*, vii. 4, 1891, pp. 73—149. Not available to me, but *cf.* the following words in H. HOLTZMANN, Literatur zum Neuen Testament, *Theol. Jahresber.* xi, 1892, p. 125: »Cramer's eingehende Erörterung, welche für die Geschichte der Exegese auf keinen Fall verloren gehen sollte, sucht zu zeigen, dass der Stelle 1. Petr. 3, 19—21 überhaupt nicht aufzuhelfen sei und demnach nichts übrig bleibe als darin eine in den Text gedrungene Randbemerkung eines Lesers ('Ενώχ, woraus ἐν ᾧ καὶ wurde, τοῖς ἐν φυλακῇ πνεύμασιν ἐκήρυξεν) zu sehen, mit welcher auch die, zum Vorangehenden doch immer spröd sich verhaltende Notiz 4, 6 in Verbindung stehe.»

[2] A. MEYER, *Die moderne Forschung über die Geschichte des Urchristentums*, 1898, p. 43.

[3] W. SOLTAU, Die Einheitlichkeit des 1. Petrusbriefes, *Theol. Stud. u. Krit.* lxxviii, 1905, p. 302ff., *id.*, Nochmals die Einheitlichkeit des 1 Petrusbriefes, *Theol. Stud. u. Krit.* lxxix, 1906, pp. 456ff. Against Soltau, 1905, C. CLEMEN, Die Einheitlichkeit des 1. Petrusbriefes verteidigt, *Theol. Stud. u. Krit.* lxxviii, 1905, pp. 619ff.

[4] D. VÖLTER, *Der erste Petrusbrief*, 1906, pp. 8f., 23. (*cf. Theol. Jahresb.* 1906, p. 296).

[5] P. SCHMIDT, Zwei Fragen zum ersten Petrusbrief, *Zeitschr. f. wiss. Theol.*, 1, 1908, pp. 42ff.

[6] A. MEYER, *op. cit.*, p. 42f.

alternately at different times. No one of them can claim priority or special legitimacy. If any theory is to be regarded as specially strong because of being relatively older and of its greater frequency it is probably the one that presumes the conversion of the »spirits» in time before the coming of Christ, for this theory can, as we have tried to show, be found already in Hippolytus and in the Latin and Syriac translations of the Bible, and it distinguishes in general the interpretation of the modern Roman Catholic Church. But this circumstance alone does not in any way convince us that this theory expresses the original meaning of the text.

It is probably also clear that all the theories we have reported either imply an acceptance of the immediate conception obtainable from this passage, namely that the verses contain the information that Christ preached the Gospel to the unbelievers immediately after His death, or an attempt to avoid, by means of a certain change or reduction of this theory, the dogmatic and practical doubts which follow from this »immediate» conception.

All theories which occur in the history of the exegesis have not been given but, as we hope, the most important historical and the most characteristic. Similarly we hope we have shown that there are certain lines and a certain system in the history of this interpretation problem, and that, in spite of all, tradition has played an important part within certain limits.

*

When, however, it is a question of finding the real meaning of this verse, we cannot depend so much upon traditional interpretations, especially as it is not possible to come near enough to the earliest Christian time. In this we can only depend upon an analysis of the text itself.

CHAPTER II.

WHO ARE »THE SPIRITS» IN VERSE 19?

To obtain a basis for a proper, complete understanding of the significance of 1 Pet. iii. 19 we must in the first place explain certain fundamental details regarding the preaching to the spirits in prison mentioned in this verse.

It may be profitable to begin with the question: Who are »the spirits in prison»?

CONNECTION WITH THE STORY OF THE FLOOD IN GENESIS.

One can see easily from the context that these »spirits», τὰ ἐν φυλακῇ πνεύματα, have a certain connection with the story of the Flood in Gen. vi—ix, for it says in iii. 20 that the spirits had been disobedient in the days of Noah when the ark was built.

But when investigating this connection more closely we are confronted with two rather different possibilities.

POSSIBLE TO THINK BOTH OF FALLEN ANGELS AND SOULS OF MEN.

(a) Either these πνεύματα can be considered as identical with the superhuman beings from the time before Noah who are termed »Sons of God» or »Giants» in Gen. vi. 1—4 and later fallen »Angels» in Jude 6: ἀγγέλους τε τοὺς μὴ τηρήσαντας τὴν ἑαυτῶν ἀρχὴν ... εἰς κρίσιν μεγάλης ἡμέρας δεσμοῖς ἀϊδίοις ὑπὸ ζόφον τετήρηκεν, and in 2 Pet. ii. 4: ἀγγέλων ἁμαρτησάντων οὐκ ἐφείσατο ἀλλὰ σιροῖς ζόφου ταρταρώσας παρέδωκεν εἰς κρίσιν τηρουμένους. These two passages clearly reveal that the beings in question are considered as bound and imprisoned in the darkness of the underworld. In the *Book* of *Enoch*, vi—xxxvi, for example, there is a description in detail of how these Angels were cast out and imprisoned. In this case the expression πνεύματα would signify superhuman beings, spirits.

(*b*) Or also the author of the Epistle is thinking of ordinary people either in general or certain people from Noah's time. More closely defined it must be the »souls» of these people bound in the Realm of the Dead who are intended by τὰ ἐν φυλακῇ πνεύματα. Augustine's statement — in his *Epist.* clxiv, which we have quoted before,[1] — that St. Peter was thinking of Noah's contemporaries during their lifetime, considered as symbolically imprisoned in the body, implies a laboured, allegorical interpretation which cannot be accepted in modern exegetics. Among other things it can be mentioned that living people cannot be termed πνεύματα and that φυλακή in N.T. language is not used of the body as a prison, but appears *e.g.* in Rev. xviii. 2 and xx. 7 as a technical term for some subterranean custody compartment.[2] Whether then there is here a question of people in general or certain people from Noah's time, the word πνεύματα must in this case signify souls of the dead.

Thus it seems that the alternative to which we must first determine our attitude is: whether here is meant spirits or dead people's souls. A lively discussion has been carried on among research workers concerning this point,[3] and different reasons can also be put forward for each interpretation.

(*a*) Support for the theory that cast-out Angels are meant by the expression πνεύματα in verse 19 is as follows:[4]

The expression in verse 22 ὑποταγέντων αὐτῷ ἀγγέλων καὶ ἐξουσιῶν καὶ δυνάμεων can well be said to be connected with the thought in verse 19. Besides this, as we have just stated, two passages in

---

[1] *Cf.* above, pp. 38f.
[2] Several other cogent objections to Augustine, in many cases going back to Bellarmine, are collected in HOLZMEISTER, *Commentarius*, pp. 347f.
[3] See, for example, K. GSCHWIND, *Die Niederfahrt Christi*, pp. 76ff. There are many references to this problem in the different editions of [E. PREUSCHEN &] W. BAUER, *Griechisch-Deutsches Wörterbuch*, *s.v.* πνεῦμα; we only refer to them here.
[4] The most representative advocate of the theory of the fallen Angels is probably F. SPITTA (*Christi Predigt an die Geister*, 1890, pp. 22ff.).

54 WHO ARE »THE SPIRITS» IN VERSE 19? [CH.

two other of the General Epistles, Jude 6 and 2 Pet. ii. 4, tend in the same direction. And it is illuminating that these evil angels in general play an important part in the Jewish and earliest Christian literature, especially in the *Book of Enoch*¹ — we shall study this fact more closely later on.

Further we have a certain argument for this theory in the fact that the word πνεῦμα actually is not used generally about the dead:² a preferable word, at least according to the older Greek language, is ψυχή³ — and 1 Pet. is certainly written in quite good Greek.⁴ To this it has been objected that πνεῦμα can be found in several passages in the N.T. where it is a question of the dead in a certain form of existence as in Luke xxiv. 37—39, Acts xxiii. 8f., Hebr. xii. 23. But this objection is not absolutely decisive, for in these cases there is, in the first place, no question of Hades or of ordinary dead people but of some kind of higher beings. Also the words ζωοποιηθεὶς πνεύματι in verse 18 do not speak of an ordinary person in the Realm of Shadows but of Christ as at least to some extent risen from the dead.⁵ A person's πνεῦμα is generally the higher, spiritual part of him, which is derived from God and after judgment enters the Divine Presence, *e.g.* 1 Pet. iv. 6, the *Book of Enoch* xiii. 6. But when the thought is of an intermediary existence in Hades the word πνεῦμα is generally not used at all. Thus, when Paul in 1 Cor. v. 5 says that a person's πνεῦμα shall be saved at the Last Day it is surely not really meant that the dead person's form of existence before, in Hades, shall be termed πνεῦμα. And in none of the passages cited is πνεύματα in the plural, except in Hebr. xii. 23.

---

¹ See above all K. GSCHWIND, *Die Niederfahrt Christi,* pp. 76ff., 111f., 130ff. Further, for example, L. JUNG, *Fallen Angels in Jewish, Christian and Mohammedan Literature,* 1926, can be mentioned.
² See R. KNOPF, *Die Briefe Petri und Judä,* 1912, p. 149. There is to be found a detailed discussion of this question.
³ E. ROHDE, *Psyche,* 1893, pp. 3ff. *e.p.*
⁴ L. RADERMACHER, Der erste Petrusbrief und Silvanus, *Zeitschr. f. d. neut. Wiss.* xxv, 1926, pp. 287ff.
⁵ *Contra* W. BAUER in *Griechisch-Deutsches Wörterbuch,* 1937, col. 1126.

ii. WHO ARE »THE SPIRITS» IN VERSE 19?

It has been customary to put forward several passages from the *Book of Enoch* as an argument that πνεῦμα can refer to the souls of the dead.[1] Some of these are not at all convincing proofs. In some passages like xxii. 3 according to the Akhmim text, and ix. 3, 10 according to Sync., πνεῦμα is given as a synonym for ψυχή, clearly only because the translators needed a variant to ψυχή in order to construct a double expression such as τὰ πνεύματα τῶν ψυχῶν or τὰ πνεύματα καὶ αἱ ψυχαί, corresponding to Semitic terms like *něshāmāh* and *rūaḥ*, which sometimes appear in couples in the literature of Enoch and similar traditions.[2] The *Book of Enoch* ciii. 3 which formerly was also used as an argument for the thesis that πνεῦμα occurs as the word for the souls of the dead,[3] now becomes, on the contrary, an argument against this thesis after the finding of a Greek version of the last chapters in the *Book of Enoch*: for in this passage the Greek term is just ψυχή.[4] In the same way ψυχαί is used of the souls of the dead in Hades in the *Book of Enoch* cii. 4, 5, 11, ciii. 7f. This last passage runs as follows: αὐτοὶ ὑμεῖς (*i.e.* the sinners) γινώσκετε ὅτι εἰς ᾅδου ‹κατ›άξουσιν τὰς ψυχὰς ὑμῶν, καὶ ἐκεῖ ἔσονται ἐν ἀνάγκῃ μεγάλῃ καὶ ἐν σκότει καὶ ἐν παγίδι καὶ ἐν φλογὶ καιομένῃ, καὶ εἰς κρίσιν μεγάλην εἰσελεύσονται αἱ ψυχαὶ ὑμῶν ἐν πάσαις ταῖς γενεαῖς τοῦ αἰῶνος. In the same way ψυχαί is used of the souls in the Realm of the Dead in the *Book of Enoch* ix. 10, xxii. 3b, *cf.* x. 3 in *Sync.* References can also be made to Wisd. iii. 1, Acts ii. 27 (= Ps. xv [xvi]. 10), Rev. vi. 9, xx. 4. Further similar evidence could probably be drawn from many corresponding literary sources.

Several of the arguments which were formerly put forward in the discussion as evidence that τὰ πνεύματα in iii. 19 should refer to the souls of the dead are thus of little value. The only instances among them which are of undoubted value in this question are some passages in the *Book of Enoch* ch. xxii where πνεῦμα is clearly used of the souls of dead people in the Realm of the Dead. It is possible that xx. 3 and 6 can also be regarded as similar arguments. These are, however, some isolated exceptions, it must be admitted, and in opposition to them is a series of places in the *Book of Enoch* where πνεῦμα absolutely signifies »spirit», as in x. 15, xiii. 6, xv. 4, 6, *e.p.*

Thus we must say that πνεῦμα is used of the souls of the dead only in certain, often specially constructed, exceptional situations.

---

[1] See *e.g.* J. MONNIER, *La première épître de l'apôtre Pierre*, 1900, p. 176.
[2] *Cf.* 3 *Enoch*, ed. by H. ODEBERG, 1928, i, pp. 174ff., ii, p. 153.
[3] *E.g.* J. MONNIER, *loc. cit.*
[4] *The Last Chapters of Enoch in Greek*, ed. by C. BONNER, 1937, p. 65.

On the other hand πνεῦμα is a usual word for »spirits», higher spiritual beings or demons.[1] With reference to the general psychological terminology τὰ πνεύματα in 1 Pet. iii. 19 ought rather to be the fallen »Angels» from Gen. vi. 1—4.

(b) Perhaps the continuation in verses 20ff., especially the idea ἀπειθήσαντες, μακροθυμία, ὀκτὼ ψυχαί and διεσώθησαν which seem to give the text a somewhat anthropological character favours such an interpretation of πνεύματα in iii. 19 that the expression should refer to the souls of the people destroyed by the Flood.[2] Above all, however, this interpretation may be favoured by the words νεκροῖς εὐηγγελίσθη in iv. 6, in so far as this passage is really connected with verse 19, and implies a reference to the preaching unto the spirits there mentioned, as many believe. And there is perhaps also reason to assume such a connection, for in this way a logical coherence in the reasoning of the author is obtained so that the motive in iv. 6 about the preaching of the Gospel to the dead does not appear so suddenly and seem so peculiar and isolated. Whether such a connection can really be considered to exist and how in that case it should be conditioned is a complicated question which cannot be decided without an analysis of each passage by itself, but in any case we can probably lay it down that a connection of some kind is imaginable. The word νεκροί in iv. 6 thus makes it probable, with a certain presumption, that πνεύματα in iii. 19 refers to the souls of dead people, *i.e.* those destroyed by the Flood.

These are two opposed theories and both are well supported: perhaps the first, about the fallen Angels, slightly more so, but even for that reason it is difficult to ignore wholly the argument we have just put forward in support of the second.

The simplest way of getting out of this dilemma is simply to reckon with both possibilities at the same time and assume that

---

[1] H. CREMER & J. KÖGEL, *Biblisch-theologisches Wörterbuch*, 1915, pp. 952, 954; BAUER, *op. cit.*, cols. 1127f.

[2] Among the representatives of this theory may be mentioned CH. BIGG, *A Critical and Exegetical Commentary*, 1902, p. 162; H. CREMER & J. KÖGEL, *op. cit.*, p. 952.

WHO ARE »THE SPIRITS» IN VERSE 19?

the fallen Angels and people from the time of Noah have been confused, purposely or not.[1] There are also positive reasons for such an assumption.

(1) The text in Genesis easily allows an intimate combination of »Sons of God», »Giants» and ordinary »people». This is at least the case in the last verse of the passage vi. 1—4 where it is difficult to avoid a mingling of the groups just mentioned

Hebr.	LXX.
המה הגברים אשר	ἐκεῖνοι ἦσαν οἱ γίγαντες οἱ ἀπ'
מעולם אנשי השם	αἰῶνος, οἱ ἄνθρωποι οἱ ὀνομαστοί.

Besides that it is, we know, the Angels who brought Sin into the world, but the people who are punished through the Flood.

(2) It also happens in the later Jewish literature that the different categories easily overlap. For example, in reading the *Book of Enoch* vi—xxxvi it is easy not to differentiate so strictly between fallen Angels, »Watchers», fallen stars, »Giants», πνεύματα and ordinary people from the time of the Flood — and all sorts of categories. Yet everything in these chapters is concerned with almost the same thing, the great sinners from the time before the Flood and their punishment. In an isolated fragment from the *Book of Enoch*, preserved by Syncellus, those to whom the castigatory sermon is directed are addressed as υἱοὶ ἀνθρώπων, verse 3,[2] in spite of the fact that a mountain has just been alluded to where there was a conspiracy, which of course must refer to the Angels' conspiracy according to ch. vi. 6 in the same Book. Further, quite as the consequence of the Genesis story is that the Angels brought Sin to the earth, while it is the people who are punished, the same transfer is clearly the basis of the reasoning in *e.g.* the *Testament of Naphtali*, iii. 5, and the Syriac *Apocalypse of Baruch*, lvi. 10—16. Compare also how Philo, in his *De gigantibus*, clearly confuses ἄγγελοι and the human ψυχαί. In Irenæus there is a passage which

---

[1] H. WINDISCH, *Die katholischen Briefe*, 1930, p. 71. E. G. SELWYN, *The First Epistle*, p. 199.

[2] *The Old Testament in Greek*, ed. by H. B. SWETE, iii, 4th ed. 1912, p. 809.

also shows a combination such as we have in view: (ἵνα) τὰ μὲν πνευματικὰ τῆς πονηρίας καὶ ἀγγέλους παραβεβηκότας καὶ ἐν ἀποστασίᾳ γεγονότας καὶ τοὺς ἀσεβεῖς καὶ ἀδίκους, καὶ ἀνόμους καὶ βλασφήμους τῶν ἀνθρώπων εἰς τὸ αἰώνιον πῦρ πέμψῃ.[1]

Besides this we also know that different groups of Angels and Spirits with varying denominations in the N.T. and similar literature cannot be so strictly differentiated. Paul, for example, speaks of Angels, Rulers, Powers & c. without making any great difference.[2] It can further probably be stated that the different groups of people in the mythical and heroic primitive ages according to the general conception of Israel and the N.T., were never quite like ordinary people — in spite of the comparison in Matt. xxiv. 37 ff. and its parallels — for the first ages really had a special character, seeing that Angels and people could then associate with each other, and the happenings of that time have, according to the Biblical conception, an institutive importance and will also to a high degree be repeated in the last days.[3] In Jude 6 and 7 the fallen Angels and the towns of Sodom and Gomorrah are combined from exactly the same angle. In *Sanh.* xi. 3 (109a) it is said that apes, spirits, *shēdīm* and *līlīn* are descended from the people who wished to build the Tower of Babel.

On the whole the boundary between Angels and people in primeval time was probably not so definite in the eyes of the author and the readers of the 1 Pet.

(3) We must specially consider the fact recently mentioned, that the available Greek versions of the *Book of Enoch* of chs. i—xxxii (we have for one thing the important Akhmim text

---

[1] *P. G.* vii, col. 552A.
[2] Regarding Angels and Spirits in the N.T. and Judaism, see *e.g.* G. Kittel, *Theol. Wörterb. z. N.T.*, *s.v.* ἄγγελος, ἀρχή &c. Some references to modern literature are also to be had in *Svensk Exeg. Årsb.* viii, 1943 pp. 52, 54 *e.p.* Particularly as to Judaism we may further mention: F. Weber, *Jüdische Theologie*, 1897 pp. 166ff.; H. Duhm, *Die bösen Geister im A.T.*, 1904, J. Scheftelowitz, *Die altpersische Religion und das Judentum*, 1920, W. O. E. Oesterley, The Belief in Angels and Demons, *Judaism and Christianity*, i, 1937, pp. 193ff.
[3] *Cf.* below, pp. 71ff.

WHO ARE »THE SPIRITS» IN VERSE 19?

and for another the fragment preserved by Syncellus), which cover a great deal of the angelological part, chs. vi—xxxvi, contain many passages with the term πνεύματα both in connection with the fallen Angels, the »Giants» & c., and the souls of dead people, so that in both cases it is certainly beings bound and in prison as a punishment for their transgressions that are referred to.

Thus πνεύματα appears of the fallen and imprisoned Angels or of their offspring the »Giants» in the following places (we refer here in the first place to the Akhmim fragment, to which the Syncellus text, as far as it is preserved, offers complete parallels): *Book of Enoch* x. 15, xiii. 6, xv. 4, 6, 7, 8 (*bis*), 9 (*bis*), 10 (*bis*), 11 (π. τῶν γιγάντων *bis*, and once only π.), 12 (according to *Sync.*), xvi. 1, xix. 1 — on the other hand πνεύματα is used in these Greek versions, strangely enough, not of the Angels who continued to be good, who sometimes, however, are called ἐγρήγοροι, »Watchers», exactly as their fallen brothers (see *e.g.* xii. 3f.).

At the same time πνεύματα appears of the souls of people, shut up in a »prison» in the Realm of the Dead, in the following passages: xxii. 3, 6, 7, 9 (*bis*), 11 (*bis*), 12, 13 (*bis*), also ix. 3, 10 according to *Sync*.

The passages xx. 3 and 6 allow of different interpretations.

Thus πνεύματα appears in the available Greek parts of the *Book of Enoch* with very great frequency and with the varying meanings »spirits» and »souls».

From all these analogical conditions it must be quite probable that πνεύματα in 1 Pet. iii. 19 can be both Angels and souls of human beings at the same time without any distinction.

RELATIONS TO THE BOOK OF ENOCH.

We have thus had an opportunity to review the remarkably great frequency with which the term πνεύματα appears in the rather short part of the *Book of Enoch* which deals with the spirits of the Flood and their imprisonment, that is just what 1 Pet. iii. 19 seems to have in view. Must we not now, especially in consideration of the extraordinary role this Book seems to have

60 WHO ARE »THE SPIRITS» IN VERSE 19? [CH.

played in early Christendom, ask ourselves whether the term πνεύματα in this passage is chosen only because of an association with that Book's angelological part where πνεύματα are so often mentioned? As a matter of fact there is much support for this assumption.[1] In any case it is highly extraordinary that the author of 1 Pet. speaks of the beings from the Flood as πνεύματα. Supported by internal evidence an attempt has often been made to explain this by saying that the author wished to procure conformity with the previous statement that Jesus went to these beings and preached to them ἐν πνεύματι — supposing this is the meaning of the words ἐν ᾧ, which introduce verse 19.[2] But firstly it is uncertain whether ἐν ᾧ refers to the previous word πνεύματι — as we shall see later;[3] and secondly it is not only exaggerated and far-fetched but also implies a serious confusion of ideas to compare πνεῦμα in verse 18, which has the character of something higher, divine, and here should actually indicate Christ's existential sphere, His life element after the Resurrection, with τὰ πνεύματα in verse 19, where the word undoubtedly is an appellative and qualifies beings who under all circumstances stand much, much lower than the Christ restored to life. If the writer had really meant to emphasize some essential relation between the Saviour vivificated in the Spirit and those disobedient »spirits» he ought

---

[1] Among those who earlier, and quite generally, wanted to maintain a dependence of 1 Pet. iii. 19 on the *Book of Enoch* may be mentioned: F. C. BAUR, *Theol. Jahrb.* 1856 pp. 215f., H. EWALD, Uebersicht, *Jahrbücher der Bibl. Wissensch.* viii, 1856, p. 191; A. HILGENFELD, Die jüd. Apokalyptik, *Zeitschr. f. wiss. Theol.* iii, 1860, p. 334; G. VOLKMAR, Einige Bemerkungen, *ibid,* iv. 1861, p. 115; *id.,* Ueber die katholischen Briefe und Henoch, *ibid.,* pp. 427ff.; FR. SPITTA, *Christi Predigt an die Geister,* 1890, pp. 34ff.; J. R. HARRIS, A Further Note on the Use of Enoch in 1 Peter, *The Expos.* vi. 4, 1901, pp. 346ff.; R. H. CHARLES, *The Book of Enoch,* 1912. *Cf.* E. G. SELWYN, *The First Epistle,* p. 199 *e.p.*

[2] *E.g.* E. KÜHL, *Die Briefe Petri und Judæ,* p. 221. *Cf.* already the text of Hippolytus, quoted above (p. 26), and Cyrillus in *Catenæ, ad loc*: Τῇ ψυχῇ (this word is clearly used instead of πνεύματι) πορευθεὶς ἐκήρυξε τοῖς ἐν ᾅδου, ὡς ψυχὴ μετὰ ψυχῶν ὀφθείς (J. A. CRAMER, *Catenæ,* viii, 1844, p. 66).

[3] Below, pp. 103ff.

ii.] WHO ARE »THE SPIRITS» IN VERSE 19? 61

to have done precisely the opposite, avoided calling them πνεύματα, and instead written ψυχαί, ἀρχαί, or something corresponding, to bring out the great difference in exaltation and rank, indeed just in »spiritualness». No, the author has certainly not thought here of any relation to Christ's πνεῦμα when he calls the beings in question πνεύματα. It is thus impossible to explain the choice of the term πνεύματα by reference to any internal, logical motive.

And yet it is scarcely possible πνεύματα is used wholly at random or in routine: for this word is an ordinary term for »spirits», especially demons and similar beings,[1] but it is probably not used of the beings from the Flood in any other place in early Christian and related literature than here in 1 Pet. and the *Book of Enoch*. In other places these beings are called »Angels»,[2] »Watchers»,[3] »Giants»[4] &c., but not πνεύματα, except in the two places we have indicated.

Thus there is very good reason to count upon an active, external reason, and such we can find just in the fact that the *Book of Enoch* in its angelological part so often uses πνεύματα of the beings from the Flood.

Now, can we really assume that the author of 1 Pet. got influenced by a Greek text of the *Book of Enoch*, so that he was directly inspired by this text when terming the spirits of the Flood πνεύματα? Yes, there is nothing to prevent us assuming that this apocryphal Book — whose origin is generally placed in the second century B.C. — was available in Greek at least in part during the first century A. D. On the contrary, the clear allusions to it[5] in 2 Pet. ii. 4, 9f., Jude 6 and especially 14f. are strong evidence for such an assump-

---

[1] *E.g.* Acts xxiii. 8f., Hebr. i. 14, Matt. xii. 43, Mark. i. 23, 26 &c., Rev. xvi, 13, xviii. 2.
[2] *E.g.* 2 Pet. ii. 4, Jude 6; Philo, *De gig.* 6.
[3] *E.g.* the *Book of Enoch* i. 5 *e.p.*; the *Book of the Secrets of Enoch* xviii. 3; the *Book of Jubilees* iv. 15; the *Testament of Reuben* v. 6f.
[4] *E.g.* Ecclus. xvi. 7; the *Book of Enoch* vii. 2 *e.p.*; the *Book of Jubilees* xx. 5.
[5] H. J. LAWLOR, Early Citations from the Book of Enoch, *Journ. of Philol.* xxv, 1897, pp. 164ff.; E. SCHÜRER, *Geschichte des jüdischen Volkes*, 4th ed., iii, 1909, pp. 284ff.; A. LODS, *Le Livre d'Hénoch*, 1892, pp. xxxviiiff.

WHO ARE »THE SPIRITS» IN VERSE 19? [CH.

tion. The supposed relation can also be inferred from other clear allusions to a book by Enoch in the *Testaments of the Twelve Patriarchs*,[1] the *Epistle of Barnabas*,[2] in Justin the Martyr,[3] &c.[4] The quotation from the *Book of Enoch* i. 9, in Jude 14f. seems even to indicate that the author of the latter had before him a text of this Book which very closely agreed just with the Greek text where we sought the word πνεύματα — *i.e.* the text which has become available to science by the discovery in Akhmim (according to modern views the MS discovered there is older than at first thought, and can be ascribed to the 5th or the 6th century).[5] Such an intimate agreement between two texts as these between Jude 14f. and the *Book of Enoch* i. 9 according to the Akhmim text is something extraordinarily rare in early Christian and similar literature. *Cf.*:

Enoch i. 9.   Jude 14f.

ὅτι ἔρχεται   ἰδοὺ ἦλθεν Κύριος
[Eth.: »with myriads of Saints»] }
σὺν τοῖς ἁγίοις αὐτοῦ   ἐν ἁγίαις μυριάσιν αὐτοῦ
ποιῆσαι κρίσιν κατὰ πάντων   ποιῆσαι κρίσιν κατὰ πάντων
καὶ ἀπολέσει πάντας τοὺς ἀσεβεῖς   καὶ ἐλέγξαι[6] πάντας τοὺς ἀσεβεῖς
καὶ ἐλέγξει πᾶσαν σάρκα
περὶ πάντων ἔργων τῆς ἀσεβείας   περὶ πάντων τῶν ἔργων ἀσεβείας
     αὐτῶν   αὐτῶν
ὧν ἠσέβησαν   ὧν ἠσέβεσαν
καὶ σκληρῶν ὧν ἐλάλησαν λόγων   καὶ περὶ πάντων τῶν σκληρῶν
καὶ περὶ πάντων ὧν κατελάλησαν   λόγων ὧν ἐλάλησαν
κατ' αὐτοῦ ἁμαρτωλοὶ ἀσεβεῖς.   κατ' αὐτοῦ ἁμαρτωλοὶ ἀσεβεῖς.

---

[1] *Cf. Test. Jud.* xviii. 1 and *En.* lxxxix. 51ff.; further *Test. Reub.* v and *En.* vi. 12, viii. 1, &c.
[2] Chs. iv. 3, xvi. 5.
[3] *Apol.* ii. 5.
[4] See also, *e.g.* SCHÜRER, *op. cit.*, with further references.
[5] F. KENYON, *The Palæography of Greek Papyri*, 1899, p. 119; *id., The Bible and Archæology*, 1940, p. 248, C. BONNER, *The Last Chapters of Enoch in Greek*, 1937, p. 3.
[6] Notice, however, ἐλέγξει in the next line in the Enoch text.

ii.] WHO ARE »THE SPIRITS» IN VERSE 19? 63

In considering these texts, which resemble each other as closely as anyone can desire, knowing the rather free way in which the N.T. and the Fathers of the Church quote the Scriptures, it is absolutely impossible to avoid the conclusion that Jude is depending on the Enoch text almost exactly as it is in the Akhmim fragment,[1] or at least one very analogous. It has been assumed that the Akhmim text and the Syncellus fragments are not primary Greek versions of the *Book of Enoch*,[2] and it is also possible that there were Greek forerunners to them. We know nothing of this for certain, and in addition, considering the usual development of ancient traditions it is not so suitable to count upon definitely limited and formally fixed translations, »editions» and »adaptations» of a certain »publication», but we ought rather to assume an organic — but not quite synchronized — transition which is dependent even on the influence from the lower stratum of living oral tradition. Under all conditions, we must consider that the Greek text from which Jude quoted was either very similar to the now available Akhmim text, or, the simplest assumption, was relatively identical with it.

It must be considered impossible that the similarities between the Enoch text and Jude should be explained by assuming a gradual assimilation of the former to the latter.[3] If the dependence had been in this direction the Enoch text would probably have been completely identical with that of Jude, and the individual, inserted expressions would have been inexplicable.[4] A quotation from the *Book of Enoch* i. 9 in [Ps.] Cyprian, *Ad Novatianum*[5] also shows clearly where the priority is to be sought. There are the words: *et perdere omnes,* corresponding to the Akhmim fragment's καὶ ἀπολέσει πάντας but differing from that of Jude's Epistle καὶ ἐλέγξαι πάντας.[6]

---

[1] *Cf.* A. Lods, *Le Livre d'Hénoch*, p. xl: »Il reste entre le texte ainsi constitué et la citation de Jude des différences notables, sans que rien toutefois force à admettre que l'auteur de l'épître a eu sous les yeux une autre recension: Tout s'explique s'il citait de mémoire.»
[2] R. H. Charles, *The Book of Enoch*, 1912, ad loc. and *The Apocrypha and Pseudepigrapha*, ii, 1913, p. 167.
[3] *Contra* Lawlor, Early Citations, pp. 165f.; *cf.* Th. Zahn, *Einleitung in das N.T.* 3. Aufl., ii, 1907, pp. 107f.
[4] *Cf.* Lods, *op. cit.*, pp. xxxix f.
[5] *S. Thasci Caec. Cypriani opera*, ed. Gv. Hartel, iii, 1871, p. 67.
[6] *Cf.* Th. Zahn, *Geschichte des neutestamentlichen Kanons*, ii, 1892, pp.

Thus the quotation from the *Book of Enoch* i. 9 in Jude 14f. proves that there was, in the time of the N.T., a Greek text to this Book, which bore at least much analogy to the Greek text we have in the Akhmim fragment.[1]

This must to a great extent support our assumption that the word πνεύματα in 1 Pet. iii. 19 is derived from the *Book of Enoch* in a Greek version.[2]

This assumption can to some extent perhaps be supported also by the fact that here in 1 Pet. iii. 19 we even find the word πορευθείς which occurs several times in the Greek parts of the *Book of Enoch* under discussion, just with regard to the appearance of the protagonist to the fallen Angels for the purpose of certain communications. Thus it says in xii. 4: Ἐνώχ, ὁ γραμματεὺς τῆς δικαιοσύνης, πορεύου καὶ εἰπὲ τοῖς ἐγρηγόροις τοῦ οὐρανοῦ, and in xiii. 3, as to how this commission was carried out: τότε πορευθεὶς εἴρηκα πᾶσιν αὐτοῖς, after which πορευθείς recurs immediately afterwards in verse 7.

If one reflects more closely over πορευθείς in 1 Pet. iii. 19 it is easy to get the impression that the pleonastic use of this word has a rather peculiar position in this connection.[3] Nowhere else in the N.T. Epistles is there a single example of the pleonastic use of πορεύομαι with a finite verb, corresponding to the Semitic use of *hlk* which we otherwise know from the Gospels written in a more popular style and coloured by Semitic idioms.[4] And just 1 Pet. is written in a particularly careful Greek, so that one must wonder why the author has used this construction.

798ff.; *id.*, *Forschungen*, v, p. 158, regarding Ps. Cyprian's quotation referring to the *Book of Enoch* and not to Jude.

[1] *Cf.* LODS, *op. cit.*, p. 100.

[2] Strangely enough the striking terminological accordance in the use of the word πνεύματα has not been noticed by FR. SPITTA, who, also, in general, does not pay much attention to the Greek text. Otherwise this investigator would have obtained a splendid instance of the thesis which, perhaps more energetically than any other, he has maintained in his book *Christi Predigt an die Geister*, namely that 1 Pet. iii. 19ff. depends upon the Enoch Tradition.

[3] Acknowledged, for example, by E. KÜHL in *Die Briefe Petri und Judæ*, p. 222; P. J. JENSEN, *Læren om Kristi Nedfart*, p. 168.

[4] W. BAUER, *Griechisch-Deutsches Wörterbuch*, *s.v.*; A. DEBRUNNER, *Friedr. Blass' Grammatik*, § 419. 2, with references.

ii.] WHO ARE »THE SPIRITS» IN VERSE 19? 65

It is impossible to assume that this πορευθείς is an analogy to the πορευθείς εἰς οὐρανόν occurring in iii. 22 and thus means »during the Ascension».[1] In this case πορευθείς ought to have been provided with some other characteristic qualifications. Now it is quite clear that the object of the action expressed in πορευθείς must be »the spirits» just because τὰ πνεύματα has grammatically been combined both with the participle πορευθείς and with the finite verb ἐκήρυξεν, but in form is governed only by the latter - quite good Greek — so the meaning is that Christ went to the spirits and preached to them.[2] Besides this it may be observed, that πορευθείς is an aorist form and indicates a momentary action. If the meaning was that Christ preached during His Ascension, the present participle ought to have been used. Yet Christ cannot first have ascended and then preached to these spirits: no one is ready to assume anything like that. It is thus impossible to place such a pregnant significance in πορευθείς in iii. 19 that it would be equivalent to πορευθεὶς εἰς οὐρανόν in iii. 22. Consequently πορευθείς in verse 19 must simply be regarded as referring to a going to the spirits combined with a preaching to them. Phrases like ἐπορεύθη εἰς τὸν ὀφειλόμενον τόπον τῆς δόξης, 1 Clem. v. 4, cf. 7, are no evidences of the other more special meaning, for we have not the verb here in an absolute form. Another thing is that perhaps we can reckon with the possibility that the spirits were in space instead of being in the underworld, as one is most inclined to believe.[3]

On the other hand we have an analogy to πορευθείς, meaning »having gone to», in the expression ἐλθὼν εὐηγγελίσατο ... τοῖς μάκραν, Eph. ii. 17. Here too, the participle has a rather pleonastic function. But in this passage there is yet a somewhat more natural emphasis on the locomotion than in 1 Pet. — notice the words τοῖς μάκραν. So we must keep to our impression that πορευθείς is a little peculiar in the connection.[4]

Here, possibly we can get some help to a better understanding by thinking that the author of the Epistle has allowed his formulation and his choice of words to be influenced by the actual words in some available earlier tradition. And it is easily seen both that the author in iii. 19 ff. in general makes use of facts already known and that nearly all the words used in these verses

---

[1] K. GSCHWIND, Die Niederfahrt Christi, pp. 89, 119 ff., is a representative of the theory of the Ascension, but he clearly does not dare to press the meaning of the word πορευθείς too far.
[2] R. KÜHNER & B. GERTH, Ausführliche Grammatik, ii. 2, 1904, § 600. 3, pp. 575 f.
[3] Cf. below, pp. 116ff.
[4] Certainly it may be said that in this way the author excludes any possibility of a spiritualising paraphrasing in the style of Augustine (so also e.g. J. E. HUTHER, Kritisch exegetisches Handbuch über den 1 Brief des Petrus ..., 1877, p. 181); but this is here not due to the author's own calculation.

5

are traditional in character and refer to different facts in Biblical accounts or similar sources. Now we have seen πορεύομαι several times in the *Book of Enoch* used of a movement followed by preaching to these fallen Angels and »spirits in prison» who seem to be identical with »the spirits» in iii. 19. And we certainly know from Jude 14f. and also, for example, from the *Epistle of Barnabas* xvi. 5,[1] that this Book was considered equal in value to the canonical O.T. in certain circles of the Early Church. It may therefore not be too bold to assume that the expressions mentioned in the *Book of Enoch* chs. xiif. — or a text somewhat similar — have given rise to the use of πορευθείς also in iii. 19. But this is, of course, only a supposition.

The imprisonment of the »spirits» is, however, a fact which must be said to be common to the angelological descriptions in the *Book of Enoch* vi—xxxvi and 1 Pet. iii. 19. The word φυλακή which here must, of course, mean »prison»[2] does not appear about the Angels' imprisonment in the Greek text we have of this Book. On the other hand we recognize the word φυλακή as the name for a place where evil »spirits» (πνεύματα) or Satan are kept in Rev. xviii. 2 and xx. 7. Yet in the *Book of Enoch* it says that the transgressors are bound, x. 4, 12, 14, xiii. 1, xviii. 16, xxi. 3f., 6, in a δεσμωτήριον (συγκλείσεως), x. 13, xviii. 14, xxi. 10, in the darkness, x. 4, 5, xviii. 2, xxii. 2, in valleys and holes in the earth, x. 12, xviii. 11, xxii. 2ff., right down into the Abyss, xxi. 7, and that their leader Azazel was flung down into the desert of »Daduel»[3] or »Dudael»,[4] x. 4, which is said to be »opened»[5] for this purpose, so

---

[1] *Cf.* above, pp. 61f., and below, p. 67.
[2] Not »watchpost» (Calvin) or anything similar. All such spiritualising or paraphrasing is, of course, in vain.
[3] The Akhmim fragment has Δαδουηλ.
[4] Syncellus has Δουδαηλ = the Ethiopic text's ዱዳኤል.
[5] A. GEIGER in *Jüd. Zeitschr.* iii, 1864/65, pp. 200ff. has assumed that Dudael = חדודו or חדודי, the abyss into which Azazel's goat was cast according to *Targ. Ps. Jon.* to Lev. xvi. 8, 10, 21 and *Mishna Joma* vi. 5. *Cf.* the notes *ad loc.* by G. BEER in E. KAUTZSCH, *Die Apokryphen und Pseudepigraphen*, 1900, and by R. H. CHARLES in his editions of the *Book of Enoch*.

that the thought goes to a swallowing up in the underworld[1] — אל דודא can also mean »God's cauldron»[2] — just as, for example, in Rev. xx. 3, 10. Compare also the *Book of Enoch* lxix. 28, lxxxviii. 3, the *Book of Jubilees*, v. 10. Sometimes also the prison is said to contain burning fire, *En.* x. 6, 13, xviii. 11, *e.p.* We recognize the prospect when we read 2 Pet. ii. 4 and Jude 6, which just treats of the fallen Angels from the time before Noah. Our passage in 1 Pet. most probably contains an allusion to these descriptions. Even if the term φυλακή is not found in the *Book of Enoch* the thing itself is widely and concretely presented there. It may be added that even dead people's πνεύματα are thought to be confined in some kind of subterranean prison, ch. xxii. We have therefore good reason also in this respect to associate 1 Pet. with the *Book of Enoch* and allow the latter to help in explaining the meaning of τὰ ἐν φυλακῇ πνεύματα in iii. 19.

On the whole we are justified in placing the *Book of Enoch* as an important background to the passage we are studying. It has been shown that this Book and the ideas connected with it has exercised great influence on early Christianity, at least in some connections. First of all, as is well known, one can consider that the idea Son of Man, which plays an important part in the Messianology of the Gospels, is intimately connected with the Enoch traditions. Further we find that much of Jesus' talk and parables have close parallels in the *Book of Enoch*.[3] As already pointed out this Book is quoted in Jude 14f. and clearly also lies behind certain other passages in 2 Pet. and Jude: ii. 2, and 6, respectively.[4] It is also quoted, definitely as a canonical writing, in the *Epistle of Barnabas* xvi. 5 (λέγει γὰρ ἡ γραφή, as it says here). Among other Early Church quotations can be mentioned *Just. Apol.* ii. 5,

---

[1] A. Lods, *Le Livre d'Hénoch*, p. 117.
[2] A. Dillmann, *Das Buch Henoch*, 1853, p. 100.
[3] In *Reich Gottes und Menschensohn*, 1940, p. 310, R. Otto says: »Die Übereinstimmung ist so gross, dass man hier geradezu von einem Schulzusammenhange reden muss.»
[4] G. Volkmar, Ueber die katholischen Briefe und Henoch, *Zeitschr. f. wiss. Theol.* iv, 1861, pp. 425ff.

Athenag. Legat. 24f., *Iren. Contra haer.* i. 15, 6, iv. 16. 2, iv. 36. 4, v. 28. 2, *Clem. Alex. Ecl. prophet.* iii. 456, 474, *Strom.* iii. 9.[1] Tertullianus fought to get the book regarded as canonical.[2] It is quite clear that it must have had great importance in the Early Church.[3] In connection with our study the reflections of the *Book of Enoch* in 2 Pet. and Jude are specially striking. But these two Epistles are not entirely without connections with 1 Pet., — on the contrary, in some respects these writings form a group by themselves[4] — this must be recognized whatever attitude one takes up as regards the question of who are their authors. Quotations from and allusions to the *Book of Enoch* in 2 Pet. and Jude are therefore very illuminating analogies.

Still another analogy to the case of reflection from the *Book of Enoch*, as we now assume regarding 1 Pet. iii. 19, is probably to be found within that Epistle. It is the interesting sentence in i. 12: οἷς (*scil.* the Prophets) ἀπεκαλύφθη ὅτι οὐχ ἑαυτοῖς ὑμῖν δὲ διηκόνουν αὐτά (*i.e.* produced their prophecies). According to our thought the following sentence in the *Book of Enoch* i. 2 is in agreement with this: καὶ οὐκ ἐς τὴν νῦν γενεὰν διενοούμην, ἀλλὰ ἐπὶ πόρρω οὖσαν ἐγὼ λαλῶ.[5] *Cf.* the term ἐκλεκτοί, important in both writings, *e. g. En.* i. 8, xxxviii. 1 ff. *e. p.*, 1 Pet. i. 1 — v. 13 *passim*.[6]

After all this we can say that there are several, some very strong, arguments for the hypothesis that the idea τὰ ἐν φυλακῇ πνεύματα in 1 Pet. iii. 19 is to a considerable extent dependent upon the idea of the fallen Angels especially such as they appear in the *Book of Enoch*, chs. vi—xxxvi.

---

[1] LAWLOR, Early Citations, pp. 164ff.; R. H. CHARLES, *The Book of Enoch*, 1912 (*cf. id.* in *The Apocr. and Pseudepigr.*).
[2] TH. ZAHN, *Geschichte des neutestamentlichen Kanons*, i, 1888, pp. 120ff.
[3] When this is denied in some quarters, it is probably for special dogmatic reasons. See, for example, the moderation of J. B. FREY in his article Apocryphes de l'Ancien Testament, *Dictionnaire de la Bible*, Supplément, i. 1928, col. 369.
[4] See for example CH. BIGG (a rather objective and unbiassed investigator) in *A Critical and Exegetical Commentary*, 1902, pp. 226f.; U. HOLZMEISTER, *Commentarius*, i, pp. 87—93, 96—103; *id.* in *Biblica* xxii, 1941, pp. 72f.
[5] *Cf.* R. HARRIS, An Unobserved Quotation from the Book of Enoch, *The Exp.* vi 4, 1901, pp. 195ff.
[6] SCHRENK, ἐκλεκτός, KITTEL, *Theol. Wört.* iv, pp. 188ff.

WHO ARE »THE SPIRITS» IN VERSE 19?

The result we have thus come to regarding the *Book of Enoch* as a source of inspiration to τὰ ἐν φυλακῇ πνεύματα in iii. 19 does not exclude the possibility that it can at the same time refer to the souls of dead people. These are also mentioned in that part of the Book which we have been considering. They are similarly called πνεύματα and these dead are also said to be shut up in some kind of prison, ch. xxii. But it is clear that the comments on the Angels are completely dominant in the connection. The dead play a very inferior part and are really only mentioned in passing. And regarding the word πορευθείς, we have only been able to show a possible agreement in two chapters of the *Book of Enoch*, where only the fallen Angels are being considered. Therefore we must say that if τὰ πνεύματα in iii. 19 is to include both »spirits» and »souls» of dead people, as appears from the reasons already given, it will be clear on the basis of the connections with this Book that in any case the most important thought must be of the fallen Angels.

The same point of view is probably also reached if in general one reflects on the great importance which the conception of the fallen Angels must have had in N.T. times. This importance appears not only from the different Books of Enoch but also from a whole series of other Jewish writers from early times, such as Wisd.,[1] Ecclus.,[2] Bar.,[3] the *Book of Jubilees*,[4] the *Damascus Documents*,[5] &c. The ordinary people from the days of the Flood, on the other hand, do not play the same role at all in the literature (in spite of the fact that they appear in Matt. xxiv. 37ff. and Luke xvii. 26f.).

Now we can preliminarily formulate as follows the answer to the question: »Who are the spirits in prison?» They are the transgressors from the time of the Flood, with no very great difference between Angels and people, but with greater stress on the *motif* complex connected with the Angels' fall. In the first place

---

[1] xiv. 6.
[2] xvi. 7.
[3] iii. 26.
[4] Ch. v.
[5] ii. 18 (S. SCHECHTER, *Fragments of a Zadokite Work*, 1910, p. xxxiii).

the thought of the writer of the Epistle can probably be illustrated from the angelological part of the *Book of Enoch*. But to complete the picture there given one can probably also put forward some similar and connected ideas from the other literature belonging to the environment of the N.T.

We shall now see what picture of the spirits of the Flood can be obtained from this literature. In doing this we shall, of course, mostly select such characteristics as really seem to be important for our study.

WHAT CAN BE LEARNED FROM THE IDEAS OF THE FLOOD BEINGS IN THE BOOK OF ENOCH AND RELATED WRITINGS.

The first thought that arises, when considering what current ideas of the beings from the Flood the author of 1 Pet. has in mind when in iii. 19 he presents them as an argument, is of course the fact also known from Matt. xxiv. 37 ff., Luke xvii. 26 f. and 2 Pet. ii. 5 that the Flood is regarded as a type for the future judgment of the world. Thus the generation from that time had not only historical interest for the authors of the N.T., but attention was drawn to them as a symbol of what was to come.[1]

It ought to be easily seen with reference to the continuation of verse 20 that this typological *motif* was current at the time when iii. 19 was formulated[2] — notice especially the words ἀντίτυπον and νῦν σώζει. And such passages as 1 Pet. i. 13, iv. 5f., 7, 17 reveal clearly that the fast approaching Judgment occupied a central point in the attention of the author.

Also in rather similar literature there are some good analogies to the idea of the Flood as the type of the coming Judgment.

Several times in the O.T. Apocrypha the generation of the Flood are reckoned with the Sodomites and others as evidence of how God punishes great sinners and makes them a »warning

---

[1] K. GSCHWIND, *Die Niederfahrt Christi*, p. 130.

[2] This is pointed out also nearly everywhere in the exegetic literature of 1 Pet. See *e.g.* J. E. HUTHER, *Kritisch-exegetisches Handbuch*, p. 177 f. *Cf.* also P. VOLZ, *Die Eschatologie der jüdischen Gemeinde*, 1934, pp. 30, 337.

example for the godless people of the future» (2 Pet. ii. 6.). This is so, for example, in Ecclus. xvi. 6ff., Wisd. x. 4ff., 3 Macc. ii. 4ff. *Cf. Test. Napht.* iii. 5, 2 Pet. ii. 5f. *Sanh.* xi. 3 (108ff.),[1] *Iren. Contra hær.* iv. 36. 4,[2] & c.

In the Apocryphal writings besides LXX we also find many examples of the typological relation between the Flood and the great world catastrophe which is still expected. In the *Book of Enoch* xciii. 4 the Flood is mentioned as »the first end», thus related to a future end of the world. In the same book ch. lxxx. 6f. the Last Days are mentioned. When here an example is given of the irregularities of Nature which foretells the destruction of the world, it is said that »many chiefs of the stars shall transgress the order and alter their orbits and tasks and not appear at the seasons prescribed to them», and thus we find that an event from primitive times, considered to have been the cause of the Flood, is thought to be repeated in the Last Days — for just the refusal of the stars to follow their ordered ways and times is given in ch. xviii. 16 and partly also in xxi. 6 as the significance of their »fall» and thus the reason for their punishment: but the stars are all the time clearly conceived as a substratum for the disobedient Angels.[3] An analogy to this is described in ch. xc. 24 where the final world catastrophe begins with a punishment of the stars who are cast out into the burning Abyss; in ch. xci. 6 it is said: »and again unrighteousness shall be consummated on the earth and all the deeds of unrighteousness and of violence and transgression shall prevail in a twofold degree», which clearly refers to the criminal and chaotic condition before the Flood; and again in xci. 15 it is said that the final punishment shall fall upon the Angels, indeed, according to certain MSS[4] even the »Watchers» are mentioned, the special name of the fallen Angels before the Flood, often used

---

[1] More materials available in H. STRACK & P. BILLERBECK, *Kommentar*, iv. 2, 1928, pp. 1185ff.
[2] *P.G.* vii, cols. 1093f.
[3] *Cf.* below, p. 72, note 1.
[4] See R. H. CHARLES, *The Book of Enoch, ad loc.*

72   WHO ARE »THE SPIRITS» IN VERSE 19?   [CH.

in the angelological part vi—xxxvi.¹ We have also in ch. x. 15ff., lx. 6, 24f. and in the *Book of Jubilees*, v. 10ff., a clear transfer of thought from the sin and punishment of the Flood generation to the final punishment of mankind according to their deeds. In the *Book of Enoch* lxvii. 12 it expressly says in the Angel Michael's explanation: »this judgment wherewith the Angels are judged is a testimony for the Kings and the Mighty who possess the earth». And speaking generally it was probable the writer's desire to direct the thought of the reader to the future judgment of the evil ones among the current generation of mankind, which caused him either in detail or shortly to touch upon the Flood and the transgressors from the time before it so many times in his description. Thus we can also take more generally the descriptions of and allusions to the Flood,² *i.e.* in the *Book of Enoch* x. 17ff., liv. 7ff., lxv, lxxxiii—lxxxiv, xci. 5, cvi, the *Book of the Secrets of Enoch* xxxiv. 2, or the *Book of Jubilees* v, as containing warning allusions to the threatening judgment which is close at hand.³ Compare the fact that in Ps. Philo, *Ant.* iii. 10,⁴ the Final Judgement of the world

¹ The term »Watchers» may also imply the connection of the fallen Angels with stars. We find the designation עירין in Dan. iv. 10, 14, 20. Further, we find that the fallen Angels are called »Watchers» *e.g.* in the *Book of Jubilees* iv. 22, viii. 3, x. 5, the *Book of Enoch* i. 5, xii. 4ff., and so on, the *Testaments of Reuben* v. 6f., *Naphtali* iii. 5, &c. There is probably in the name itself an allusion to the »watchfulness» of the heavenly bodies. See the *Book of Enoch* lxi. 12, c. 10, the expression »the Watchers of Heaven», xii. 4, the *Damascus Documents* ii. 10, but above all the *Book of the Secrets of Enoch*, *passim*, where »the Watchers'» celestial character is apparent. The seasons have also a kind of »Watchers» according to the *Book of Enoch* lxxxii. 10. *Cf.* also the Cherubim, *e.g.* in Ezech. i and x, and the Phenician so-called Ζωφησαμιν (צופי שמים) which Philo Byblius defined as οὐρανοῦ κατόπται according to Eusebius, *Prep. ev.* i. 10 (*P.G.* xxi, col. 76A). See also E. SCHRADER, *Die Keilinschriften und das Alte Testament*, 3. Aufl. 1903, p. 629.

² K. GSCHWIND, *Die Niederfahrt Christi*, p. 130.

³ In 4 Ezra iii. 9 the Flood is mentioned for quite another reason: Here the question is the problem of theodicy. The difference has not been noticed by several who quote this passage among those mentioned above to illustrate the character of the Flood as a type of the Last Judgment.

⁴ *The Biblical Antiquities of Philo* translated by M. R. JAMES, 1917, p. 81.

is described directly after the Flood. It is only by means of this logical relation that the graphic descriptions and the serious tone which stamps the presentment in these passages can be explained.

A special aspect of this complex of ideas is formed by the quite ordinary conceptions in early Christendom and its immediate surroundings that as the world in ancient time was destroyed by a flood of water, the coming catastrophe would take the form of a flood of fire.[1] This view is quite distinct in 2 Pet. iii. 6f. Comp. also *Vita Adæ* ch. xlix. Later we find them again in for example a homily by Ps. Melito[2] where three different world catastrophes are mentioned: 1) through a tempest (by this apparently is meant a catastrophe in Enosh's time, mentioned elsewhere),[3] 2) a flood of water, and 3) a flood of fire, which is to come at the end of time. In the *Sibylline Books*, for example iv. 172ff., the burning of the world is mentioned.[4] Here the speculations as to cosmic periods by Greek and Oriental thinkers form an important, more general, back-ground.[5]

There are thus many links between the Flood and the coming Judgment. Ideas concerning such a connection are characteristic of many writings in the N.T. and related literature.

It would be very peculiar if 1 Pet. was very different from the traditions mentioned. On the contrary, we must think that this Epistle follows wholly the current Early Christian and Jewish conceptions on this point. The internal evidence of the text, as we have just said, also favours the assumption of a connection between the Flood and the coming Judgment. In mentioning the spirits in prison, which has with it an idea of the Flood, the author has had in mind the coming destruction of the world, and in this way wishes to admonish, or comfort, in some respects, those he is addressing.

If the idea of the Flood catastrophe can in itself be considered as likely to have a counterpart in the great destruction at the Last Day, then it is reasonable to think that also the transgressors, for

---

[1] P. Volz, *Die Eschatologie der jüdischen Gemeinde*, pp. 335ff. *Cf.* C. M. Edsman, *Gezelii bibelverk*, 1941, pp. 42ff.
[2] I. C. Th. Otto, *Corpus apologetarum*, ix, 1872, p. 510f.; translation p. 432.
[3] *Cf. Gen. R.* v. 6, xxiii. 7.
[4] See further Volz, *loc. cit.*
[5] Edsman, *op. cit.*, pp. 47ff.

74 WHO ARE »THE SPIRITS» IN VERSE 19? [CH.

whose sake God allowed this catastrophe to fall upon the early world, are considered as having a special counterpart to-day — or at least that they will have such a counter-part in the Last Day. We have already seen in some of our examples that certain people at the end of time — whether this time is considered as at present or far away in the future — are pointed out as analogies to the transgressors and sinners of antediluvian times. This is to a certain extent the case with the stars in the *Book of Enoch* lxxx. 6f.[1] But much more distinct is the interesting passage lxvii. 12,[2] where Michael expressly declares that the doom of the Angels is a testimony for the Kings and the Mighty of the present. Thus we see that the beings punished at the Flood can be conceived as a type of certain beings in the present.

But if a person or a thing in the past is considered as a »prototype» for something in the present, the thoughts of the N.T. as well as of the Jewish theological writers liked to express themselves in such a way that the typical phenomenon is not merely a picture, a comparison, or a parable from the past, which has a certain sentimental value or can be used as a pedagogic illustration in the interest of esthetics or education: but the prototype has a much more active function as a principle, origin, »father», authority and protector in relation to the present day counterpart. Thus, for example, 1 Pet. speaks of Sarah as a model for the Christian women of this day, a model of purity and faithful submission, and in that way urges them to resemble her in »good deeds», and so become her children, iii. 6. And this is certainly no poetical picture but implies a quite concrete relationship. Paul's reasoning as to who are the descendants of Abraham and Isaac in Rom. iv. 11ff., ix. 6ff., Gal. iv. 22ff. &c. are instructive analogies. Notice also for example the following sentences from John viii. 39ff.: (39) ... εἰ τέκνα τοῦ Ἀβραάμ ἐστε, τὰ ἔργα τοῦ Ἀβραάμ ποιεῖτε. (40) νῦν δὲ ζητεῖτέ με ἀποκτεῖναι ... τοῦτο Ἀβραάμ οὐκ ἐποίησεν. (41) ὑμεῖς ποιεῖτε τὰ ἔργα τοῦ πατρὸς ὑμῶν ... (44) ὑμεῖς ἐκ τοῦ πατρὸς τοῦ

[1] See above, p. 71.
[2] See above, p. 72.

διαβόλου ἐστὲ καὶ τὰς ἐπιθυμίας τοῦ πατρὸς ὑμῶν θέλετε ποιεῖν. ἐκεῖνος ἀνθρωποκτόνος ἦν ἀπ' ἀρχῆς ... Here it appears clearly that a Biblical figure, important as to principle, under whom one places oneself by one's action and reasoning can be regarded as a spiritual »father», and thus the relationship can be considered more intimate and significant than the real physical descent from a person. It is also important that the Devil in this passage is called a homicide from the very beginning. Priority according to Biblical reasoning is very much the same as logical and practical authority in principle (see *e.g.* Gen. iv. 20—22). The relation to the authority or principle under which a man places himself is for Biblical writers quite concrete and palpable. Naturally we must reckon with different degrees of firmness and concreteness in these ideas, but in general we must probably assume a considerably more active and functional importance in the different »prototypes» from the Scriptures than these would have if they were merely pictures without the characteristic of reality.[1]

We may also remember that the primeval characters according to Early Christianity, as to Judaism (at least Pharisaism), were not at all outside existence, even if they had left the earthly life. They still had a real importance in Heaven as on earth, possibly also in the underworld, for as it is said, »He is not the God of the Dead but of the living, for all live unto Him», Luke xx. 38. We constantly meet examples of the fact that many personalities of the O.T. are thought of as still existing and actual realities, *e.g.* Moses, David, or Elijah, who would later come to be actual.

Regarding these circumstances we should be prepared to conceive Michael's words about the beings of the Flood in the *Book of Enoch* lxvii. 12: »This judgment wherewith the Angels are judged is a testimony for the Kings and the Mighty who possess the earth», or similar evidence, as indications of a closer, more essential

---

[1] The common typology as described by L. GOPPELT in his *Typos*, 1939, and implying a relation of presage and fulfilment, is not quite the same thing as these relations between an active personal prototype and his dependants.

and functional relation between the »prototype» and the present-day counterparts than an uninitiated modern reader is perhaps at first inclined to think. We may also be able to understand that the beings from the Flood were not considered by the author of 1 Pet., as by his environment, to be quite absent from existence, but in spite of all were still able to have some influence on mankind and their world. Certainly God had wiped out all beings from the earth through the Flood (Gen. vii. 23), but one could not help thinking that these transgressors were still to be found somewhere — *e.g.* ἐν φυλακῇ! — and could assert themselves in some way.

The following observations from the *Book of Enoch* and other writings closely related to it, also from the N.T. and the literature of the Early Church, will support the ideas of the Flood beings in the N.T. surroundings as having the general characteristics of such functional and actual aspects.

Let us first point out the circumstance, extremely important in principle, that the *Book of Enoch* incontrovertibly, although not in a directly apparent way, attributes to the fall of the Angels a unique importance in principle: for to this book the Angels' fall is actually, even though not expressly so stated, the historical explanation of the coming of Sin into the world, in the same way as Adam's fall is the explanation of the same fact according to other holy writings in Israel and Christianity. In the *Book of Enoch* Adam's fall is not mentioned, but the fall of the Angels is the pervading chief theme and is the whole time related to Sin and the Judgment, and this in such a perspective that the thought of the reader is constantly directed from the historic past to the present and the future. This circumstance has been characterized by ADOLPHE LODS — a prominent investigator in this field — in the following way:[1]

»La chute des anges explique l'état actuel du monde. Le narrateur n'a pas su mettre cet aspect de sa pensée en pleine lumière. De ces pages maladroites et enfantines se dégage cependant toute une conception du monde,

---

[1] A. LODS, La chute des anges. Origine et portée de cette spéculation, *Rev. d'hist. et de philos. rel.* vii. 1927, p. 301.

toute une philosophie de l'histoire qui était nouvelle en Israël.[1] Il attribue, en somme, à la chute des anges et à ses suites le même rôle que Paul dans le christianisme, les auteurs du quatrième livre d'Esdras et de l'apocalypse de Baruch dans le judaïsme devaient assigner, deux siècles plus tard, à la faute d'Adam: c'est la cause première du mal qui caractérise l'éon actuel.»

It seems also clear that, on the basis of Gen. vi. 5, viii. 21 there is reason to connect the evil instinct, יצר הרע, which played such an important part in later Judaism's theology as an explanation of the fact of Sin, with the transgressors from the Flood.

Besides the primary Fall, the desire for the women of the earth, the *Book of Enoch* mentions several different transgressions and sins for which the fallen Angels are responsible. Thus in ch. xiii. 2 the unrighteous and sinful acts, which they taught mankind, are spoken of quite generally.

Among the special crimes committed by these Angels perhaps should be first mentioned that they taught men the use of certain dangerous, technical tools, such as weapons for use in war and the shedding of blood. This is given in the *Book of Enoch* viii. 1, lxv. 6f. Naturally the thought here is not merely of those who perished in the Flood but also of mankind of later times. Thus the Angels are at the back of such cultural curses as war and similar things.

We see also in the *Book of Enoch* vii. 1, viii. 3[2] (especially according to *Sync.*) &c., that the fallen angels taught mankind magic. And according to ch. xix. 1 they taught men, when they led them astray, to offer to demons as to gods, thus they have also introduced idolatry. Compare also viii. 3, ix. 6f., lx. 6 (they take the name of God in vain), lxv. 6, 11 in the same Book.

The Angels must also be considered as partly responsible for the heathenish sin of blasphemy. This seems to appear from the introductory chapters to the *Book of Enoch*, where we find an address

---

[1] That is perhaps not quite certain. The theory in question may also very well have existed for a long time beside other theories, though it was not represented in canonical literature.

[2] »Der Fall der Engel dient hier als Erklärungsgrund für allerlei Zauberei in der Welt», G. BEER, *ad loc.*, in E. KAUTZSCH, *Die Apokryphen und Pseudepigraphen*, ii, 1900.

78 WHO ARE »THE SPIRITS» IN VERSE 19?

of exhortation which must have been regarded as referring both to the fallen Angels and their followers in Sin among the people of the earth; see ch. i. 9, v. 4. *Cf.* xxvii. 2.

The fallen Angels are at the same time themselves the origin of the evil demons.[1] They begat the Giants by the women of the earth, as is known, and the Giants appeared on the earth as evil spirits. In the *Book of Enoch* xv. 3 and 8 ff. it says:

(3) »Wherefore have ye (*i.e.* the fallen Angels) left the high, holy and eternal heaven, and lain with women, and defiled yourselves with the daughters of man and taken yourselves wives, and done like the children of earth, and begotten giants as sons? ... (8) And now the Giants, who are produced from the spirits and flesh, shall be called evil spirits upon the earth, and in the earth shall be their dwelling.[2] (9) Evil spirits have proceded from their bodies because they are born from men,[3] and from the holy Watchers comes the origin of their creation and their fundamental principle.[4] They shall be evil spirits on earth, and evil spirits shall they be called. (10) As for the spirits of heaven, in heaven shall be their dwelling, but as for the spirits of the earth which were born upon the earth, on the earth shall be their dwelling. (11) And the spirits of the Giants are oppressing the clouds[?],[5] destroying, attacking, fighting, and working destruction on the earth, the harsh spirits of the Giants, and they are spirits causing trouble, taking no food but hungering and thirsting,[6] and offensive. (12) And these spirits shall rise up against the children of men and women, because they have proceded from them.»

Here it is quite clear that even if the *Book of Enoch* speaks in principle of phenomena in the time before the great Flood, the thought runs all the time to current conditions and the actual purpose of the description is to illuminate certain of them. The

---

[1] *Cf.* H. STRACK & P. BILLERBECK, *Kommentar*, iv. 1, 1928, pp. 505 f.
[2] Or: »on the earth», as in *Sync.*
[3] The Akhmim text and the Ethiopic text have »from those above».
[4] In Greek: ἐκ τῶν ἁγίων ἐγρηγόρων ἡ ἀρχὴ τῆς κτίσεως αὐτῶν καὶ ἀρχὴ θεμελίου.
[5] The Akhmim fragment has νεφέλας, which is perhaps somewhat peculiar; the Ethiopic text has a corresponding expression, while *Sync.* has one perhaps still more peculiar νεμόμενα. Possibly the designation נפילים, »Giants», Gen. vi. 4, lies behind this: but this is, of course, not quite certain. Perhaps the »clouds» really belongs here. See the discussion by G. BEER in E. KAUTZSCH, *Die Apokryphen und Pseudepigraphen*, ii, 1900, *ad loc.*
[6] *Cf.* the Djinns of the Arabs, who have a lion's hunger but are not able to eat, J. WELLHAUSEN, *Reste arabischen Heidentums*, 1897, pp. 149 f.

evil spirits, πνεύματα, who are the forms in which the Giants appear on earth, are thought to belong not only to the past but also to the contemporary world.

And the punishment that awaits the Angels, »the Watchers», is not for the evil spirits: they are allowed to hold sway among mankind with their depravity until the final Judgment.[1] For this reason the verse immediately following, xvi. 1, is as follows:

»Ever since the days of the slaughter and destruction and the death of the Giants, the *něphīlīm*, the strong on the earth, the great celebrities, the spirits which issue from their souls, although they be of flesh, shall exercise destruction without any punishment. Thus shall they destroy until the day of the consummation, the great Judgment in which the great Eon shall come to an end. It shall come to an end all at once.»[2]

But if the fallen Angels are behind these evil spirits who are still active on the earth — and it is specially stated, as we saw in xv. 9, that the origin of the creation of the spirits and their basic principle is to be sought in the »Watchers» — then the fallen Angels are not without influence upon the life on the earth, in spite of their being bound in the dark prison. On the contrary, we see from this that the Angels are the extreme principle of the demons' existence and the actual root and source of power for their wicked activity in the world.

The same facts appear with all desirable distinctness in the *Book of Jubilees* x. 5ff., a passage which we will present *in extenso*. First Noah speaks and addresses God, interceding for his children who after the Flood began to be attacked by impure spirits: then the text passes to a description of the partial imprisoning of the spirits; and although it here refers to a period after the Flood, this imprisoning is certainly the direct counterpart to the imprisoning of the disobedient angels according to the *Book of Enoch*:

»(5) And Thou knowest how Thy Watchers, the fathers of these spirits (N.B.), acted in my days. And these spirits which are living, imprison them and hold them fast in the place of condemnation, and let them not bring

---

[1] R. H. CHARLES, *ad loc.*

[2] This passage has been translated in the first place from the text of Syncellus. The meaning in the other texts is, however, the same, although the form of the language is worse.

destruction on the sons of Thy servant, my God, for they are malignant, and created in order to destroy. (6) And let them not rule over the spirits of the living, for Thou alone knowest the power over them. And let them not have power over the sons of the righteous from henceforth and for evermore. (7) And the Lord our God bade us to bind all. (8) And the chief of the Spirits, *Masṭēmā*, came and said: 'Lord, Creator, let some of them remain before me, and let them hearken to my voice, and do all that I shall say unto them. For if some of them are not left to me, I shall not be able to execute the power of my will on the sons of men. For these are for corruption and leading astray before my judgment, for great is the wickedness of the sons of men.' (9) And He said: 'Let the tenth part of them remain before him, and let nine parts descend into the place of condemnation'. (10) And one of us He commanded that we should teach Noah all their medicines. For He knew that they would not walk in uprightness, nor strive in righteousness. (11) And we did according to all His words. All the malignant evil ones we bound in the place of condemnation, and a tenth part of them we left that they might be subject before Satan on the earth.»

Here it appears first that the demons are the descendants of the fallen Angels: that further the evil spirits on this occasion are considered as being imprisoned exactly in the same way as the Angels in the *Book of Enoch* vi. ff. (or the *Book of Jubilees* v. 6 ff.). But their power is not wholly paralyzed because a tenth part of their company is still free to exercise the deeds of their prince *Masṭēmā* or Satan among mankind.

In Christianity the conception of the demons originating from the fallen Angels is preserved *i.a.* by Justin the Martyr, who, in his *Apol*, II. v, says:[1] οἱ δ'ἄγγελοι, παραβάντες τήνδε τὴν τάξιν, γυναικῶν μίξεσιν ἡττήθησαν, καὶ παῖδας ἐτέκνωσαν, οἵ εἰσιν οἱ λεγόμενοι δαίμονες,[2] and by Athenagoras, in *Leg. pro christ.* xxv: οὗτοι τοίνυν οἱ ἄγγελοι οἱ ἐκπεσόντες τῶν οὐρανῶν, περὶ τὸν ἀέρα ἔχοντες καὶ τὴν γῆν, οὐκέτι εἰς τὰ ὑπερουράνια ὑπερκύψαι δυνάμενοι. καὶ αἱ τῶν γιγάντων ψυχαί, οἵ περὶ τὸν κόσμον εἰσὶ πλανώμενοι δαίμονες, ὁμοίας κινήσεις, οἱ μὲν αἷς ἔλαβον συστάσεσιν, οἱ δαίμονες, οἱ δὲ αἷς ἔσχον ἐπιθυμίαις, οἱ ἄγγελοι, ποιούμενοι[3] (notice here the remarks about sensual cravings).

---

[1] *P.G.* vi, col. 452.
[2] *Cf.* also *Apol.* I, v.
[3] *P.G.* vi, col. 948 f.

Compare also a passage from Minuciux Felix, *Octavius*, xxvi: *Spiritus sunt insinceri, vagi, a coelesti vigore terrenis labibus et cupidatibus degravati. Isti igitur spiritus, posteaquam simplicitatem substantiæ suæ, onusti et immersi vitiis, perdiderunt, ad solatium calamitatis suæ non desinunt perditi jam perdere, et depravati errorem pravitatis infundere, et alienati a Deo, inductis pravis religionibus a Deo segregare. Eos spiritus dæmonas esse poetæ sciunt, philosophi disserunt*, &c.[1] (Here the teaching of the fall of the Angels is, however, very attenuated and presented in a general, philosophically sensible, abstract style.) See further the expression *dæmoniis et apostaticis spiritibus* in *Iren. Contra hær.* v. 28. 2.[2] Commodianus has in a poem in his *Instructiones adv. gent. deos*, iii, called *Cultura dæmonum*, expressly derived the demons or the false gods and their worship from the fall of the Angels:

> *Cum Deus omnipotens exornaret mundi naturam,*
> *visitari voluit terram ab Angelis istam.*
> *Legitima cuius spreverunt illi dimissi:*
> *tanta fuit forma feminarum quæ flecteret illos,*
> *ut coinquinati non possent coelo redire,*
> *rebelles ex illo contra Deum verba misere.*
> *Altissimus inde sententiam misit in illos.*
> *De semine quorum gigantes nati feruntur,*
> *Ab ipsis in terra artes prolatæ fuerunt,*
> *et tingere lanas docuerunt, et quæcumque geruntur.*
> *Mortales et illis mortuis simulacra ponebant.*
> *Omnipotens autem, quod essent de semine pravo,*
> *non censuit illos recipi defunctos e morte:*
> *Unde modo vagi subvertunt corpora multa:*
> ***maxime quos hodie colitis deos et oratis***.[3]

We also find in Philo, *De gigantibus*, an instance of the idea that the demons are descended from the fallen Angels, although he too, of course, has quite another, more enlightened and philo-

---

[1] *P.L.* iii, cols. 321f. — Regarding the heathen philosophers *cf. Herm. Irris. gent. phil.* i. 1 (*P.G.* vi, col. 1169).
[2] *P.G.* vii, col. 1199B. — See also the interesting remarks in *Iren.* Εἰς ἐπίδ., ch. xviii (Patrol. Orient. xii, p. 672).
[3] *P.L.* v, cols. 203f.

sophical conception of who the demons are than, for example, the *Book of Enoch*.[1]

That the demons are free and are allowed to work on earth until the Last Judgement in order to attack people is also in harmony with the views in the N.T. and especially in the Synoptic Gospels. See Matt. viii. 29, where the demons in a man possessed in the country of the Gadarenes call out to Jesus: »What have we to do with thee, thou Son of God? ἦλθες ὧδε πρὸ καιροῦ (prematurely to) βασανίσαι ἡμᾶς;» Thus here the demons themselves rely on being allowed to hold sway till the end of the world. According to the parallel account in Luke they really fear to be forced by Jesus into the Abyss, Luke viii. 31.

In connection with this may be mentioned a few places in the N.T. where the fallen Angels from Gen. vi. 1—4 appear to some extent as still active factors in the world. In 1 Cor. xi. 10 Paul says that the women ought to have an ἐξουσία on the head διὰ τοὺς ἀγγέλους. It is difficult here to avoid thinking of the well-known account[2] of how the Angels in prehistoric times were lured by the physical beauty of the women on earth.[3] It may be noticed that 1 Cor. xi is dealing with women as they exercise their cult and pray. And then they were of course in a special way exposed to attack from higher beings like the Angels. If the passage really alludes to the fall of the Angels we have still another proof of their constant potential activity. In Jude 13 the apostates are declared to be ἀστέρες πλανῆται for whom the darkness is preserved for eternity, and then follows in verse 14f. the quotation from Enoch's severe lecture in the *Book of Enoch*, i. 9. This passage also reveals the close connection between the fallen Angels — who are also thought

---

[1] See, for instance, *De gig.* 6, 16.

[2] *Cf.* also H. STRACK & P. BILLERBECK, *Kommentar*, iii, 1926, pp. 437ff.

[3] Among later investigators LODS also desired to take this passage as an allusion to the fall of the Angels, La chute des anges, *Rev. d'hist. et de philos. rel.* vii, 1927, pp. 299ff. Many other theories have certainly been put forward, see L. BRUN, »Um der Engel willen» 1 Kor. 11, 10, *Zeitschr. f. d. neut. Wiss.* xiv, 1913, pp. 298ff., or W. FOERSTER, *s.v.* ἐξουσία in G. KITTEL, *Theol. Wört.* ii, 1935, pp. 570f.

of as stars, *e.g.* in the *Book of Enoch* xviii. 13[1] — and contemporary sinners. The continued influence on the earth of the fallen Angels, in spite of their imprisonment in primitive times, also appears from the following special circumstances. The leader of the Angels is in some passages in the *Book of Enoch* called »Aza(z)el», viii. 1, x. 4, *e.p.* That is the same name as the demon to whom the scapegoat was offered, according to Lev. xvi.[2] (Perhaps the other name for the Prince of the Angels, Semiaza, vi. 3 *e.p.*, can be associated with the Sammaël[3] of rabbinic Judaism, the name of the Prince of the Demons.)[4] In the *Book of Enoch* xix. 2 the women who had intercourse with the Angels are said to become »sirens», *i.e.* haunting, female demons (σειρήν = זן in Job xxx. 29, Isa. xxxiv. 13, xliii. 20; = יענה in Isa. xiii. 21, Jer. l. 39, Mic. i. 8).[5] The word γίγαντες is used in the LXX as translation of רפאים.[6] In several places in the O.T. one has reason to think of the »Giants» in Gen. vi. 4, when it is actually a question of »the Rephaim» or »the shades», *e.g.* Jos. xiii. 12, Job xxvi. 5, Isa. xiv. 9: but from this one gets also the impression that these »Giants» still appear on or under the earth in different ways. *Cf.* also Symmachus' repeated translation of

---

[1] *Cf.* above, p. 72 note 1, and below, p. 84.
[2] For the name Azazel, עזאזל, see M. SCHWAB, Vocabulaire de l'angelologie, *Mém. prés. à l'Acad. des inscr.* I. x. 2, 1897, p. 321. There the rather similar name עזאל »rebelle à Dieu» is also treated; this occurs in Jewish literature together with *Shamḥāzi* whereby we obtain an analogy to Azazel and Semiaza. *Cf.* the next note.
[3] *Cf.* L. BERTHOLDT, *Christologia Iudaeorum*, 1811, p. 182f.; A. LODS, *Le Livre d'Hénoch*, p. 107. Actually, indeed, Semiaza = *Shamḥāzai*, or something similar, but note that of the other Angels listed in the *Book of Enoch* nearly all have a name ending in *-el*. — In *Pirqe de R. Eliez.* xiii the leader of the apostate Angels, Semiaza, is also called Sammaël.
[4] More about these Angels in M. GRÜNBAUM, Beiträge zur vergleichenden Mythologie aus der Hagada, *Zeitschr. d. Deutsch. Morg. Ges.* xxxi, 1877, pp. 225ff.; more references in *Encyklopädia Judaica*, *s.v.* Azazel, and similar works.
[5] *Cf.* several places in *Aq.*, *Symm.* and *Theod.*, according to E. HATCH & H. A. REDPATH, *Concordance*, *s.v.* — Jer. l. 39 = xxvii. 39 in the LXX.
[6] See HATCH & REDPATH, *Concordance*, *s.v.* γίγας.

רפאים by θεομάχοι.[1] The word רפאים is also interpreted in later Jewish literature[2] as clearly referring to the beings before the Flood.[3] We can further reflect somewhat more closely over the fact that the fallen Angels are often combined with the stars, as in the Book of Enoch xviii. 13, xxi. 6. The passages Isa. xiv. 12—21, xxiv. 18—22 are O.T. types of this combination — otherwise this motif is perhaps also directly inspired by Chaldean astral theories.[4] However, if the fallen Angels could be identified in this way with the planets or other heavenly bodies, their imprisonment was naturally only theoretical and in principle: for in practice, at the same time, one felt quite well the pressure and strong influence of the heavenly bodies on human life, as the astrological view of life postulated it, and in that way, too, the fallen Angels obtained a powerful and influential position in the world. How widely this identification between the fallen Angels and the stars actually stretched in N.T. environments we cannot investigate here. In Jude 13 for example, however, it is indicated, and further may be named Philo, *De æternitate mundi* 47 and *De somniis* I, 22, where the theory is indicated that the celestial bodies are in prison (δεσμωτήριον) which, of course, here is thought of more philosophically.[5] A glance at the passages quoted above from Athenagoras and Minucius Felix also shows that the astral perspective was very near in thought.

---

[1] Ps. lxxxvii (lxxxviii). 11, Job xxvi. 5, Prov. ix. 18, xxi. 16. H. J. Schoeps, Mythologisches bei Symmachus, *Biblica* xxvi, 1945, pp. 100ff.
[2] *E.g.* Pirqē de R. Eliezer xxxiv, who makes Isa. xxvi. 14: »the Rephaim shall not rise», indicate the generation of the Flood.
[3] ענקים is also rendered in LXX by γίγαντες, Deut. i. 28.
[4] W. Bousset & H. Gressmann, *Die Religion des Judentums*, 1926, pp. 73f. *Cf.* H. L. Jansen, *Die Henochgestalt*, 1939, pp. 9f., 13ff., *e.p.*
[5] Compare also *e.g.* the following poetic fragment quoted by Athenagoras in *Leg. pro christ.* xviii:

κούρους δ'οὐρανίωνας ἐγείνατο πότνια Γαῖα,
οὓς δὴ καὶ Τιτῆνας ἐπίκλησιν καλέουσιν,
οὕνεκα τισάσθην μέγαν οὐρανὸν ἀστερόεντα

(*P.G.* vi, col. 928 B).

However, if the fallen Angels were still believed to be active in the world through the demons, there is one region in which their influence is generally believed to make itself felt in a quite special way, and one for us who study 1 Pet. particularly interesting: The fallen Angels and their representatives, the demons, are regarded as having specially close relations with the heathen, especially with the rulers of the heathen, their kings.[1] This is connected, of course, with two circumstances: partly that the fallen Angels are considered to be the origin of magic and idolatry, and partly that they had as their representatives on earth the demons who are of course almost identical with the false gods of the heathen — it is stated quite clearly, *e.g.*, in the *Book of Jubilees* xv. 31, that the »spirits» misled the peoples to apostasy from God. These connections between the fallen Angels and the kings of the heathen and other rulers appear in several places in the *Book of Enoch*.

In that part which contains the so-called »Parables», the »Kings and the Mighty and those who reside on the earth» are often mentioned: lv. 4, lxii. 1, 3, 6, 9, lxiii. 1, 12, lxvii. 8, 12, and this in such a way that it seems in reality to be these kings &c. who are referred to whenever it is a question of the Final Judgment, as for example chs. lxii f. show.

It is quite clear for anyone who knows the O.T. notion of the heathen in the Last Time and their rulers' doom and prostration before the Messiah on Sion at the great catastrophe (*e.g.* in Ps. lxxii. 10ff., Dan. vii. 14, Mic. vii. 16f.), that it here in the *Book of Enoch* also must be reference to the kings and rulers of the heathen. See also *e.g.* the *Book of Enoch*, lvi.

»Those who reside on the earth» seems in these places to be a special expression for the rulers of the heathen world. Looked at superficially it

---

[1] These circumstances and their importance for our subject have already to some extent been meritoriously observed by K. GSCHWIND in his *Die Niederfahrt Christi*, pp. 133ff. Our exposition is here mostly constructed from our own material, as Gschwind's argumentation is actually neither particularly detailed nor even always correct, for he sometimes builds upon facts which are somewhat unconnected with what is here essential. Nor has he seen what we consider the most important, the connection of the Angels with the heathen kings. But for the rest, we gladly acknowledge the extraordinary value of his suggestion, which ought to have left considerably more traces in the later scientific literature than is the case.

only means »those who sit, live on the earth»[1] but in our view, at least in this case, when connected with the kings and the rulers, it is a reproduction of the O.T. expression יושבי הארץ, interpreted so that ישב, »sit», has the meaning »be enthroned (as a ruler, a judge) over».[2] This interpretation of the verb ישב is very usual in the O.T. and is a characteristic aspect of this verb: see, for example, Ex. xviii. 14, Ps. ii. 4, lxi. 8, &c. In Rev., too, we find that οἱ κατοικοῦντες or οἱ καθήμενοι ἐπὶ τῆς γῆς, or similar expressions, derived from the LXX mode of rendering the same Hebrew phrase, probably have the meaning »those who rule on the earth», at least in vi. 10 and xvii. 2, considering the context (see these passages).[3] Thus, only by postulating the meaning »those who rule over» or »preside over the earth» do we consider it possible to obtain a reasonable understanding of the phrase in question in the passages in the *Book of Enoch* where there is a distinct traditional combination of »the Kings» and »the Mighty», so that a triple formula has arisen.

Where then these Kings, Mighty, and Rulers of the earth are said to be placed under judgment, the fallen Angels constantly come into the field of vision and are thus placed in intimate relation to these Kings, &c. Probably this is most clear in the *Book of Enoch* lxvii. 4—lxix. 1. We have already stated that the judgment over the Angels is there expressly said to be a testimony to the Kings of the earth, lxvii. 12.[4] The whole context emphasizes the same fact. The thought oscillates the whole time between the Angels and the Kings. Unfortunately we cannot quote this interesting passage here. Yet almost the same oscillation is to be found in chs. liv—lv, and this passage we have perhaps space to quote:

---

[1] The expression is generally so translated by DILLMAN, CHARLES and others. The former speaks of those »welche die Feste inne haben», and BEER has »die auf dem Festlande wohnen». But this is very strained in connection with the kings and the powerful.

[2] Besides the passages mentioned above similar phrases can also be found in chs. liv. 6, 9, lv. 1, 2, lx. 5, lxv. 6, 12, lxvi. 1, lxvii. 7, lxix. 1, but there it seems to be a question of mankind in general — and the situation is here not the Judgment but the transgression at Noah's time — so that the translation must be »those who dwell on the earth» &c.

[3] In Rev. this expression always refers to the heathen world. See E. LOHMEYER, *Die Offenbarung des Johannes*, 1926, p. 121. R. H. CHARLES, *The Revelation*, 1920, ii, p. 13, wishes, however, to except xiv. 6, where he prefers to understand the expression *in bonam partem*.

[4] *Cf.* above, p. 72.

»liv. (1) And I looked and turned to another part of the earth, and saw there a deep valley with burning fire. (2) And they brought the Kings and the Mighty, and began to cast them into this deep valley. (3) And there mine eyes saw how they made these their instruments, iron chains of immeasurable weight. (4) And I asked the Angel of Peace who went with me saying: 'For whom are these chains being prepared?' (5) And he said unto me: 'These are being prepared for the hosts of Azazel, so that they may take them and cast them into the abyss of complete condemnation, and they shall cover their jaws with rough stones as the Lord of Spirits commanded.' (6) And Michael, and Gabriel, and Raphael, and Phanuel shall take hold of them on that great day, and cast them on that day into the burning furnace, that the Lord of Spirits may take vengeance on them for their unrighteousness in becoming subject to Satan and leading astray those who dwell on the earth.' (7) And in those days shall punishment come from the Lord of Spirits, and He will open all the chambers of waters which are above the heavens, and of the fountains which are beneath the earth. (8) And all the waters shall be joined with the waters ... (9) And they shall destroy all who dwell on the earth and these who dwell under the ends of the heaven. (10) And [when?] they have recognized their unrighteousness which they have wrought on the earth, by these shall they perish. lv. (1) And after that the Ancient of Days repented and said: 'In vain I have destroyed all who dwell on the earth.' (2) And He swore by His great Name: 'Henceforth I will not do so to all who dwell on the earth. And I will set a sign in the heaven, and this shall be a pledge of good faith between Me and them for ever, so long as Heaven is above the earth. And this is in accordance with My command.'

(3) 'When I have desired to take hold of them by the hand of the Angels on the day of tribulation and pain, because of this I will cause My chastisement and My wrath to abide upon them', saith God, the Lord of Spirits. (4) 'Ye Kings and Mighty who reside on the earth, ye shall have to behold Mine Elect One, how He sits on the throne of glory and judges Azazel, and all his associates, and all his hosts in the name of the Lord of Spirits.'»

Now if we disregard all doubtful theories of different sources and interpolations,[1] but read the text as it is, we must recognize that the combination of the fallen Angels and the earthly kings here is quite complete. It is scarcely known at all whether the question here is a judgment in the past or in the future. We must remember that these are visions which Enoch, the seventh from Adam, had — that is before the Flood. In the middle of the passage about the valley with burning fire in which the kings are to be cast comes a long quotation from the account of the Flood. This passage

---

[1] Something that occurs quite generally about the *Book of Enoch*.

cannot reasonably have been put in here at random, some logical connection between the different notions must have been felt. And it is clear from the context of ch. liv. 5, that the Kings and the Rulers who, it has just been said, will be tormented with heavy iron chains, are called Azazel's hosts; it seems thus that they are directly subservient to the fallen Angels' ruler, he who has the same name as the demon to whom the scapegoat was offered, according to Lev. xvi.[1] Notice too that the punishment of Azazel's hosts with these rough stones in the Abyss, *ibid.*, is much the same as falls upon Azazel according to ch. x. 4f.

In ch. xc. 22—25, in connection with the judgment of the world, there is a similar oscillation between the Princes of the earth and their celestial centres of power, in this case not the fallen Angels, but their corresponding stars. It states as follows:

»(22) And He spoke to that man who wrote before Him, being one of those seven white ones, and said unto him: 'Take those seventy shepherds[2] to whom I delivered the sheep,[3] and who taking them on their own authority slew more than I commanded them.' (23) And behold, they were all bound, I saw, and they all stood before Him. (24) And the judgement was held first over the stars, and they were judged and found guilty, and went to the place of condemnation, and they were cast into an abyss, full of fire and flaming, and full of pillars of fire. (25) And those seventy shepherds were judged and found guilty, and they were cast into that fiery abyss.»

From these and other similar evidences it is clear that the *Book of Enoch* considers the fallen Angels to have a special position as the celestial counterpart of and a source of inspiration to the kings and rulers of the heathen world.

The remarkable passage Isa. xxiv. 18—22 gives an interesting precedent of this view. It says there in verse 18 that the windows on high are opened, whereby one is driven to think of the account of the Flood (in Gen. vii. 11 it says the windows of heaven were opened). Then is described the violent action on earth by the Lord, and afterwards it says: »In that day the Lord shall punish the host

---

[1] *Cf.* above, p. 83.
[2] *I.e.* the heathen rulers of the Jews, first mentioned in ch. lxxxix. 59. See also A. DILLMANN, *Das Buch Henoch*, pp. 264ff.
[3] *I.e.* the people of Israel.

WHO ARE »THE SPIRITS» IN VERSE 19? 89

of the high ones on high, and the kings on the earth upon the earth», verse 21. Thus here the stars are associated with the earthly kings, just as in the *Book of Enoch* — and from the perspective of the Flood it is easy to identify the stars with the fallen Angels.[1] See further in the following passage from the *Testament of Naphtali*, iii, how the connection between the fallen Angels and the heathen world is reflected in other places in the literature belonging to the N.T. environment: (2) μὴ ἀλλοιώσητε νόμον Θεοῦ ἐν ἀταξίᾳ τῶν πράξεων ὑμῶν. (3) ἔθνη πλανηθέντα καὶ ἀφέντα Κύριον ἠλλοίωσαν τὴν τάξιν αὐτῶν, καὶ ὑπήκουσαν ξύλοις καὶ λίθοις, πνεύμασι πλάνης. (4) ὑμεῖς δὲ μὴ οὕτως, τέκνα μου, γινώσκοντες ... ἐν πᾶσι τοῖς δημιουργήμασι Κύριον τὸν ποιήσαντα πάντα,[2] ἵνα μὴ γένησθε ὡς Σόδομα, ἥτις ἐνήλλαξε τάξιν φύσεως αὐτῆς. (5) ὁμοίως δὲ καὶ οἱ Ἐγρήγοροι ἐνήλλαξαν τάξιν φύσεως αὐτῶν, οὓς κατηράσατο Κύριος ἐπὶ τοῦ κατακλυσμοῦ, δι' οὓς ἀπὸ κατοικησίας καὶ ἄκαρπον τάξας τὴν γῆν ἀοίκητον. Here it is true that the watchers are not described as a source of inspiration to the heathen and as the active principle behind them — this would perhaps not harmonize with the more moralizing and »enlightened» spirit of the *Testaments* — but their apostasy appears in any case as a rather natural pattern for the heresy of the heathen, and their fate is a warning example in this connection.

Thus we have seen, in several distinct examples, that the fallen Angels were considered to have a special connection with the heathen world and the earthly kings and rulers. In the main it may be said that the fallen Angels in this spiritual environment were regarded as being at the back of heathenism and its delusions. These Angels, it was thought, had introduced magic and idolatry into the world. They still work on earth through their descendants the demons. And the demons have an important task in misleading the heathen

---

[1] *Cf.* below, ch. xi.
[2] Compare with this idea that God is revealed in His works, the *Book of Enoch* ii—v. One can also think of Rom. i. 19f.; see in this respect A. FRIDRICHSEN, Zur Auslegung von Röm. 1, 19f., *Zeitschr. f. d. neut. Wiss.* xvii, 1916, pp. 159ff.

and inspiring them to the worship of false gods.[1] But there is also a direct connection between the Angels and the Princes of the world according to clear evidence. This connection which is specially considered in an eschatological association, when there is a question of the great rendering of account and the Last Judgment, ought to be of special interest in studying 1 Pet. iii. 19.

CONCLUSION.

The answer to our question: Who are the spirits in prison?, can thus be shortly formulated as follows:

On the basis of the context it seems that 1 Pet. with πνεύματα in iii. 19 can allude both to spirits in the meaning of Angels and to the souls of dead people. Considering the quite clear connection with the *Book of Enoch*, it is probably most important to think of the fallen Angels and their descendants mentioned in Gen. vi. 1—4, who play a very great role in the *Book of Enoch* and similar writings. They were possibly also important in 1 Pet.'s environment, as appears from the analogies in 2 Pet. and Jude. Among the descriptions to which are linked the fallen Angels in the *Book of Enoch* and other similar writings, the following are of special importance for the study of 1 Pet. iii. 19: the chief task of the Angels to be a type for the sinners at the Last Judgment, their clear part as the originators of the demons, the evil spirits and the false gods, and finally their position in principle, as a continuous active source of inspiration to the heathen and the earthly rulers. These different tasks and functions show that these Angels, in spite of their imprisonment, were in no way hindered from having an active effect on the life of the world. On the contrary, they have a fatal influence on mankind and their lives even to-day. This is thought to take place directly and indirectly: in the latter case through the demons.

In this way the spirits in prison are actually nearly identical with the demoniac spiritual powers in general, Angels, Powers,

---

[1] *Cf.* GSCHWIND, *Die Niederfahrt Christi*, pp. 134 ff.

Rulers, or whatever they may be called. This ought to be clear also from 1 Pet. iii. 22, where some of these classes are mentioned, possibly in some connection with the thought in iii. 19. It is not possible to set any definite limits to all these different groups: altogether they form a fairly homogeneous mass with rather similar functions.

At the same time we must however observe that the author of 1 Pet. in iii. 19 chose to speak only of the spirits in prison and no others. It must be to certain peculiar descriptions connected with just these spirits that he holds. An important reason for this special choice is probably that the fallen Angels according to what we have found in the *Book of Enoch* and similar writings were considered as being themselves the origin of all the other demons on earth. Another important fact is the special relation to the heathen world, the heathen disguised religion and the earthly kings, which the fallen angels are considered to have. In this way it is clear that the preaching to »the spirits in prison» must be understood as directed to certain beings who form the actual principles behind the heathen.

It is not too fantastic to assume that 1 Pet. depends to such a high degree on the ideology of Enoch. The theology and conception of the world which is connected with the Enoch literature has really had, as we have emphasized several times, an extraordinary importance in early Christianity, particularly in the General Epistles.[1] Even those to whom 1 Pet. is addressed must have had some knowledge of it. Only in this way can we explain how the author could present those peculiar »spirits» in such an intimating and self-evident way, as he clearly does, as phenomena well-known to those he is addressing.

*

After these observations regarding the spirits in iii. 19 we must now first devote a short study to certain other particular questions arising from this verse and often discussed by interpreters of our

---

[1] *Cf.* above, pp. 66 ff.

Epistle. By means of the perspective now obtained, however, we ought already to have answered the most important question for a following synthetical explanation of iii. 19. None of the problems discussed in the next chapter do we consider as being of central importance: candidly speaking, sometimes they even seem to be rather subtle. But they have in general been much debated in scientific literature, and we have also certain substantial reasons for treating them before we can try to obtain a comprehensive view of this verse in chapter iv.

CHAPTER III.

OTHER PRELIMINARY QUESTIONS IN VERSE 19.

Having considered it possible in the previous chapters to state that the idea »the spirits in prison» has in many respects connections with the descriptions of the fallen Angels especially in the *Book of Enoch*, logical necessity now leads us to study the following question:

WHO SHOULD BE CONSIDERED TO HAVE PREACHED IN III. 19?

May not this connection with the description of the fallen Angels in the *Book of Enoch* mean that it really ought to be Enoch who is thought to preach to the spirits in this passage, and not Christ, as is probably thought in the first place? If the author of 1 Pet. here really alludes to those fallen Angels, as we tried to show, is it not most natural to imagine that he also thinks of just that person as preacher who plays the main role in the angelological descriptions in the *Book of Enoch*, and there actually presents certain messages to the imprisoned Angels and speaks to them — viz. Enoch himself?

Many investigators have also assumed that the subject in this passage was actually Enoch. They are divided however into different groups in respect of the way in which they want to force Enoch in as the subject. Indeed their differences are really highly essential and we must decide upon our attitude to these theories in essentially different ways.

(1) First we have the well-known effort to alter the text, which

implies that ἐν ᾧ καί in the passage should really be read 'Ενώχ or ἐν ᾧ καὶ 'Ενώχ or something similar.[1] By means of such manipulations an attempt is made to smuggle in Enoch as the subject and in this way to obtain an almost complete connection with the *Book of Enoch*.

This interference with the text must, however, be absolutely repudiated for two serious reasons. In the first place the text is unanimously handed down in the form ἐν ᾧ καί. There is no hint of Enoch in the tradition of the text. In the second a sudden transference of the thought to Enoch would here be highly unnatural and illogical. On the contrary, it is clear that the person who performed the action indicated in verse 19 must be the same as that in the preceding verse, viz. Christ, whose genius also hovers over the whole context as is especially proved in verses 21—22. We have no cause to assume such a curious and fanciful process of thought in the Epistle, that it should suddenly begin to speak of Enoch in the same breath as it speaks of the significance of Christ's Death and Resurrection for those suffering in faith, verse 18 — *i.e.* the most intimate fundamental facts of the Christian faith. Instead of that the author reveals in general a controlled logic, and has the ability to keep to a fundamental thought with almost obstinate consistency even in the course of long expositions. The previous passage in ii. 21—25 is especially illuminating because of its great similarity to iii. 19—22. There Christ Himself stands

---

[1] *Cf.* our bibliographical survey on pp. 41f. above. As the reader can see there, several older writers have also made such attempts. The most important modern advocate of this conjecture is J. CRAMER in his essay Het glossematisch karakter van 1. Petr. 3, 19—21 en 4, 6 (see also p. 50 above); *cf.* J. M. S. BALJON, Bijdragen op het gebiet der conjecturalkritiek, *Theol. Stud.* 1892, pp. 429f. Later appeared, quite ignorant of any predecessor: J. R. HARRIS, A Further Note on the use of Enoch in 1 Peter, *The Exp.* vi. 4, 1901, pp. 346ff.; *id.*, On a Recent Emendation in the Text of St. Peter, *ibid.*, vi. 5, 1902, pp. 317ff. Harris seems to be the best known representative of the hypothesis. Among those who immediately agreed with Harris's thesis are: M. R. JAMES according to Harris in *The Exp.* vi. 5, p. 317f., E. NESTLE in *Theol. Lit.-Bl.* xxiii, 1902, col. 166. See further our notes on p. 42.

iii.] OTHER PRELIMINARY QUESTIONS IN VERSE 19 95

in the centre the whole time during the argumentation. See also how in iv. 1 ff. the author logically resumes the contact with what was put forward in iii. 13 ff. and especially iii. 18.

Nor can one wholly avoid the disadvantage of spoiling with this alteration all the simplest logic and the most elementary connection of the text by declaring that the whole passage about the spirits in prison &c. is an interpolation, because an original marginal note has come into the text during a change of the language form.[1] This way of avoiding all interpretation difficulties caused by our old texts only implies taking another devious way and making the material still more troublesome. The interpolation hypothesis has here no other basis than the incapacity of the interpreter to penetrate the meaning of the text. It is a method of capitulation which only pushes aside and increases the difficulties without solving any one of them.

(2) Then we must mention another theory quite different as to method, which nevertheless also implies an attempt to place Enoch in the passage as some kind of subject, namely, that although Christ is the actual subject of the clause the author's thought is, at the same time, that Christ preached to »the spirits» in the person of Enoch, *i.e.* in a pre-existent form. Thus Christ would only be indirectly behind the action mentioned, Enoch would be the active instrument, and the statement of the passage could thus be easily identified with traditions otherwise well known, namely Enoch's appearance to the fallen Angels in the *Book of Enoch*.[2]

In this connection we must mention the peculiar but historically important theories that Christ preached in a pre-existent appearance with Noah, the Prophets, or even other corresponding persons, as a mouthpiece. We have earlier seen that Augustine put forward

---

[1] J. CRAMER, *op. cit. Cf.* H. HOLTZMANN in *Theol. Jahresber.* xi, 1892, p. 125 (»Cramer's ... Erörterung, welche für die Geschichte der Exegese auf keinen Fall verloren gehen sollte ...»). See further literature above on p. 50, and *cf.* our remarks *ibid.*

[2] It was chiefly FR. SPITTA who energetically tried to get accepted this conception of the preaching to the spirits, *Die Predigt Christi an die Geister*, pp. 21 ff. *Cf.* above, p. 42.

such a conception and found many followers.¹ In this way one can refer to 2 Pet. ii. 5, with its idea of Noah as a δικαιοσύνης κῆρυξ. It must, however, be declared impossible that Christ should be considered as having preached to the spirits through Noah or any other such Biblical figures. For in that case one has no correct explanation of the words ἐν φυλακῇ. We have already stated that from the modern exegetic point of view it is clear that this expression must be taken literally and not allegorically.² But Noah or any other possible corresponding representatives of Christ could not very well be considered as having gone and preached to spirits who were already in prison, for we hear nothing of this anywhere and we have no cause to assume such a tradition. The words πνεύματα and ἐν φυλακῇ must however indicate that the beings in question already at the time of the preaching were »spirits» and were shut up in prison. It is an unreasonable assumption³ that these words should instead be a metaphorical expression for »beings who now (contemporary with the author writing) are spirits shut up in prison» or something similar. Such an argument would properly have demanded at least a νῦν in front of ἐν φυλακῇ.⁴ And this kind of expression must certainly be said to be very much more strained than if we, for example, should say: »Jesus has appeared to the Apostle Paul» although at that time he was not an apostle.⁵ The epithet »Apostle» is here connected with the name Paulus quite conventionally. But why should the more original qualifications »spirits» and »in prison» be dragged in, if the author wishes really

---

[1] *Cf.* above, pp. 40ff. — In later times the most important representative of this theory has been J. HOFMANN, *Die Heilige Schrift*, vii. 1, p. 132, and after him G. WOHLENBERG, *Der erste und zweite Petrusbrief*, pp. 112ff.

[2] Above, pp. 53, 65 note 4, 66ff. — See also Isa. xxiv. 22 (*cf.* above, pp. 88f.).

[3] Yet made by HOFMANN, *op. cit.*, p. 132, and WOHLENBERG, *op. cit.* p. 113.

[4] This is also admitted by WOHLENBERG, but he tries, nevertheless, to keep to HOFMANN's theory, *op. cit.*, p. 113.

[5] HOFMANN, *op. cit.*, p. 132, has tried to strengthen his theory just by stating that such a phrase would be a perfect analogy to »the spirits in prison» conceived in the metaphorical way mentioned. This is, however, not at all correct. The epithet »Apostle» can be much better added mechanically than the more curious expression »spirits» and »in prison».

to speak of these beings at a time before they became »spirits in prison»? The words mentioned are in that case wholly unnecessary and only confusing. It is thus impossible to consider Noah as the active instrument of the preaching in verse 19.

On the other hand one could quite well, as to the expression ἐν φυλακῇ, suppose Enoch to be the one who preached. For Enoch's transactions with the fallen Angels in the *Book of Enoch* occur in such circumstances that it is actually not quite clear whether these Angels are already imprisoned in the underworld when Enoch comes to them, or only are to be so afterwards. The former is quite possible if one first reads in ch. x of the order to cast out and imprison the Angels and then in xiiff. of Enoch's appearance to them.[1]

Thus the theory of Enoch as a mouthpiece for Christ really is to some extent thinkable. And it implies, too, the advantage mentioned above, to obtain also in what concerns the preaching person an intimate connection with traditions earlier known, that is the reports of Enoch's appearing to the fallen Angels in the *Book of Enoch*.[2]

It seems also that one can support the assumption of such a preexistent appearance of Christ through Enoch by certain special circumstances. First can be mentioned some details in 1 Pet.'s text. If the expression ἐν ᾧ, in iii. 19, can be supplemented by the word πνεῦμα just mentioned, the meaning is that Christ went to the »spirits in prison» ἐν πνεύματι, in the shape of the Spirit, or with the help of the Spirit, or something similar. In this way it is possible to consider the reasoning as being that the Spirit of Christ has inspired Enoch and spoken through him. This agrees very well with the remark in i. 11, that Christ's Spirit active in the prophets imparted revelations to them regarding the sufferings associated with Christ.[3] As an especially illuminating analogy to such a preexistent appearance it can be mentioned that in 1 Cor. x. 4 the pneumatic rock during the wanderings in the desert

---

[1] SPITTA supposes a preaching by Christ as Enoch to spirits who were afterwards shut up in prison, *op. cit.*, pp. 28ff. On this basis we cannot accept his theory. But yet it may be possible to keep to this theory because of the vagueness with regard to the position of the Angels on the occasion of the preaching. This problem Spitta has not considered necessary to examine.
[2] It is indeed also this which SPITTA considers so important.
[3] Regarding the conception τὰ εἰς Χριστὸν παθήματα in this passage see C. A. SCOTT, The Sufferings of Christ, *The Exp.* vi. 12, 1905, pp. 234ff.

is identified with Christ Himself.[1] Enoch even, on account of his strongly »messianic» character in the *Book of Enoch*, would be specially suitable to appear as a subject of an incarnation of Christ in a pre-existent form.[2] Further it may seem that after attention is directed in iii. 20 to several occurrences in the time of Noah, one may wonder whether the preaching to these spirits ought not to belong to the same time; and only in that way — it may be imagined — can one obtain a logical connection between the preaching in verse 19 and the comments in 20ff.[3]

However, quite serious objections can be made to this preexistence theory.

(a) The text in no way indicates that Enoch is here in question, nor anybody else than Christ Himself. If the author had wished to direct the thought to Enoch he ought in all reason to have indicated it in some way, but this he has not done. Only by a prejudiced desire at any cost to show dependences on the *Book of Enoch*[4] is it possible to read in Enoch as the acting subject.[5]

(b) There would have been no sense in putting forward in this connection a preaching by Christ wholly identical with that done by Enoch in the time before the Flood. Enoch's proceedings with the fallen Angels according to the *Book of Enoch* did not lead to any effect, for they continued being subject to the punishment once decided, and the result of Enoch's intervention was nil. But it is probable that the comments on the preaching in iii. 19 have some purpose of a practical and appealing kind in the context. Verse 18 appears as a reason for the previous exhortation. The patience of the Christians in suffering is here given an exhortative prototype through the remembrance of Christ's innocent Suffering and Death. After this comes verse 19 with a καί which clearly

---

[1] *Cf.* also, *e.g.*, John viii. 58, Eph. ii. 17.
[2] SPITTA, *op. cit.*, pp. 37ff.
[3] *Cf.* SPITTA, *op. cit.*, p. 48.
[4] And it is just such a rash, deductive attitude which SPITTA has in this matter.
[5] For comparison it may be noticed that H. GUNKEL, who was one of SPITTA's chief followers in the question of linking 1 Pet. iii. 19 in general to the *Book of Enoch*, characterized the attempt to make Noah or Enoch the real subject of this passage as »Krone der Willkür», *Die Schriften des Neuen Testaments*, ii, 1908, p. 562.

iii.] OTHER PRELIMINARY QUESTIONS IN VERSE 19 99

indicates that even this sentence is to justify what has just been said, but from a somewhat different point of view. This argument would be quite valueless, or even work in the opposite direction, if it was a reference to a preaching by Christ wholly identical with the appearance of Enoch to the fallen Angels as it is described in this Book.

(c) If ἐν ᾧ in verse 19 formally referred to the just mentioned πνεῦμα in ζωοποιηθείς πνεύματι but here actually indicated a shape of the pre-existent Christ, there would be a discrepancy between two kinds of πνεῦμα with quite different functions.[1] For the πνεῦμα which may serve as a basis for the pre-existent Christ certainly belongs to another sphere than the πνεῦμα which appears as a person's vital principle after the destruction of his body — even if there is at bottom only one πνεῦμα. We must indeed find the transference rather sudden between the πνεῦμα mentioned in verse 18 as surviving Christ's physical Death, and this supposed pre-existent πνεῦμα in verse 19.

(d) The qualifier of πνεύμασιν in verse 20, viz. the participle ἀπειθήσασιν, is an aorist form and cannot express an action in the present, such as must be assumed if the author indicated a preaching through Enoch at the time »when God's patience held out during the construction of the ark in the days of Noah». The attempt to avoid this difficulty by making the meaning of the participle pluperfect in relation to that determination of tense, and say that the spirits had been disobedient before God's patience held out in the days of Noah, is really unnatural and linguistically impossible because of the correspondence between ποτέ and ὅτε.[2] The implication must naturally be that the spirits were disobedient a long time ago during the time when God's patience held out during the days of Noah. The aoristic participle is here used to indicate a given fact (»complex aorist»). Thus the disobedience of the

---

[1] Cf. however below, pp. 104ff., regarding ἐν ᾧ.

[2] It is difficult to understand how SPITTA could be guilty of such extraordinary reasoning, op. cit., pp. 31f., but he has, of course, rightly perceived that otherwise his consistent Enoch theory would receive a blow at a very serious point.

spirits is not considered as contemporary with the *kerygma*, but as a fact already then completed, and the *kerygma* must necessarily belong to a later time.

We are therefore compelled also to reject the pre-existence theory, and state that the preaching must under all circumstances have been carried out by Christ Himself in some way in connection with His Death and Resurrection. This is, too, absolutely the most usual conception. And we should indeed not have questioned the matter except for the fact that as regards the earlier combinations with the *Book of Enoch* it was interesting to see whether the relations to this apocryphal book could be made still more intimate than what concerns the object of the preaching, so that the preacher should also be the same in both cases. This we must deny.[1] The person who preaches in iii. 19 is Christ Himself, not Enoch, not even indirectly.

Here, however, we face the question of what kind, viewed more closely, the relationship between the *Book of Enoch* and 1 Pet. iii. 19 may be, if the connections observed between the fallen Angels and the imprisoned spirits are to be appropriately considered.

CHRIST AS THE NEW ENOCH.

On the one hand we have found that the preaching to the »spirits» in our passage clearly depends upon the descriptions of the fallen Angels especially in the *Book of Enoch*. On the other hand, we have found that every attempt to smuggle in Enoch as the real subject in verse 19 must be rejected, so that the preaching spoken of in 1 Pet. cannot be quite identical with Enoch's appearance to the fallen Angels in the *Book of Enoch*.

On account of these observations we can probably state there is reason to consider the preaching to the spirits in 1 Pet. as a tradition concerning Christ in the first place which yet, because of the obvious agreement with the *Book of Enoch* especially as regards those to whom he appears, should be explained as very

---

[1] Principally in regard to SPITTA, *op. cit.*

much dependent on Enoch's appearance to the fallen Angels and may be best understood as a duplicate or a typological correspondent to it. Thus Christ appears at this point as a new Enoch.[1] He addresses himself to the same beings, imparting a revelation of some kind. This revelation is evidently not identical with the ineffective one which Enoch had to impart to the Angels according to the *Book of Enoch*, for it would not have had any meaning in the parenetical connection in the context of verse 19, and Christ, the chosen Corner Stone, must indeed have had something superior to bring — whether as regards punishment or pardon — than His antitype Enoch, whose intervention for the sake of the Angels did not cause any change in their state. Nevertheless we must probably assume a typological agreement between Enoch and Christ at this point, such that Christ as a new Enoch is a fulfilment of the prophecies which Enoch's action here implies.

As a matter of fact it cannot be regarded as so peculiar that Enoch should here be conceived as an antitype of Christ, so that Christ has come to appear as the fulfiller of the prophesy implied in the experiences of Enoch. Already at the beginning of the *Book of Enoch* the principal person himself says that he really does not think of his own time but of generations to come far later: ἐπὶ πόρρω οὖσαν (γενεὰν) ἐγὼ λαλῶ. *Cf.* the *Book of Jubilees* x. 17: »For Enoch's office was ordained for a testimony to the generations of the world.» We have earlier stated that a fundamental tendency in the *Book of Enoch* is the actual direction of attention to the coming end of the world.[2] It must also be remembered that Enoch's experiences appear to a great extent as visions, *e.g.* the *Book of Enoch* xiii. 8, xvii. 1, xxxvii. 1ff., liv. 1ff. &c., and the *Book of the Secrets of Enoch*, *passim*. Thus Enoch is largely considered as an apocalyptic prophet. So has he also been conceived within N.T. circles to judge from Jude 14. Then according to this last

---

[1] *Cf.* H. GUNKEL's views in *Die Schriften des Neuen Testaments*, ii, 1908, p. 562: »In der altchristlichen Überlieferung ist also Christus hier an die Stelle Henochs getreten.»

[2] See above, pp. 70ff., 85ff.

passage Enoch's prophecies really refer to the Messianic period. It is also quite clear that early Christianity which apparently to a high degree was connected with the Enoch traditions and to some extent honoured the *Book of Enoch* as holy writing[1] must have considered the pronouncements about Enoch as alluding to the Messianic time. And in this way, of course, it was natural to consider Enoch as a type of Christ. Only by means of such an intimate connection between Enoch and Christ can, for example, the striking agreement between certain parenetic passages in the *Book of Enoch* and some of Jesus' words[2] be explained. Another thing that made Enoch specially suitable as a type for Christ was the manner of his departure, Gen. v. 24, *cf.* Ecclus. xlix. 14 (16).[3] Elijah also partly serves in this way as a type for Christ in that the pronouncement about Jesus, ἀνελήμφθη εἰς τὸν οὐρανόν, can clearly be connected with corresponding pronouncements about Elijah in the O.T.[4] Besides, this prophet is placed in intimate relation to John the Baptist, Matt. xi. 9ff. with parallels. The most important fact is, however, that in the *Book of Enoch* the idea of the »Son of Man» plays such a prominent role, *e.g.* in ch. lxxi. We ought also to think of Enoch's character as »Primal Man» and the usual combination of this figure in primitive times with a corresponding figure in the last days, such as are shown by speculations as to the First and the Second Adam. And of course much more could be presented in support of the idea of Enoch as a type for Christ.

The fact that in the *Book of Enoch* it is expressly stated to be Enoch himself who lives through the events which we here consider probably to have been typological patterns to certain of the actions later done by Christ, he himself who goes and speaks with the fallen Angels &c., causes no difficulty at all in maintaining the theory now put forward concerning the prophetic references to the Messi-

---

[1] *Cf.* above, pp. 66ff.
[2] Regarding this see R. OTTO, *Reich Gottes und Menschensohn*, 1940, pp. 310ff.
[3] See also Ecclus. xliv. 16, Hebr. xi. 5, *Jos. Ant.* i. 3. 4.
[4] L. GOPPELT, *Typos*, 1939, p. 96.

anic time or concerning the typological correspondence between Enoch and the coming Messiah. A prophet or similar figure is thought sometimes to experience actively in his own person what later in complete reality shall happen to the Messiah. Let us only think of Jonah and his »sign», Matt. xii. 39ff. with parallels. Also in the form of a vision the same experience referring to the Messiah can occur to a prophet or similar person. A proof of this is Ezechiel's vision of the resurrection of the dry bones with the prophet's own cooperation in Ezech. xxxvii, which by Early Christianity was considered a prophetic pattern of how Christ awakens the dead, 1 Clem. 1. 4, *Just. Apol.* I, lii, *Iren. Contra hær.* v. 15. 1, v. 34. 1, &c.[1] According to this reasoning the prophet himself in anticipation plays the role of the coming Messiah.

If we consider the points of view here put forward we ought to understand the formal relations between the *Book of Enoch* and 1 Pet. iii. 19 in a logical and practically satisfactory way, without having to take up any too rash hypotheses or to carry out any violent manipulation.

At the same time we have obtained an indication of an important genetic explanatory basis for the idea expressed in this passage. We shall return to this question later.[2]

We must first, however, consider certain other questions of detail in iii. 19, before taking up the central subject. For there is really cause to agree with v. ZEZSCHWITZ concerning this passage: *quot verba, tot ænigmata.*[3]

WHAT DOES ἐν ᾧ MEAN?

The ordinary opinion is that ἐν ᾧ in 1 Pet. iii. 19 refers to the πνεύματι in verse 18 immediately preceding it.[4] The matter, however,

---

[1] W. NEUSS, *Das Buch Ezechiel*, 1912, pp. 24ff.
[2] See below, ch. xi.
[3] C. A. G. v. ZEZSCHWITZ, *Petri Apostoli ... sententia*, p. 22.
[4] This opinion is accepted with almost 100 % unity and certainty. Examples: H. VON SODEN in *Handcommentar zum N.T.*, 1891, p. 131f.; E. KÜHL, *Die Briefe Petri und Judæ*, p. 219; J. MONNIER, *La première*

is in no way self-evident. The arguments usually put forward for the statement are not quite incontestable by a sceptical critic. Among other things it has been thought that the supplementing of ἐν ᾧ with πνεύματι could be supported by the fact that it is followed by πνεύματα, so that in such a way we can bring out a correspondence between Christ's πνεῦμα and this later πνεύματα as the term for the beings in prison.[1] The absurdity of this reasoning we consider we have already shown.[2] If the word πνεῦμα is to be presumed after ἐν ᾧ it must be considered as a qualification of the existence form of the Risen One and so have quite a different value from what the same word has later as a qualification for the evil beings in prison. First of all, however, it has been argued that πνεύματι in verse 18 stands immediately before ἐν ᾧ.[3] This reasoning is, of course, not faulty but it has only a limited value. Our author does not always use the so-called »relative connection»[4] in the way that it would then be formulated here, in direct contact with the antecedent, but there are often also some words between the antecedent and the relative pronoun, as for example in i. 10, 12, ii. 8, 10 &c. In any case it is not necessary that ἐν ᾧ, because of its position, should refer to πνεύματι. This argument is not absolutely binding, as a proof. There is on the whole nothing that necessitates the combination of ἐν ᾧ with πνεύματι.

On the contrary there are possibilities of presenting serious reasons against this theory.

Of late years an important objection has been put forward by F. ZIMMERMANN,[5] because of an example of ἐν ᾧ in a papyrus text from Oxyrhynchus examined by him. He thinks that in 1 Pet. iii. 19 it »ganz ausgeschlossen ist, ἐν ᾧ auf πνεύματι zu beziehen». »Dort ist σαρκί», he declares, »ebenso wie épître, p. 173; U. HOLZMEISTER, *Commentarius*, p. 299. See also C. CLEMEN, »*Niedergefahren zu den Toten*», p. 124.

[1] See also VON SODEN, *loc. cit.*
[2] See above, pp. 60f.
[3] *E.g.* W. STEIGER, *Der erste Brief Petri*, 1832, p. 349, or MONNIER, *op. cit.*, p. 173, lay stress on that.
[4] Which is otherwise actually a typical construction in 1 Pet.; *cf.* G. WOHLENBERG, *Der erste und zweite Petrusbrief*, p. 106.
[5] F. ZIMMERMANN, Verkannte Papyri, *Arch. für Papyrusforsch.* xi, 1935, pp. 165 ff.

πνεύματι Dat. der Beziehung, und mit Vers 18 schliesst der Gedanke, dass Christus für uns gelitten hat, um uns zu erlösen, dafür starb er — leiblich — und lebte — geistig. Dann beginnt ein neuer Gedanke ...»[1] Instead Zimmermann wants to take ἐν ᾧ in verse 19 as analogous to the same expression in a similar syntactical connection in the papyrus text, where ἐν ᾧ is clearly a temporal conjunction with a concessive or adversative secondary sense — Zimmermann renders this expression in the papyrus text by *indessen*.[2]

In considering the matter carefully it must also be acknowledged that if σαρκὶ and πνεύματι in verse 18 are cases of dative of reference, *dativus limitationis* or *respiciendi* (»Dativ der Beziehung») as is quite probable, this ἐν with a supposed πνεύματι in verse 19 cannot possibly form any syntactical analogy to it, even if ἐν with the dative can in other cases quite well replace a *dativus respiciendi*, as in ἐν μηδενὶ λειπόμενοι, James i. 4, and also in ἐν ᾧ according to 2 Cor. xi. 12, 21, where the expression is, however, adverbial. The real peculiarity in the *dativus limitationis* or *respiciendi* is that by it a more limited sphere is indicated, one in which a judgement regarding a certain quality or a certain condition shall be considered to apply, or, as is said in our most important Greek grammar: »... der Dativ als sogenannter Dativ der Beziehung (neben dem weit üblicheren Akkusativ) [bezeichnet] den Gegenstand, woran oder worin sich ein *Zustand*[3] äussert.»[4] To say that Christ, »as regards the spirit», went away and preached, is not possible — indeed, even if it were so,[5] the expression could under no circumstances be regarded as analogous to the phrases »He died as regards the Flesh, rose to life as regards the Spirit», for the kind of activity expressed in the predicate would be quite different in the two cases. The conception »as regards the spirit» demands that the predicate contains a statement regarding the inner condition of the person. But this is not at all the case when πορευθεὶς ἐκήρυξεν follows.

[1] ZIMMERMANN, *op. cit.* p. 174.
[2] *Op. cit.*, pp. 171 and 174.
[3] Our italics.
[4] R. KÜHNER, *Ausführliche Grammatik*, ii, Syntax, 3rd ed. by B. GERTH, ii, 1898, § 425. 12, p. 440.
[5] W. BAUER is one who has this interpretation in his *Griechisch-Deutsches Wörterbuch*, 1937, *s.v.* ἐν, col. 433. There he first gives the translation »was dieses anbetrifft» to 1 Pet. iii. 19.

The only correct conception of πνεύματι in iii. 19 must also be that it is an example of the *dativus respiciendi*. Above all this assertion is supported by σαρκί and πνεύματι in 1 Pet. iv. 6 which cannot be any other kind of dative. It is also really impossible to take σαρκί in verse 18 as anything else than the *dativus respiciendi*. The antithetical contrast between σαρκί and πνεύματι thus makes it almost certain that the latter word also is the same kind of dative. This is true in spite of the rule in John vi. 63 that τὸ πνεῦμά ἐστιν τὸ ζωοποιοῦν (*cf.* Rom. viii. 11, 1 Cor. xv. 45, 2 Cor. iii. 6), for this principle refers to the effect of Christ's Spirit upon others. It is also possible to hear, for example, that τὸ πνεῦμα ζωή (ἐστι) διὰ δικαιοσύνην, Rom. viii. 10. If now it really says in verse 18 that Christ was brought to life »as regards» the spirit, the spirit must be considered as the substance to which the qualification »life» belongs (*cf.* Rom. viii. 10). It is then actually the spirit itself which is brought to life (which, of course, does not here imply that it passes from death to life, for the spirit has never been dead, but only that it becomes the bearer of the new Life which follows upon the humiliation of the body). Thus πνεύματι in verse 18 has an intimate subjective meaning. It is actually a sudden transference of thought which ought not to be regarded as permissible nor in agreement with the usual language of 1 Pet., if the author immediately afterwards considers it right to refer to the word πνεῦμα but now uses it in one or another objective meaning of the Resurrection form of Jesus or something similar. This will be just as unnatural as to say for example: »His Soul was made alive and in that He went and preached.» For this reason any translations of the type »in the spirit» and such like are also excluded.

Perhaps one could, also after paying attention to the intimate subjective function of πνεύματι in verse 18, think of the meaning »in the form of which», »as which»[1] or something similar, *i.e.* corresponding to such an expression

---

[1] This meaning has no relation to the one, »with reference to», as seems to be assumed by W. BAUER, *loc. cit.*, in that the translation of 1 Pet. iii. 19 »was dieses betrifft» is combined with »Geist, als welcher». — The latter interpretation appears also, for example, in H. GUNKEL in *Die Schriften des N.T:s*, iii, 1917, p. 281, and it is probably not so unusual.

iii.] OTHER PRELIMINARY QUESTIONS IN VERSE 19 107

as ἐν δωρεᾷ in 2 Macc. iv. 30, ἐν μυστηρίῳ in 1 Cor. ii. 7 &c.?[1] Indeed, it may be said that just as the phrase »He was brought to life as regards the spirit» is quite equivalent to »He was brought to life as spirit», a continuation with »as which — i.e. as spirit — He also went and preached» or something similar is not quite unnatural. Yet for other reasons this translation is rather improbable. For one thing it must be doubted that there was any interest in stating in which form Christ appeared to the spirits. For it can scarcely have been interesting for the author of the Epistle to communicate to his readers any subtle Christological theory of matter in this connection which is so strongly parenetical and practically directed, where except the references to certain well-known O.T. facts we have only to deal with the fundamentals of the Christ drama and the basic demands of the Christian life. Information as to the nature which Christ took upon Himself on this occasion would have been quite irrelevant, as it has only an abstract theoretical interest. For another thing it is very improbable that the author has considered τὸ πνεῦμα to be the essence of Christ in the prison mentioned, in so far as the question is of a preaching in the underworld directly after Christ's death, because πνεῦμα is — as we have already stated — not the usual term for that part of man which goes to the underworld; for that ψυχή is preferred, as in Ps. xv (xvi). 10 (= Acts ii. 27). Notice also that in 1 Pet. iv. 19 ψυχή is used in contradistinction from πνεῦμα in the Bible words lying behind it, Ps. xxx (xxxi). 6 and Luke xxiii. 46.[2] These terminological misgivings must indeed become much greater if we remember that it has just been a question of that part of Christ's Person which was brought to life. It is, of course, certainly to some extent possible to translate an ἐν ᾧ by »in the form of which, as which» &c. analogous to the examples given, ἐν δωρεᾷ &c., but this meaning is not readily found and there is not, at least in the N.T., any relative expression of this kind. Therefore this translation is actually far from being plausible.

If we consider verse 18 as a whole we find further that the appositions θανατωθεὶς μὲν σαρκί, ζωοποιηθεὶς δὲ πνεύματι appear in parenthesis in the sentence, inserted as a clearer explanation of the main action, but on the other hand based on well-known christological formulæ of an elementary character. It is not probable that ἐν ᾧ is connected to this πνεύματι, here accompanying rather cursorily. Nor would it be natural if one of the two antithetical ideas, σαρκί and πνεύματι, was suddenly taken out of the context

---

[1] Cf. κατά with the accusative, having the same meaning, e.g. in κατὰ χάριν, ὀφείλημα, Rom. iv. 4.
[2] Particularly contra R. KNOPF, Die Briefe Petri und Judä, 1912, p. 148, who at the same time, p. 149, is specially eager to maintain ψυχή as the correct term for the souls who go down into Hades.

and formed a basis for the whole of the following sentence. But above all it is unnatural to make a dative of reference serve as antecedent to a relative pronoun.[1]

Let us therefore, to avoid all these philological, logical and material doubts, try to interpret ἐν ᾧ without reference to the preceding πνεύματι and instead take these words as a relative adverb serving as a conjunction.[2] In such a form, as a conjunction, ἐν ᾧ appears in several passages in the N.T., and this even in 1 Pet. so that we shall have several good analogies to show.

Thus ἐν ᾧ is clearly a temporal conjunction (equal to ἐν ᾧ χρόνῳ,[3] καιρῷ or similar expressions) and means »whereat», »on which occasion», »while», »at the same time as», »in doing which» &c. — in the case of relative connection »thereat» &c. — in the following undoubted passages in the N.T. not counting 1 Pet.:

Mark ii. 19[4] = Luke v. 34:[4] ἐν ᾧ ὁ νυμφίος μετ' αὐτῶν ἐστιν.[5]

Luke xix. 13: ἐν ᾧ ἔρχομαι (»while I am on the way»).[6]

John v. 7: ἐν ᾧ ἔρχομαι.[7]

To this we will add Rom. ii. 1: ἐν ᾧ γὰρ κρίνεις τὸν ἕτερον, »in[8] judging another», where ἐν ᾧ has probably a temporal purport with a conditional by-significance — the purport is probably not causal or instrumental, as the relation between the relative clause

---

[1] F. ZIMMERMANN, Verkannte Papyri, p. 174. Cf. E. G. SELWYN, The First Epistle, p. 197: »The antecedent cannot be πνεύματι for there is no example in N.T. of this dative of reference, or adverbial dative as I should prefer to call it, serving as antecedent to a relative pronoun.»

[2] K. GSCHWIND's suggestion in Die Niederfahrt Christi, p. 118, to consider ἐν ᾧ as referring to the message with which Christ went and preached to the spirits, is made improbable by the fact that ἐν ᾧ like τοῖς πνεύμασι belongs grammatically to ἐκήρυξεν, but it cannot be said ἔν τινι κηρύσσειν in the meaning »to preach, announce, something».

[3] F. VIGERUS, De præcipuis græcæ dictionis idiotismis liber, 1834, p. 606.

[4] A. DEBRUNNER, F. Blass' Grammatik, 1943, § 455. 3, p. 208.

[5] In the parallel passage in Matt. ix. 15: ἐφ' ὅσον.

[6] With J. VITEAU, Étude sur le grec du N.T., i, 1893, p. 129f.; contra DEBRUNNER, op. cit., § 383. 1, p. 168. We should probably have the same meaning as in John v. 7, i.e. the following example.

[7] DEBRUNNER, op. cit., § 455. 3, p. 208: »während».

[8] So e.g. H. LIETZMANN, An die Römer, 1933, p. 38 (»indem»).

OTHER PRELIMINARY QUESTIONS IN VERSE 19

and the main sentence is not that of reason and consequence or of cause and effect, but contemporaneity and identity, so that we have two different phases of the same act.[1] The same temporal conjunction in the form ἐν οἷς appears in the writings of Luke: Luke xii. 1: ἐν οἷς ἐπισυναχθεισῶν &c. (»when in this situation»). Acts xxiv. 18 *var. lect.*: ἐν οἷς εὖρόν με (»when», »on which occasion»). Acts xxvi. 12: ἐν οἷς πορευόμενος (»when I then»). This conjunction ἐν ᾧ appears, of course, in other places besides the N.T. as *e.g.* in *Soph. Trach.* 929, *Xenoph. Oecon.* xvii. 10 (*cf.* ἐν ὅσῳ with the same function in *Aristoph. Eccl.* 1152f.).[2] An interesting case is the one in the Oxyrhynchus papyrus noted by F. ZIMMERMANN[3] (it contains a text from Arrian's Τιλλιβόρου βίος):[4] "Ω μοι τῶν ἁμαρτηθέντων ἔ[φη· νῦν ἐγὼ ὁ ἀσεβὴς μαθὼν τὰ τ]οῦ σώματος αἰκιζομένου [αἰδῶ νέ]μ[ει]ν β[ούλομαί σοι σοῦ εὐ]ωχούμενος· ἐν ᾧ ἔδει με κ[ρ]ε[ίτ]τον[ας δίκας ἢ μοιχάδας τίν]ε[ι]ν τὰς ἴσας ἀναδεδεγμ[έ]νας.[5] In this passage ἐν ᾧ has clearly the character of a conjunction. This conjunction here, however, has a modal quality, has thus not merely the significance of tense but a concessive or adversative meaning and should be translated *e.g.* by »although», »in spite of the fact that» or »and yet».[6] In other languages, too, it is possible to find an oscillation in similar expressions between a meaning purely temporal and one more modally coloured, as concessive, *e.g.* the German *indessen*, or causal or explicative, *e.g.* the Latin *dum*, and the English »in that».

The expression ἐν ᾧ as a causal, instrumental or explicative conjunction, with the meaning »because», »seeing that», an explan-

---

[1] *Contra* DEBRUNNER, *op. cit.*, § 219. 2, p. 101 (causal interpretation); W. BAUER, *Wörterbuch, s.v.* ἐν, col. 433 (local interpretation).
[2] See also *e.g.* F. VIGERUS, *op. cit.*, pp. 606f.; A. N. JANNARIS, *An Historical Greek Grammar*, 1897, §§ 233, 1392, 1776 &c.
[3] Verkannte Papyri, pp. 170f., 174.
[4] B. P. GRENFELL & A. S. HUNT, *The Oxyrhynchus-Papyri*, iii, 1903, no. 416, pp. 60f.
[5] We give here ZIMMERMANN's text. The many uncertainties in the text do not affect the present question.
[6] ZIMMERMANN, p. 174, has *indessen*.

atory »in that», or with a relative connection »and therefore» &c., is found in the following places in the N.T. besides 1 Pet.: Rom. viii. 3: explicative »in that»; Hebr. ii. 18: »as»; Hebr. vi. 17: »on account of which.»[1] In 1 Pet. ἐν ᾧ occurs in the following passages:

i. 6 ἐν ᾧ ἀγαλλιᾶσθε.
ii. 12 ἐν ᾧ καταλαλοῦσιν ὑμῶν.
iii. 16 ἐν ᾧ καταλαλεῖσθε.
iii. 19 ἐν ᾧ καὶ ... ἐκήρυξεν.
iv. 4 ἐν ᾧ ξενίζονται.

Of these ii. 12 and iii. 16 are different from the others and rather similar to each other. The usual idea is that ἐν ᾧ there is the same as ἐν τούτῳ, ἐν ᾧ or something similar, so that we should not have any conjunction here.[2] In that case the meaning would be that the heathen come to shame in the respect in which they reproach the Christians. It is perhaps possible to support this idea with a Greek inscription: ἵνα μηδ' ἐν τούτοις ἔχωσιν ἡμᾶς καταλαλεῖν οἱ ..., W. DITTENBERGER, *Sylloge*, 3rd ed., ii, no. 593, *l.* 6. This interpretation, however, is impossible in 1 Pet. ii. 12 for the main sentence speaks of praising God, but it is nonsense to say that the Heathen will praise God »in that respect». Further a supposed ἐν τούτῳ in ii. 12 must compete in a peculiar way with ἐκ τῶν καλῶν ἔργων as a modification of the verb δοξάσωσιν.[3] For the same reason ἐν cannot here have a causal meaning, It is unnatural to consider a causal ἐν τούτῳ explained by a following apposition ἐκ τῶν καλῶν ἔργων. No, even in 1. Pet. ii. 12 ἐν ᾧ must certainly be a conjunction, probably of a pure temporal character[4] so that the meaning is: »just as they slander you» (note that ἐν ἡμέρᾳ ἐπισκοπῆς is here not the Last Day but the day in earthly life when the person in question is converted by reason of his realization of the blamelessness of the

---

[1] DEBRUNNER, *ibid.*: *weswegen*.
[2] *E.g.* E. KÜHL, *Die Briefe Petri und Judæ*, pp. 158, 205; CH. BIGG, *Commentary*, pp. 136f., R. KNOPF, *Die Briefe Petri und Judä*, p. 103.
[3] Also acknowledged *e.g.* by KÜHL, *op. cit.*, p. 158.
[4] Thus H. WINDISCH, in *Die katholischen Briefe*, 1930, p. 62, also understands ἐν ᾧ in this passage.

iii.]   OTHER PRELIMINARY QUESTIONS IN VERSE 19   111

Christians, as is clear from the instructive analogy in iii. 1f.).[1] In all probability ἐν ᾧ in iii. 16, a passage which so clearly agrees with ii. 12, must be interpreted in exactly the same way, as a temporal conjunction. In both cases we obtain, by such an interpretation, a natural content as to matter and language and a considerably more comfortable translation than the usual involved phrases »in the respect in which» &c. We have thus two examples of ἐν ᾧ as a temporal conjunction.

If we now look at 1 Pet. i. 6 and iv. 4 we find that ἐν ᾧ has the character of a causal conjunction. To consider the relative pronoun in i. 6 as referring to the previous ἐν καιρῷ ἐσχάτῳ is indeed impossible, as ἀγαλλιᾶσθε with respect to its parallelism with verse 8 cannot have a future significance, which one must then demand on the basis of the idea καιρὸς ἔσχατος.[2] The most suitable translation, considering the »relative connection» must be: »therefore» or »because of that», namely, therefore that the Christians now have this living hope, &c.[3] In iv. 4 we have the same condition. It is quite clear that ἐν ᾧ here fits best into the context if it is translated by »therefore» or something similar. The reasoning seems to be quite simply that the heathen are surprised no longer to find the believers taking part in the depravity mentioned just because the recently converted Christians had previously taken part in it for some considerable time.[4] Thus there are two cases of ἐν ᾧ as a causal conjunction in 1 Pet.

Reflecting again over 1 Pet. iii. 19, we must state, in the face

---

[1] *Cf.* Matt. v. 16, and analogies quoted to it in H. STRACK & P. BILLERBECK, *Kommentar*, i, 1912, pp. 239f.

[2] See, *e.g.*, KÜHL, *op. cit.*, pp. 82ff., J. MONNIER, *La première épître*, p. 39, U. HOLZMEISTER, *Commentarius*, p. 204.

[3] KÜHL, *op. cit.*, p. 84; R. KNOPF, *op. cit.*, p. 47; U. HOLZMEISTER, *loc. cit.* The logical and language difficulties indicated are ignored by BIGG, *op. cit.*, pp. 102f., H. WINDISCH, *op. cit.*, p. 53 and others. Yet we cannot avoid considering these doubts decisive in this case.

[4] *Cf.* E. HUTHER, *Kritisch exegetisches Handbuch*, p. 204, KNOPF, *op. cit.*, p. 165 (who also here quotes the names B. WEISS, KÜHL, USTERI, v. SODEN). The passage is also understood in this way in the Swedish translation of the Bible 1917.

of the material here presented, that there are many good examples in the N.T. which make it probable that this latter passage also contains ἐν ᾧ as a conjunction. Above all it must be noticed that the author of 1 Pet. displays a clear preference for the conjunction ἐν ᾧ when he uses it in four places, even quite near to iii. 19. And by means of such a conception we can wholly avoid the logical and language difficulties which, as we have shown, easily arise when ἐν ᾧ is connected with the previous πνεύματι, as is prevalent. For this reason we consider we ought to prefer to understand ἐν ᾧ as a conjunction in iii. 19.

Then the question will be: What kind of conjunction? Looking at the context and also considering what categories of ἐν ᾧ as a conjunction we have otherwise in the N.T., there are really only two possibilities: Either ἐν ᾧ in this passage is a purely temporal conjunction, in this case meaning »whereat» or »thereat», »on which occasion» &c.: or also it is a causal conjunction meaning »wherefore» or »therefore», »for this reason» &c.

The causal conception is supported by a patristic tradition based upon the theory of an allusion to Christ descending to win sinners to God. »Œcumenius» says in his commentary to 1 Pet. regarding ἐν ᾧ in iii. 19, that it ἀντὶ τοῦ διὸ κεῖται αἰτολογικῶς, after which he declares: εἰπὼν γὰρ ὅτι ὑπὲρ τῶν ἀδίκων ἡμῶν ἀπέθανε, καὶ ἐκ τούτου δοὺς ἔμφασιν ὅτι ὑπὲρ σωτηρίας ἁπάντων ἀνθρώπων τὸν θάνατον ὑπέστη, λέγει ὅτι διὸ καὶ τοῖς ἐν τῷ ᾅδῃ κατεχομένοις ἐκήρυξεν.[1] This statement is also found in Theophylactus' commentary,[2] and even among modern investigators it is possible in rare cases to find an interpretation of this kind.[3] Against this theory however it can be pleaded that there is a certain obscurity as to the extent in which a purely causal relation can really be discovered here. It is not possible to bring out such a causal relation that the conclusion as to the preaching to the spirits appears as a clearly logical con-

---

[1] P.G. cxix, col. 560 A.
[2] P.G. cxxv, col. 1232 C.
[3] E. GÜDER, Die Lehre von der Erscheinung Jesu Christi unter den Todten, 1853, p. 42.

sequence of the given premisses. An allusion to ἵνα &c. should, further, preferably have been expressed by εἰς ὅ, in which case the reasoning would be final. The causal interpretation does not, on the whole, give any clearly logical connection.

By a temporal interpretation on the other hand of ἐν ᾧ we can obtain the following natural meaning: »on which occasion» or »on that occasion», namely when He died (preferably not: »when He was made alive» because of the parenthetical character of those appositions) Christ went and preached also to the spirits. This gives a highly logical and natural purport to our passage, the translation is simple and intelligible, and a good formal analogy can be shown in the immediately preceding verse 16, apart from other analogies which we have already touched upon — it may also be observed that the Oxyrhynchus papyrus referred to above is good evidence that ἐν ᾧ can allude to the previous situation, and continue the reasoning after a short pause.[1] If then we are to choose between a conception of ἐν ᾧ as a causal and as a temporal conjunction we must prefer the latter. In the temporal interpretation there is the very best possibility to understand this ἐν ᾧ, which otherwise causes so many misgivings.[2]

The καί which in 1 Pet. iii. 19 follows directly upon ἐν ᾧ will by this temporal interpretation best connect ἅπαξ ἀπέθανεν ... ἵνα ὑμᾶς ... with τοῖς ... ἐκήρυχεν. This too gives a good and natural meaning.

Finally, to confirm this theory of ἐν ᾧ as a conjunction in a temporal meaning we can draw a few examples from Greek literature in general for the purpose of comparison.

---

[1] *Cf.* ZIMMERMANN, *op. cit.* p. 174, regarding the syntactical agreements between the passage in this papyrus and 1 Pet. iii. 19.

[2] An earlier proposed interpretation of ἐν ᾧ in that way is to be found in *The Twentieth Century New Testament*, [1903] 1904: »And it was then that He went» ... *Cf.* E. GOODSPEED, *Problems of New Testament translation*, p. 197. — In a similar way E. G. SELWYN, *The First Epistle*, p. 197, says: »ἐν ᾧ: in which state ... or better and more broadly: 'in which process', 'in the course of which', referring to Christ's passion and resurrection generally.»

We have already stated that the temporal character of ἐν ᾧ appears also in classical Greek.[1] Some examples from Plato may elucidate that peculiarity: *Phæd.* xi (67 A): καὶ ἐν ᾧ ἂν ζῶμεν ("as long as"); *Conv.* xi (185 D): ἐν ᾧ δ' ἂν ἐγὼ λέγω ("while I speak"); *Resp.* vi. 11 (498 B): ἐν ᾧ βλαστάνει; vii. 2 (516 E): ἐν ᾧ ἀμβλυώττει, *cf.* Herodotus, vi. 89: ἐν ᾧ ὧν Κορινθίων ἐδέοντο χρῆσαι σφίσι νέας, ἐν τούτῳ διεφθάρη τὰ πρήγματα. Seeing that ἐν ᾧ in 1 Pet. iii. 19, although a relative expression, has a demonstrative meaning ("relative connection"), it is really equal to ἐν τούτῳ. This expression often has just the meaning which we have here assumed as regards ἐν ᾧ, namely "thereat", "on this occasion".

This is quite usual in Xenophon, *e.g. Inst. Cyr.* iii. 2. 12: ἐν δὲ τούτῳ προσάγουσι τῷ Κύρῳ τοὺς αἰχμαλώτους ("in this situation"), *ibid.*, iii. 3. 48: ἐν τούτῳ δ' ἦλθε Χρυσάντας.

In Herodotus, too, we find similar expressions, *e.g.* the passage just quoted, or in vii. 26. 1: ἐν ᾧ δὲ ... ἐν τούτῳ ...
Cf. Parthen. Erot. ix. 5: καὶ ἐν τούτῳ δὴ τοῖς Μιλησίοις ἑορτὴ ἐπῄει ... τότε ...

Such an ἐν ᾧ = ἐν τούτῳ could also sometimes correspond in some way to the adverbial use of ἐν in the expression ἐν δέ or ἐν δὲ καί. The former appears for instance in Sophocles: *Oed. T.* 27: ἐν δ' ὁ πυρφόρος θεός; *Trach.* 207: ἐν δὲ κοινὸς ἀρσένων ἴτω κλαγγά; *Ant.* 420f.: ἐν δ' ἐμεστώθη μέγας αἰθήρ. We have also perhaps a case of this adverbial ἐν δέ in the N.T., namely in Phil. iii. 13 (instead of the difficult ἕν δέ).[2] *Cf.* ἐν δὲ τούτῳ in 2 Pet. iii. 8 *var. lect.*[3] In the form ἐν δὲ καί we have sometimes the same expression meaning "then also", with a temporal character, *e.g.* Ps. Lucian. *De astrol.* iv (362):[4] ἐν δὲ καὶ οὐνόματα αὐτέοισιν ἐπέθεσαν.

The expression ἐν τῷ αὐτῷ meaning "at the same time"[5] is also

---
[1] *Cf.* above, p. 109.
[2] A. FRIDRICHSEN, Exegetisches zum N.T., *Symb. Osl.* xiii, 1934, pp. 44ff. ("dabei aber").
[3] *Ibid.*, p. 45.
[4] *Ibid.*, p. 46.
[5] F. PASSOW, *Handwörterbuch*, i, 1841, col. 454a.

iii.]   OTHER PRELIMINARY QUESTIONS IN VERSE 19   115

an example of a corresponding temporal use of ἐν. This comes out clearly just in correspondence with ἐν ᾧ (καί) in *Parthen. Erot.* ix. 7: φασὶ δέ τινες καὶ Διόγνητον ἐν τῷ αὐτῷ καῆναι, ἐν ᾧ καὶ ἡ παῖς. In such phrases we can therefore discover close analogies to ἐν ᾧ in 1 Pet. iii. 19, as we prefer to interpret it.

With the conception of ἐν ᾧ which we prefer all subtle speculations are made impossible as to the form in which Christ appeared at the preaching to the spirits in prison, such speculations as often engaged the attention of the older theologians — especially those of orthodox Protestantism — as regards 1 Pet. iii. 19.[1]

WHEN AND WHERE WAS THE KERYGMA PERFORMED?

From our earlier observations it may be clear that the preaching is not regarded as being in Noah's time and by the pre-existent Christ but a preaching in connection with the Saviour's death. The correctness of combining the preaching in some way with the Christ drama in general ought not to be in doubt.

We may not, however, only speak of Christ's suffering and death in quite general terms, but must also go deeper and ask at what point of time in the drama of Salvation the preaching took place. Is it a preaching during the time between the Death on the Cross and the Resurrection, the *triduum mortis* — so that here we should have an announcement of the *descensus ad inferos* — or a preaching at or after the Resurrection — so that we should have an announcement of the *ascensus*? This problem has aroused much discussion.[2]

The reader who wishes to follow our suggestion as to the interpretation of ἐν ᾧ must naturally prefer the Descent theory, for in

---

[1] See the good reviews in C. F. KEIL, *Commentar*, 1883, pp. 128f.; and P. J. JENSEN, *Læren om Kristi Nedfart*, pp. 124ff., 157ff.

[2] Most students, of course, follow the traditional Descent theory. See the bibliographical references in U. HOLZMEISTER, *Commentarius*, pp. 307ff. The Ascent theory is taken in different ways *e.g.* by P. J. JENSEN, *Læren om Kristi Nedfart*, pp. 180ff.; K. GSCHWIND, *Die Niederfahrt Christi*, pp. 119ff.; H. SCHLIER, *Christus und die Kirche im Epheserbrief*, 1930, p. 17.

that way the meaning is that Christ went and preached to the spirits on the occasion of His Death.

The problem can, however, also be regarded from a purely matter of fact point of view. This question of time is intimately connected with the question: Where is the prison in which the spirits are? For it is extremely likely, indeed the only natural thing, to think that if the prison is in the underworld, Christ preached to the spirits at His descent immediately after Death, but if it is somewhere in space, the preaching took place in connection with the ascension. *Tertium non datur*. It is really not credible that the preaching in question formed an act unconnected with these phases of the Christ drama.

As regards the situation of the prison we must at once state that the first and simplest thought is to place it in the underworld. To judge from 2 Pet. ii. 4 and Jude 6, the rebellious beings from the time of Noah should be thought of as cast down into the Tartarus. The scenes in the *Book of Enoch* make it also most probable that the prison was in the underworld. Further φυλακή is, as already mentioned,[1] a designation for the underworld prison according to Rev. xx. 7 compared with xx. 3. Finally we have a tradition of Christ's Descent indicated in other parts of the N.T. and related literature which do not need to depend upon 1 Pet. iii. 19, *e.g.* Matt. xii. 40, Acts ii. 24, 27. Rom. xiv. 9, Eph. iv. 8f.,[2] so that here we can quite well count upon an idea which also appears elsewhere.

However, on the other hand one can refer to descriptions in certain writings which resemble the N.T. of a prison for the fallen Angels somewhere in space. Thus Enoch in the *Book of the Secrets of Enoch* meets the fallen Angels, called *grigori*, »Watchers«, shut up partly in the second heaven, ch. vii, and partly in the fifth, ch. xviii, where they are said to be bigger in form than the biggest giants. In the *Greek Apocalypse of Baruch*, ii.f., the sinners from the Tower of Babel are similarly shut up in the first and second

---

[1] *Cf.* above, pp. 53, 66f., 96.
[2] *Cf.* P. J. JENSEN, *op. cit.*, p. 32; K. GSCHWIND, *op. cit.*, pp. 157ff.

heaven;[1] *cf.* the parallel in the *Slavonic Apocalypse of Baruch*, iif.[2] Such descriptions are certainly connected with a tendency to spiritualizing the older, more primitive and concrete descriptions of the underworld, a tendency which appears in several theological or philosophical tracts especially from later times and which implies that the place where the dead are kept is moved up to some higher sphere, *e.g.* the sphere of the planets — here we can especially think of gnosticism.[3]

No absolute difference between these varying descriptions of the Realm of the Dead should, however, be maintained. It is best to count upon an oscillation of thought according to more or less philosophical conceptions. It is possible that the author of 1 Pet. was able to oscillate in the same way between a more concrete and a more spiritualized idea of this »prison», and perhaps also his readers. But there is on the other hand no special reason to assume that this author or his readers wished in principle to free themselves from the more concrete conception of a prison in the underworld, something like the descriptions in the *Book of Enoch*. For this reason it will be best to keep to the theory of the prison being in the underworld and of the preaching being connected with Christ's *descensus ad inferos*.[4]

It certainly seems as if the sequence of the *motifs* in 1 Pet. iii. 19 favours a preaching at the Ascent. The kerygma is mentioned immediately after ζωοποιηθεὶς πνεύματι and a little later the author recalls that Christ was exalted above Angels and Powers. Yet a strict, deliberate chronological order in the text must not be

---

[1] M. R. JAMES, *Apocrypha anecdota*, Texts and Studies v. 1, 1897, pp. 85f.
[2] *Ibid.*, pp. 96ff.
[3] Thus we are obliged to suppose a development in a direction quite opposite to H. SCHLIER's exposition in his *Religionsgeschichtliche Untersuchungen*, 1929, pp. 72ff., and *Christus und die Kirche*, 1930, pp. 16, where he often seems to regard the gnostic ideas of a celestial prison as more original. The gnostic theories of a celestial Hades must, of course, in general be a secondary stage in relation to the simpler popular ideas of the Realm of the Dead and the prison of the souls as placed in the underworld.
[4] As most scholars do. *Cf.* above, p. 115 note 2.

assumed.¹ In the world of ideas of the N.T. there are often shiftings in the chronological order, even especially in the eschatological traditions. Even in the Haggadah of Judaism — and here in iii. 19 ff. it may be said that we have a bit of Haggadah — there is great freedom in respect of chronology.² An old Jewish rule for the exposition of the Scriptures run אין מוקדם ומאוחר בתורה, »there is no before and after in Scripture».³ Finally ζωοποιηθείς is certainly not the same as *ascensus*: at the most ζωοποιέω is the same as ἀνίστημι,⁴ even if there is besides a special significance in this term. Thus we have no reason to maintain an Ascensus theory on the basis of the connection with the context.

We prefer to think of a preaching in the underworld carried out by Christ in connection with his descent during the *triduum mortis*.

This supports our assumption that ἐν ᾧ is a temporal conjunction meaning »whereat» and referring to ἅπαξ ἀπέθανεν in the previous sentence.

THE CONTENT AND THE EFFECT OF THE PREACHING.

What did the preaching mean to the imprisoned spirits? What effect had it on them?

This is perhaps theologically the most intricate of all the questions presented by 1 Pet. iii. 19, and there has been hot discussion about it within the sphere of research. There has been,

---

[1] Correct observation by P. LUNDBERG, who in his *La typologie baptismale dans l'ancienne Église*, 1942, p. 106, in this matter opposes H. SCHLIER, *Christus und die Kirche im Epheserbrief*, p. 17.

[2] *Cf.* the following words by M. GRÜNBAUM, Beiträge zur vergleichenden Mythologie aus der Hagada, *Zeitschr. d. Deutsch. Morg. Ges.* xxxi, 1877, p. 194: »Wie die genealogische, so ist auch die chronologische Reihenfolge der Hagada gleichgültig. Der Anachronismus ist der Lebensprincip der Hagada; oder vielmehr sie ist achronistisch, sie betrachtet alle Dinge sub specie æternitatis.»

[3] W. BACHER, *Die älteste Terminologie der jüdischen Schriftauslegung.* 1899, pp. 167 f.; *cf.* D. DAUBE, Two Haggadic Principles, *The Journ. of Theol. Stud.* xliv, 1943, p. 150.

[4] According to MELITO, *The Homily on the Passion*, § 101, *l.* 12 f.

however, in general a desire to know too much, far more than there is in the text.

If we keep to Christ as the preacher and the time immediately after His death as the occasion of the preaching we have the following main possibilities for answering these questions as it seems: (1) Christ offered the spirits, all or at least certain better ones among them, salvation.[1]

(2) He exhorted them to repent.[2]

(3) He confirmed their eternal damnation.[3]

(4) He told them the secret of the Gospel, quite generally, without any information of their release &c.[4]

(5) He showed them His true glory, so that they were put to shame;[5] possibly He also reprehended them. The difference between the last two cases is not very great, as the content of the Gospel is just Christ's true glory, but a little difference may indeed be maintained.

How we shall answer the question as to the content of the preaching depends in the first place on how we take the expression ἐκήρυξεν. What we here seem to have to consider in the first instance is perhaps its possible relation to εὐηγγελίσθη in iv. 6. But we cannot *a priori* take it for granted one has a right to combine the preaching in iii. 19 with the evangelization in iv. 6. There is no question of any quite identical facts for at least the receivers of the revelation were not quite the same in both cases. It seems too

---

[1] This theory is, as already stated, in many variations absolutely dominant in modern research. See *e.g.* C. CLEMEN, »*Niedergefahren zu den Toten*», pp. 133 ff.; J. MONNIER, *La première épitre*, p. 177; U. HOLZMEISTER, *Commentarius*, pp. 349 ff. Compare our historical review, above pp. 42 ff., 47 ff.

[2] This theory is, in fact, also possible, even if there seems to be no outstanding modern representative of it.

[3] *E.g.* J. FRINGS, Zu 1 Petr. 3, 19 und 4, 6, *Bibl. Zeitschr.* xvii, 1925, p. 86. *Cf.* above, pp. 44 f.

[4] Also an imaginable case, but no more important representative can here be mentioned, who does not at the same time think of Christ's triumph over the spirits, as in the 5th case above. These cases are also very similar.

[5] This is the main theory of the question in P. J. JENSEN, *Læren om Kristi Nedfart*, p. 185, K. GSCHWIND, *Die Niederfahrt Christi*, pp. 124 f., and E. G. SELWYN, *The First Epistle*, pp. 200, 353. — *Cf.* above, p. 45.

audacious to assume such an analogy quite *a priori*. We shall return later to this problem.¹ It may only be stated here that it is not advisable to include this εὐηγγελίσθη too hastily when expounding the ἐκήρυξεν. We had better analyse the latter verb by itself. Now in most cases in the N.T. the verb κηρύσσειν is connected with εὐαγγέλιον. Even when it appears without this noun as its object it is predominantly a technical term for to preach the Gospel. We have certainly also such objects as μετάνοιαν, Luke xxiv. 47, Μωϋσῆν, Acts xv. 21, μὴ κλέπτειν, Rom. ii. 21, περιτομήν, Gal. v. 11, καταστροφήν, 1 Clem. vii. 7. But these are only isolated exceptional cases. As a rule κηρύσσω is the special term for preaching the Gospel. Here are a few typical examples: Matt. iv. 23: διδάσκων ἐν ταῖς συναγωγαῖς αὐτῶν καὶ κηρύσσων τὸ εὐαγγέλιον τῆς βασιλείας, = Luke iv. 44: καὶ ἦν κηρύσσων εἰς τὰς συναγωγὰς τῆς Ἰουδαίας; 1 Cor. i. 23: ἡμεῖς δὲ κηρύσσομεν Χριστόν; 1 Tim. iii. 16: ἐκηρύχθη ἐν ἔθνεσιν. It may also be observed that κηρύσσω does not mean »make a speech» or something of that kind in a more or less rhetorical manner; the etymological purport of the word is »to cry out as a herald», »to proclaim»,² which is something more dramatic and has more emphasis on a fact solemnly communicated than our »to preach». (In the Fourth Gospel and the Epistles of John there is instead of κηρύσσειν the similarly solemn μαρτυρεῖν.³)

We have probably the best reason to assume that κηρύσσω also in 1 Pet. iii. 19 has the same meaning as usually in the N.T., »to preach or proclaim the Gospel».⁴ As the Gospel is the same as the message about Christ we must thus opine that Christ went to the spirits and communicated to them the secret about Himself as the humbly suffering, and thereby victorious, Messiah.

This is actually all that we can get from the text. There is not a scrap of information about a preaching of such a special kind as must be implied by the first three of the above proposals for

---

[1] *Cf.* below, pp. 204 ff.
[2] G. FRIEDRICH, κηρύσσω, in G. KITTEL, *Theol. Wört.* iii, 1938, p. 702.
[3] *Ibid.*
[4] See also *i.a.* G. FRIEDRICH, *op. cit.*, p. 706.

OTHER PRELIMINARY QUESTIONS IN VERSE 19

the reply to our question. It does not say that the spirits were released from prison, it does not say that all or some of them became believers, probably after long discussions, it does not say that Christ pronounced any special judgement over them. The only thing there is in iii. 19, is that Christ preached, *i.e.* proclaimed the message about Himself as the Messiah. However, seeing that these spirits had distinguished themselves by disobedience, defiant and rebellious behaviour we can perhaps be certain of the effect that they were astonished and ashamed to find the glory of the Messiah in such a humble form as Christ. They possibly also became subject in principle to Christ, as it clearly states ὑποταγέντων αὐτῷ ἀγγέλων καὶ ἐξουσιῶν καὶ δυνάμεων in iii. 22. That is, in all probability, what the text is meant to convey. Thus only the 4th and the 5th of the above proposals are acceptable. The difference between these possibilities is very small, and perhaps it does not matter which case we choose.

It is most probable that the author refrains quite purposely from expressing himself more clearly as to the content and effect of the preaching. He only wished to state that the spirits actually learned the great Messianic secret.

Here we may recall what we previously considered one could state, that as far as the spirits in prison are the fallen Angels from Gen. vi. 1—4 and certain O.T. Apocrypha they have a significance, important as to principle, in relation to the spirit world, the Angels, the Powers, the demons in general, and can in a certain way represent the whole world of fallen Angels. Therefore, after the determinations made regarding the kind of preaching in our passage, we may now remind especially of the following N.T. passages:

1 Pet. i. 11 f.: τὰ εἰς Χριστὸν παθήματα καὶ τὰς μετὰ ταῦτα δόξας ... ἃ νῦν ἀνηγγέλη ὑμῖν ... εἰς ἃ ἐπιθυμοῦσιν ἄγγελοι παρακύψαι.

1 Cor. ii. 7 ff.: θεοῦ σοφίαν ... ἣν οὐδεὶς τῶν ἀρχόντων τοῦ αἰῶνος τούτου ἔγνωκεν· εἰ γὰρ ἔγνωσαν, οὐκ ἂν τὸν κύριον τῆς δόξης ἐσταύρωσαν.

Col. ii. 15: τὰς ἀρχὰς καὶ τὰς ἐξουσίας ἐδειγμάτισεν ἐν παρρησίᾳ, θριαμβεύσας αὐτούς ...

1 Tim. iii. 16: ἐδικαιώθη ἐν πνεύματι, ὤφθη ἀγγέλοις.

The first passage seems to assume that the Angels have actually not yet learnt the Gospel secret. Thus there is a certain contradiction of the other passages, but it is not so important. 1 Pet. i. 12 only speaks of the eagerness of the Angels to learn about the Christian Mystery as a whole. Further we must not be too strict in our demand for systematic consistency in the eschatological conception in the N.T. Thus we could really say that all the four passages quoted are different ways of saying that the Messianic drama is a secret which was at first kept from the world of the Angels but was communicated to them after Christ's death and victory. To this we have an analogy in iii. 19.

The author of 1 Pet. did not want to say more than what appears from these passages — that the secret of the Messiah was communicated to the Angel world in connection with Christ's victory in death. The announcement of this must certainly not stand quite alone but can be placed in a special kind of connection with the context as we shall later see. But the author does not at all wish here to give any information about the later fate of the Angels, their possible release &c. In this respect he is considerably more careful than the Bible interpreters of this passage in later times. We are thus compelled not to read into the text more than it actually contains.

On the other hand it can of course be interesting to see what fate, outside 1 Pet. iii. 19, is thought to await the fallen Angels or the sinful antediluvian generation. But it must be observed here that in most of the cases now to be quoted it is a question of the end of the world and time, while in our passage it is only a question of an event in connection with Christ's death.

We can thus first observe that certain Bible passages incontestably produce a strong impression of all creatures being considered as finally received by God. Such a teaching of the general reestablishment is not so often put forward in the N.T., but Paul really alludes to it, e.g. in Rom. xiv. 9, Eph. i. 10.[1] Also 2 Pet. ii. 4 and Jude 6 admit a similar theory, seeing that they only speak of the fallen

---

[1] Cf. A. OEPKE, ἀποκατάστασις, G. KITTEL, Theol. Wört., i, 1933, pp. 390f.

Angels' imprisonment until the Last Day. In Judaism one is often strict towards the generation of the Flood to the very last, and counts upon a complete annihilation of them, but there is no complete agreement on the matter.[1] Thus *Talm. Bab. Sanh.* xi. 3 (108a) denies that these people shall partake in the Resurrection: *cf.* Isa. xxvi. 14 and *Tos. Sanh.* xiii. 6, *Gen. R.* xxviii. 8,[2] *Pirqē de R. Eliezer* xxxiv. According to *Gen. R.* xxviii. 3, the *lūz*, the bone which is substantial for the Resurrection is removed from the generation of the Flood. In the *Sibylline Books* ii. 230 ff. the appearance of the »Titans» and the »Giants» for condemnation at the Last Day is mentioned. In the *Book of Enoch* a double punishment is counted upon for the fallen Angels, one at the time of Noah and one at the end of the world, for this must be the reason why double places of punishment for them are described in several places in the chapters vi—xxxvi. How it will be for them in the final judgment is not clearly stated. Yet this book seems to believe in everlasting damnation for the fallen Angels, *e.g.* x. 5, xvi. 4. In this connection it is also of a special importance that Enoch, in chs. xii ff., fails in his intervention on behalf of the Angels although he clearly gets them to feel remorse and terror.

In the *Book of the Secrets of Enoch* ch. xviii it is stated, however, quite clearly that the fallen Angels, the »Watchers», at Enoch's appearance to them were converted and began to praise God. Thus we have a more positive idea of this question in the Enoch tradition. Also in the *Book of Enoch* there are really certain expressions which indicate a tendency to a teaching of ἀποκατάστασις πάντων in opposition to the condemnation theory which, at least superficially considered, is predominant. Thus in the Greek text of this book it clearly states that the »Watchers» will at the revelation of the Lord »come to believe», πιστεύσουσιν, i. 5; yet perhaps the

---

[1] *Cf.* H. STRACK & P. BILLERBECK, *Kommentar*, iv. 2, 1928, pp. 1185f.
[2] BILLERBECK, *loc. cit.*, probably does not conceive this passage correctly, when he makes it contain favourable judgements regarding the future fate of the generation of the Flood. Compare the quite opposite translation in *Midrash Rabba*, translated under the editorship of H. FREEDMAN & M. SIMON, i, 1939, which seems to render the text more correctly.

text is not quite reliable here as the Ethiopic translation has no directly corresponding expression. In ch. lxvii. 11 we have, however, a clear indication that the punishment of the Angels is thought to be gradually mitigated.[1] According to xviii. 16, xxi. 6 their punishment lasts 10.000 years, according to x. 12 seventy generations. In the *Hebrew Book of Enoch* (3 Enoch), ch. xlvii, it is said that the bodies of the Angels are punished in streams of fire, while their souls return to Shekina. Finally we can point to a few passages in the Ethiopic *Book of Enoch* where it speaks of everybody prostrating before the Messiah, especially the Kings and Powers, namely in xlviii. 10, lxii. 3ff., lxiii. 1ff. In ch. lxix. 26 it says — just after the fallen Angels have been mentioned — somewhat resembling the *Book of the Secrets of Enoch* xviii, that »great joy prevailed among them» and that they »blessed, glorified and extolled because the name of that Son of Man had been revealed unto them». It is certainly considered that this verse was not originally in this position,[2] but it is also not sure that one has the right to move it. We have in that way several examples to show that sometimes the Enoch traditions reveal a less strict attitude to the sinners from the time before the Flood. According to *Talm. Jer. Sanh.* x. 3, or *Gen. R.* xxviii. 8, there have also been certain rabbinic theologians who questioned the participation of the generation of the Flood in the world to come.

Thus it is seen that opinions as to the antediluvian sinners differ very much in the literature we must chiefly consider. We repeat, however, that the cases quoted refer as a rule to the prospects at the Last Day. With the exception of the account of Enoch's intervention on behalf of the Angels in the *Book of Enoch* xii.ff., only the *Book of the Secrets of Enoch* xviii among the examples quoted really deals with an earlier occasion corresponding to the appearance to the spirits in prison in 1 Pet. iii. 19, and we also

---

[1] The peculiar ideas of the hot water in this chapter can be illuminated by certain reflections in *Gen. R.* xxviii. 8.

[2] See *e.g.* G. BEER in E. KAUTZSCH, *Die Apokryphen und Pseudepigraphen*, ii, p. 276.

OTHER PRELIMINARY QUESTIONS IN VERSE 19

in this passage seem to have a certain analogy to it because we find there the idea of Enoch's meeting the fallen Angels developed in a more positive direction than in the *Book of Enoch*. Notice however that not even here is anything more said than that the »Watchers» surrendered in the presence of the Revealer of the Divine Glory. It does not say that they were released, nor anything of that kind.

*

We have now concluded the discussion of these preliminary questions of detail. It seemed necessary to state our attitude to them chiefly because they have been so keenly discussed by interpreters in all ages. As a matter of fact we ourselves do not attach such extraordinary importance to all these possible, minute differences in the interpretation of the different factors in the preaching to the spirits. The points of view here put forward have been intended to give some picture of the most probable way in which the author of our Epistle and his readers thought of this preaching. Seeing that the author has not stated in detail where the spirits were, what Christ preached to them &c., &c., we may imagine he assumed that his readers had their own conception of these matters, quite likely on the basis of a certain Christian education. But this idea can very well have been considered rather approximate.

The main thing is, of course, in all circumstances that Christ did preach and just to those spirits who had been disobedient in the time of Noah.[1] In this we have our most important factor to consider when we now go on to a summarized consideration of 1 Pet. iii. 19, and its task in the context.

---

[1] *Cf.* H. ODEBERG, »Nederstigen till dödsriket», *Bibliskt Månadshäfte* xviii. 12, 1944, p. 358.

CHAPTER IV.
COMPREHENSIVE STUDY OF VERSE 19.

WE MUST SEEK FOR THE AUTHOR'S PURPOSE WITH VERSE 19.

The author must absolutely have had a definite purpose in writing verse 19. It is true that the whole passage 18—22 is often considered as connected with the traditional Christological formulæ which made up the rudimentary origins of a creed.[1] The words and the ideas would thus be formally decided by a previously determined basis, and a personal contribution by the author of the Epistle cannot be very likely. If this assumption holds good as regards the whole passage — but it must not be over-emphasized — it is also not difficult to assume that an appearance of Christ to »the spirits» is to be found in some Christological formula used here, for there is an analogy to it in 1 Tim. iii. 16: ὤφθη ἀγγέλοις. But this creed formula cannot have spoken of the spirits in prison in just the way as we find them treated here, for in that case there would be no necessity to characterize them in such a strikingly circumstantial way. We think, then, that even if 18—22 as a whole is built upon certain traditional ideas and formulæ, the detailed description of the spirits to whom the Saviour preached, and also the interest it clearly aroused, were a personal contribution of the author[2] made with a certain object.

This object we must also try to find, and the task is the most important in an investigation of our subject. Investigators have

---
[1] *Cf.* C. CLEMEN, »*Niedergefahren zu den Toten*», p. 104; P. LUNDBERG, *La typologie baptismale*, p. 100ff.
[2] *Cf.* LUNDBERG, *op. cit.*, p. 103ff.

in general inquired too extensively about the more detailed circumstances of the preaching and similar apocalyptic and curious problems. As regards these we have only a vague conception. What we must try to determine more exactly is the main purpose of the author with this *motif* in verse 19. In this way we shall finally issue from the forest of futile questions in which the interpreters as a rule have remained.

Thus: why does the author direct the thought here to Christ preaching to the sinners from the time of Noah and allow this fact to have such a prominent place in the presentation? The answer to this we must, of course, obtain by considering the context.

A GLANCE AT THE CONTEXT: ESPECIALLY VERSE 18 AND THE PARENESIS IN 13—16.

Verse 18 begins with a ὅτι which shows that it is a reason for the previous statement. In the first place it seems to have a logical relation to verse 17 and be an argument in support of the thesis there expressed.

From this it might perhaps be concluded that the verses 19ff. should also serve as an argument for the same thesis but from another point of view. This theory has also been held by certain investigators, who believed that in this way they could show a logical connection between verses 19ff. and the context.[1] This belief is certainly very praiseworthy and should certainly be preferred to all theories of an interpolation or a digression.[2] None the less the attempt to base verses 19ff. just upon verse 17 must be regarded as connected with clearly logical difficulties. That Christ preached to the sinners in prison, these hardened sinners: how can this be regarded as a reason for the thesis in verse 17 that it is »better» (κρεῖττον) to die

---

[1] With some exaggeration P. J. JENSEN says that everyone considers the verses 18—22 to be an illumination of the saying in verse 17, *Læren om Kristi Nedfart*, p. 172. Otherwise it is principally K. GSCHWIND who likes to make verses 19ff. dependent on verse 17, *Die Niederfahrt Christi*, p. 109.

[2] *Cf.* above, p. 46, note 1.

while doing »good deeds» than evil? Perhaps the preaching could be considered as a »good deed» but what advantage had Christ from it? Did Christ obtain through His suffering and death an opportunity to preach to these strange spirits? But what advantage was there in it for Him? Whether the preaching is assumed to have been positive or negative, it is not possible thereby to obtain any intelligible illustration of the thesis that the death of the innocent sufferer is something »better».[1] Those who wished to put forward this theory have not brought out any natural logic in the text. Thus it is not possible to conceive the verses 19 ff. as an argument parallel to verse 18 for the thesis in verse 17.

Besides it is actually not so that the transition of thought in verse 18 to Christ's suffering and death was intended as a concrete example of the general principle formulated in verse 17. For this thesis has no independent, abstractly theoretical interest but only stands out as a reason for what immediately precedes it, 13—16, the exhortation to patience and courage before the heathen. This is also clear from the language. In verse 17 there is a γάρ pointing direct to the previous exhortation. But the ὅτι introducing verse 18 does not indicate that this in its turn shall be subordinate to verse 17 as an explanation. For we find that our author, like other Greek writers, can use such expressions as γάρ and ὅτι — which undoubtedly are rather equivalent — in a blunted, routine function, so that they do not only imply a reference to a point immediately preceding but also link it to a more distant general thesis, something like the German *ja, bekanntlich,* »we know», or similar expressions.[2] In such cases these Greek particles can often

---

[1] As is well known GSCHWIND's idea of the preaching is negative. In this way he tries to take verses 19f. as an example of suffering in return for misdoings mentioned in the last part of verse 17 (*loc. cit.*). The first part of this verse would then be illustrated by verse 18. But now, verses 19f. do not at all discuss »suffering for misdoing» but the preaching of Christ. Gschwind's attempts at solution are really very far-fetched.

[2] J. A. DENNISTON, *The Greek Particles*, 1934, has also noted that γάρ sometimes refers, not to the immediately preceding sentence, but to something further back, *op. cit.*, p. 63, and that successive γάρ's may have the same reference, p. 64, and gives examples of that from the classics.

not be translated every time with anything else than »and». See for example the passage 1 Pet. ii. 19—21. There γάρ occurs several times, once in every phrase, but the one instance does not refer exclusively to what immediately precedes it, but each γάρ refers also again to the once given exhortation in ii. 18. It is precisely the same with ὅτι in verse 21 which is just equivalent to these preceding γάρ's[1] — we can even say that a ὅτι may have a still clearer reference to a generally accepted principle, as for instance a Christological item. These different cases of γάρ and ὅτι are thus not only subjected to each other but coordinated. The same phenomenon also occurs elsewhere in the N.T.[2] In the same way we ought to consider ὅτι in iii. 18 as mainly coordinated in relation to γάρ in verse 17. Both particles refer to the exhortation in verses 13—16, which form the starting point for the whole reasoning.

Thus verse iii. 18 should also be seen in relation to the immediately preceding exhortations to patience and frankness before the heathen. Here attention should first be paid to verses 13—15 a. Then the following reasoning is discovered: Just as Christ once died — or suffered[3] — περὶ ἁμαρτιῶν but rose again, so shall also the Christians with dutiful steadfastness and confidence bear any possible suffering for the sake of the heathen. For Christ is the pattern, τὸ ὑπογραμμόν, according to which the Christians must arrange their lives. In ii. 21 we have this put forward, in precisely similar reasoning: Just as Christ in His time suffered for the servants here addressed, so they should be prepared to suffer for the sake of their pagan masters. The Christians are also similarly exhorted in iii. 15 to hold the Lord Christ sacred in their hearts, which here must mean that in their hearts they should consider Christ as an encouraging pattern. Notice also that there is a complete language and logical analogy between ὅτι καὶ Χριστός in ii. 21 and iii. 18. In both cases

---

[1] In front of this ὅτι there should be a full-stop, not a comma as E. NESTLE has it.
[2] Cf. W. BAUER, Griechisch-Deutsches Wörterbuch, s.v. γάρ, col. 252. See also Matt. xvi. 25—27 with parallels (γάρ); Matt. vii. 13f., John i. 15f. (ὅτι = γάρ); Matt. xi. 29f. (ὅτι and γάρ probably co-ordinated).
[3] According to some MSS.

these words introduce an exhorting argument with reference to their exalted pattern, Christ, and this argument is in both cases inserted as a complement to the previous arguments in different sentences introduced by γάρ. We have thus in both these passages an example of conclusions with a parenetical object according to the rule of logic *a maiore ad minus*.

THE SOLUTION OF OUR MOST IMPORTANT PROBLEM.

Considering these relations between the verses 17—18 and the previous parenesis in 13—16 we must ask: Is not iii. 19 also connected with the previously expressed exhortations? Certainly this question must be answered in the affirmative. For by placing the verses in such a connection we at last have an explanation of the author's intention with the curious preaching to the spirits, and can solve what is really the basic problem of our text.

We find in iii. 14b and the following words, that the Christians are exhorted not to fear the pagans,[1] but, sanctifying the Lord Christ in their hearts, always be ready to answer (ἕτοιμοι πρὸς ἀπολογίαν) before everyone who demands an account of the Christian hope, *i.e.* the Gospel, 15, yet not arrogantly but with an humble respect (μετὰ πραΰτητος καὶ φόβου), and with a good συνείδησις, in order that any possible slanderers shall be put to shame, 16. If these exhortations are combined with the introductory remarks in verse 13, »who will do you evil», one obtains the following reasoning: There is no one so hardened, no such evil being, that the Christians ought not to let them know of the Christian hope, the Gospel, with real courage.

On this thesis, on this exhortation to confess with frankness their Christian faith and communicate the Gospel to the heathen verse 19 is an argument *a maiore ad minus*: Christ in connection with His suffering and death preached the Gospel also (καί) to the

---

[1] Here, of course, αὐτῶν is objective genitive, not subjective as in the Isaiah text. It is quite clear from the whole context that the pagans are here referred to.

imprisoned spirits from the time of Noah, these giants in the sin of disobedience. In the same way the Christians, even if it means suffering and death for them, should courageously tell the most hardened, possibly, those in high position on the earth, what is the hope of the believers, the secret of the Messiah, the Resurrection and all concerning it.

The reference to Christ preaching to the spirits in prison is thus also introduced in this connection to give support to the previous exhortation. Here the main thing is the exhortation in verse 15, a bold communication of the Gospel to the pagans. So verse 19 should be most closely connected with the words ἕτοιμοι ἀεὶ πρὸς ἀπολογίαν παντὶ τῷ αἰτοῦντι ὑμᾶς λόγον περὶ τῆς ἐν ὑμῖν ἐλπίδος in iii. 15. But in the last resort there is also a connection with the whole of the exhortation pericope 13—16. In this way verse 19 appears as the third argument in support of these exhortations, after the two arguments in verses 17 and 18. We find here a chain of arguments to support the previous parenesis, which regarded philologically and logically forms a complete parallel to the chain of arguments in ii. 19ff.

And here, too, Christ is described as the great Pattern. Just as He announced the Gospel for the beings from the Flood, so should the Christians without fear or selfish reserve tell of the Gospel to the pagans in their environment. But these two objects of the imparting of the Gospel correspond, as we have already found. From this certain important conclusions can be drawn.

THE BEINGS FROM THE FLOOD AND THE PAGAN WORLD.

We can now link up the result we have come to above from the study of the beings from the Flood in the *Book of Enoch* &c.[1] It appeared that these beings are the power at the back of the pagans in general — with their magic, idolatry and the demons behind it — and of the special representatives of the pagan world, the pagan kings and powers. In all these respects the fallen Angels are the chief inspiration and source of the errors of paganism.

---

[1] See above, ch. ii.

This perspective at last gives us a really satisfactory explanation of the reason why the author of the Epistle has selected just these beings from the Flood for his argument. Christ has communicated the Messianic Secret, the Gospel, to these beings who are the deepest root and the real source of heathendom, indeed, its most prominent patrons at the present day, so that they are put to shame before this humble, suffering and loving and at the same time so highly exalted Messiah — thus we determined the content and result of the preaching. In that way Christ has also turned the edge of all that heathendom means.[1] The pagan nations and individuals at the present time have no longer any support from the fallen Angels, in any case not by a long way such energetic support as before. They are in general no longer so dangerous, for they can no longer do the Christians any real harm. But, above all, they can no longer harden their hearts when in contact with the Gospel and seeing its concrete expression in the practical life of the Christians. On the contrary they are easily driven to conversion.

THE CONVERSION OF THE HEATHEN.

Here we have the most definite, the most energetic and at the same time the most optimistic mission views. The Gospel shall be spread to all beings, while there is time. Judgment will soon come, iv. 7. Until then all, or at least as many as possible, must have come in contact with the Gospel: for on the basis of his attitude towards it each will be judged, — indeed, for that very reason the Gospel has been preached to the dead also, iv. 6. This spreading of the Gospel is to be done by all Christians in all situations. It does not mean that they must be always preaching and making speeches, but they shall work just as much through their behaviour, their patience, their love, their faithfulness, as is stated in iii. 1: ἄνευ

---

[1] This has apparently also been perceived by E. G. SELWYN, *The First Epistle of St. Peter*, 1946, p. 328: »Meanwhile, Christ Himself had gone to the very fountain-head of cosmic and human evil, and had proclaimed His sovereignty and God's, over the spiritual world, even over these typically rebellious spirits of Noah's day.«

λόγου κερδηθήσονται, and similarly several times ἀναστροφὴ καλή is mentioned or something similar as a means of affecting others, ii. 12 &c. And the Gospel of Suffering has within it a power that conquers all: of this the Christians can be convinced in principle. No important opposition will be able to harm them, this is the given hypothesis of work. Practically speaking all those who harden themselves and abuse the Christians' way of life will be forced to be ashamed when they really have the opportunity of getting to know the Christians' patient humility and blamelessness. This can be clearly read in the verse iii. 16, if one pays attention to the immediate context of verse 19. Otherwise it is also a prevailing thought in all the different parenetical parts of our Epistle. See ii. 12, 15, iii. 1 and 5f. (cf. Matt. v. 16). There is no difference in principle whether the parenesis is directed to all Christians or to a certain category of Christians such as servants or women. It is in any case the pagans surrounding them that the Christians have to deal with. In iii. 6 it is interesting to observe that the expression ἀγαθοποιοῦσαι καὶ μὴ φοβούμεναι μηδεμίαν πτόησιν refers to Prov. iii. 25: καὶ οὐ φοβηθήσῃ πτόησιν ἐπελθοῦσαν οὐδὲ ὁρμὰς ἀσεβῶν ἐπερχομένας, so that here too it is clearly the heathen in these women's environment who are under consideration, *i.e.* primarily their paganish husbands.

THE SPIRITS OF THE FLOOD AND THE EARTHLY POWERS.

It appears from the indication in iii. 15 of those who demand an account from the Christians for their faith, that in the parenesis iii. 13ff. there is not only a reference to pagan private individuals, but that the author is probably also thinking of state authorities, officials, local governors, princes, who in the interests of the Roman State and Empire had to make arrangements for an investigation into the tendency of the new religiousness. The expression ξενίζονται in iv. 4 probably reveals the same connection: It may be said to indicate euphemistically that the Christians to a large extent are officially being called upon to state their reasons for not participating in the heathen cult and the debauches connected with it. Notice also that in the following verse the author reveals the direction of his thought by turning the matter round and stating that the people in question will in their turn have to give an account to the great Judge. All the time these indications are only euphemistic[1] — no such clear words as *e.g.* in Mark xiii. 9 ff. with parallels — but we think it can in any case be discerned that the writer is carefully referring to pagan official situations. The delicate subject was also very important and valuable to be touched upon in the exhortation to the ἀρτιγέννητα βρέφη (ii. 2), who would now enter an enemy world as Christians.

If then in iii. 13 ff. the pagan authorities and holders of power are being considered, the representatives of the Roman Empire and its Emperor, we have the spirits in verse 19 in deeper relief if we remember that the fallen Angels in the *Book of Enoch* &c. have a special relation to the Kings, the Mighty and those who reside on the earth.[2] The state authorities are no longer so dangerous. The personal representatives of the pagan state can now in principle more easily be brought to conversion and an insight into the loftiness and value of a Christian's faith. For their patrons and source of inspiration in the spirit world have heard the Gospel through Christ Himself.

In passing we notice, as regards the Spiritual Powers behind the state authorities, that the Angels and other Spirits clearly, in the view of the Bible, stand behind the political bodies. We can think in the first place of the »Gods» in Ps. lxxxi (lxxxii), »the Prince of this world» in John xiv. 30,[3] the Powers of this Age in 1 Cor. ii. 6,[4] and αἱ ἐξουσίαι and οἱ ἄρχοντες in Rom. xiii. These latter categories are probably thought of not only as human but also as supernatural beings,[5] in accordance with the view of

---

[1] *Cf.* R. KNOPF, *Die Briefe Petri und Judä*, pp. 165 f.
[2] *Cf.* above, pp. 85 ff.
[3] Å. V. STRÖM, *Vetekornet*, 1944, pp. 392 ff.
[4] *Op. cit.*, pp. 387 f., with note.
[5] G. DEHN, Engel und Obrigkeit, *Theol. Aufsätze, Karl Barth z. 50. Geb.*, 1936, pp. 90 ff.; O. CULLMANN, *Königsherrschaft Christi*, 1941, pp. 25 f., 33, 44—48. *Cf. Svensk Exeg. Årsb.* viii, 1943, p. 62.

antiquity as regards the state and politics, a view which was far from being religiously neutral: we must preferably here assume an oscillation of thought between natural and supernatural beings.

THE LOGICAL CONNECTION WITH THE TEXT.

Thus, quite simply by connecting iii. 19 to the parenesis in the previous verses and especially verse 15, one can actually place it in correlation with the context in a completely intimate, logical and natural way. By this means we can find not a loose series of associations of ideas in which the one link gives rise to the next, but from the author's point of view a firm line of completely logical proofs in support of the earlier exhortation. We find notions which in many respects pass into each other with systematic consistency and which make the whole into an organic connection sufficiently intelligible to any reader who had some knowledge of the ideology controlling the author's thought. This ideology rests in the first place on a knowledge of such writings as the *Book of Enoch*, but also agrees in a high degree with the general point of view in the N.T. It is clear that the readers of the Epistle could react to the description and have enough knowledge to follow the author's reasoning. Only on this assumption could he express himself so confidentially. Besides this we should notice that he here addresses himself to baptisees (iii. 21) who had clearly just received the teaching in the Christian Faith and the Holy Scriptures current for a catechumen. And these catechumens who have just completed their training have presumably a better insight on many points in the thought world of these Scriptures than we moderns can easily procure.

Thus it cannot be said that verse 19 contains a digression or anything strange to the context. The thought goes strictly forward with clear logic — that is according to the reasoning of the Biblical world.[1]

---

[1] This thesis is the central purpose of our presentation. It implies a criticism of earlier writers in general, on account of the general predilection for the digression theory. See *e.g.* R. KNOPF's representative commentary.

It is not enough that the author has found in Christ's preaching to the »spirits» before the Flood a tolerable and, for his environment, a wholly intelligible model for the correct behaviour of the Christians towards the pagans around them. No, the spirits from Noah's time are also so resourcefully chosen that the author in verses 20—22 can connect to these figures a whole series of typological combinations, which according to the early Christian conception must also have formed a really striking proof of the thesis put forward in the parenesis, that the Christians must appear before the pagans without fear for their worldly power. Nearly every word also in these verses gets a special meaning seen against the background of the earlier parenetic passage in iii. 13—16, if one discovers the analogies between the O.T. comments here and the situation in the parenesis.

What, therefore, we have here is certainly not some arbitrary association of ideas but all is practically thought out and intended to be applied to life.

*

We shall now illustrate these statements by going through iii. 20 —22 in order to draw up the perspective. Also iv. 6 can then be included in the discussion. After that we will turn back to give iii. 17—18 some further illumination.

Die Briefe Petri und Judä, pp. 143 (»Erweiterungen»), 147 (»Spekulation»), 170 (»Abschweifungen»). And we hope to have discerned the connections in the text in a more elucidative way than the few scholars who have earlier opposed the digression theory (*cf.* above, pp. 3f.).

CHAPTER V.

INVESTIGATION OF VERSES 20 AND 21 A.

In verse 20 the first phrase, being an apposition to πνεύμασιν in verse 19: ἀπειθήσασίν ποτε ὅτε ἀπεξεδέχετο ἡ τοῦ θεοῦ μακροθυμία ἐν ἡμέραις Νῶε, is a logical unity, and should be read out without a pause, as all the words after ἀπειθήσασιν clearly serve to indicate certain nearer circumstances under which the disobedience took place, but then the expression ἐν ἡμέραις Νῶε undoubtedly is the most important and the most necessary, giving the emphasis in the whole phrase. On the other hand after this phrase a pause may be made and preferably a comma placed before the next part of the sentence,[1] which is absolute genitive, for the words about the building of the Ark lead the thought to a side *motif* which has no such intimate connection with the spirits' disobedience. In the former phrase, however, all the words are intimately connected, as if there was only ἀπειθήσασιν ἐν ἡμέραις Νῶε. Why has the author quite simply not been satisfied with this short phrase? Why has he put in the words about how God's longanimity waited? Were they not really unnecessary?

Of course the words about God's longanimity are added in order to lead the thought to the present day when His longanimity is similarly giving the world a short respite before the catastrophe comes. Thus we find here an example of parallelling the time of the Flood with the present time before the Judgment of the world, which also clearly appears in verse 21. Therewith it is also clear

---

[1] This has, unfortunately, not been done in E. NESTLE's edition of the text.

that the disobedience is not mentioned only as a characteristic of or an analytical judgment on these spirits, defining their essence, but the whole time the thought is concerned with modern circumstances, here chiefly those who are now disobedient to the Christian message *i.e.* the heathen — the judgment is thus synthetic. We could illustrate the logical connection by saying in the translation for example: they who on their side, in their turn, were disobedient in Noah's days. The word ἀπειθήσασιν is thus intended to lead the thought to the disobedient in the present environment of the Christians.[1] Note that the pagans in ch. ii. 8 are expressly called τῷ λόγῳ ἀπειθοῦντες, similarly in iii. 1, and also in iv. 17 they are qualified as ἀπειθοῦντες τῷ θεοῦ εὐαγγελίῳ, so that the verb ἀπειθεῖν especially characterizes the heathen in this Epistle.

That »God's longanimity waited» surely refers to the 120 years which were granted to the beings before the Flood according to Gen. vi. 3.[2] In the same way even now the catastrophe is to be expected after a definite period, 1 Pet. iv. 7. It is of special interest for us to see that the *Book of Enoch* also contains references to God's »longanimity» in this situation, ch. ix. 11[3] (ὁρᾷς ταῦτα καὶ ἐᾷς αὐτούς), lx. 5 (»He hath been merciful and long-suffering towards those who dwell on the earth») as also to a »waiting», xciii. 3 (»while Judgment and Righteousness still endured»[4]).

The building of the Ark is mentioned naturally not in order to make the situation, when the spirits were disobedient, more lively and concrete, but this fact also clearly refers to the present time. The building of Noah's Ark is referred to in Hebr. xi. 7 as a type with an allusion to the future. In the *Book of Enoch* lxvii. 2 it is said that the Angels have built these »pieces of wood», from which

---

[1] See also the valuable expositions on ἀπειθεῖν in P. LUNDBERG, *La typologie baptismale*, pp. 108 ff.
[2] So, *e.g.*, also E. HUTHER, *Kritisch exegetisches Handbuch*, p. 184; E. KÜHL, *Die Briefe Petri und Judæ*, p. 229; J. FELTEN, *Die zwei Briefe*, p. 111.
[3] H. GUNKEL, Der erste Brief des Petrus, *Die Schriften des N.T:s*, iii, 1917, p. 282.
[4] On this rendering see A. DILLMANN's arguments in *Das Buch Henoch*, p. 294.

a seed of life shall proceed. The passive form in this passage in 1 Pet. can perhaps be connected with such a tradition of the Angels' activity. In our passage the Ark is clearly put forward as a means of rescue. The Christian counterpart which first comes to mind is the Church, seeing that the Ark in the typology of the Early Church so often seems to have been connected with it.[1] This is also supported by the expression κατασκευαζομένης; in connection with this we can refer to ii. 5 where the Church is called a spiritual house as which the believers shall allow themselves to be built up. Another possibility is that the Ark alludes to the wood of the Cross. This is made probable by *Just. Dial.* ch. cxxxviii.[2] There it is told of the generation reborn by Christ as having the mystery of the Cross in the same way as ὁ Νῶε ἐν ξύλῳ διεσώθη ἐποχούμενος τοῖς ὕδασι μετὰ τῶν ἰδίων.[3] As a background to this *lignum* typology may be mentioned the newly quoted passage in the *Book of Enoch* and two passages in Wisd. which disclose much verbal resemblance to our verse, namely x. 4: ... κατακλυζομένην γῆν πάλιν διέσωσεν σοφία, δι᾽ εὐτελοῦς ξύλου τὸν δίκαιον κυβερνήσασα, and xiv. 5: διὰ τοῦτο καὶ ἐλαχίστῳ ξύλῳ πιστεύουσιν ἄνθρωποι ψυχὰς καὶ διελθόντες κλύδωνα σχεδίᾳ διεσώθησαν — notice here διασῴζειν as in 1 Pet. iii. 20, and also ψυχαί. But because of the εἰς ἥν following κιβωτοῦ it is perhaps more reasonable to think of the Church or a similar sphere of salvation as a counterpart to the Ark? Well, but it is probably best to count upon both connections.[4] The μηχανή men-

---

[1] *E.g.* Tert. *De bapt.* viii (*P.L.* i, col. 1209): *ecclesia est arca figurata*. See also H. LECLERQ, *s.v.* Arche, *Dict. d'arch. chrét.*, i. 2, 1907, cols. 2709f.
[2] *P.G.* vi, col. 793.
[3] P. LUNDBERG, *La typologie baptismale*, pp. 86, 186.
[4] We do not consider it so important to discuss which typology of the Church's history is the most ancient. It seems to us that typologies, like other exegetic combinations in the Biblical religions, have frequently arisen spontaneously, *ad hoc*, without any special background of older or newer traditions. Therefore our standpoint must be somewhat different from that of P. LUNDBERG, who in his *La typologie baptismale* often concerns himself with the age of different typologies, and assumes different periods and strata of tradition and so on. See, especially in this question, *op. cit.* pp. 86, 186.

tioned by Ignatius in *Ad Eph.* ix. 1[1] can also be thought of. Here the Cross is the instrument which draws the Christians to the heights so that they can be placed as stones in God's temple.[2] There we have both *motifs*, the Cross as a vehicle and the building, united.

The three components of which the scene now consists: the defiance of the Flood beings, the approaching catastrophe, and the arrangement of a protected refuge for certain elect, have thus all their counterparts in the situation in the parenesis.

»Into the Ark» (this Epistle does not confuse εἰς and ἐν more than possibly in v. 12, which belongs to the special ending)[3] »some few» were rescued. The small number is, of course, mentioned with a thought of the fewness of the Christians in comparison with their environment[4] (*cf.* Matt. vii. 14). They were more definitely »8 souls» (*cf.* 2 Pet. ii. 5). This information is given, not only because of the actual circumstances of the Noah story, but because it has also a deeper significance. The figure 8 was strongly symbolic. It had among other meanings that of completeness, namely in the speculations of the Ancient Church and gnosticism regarding the ogdoad as the highest heavenly stage.[5] It had also special reference to the Lord's day, ἡ κυριακή, the day of rest, the day of the Resurrection of Jesus and the day of the Ascension.[6] See, for example, the *Epistle of Barnabas* xv. 8 where God speaks of this day, ἐν ᾧ καταπαύσας τὰ πάντα ἀρχὴν ἡμέρας ὀγδόης ποιήσω, ὅ ἐστιν ἄλλου κόσμου ἀρχήν, and the next verse: διὸ καὶ ἄγομεν τὴν ἡμέραν τὴν ὀγδόην εἰς εὐφροσύνην, ἐν ᾗ καὶ ὁ Ἰησοῦς ἀνέστη ἐκ νεκρῶν καὶ φανερωθεὶς ἀνέβη εἰς οὐρανούς; notice here the words of the origin of a new world. There is also in *Just. Dial.* ch. cxxxviii[7] a com-

---

[1] H. Schlier, *Religionsgeschichtliche Untersuchungen*, 1929, pp. 110ff.
[2] *Cf. Herm. Sim.* ix.
[3] A. Debrunner, *F. Blass' Grammatik*, § 205, p. 95.
[4] *Cf.* E. Huther, *Kritisch Exegetisches Handbuch*, p. 188.
[5] W. Bousset, *Hauptprobleme der Gnosis*, 1907, pp. 9ff.; C. Schmidt in *Texte und Untersuch.* xliii, 1919, pp. 275ff.
[6] C. Schmidt, *loc. cit.*, pp. 279ff.
[7] *P.G.* vi, col. 793.

bination of the Resurrection day with our passage. There is perhaps also a play on words with the name Noah, which according to Gen. v. 29 was regarded as meaning »rest»,[1] and on the other hand the day of rest, or the »rest» as a name for the highest sphere. Often in these ogdoad speculations there is mention of the »rest», in combination with the eight day or the ogdoad as the highest sphere,[2] as in *Acta Thom.* xxvii: »Come, mother over the seven houses (the spirit) that you may rest in the eighth house.» Further the chapel of baptism and also the baptismal bath were in the Ancient Church often 8-sided which also was interpreted symbolically.[3] Finally Noah is himself a symbol of the resurrection, as appears *e.g.* in the *Biblical Antiquities of Philo*, iii. 10, where God tells Noah his intention to »quicken the dead and raise up from the earth them that sleep», so that »the world shall rest, Death shall be quenched and Hell shall shut his mouth».[4] Here there is a possibility for several associations of ideas between the saving of Noah and of the Christians. And it is certain that the author has purposely wished to bring out many of the different possibilities, to console the Christians thus: for this is often the current way of the Biblical authors to witness and persuade — compare the Jewish exegetics in the Talmud &c. The saving of the eight souls is thus a type of the Christian salvation resting upon many connections, and their mention is regarded as a convincing proof of the Christians' being rescued from destruction now and in the future.

Noah's family was rescued in the Ark »through water». It is scarcely possible that the author here thinks of a tradition like that in *Gen. R.* xxxii. 6,[5] of how Noah stood with the water up to his

---

[1] *Cf.* C. STERN, *Philo und der Midrasch*, 1931, p. 20.
[2] C. SCHMIDT, *loc. cit.*, pp. 278ff. Also P. LUNDBERG, *La typologie baptismale*, pp. 79ff., gives many good instances of these speculative combinations.
[3] F. J. DÖLGER, Zur Symbolik des altchristlichen Taufhauses, *Antike und Christentum* iv, 1934, pp. 153ff.; K. SCHNEIDER, Achteck, *Reallex. für Ant. u. Christ.*, cols. 78ff.
[4] M. R. JAMES, *The Biblical Antiquities of Philo*, pp. 81f.
[5] *Cf.* FR. SPITTA, *Christi Predigt an die Geister*, p. 51; R. KNOPF, *Die Briefe Petri*, p. 155.

ankle before he climbed into the Ark,[1] for this tradition is too specialized, and is based upon the ובמי in Gen. vii. 7. But the expression δι' ὕδατος should in any case primarily have a local meaning, indicating a passage through the element water, for in the LXX it says διὰ τὸ ὕδωρ which actually is causal but can be interpreted locally, on the other hand not instrumentally, and the passage Wisd. xiv. 5 just quoted,[2] which may be considered as a very important model of the phrase in 1 Pet., undoubtedly indicates the thought of a passage through the water.

> It has been much discussed whether διά here shall be understood in a local or instrumental meaning.[3] A purely instrumental interpretation seems to us improbable for several reasons. Even if the verb διασῴζειν sometimes both in the LXX[4] and in the N.T.[5] means almost the same as σῴζειν, διά should probably in this combined verb form not be so meaningless that the unsuitability of letting it be followed immediately by an instrumental διά was not felt. Further the water is not at all a means of rescue, just as little as the fire in Paul's words σωθήσεται ... ὡς διὰ πυρός in 1 Cor. iii. 15, although it is of course a necessary accident. *Cf.* also διὰ τῆς θαλάσσης διῆλθον, used of a process corresponding to Baptism in 1 Cor. x. 1.[6] Finally the author of the Epistle himself indicates in verse 21 that it is certainly not the water which has effect, by speaking clearly and distinctly of Baptism as an action and not as an element, and declaring that the saving power of Baptism depends upon Christ's Resurrection. But it is possible that the thought has glided over from a local to an instrumental consideration seeing that the allusion is to a passing which is a necessary condition for salvation.[7]

Under all circumstances, however, it is remarkable that the author does not think of what usually comes to our minds in the question of Noah's rescue in the Ark: that these just people were rescued from the destroying water, for then he would not have

---

[1] *Ad* Gen. vii. 7, »through the water of the Flood«: »R. Jochanan said: He lacked Faith. Had not the water reached his ankles he would not have entered the Ark.«

[2] See above, p. 139.

[3] Earlier discussions reported in E. HUTHER, *Kritisch exegetisches Handbuch*, pp. 187f.

[4] *E.g.* Wisd. x. 4, concerning the saving of Noah.

[5] Matt. xiv. 36, Luke vii. 3, Acts xxiii. 24, *e.p.*

[6] P. LUNDBERG, *La typologie baptismale*, p. 112.

[7] E. G. SELWYN also thinks that the two views are not mutually exclusive, *The First Epistle*, p. 202.

been able to speak of a rescue »through» water. What then was Noah saved from according to this passage in 1 Pet.? It must have been from his dangerous environment, the disobedient beings of his time, in the same way as Lot according to 2 Pet. ii. 7 was rescued from the lawless of his time, and as Peter in Acts ii. 40 exhorts the people to let themselves be rescued »from this evil generation» by means of Baptism.

Here again we have a proof that the parenesis situation is the logical basis also in verse 20. Just as Noah was saved from the disobedient in his environment — who according to the *Book of Enoch* chs. vii ff. outraged people in many different ways, so that they began to cry to Heaven — so should the Christians by Baptism be rescued from their disobedient, godless surroundings: the pagans. For this reason they ought to be able to appear before them without fear and preach the Gospel in word and action. Noah preached also righteousness to his evil environment, but yet was saved according to 2 Pet. ii. 5: ὄγδοον Νῶε δικαιοσύνης κήρυκα ἐφύλαξεν.

THE FIRST PART OF VERSE 21.

Now comes the express formulation of the thought lying behind each detailed description in the earlier story of Noah's rescue: that this is a counterpart in prefigurative form to the Christians' salvation by Baptism. The language is, however, extremely difficult and it has been discussed endlessly within research with no satisfactory result.[1] Its theological content can certainly always be surmised to some extent. But as it may be interesting to understand it so as to give satisfaction also philologically we shall, in spite of all previous vain efforts, make an attempt to reach a reasonable linguistic understanding as a basis for our continued theological discussion.

---

[1] Examples: E. HUTHER, *Kritisch exegetisches Handbuch*, pp. 188 ff.; R. KNOPF, *Die Briefe Petri*, p. 156; U. HOLZMEISTER, *Commentarius*, p. 302; E. G. SELWYN, *The First Epistle of St. Peter*, pp. 203 f.

As the reader will remember the phrase runs as follows: ὃ καὶ ὑμᾶς¹ ἀντίτυπον νῦν σώζει βάπτισμα. One thing concerning this sentence may be stated at once as quite certain. It is incorrect, if as unfortunately so often happens, one allows ὃ to refer to ὕδωρ in the expression δι' ὕδατος in the preceding verse. The author has himself prevented such a misunderstanding by writing immediately after it: οὐ ... ἀπόθεσις ... ἀλλὰ ... ἐπερώτημα, which clearly shows that what saves the Christians is an action and not an element. If this is understood one is perhaps impelled to make ὃ allude to the whole sentence διεσώθησαν δι' ὕδατος.² Then the following reasoning is obtained: Noah and his family were saved by water, which now also saves you, *i.e.* the fact that Noah was saved is now your salvation. This does not give a satisfactory meaning, for it is not thanks to Noah's marvellous rescue that the Christians are now saved, but thanks to Christ's resurrection, verse 21. Further, both these interpretations involve two other difficulties. For one thing what shall we do with the words ἀντίτυπον and βάπτισμα? If both are made predicative attributes, as so often is done, the clause has a quite abnormal form with these two independent but analogous qualifiers of the predicate and is far from easy to translate, as for instance »which now as a counterpart saves also you in the form of baptism». If on the other hand βάπτισμα is made an apposition or epexegesis and translated: »namely Baptism», it is difficult to justify the lack of the article to βάπτισμα. Then it is also difficult to explain how ἀντίτυπον can be used of Christian Baptism, when the word preferably should mean »image», »copy» &c. or as an adjective »imitated» &c., in any case something secondary in relation to the original, ὁ τύπος, as appears clearly from Hebr. ix. 24: ἅγια ... ἀντίτυπα τῶν ἀληθινῶν, or 2 Clem. xiv. 3: ἡ γὰρ σὰρξ αὕτη ἀντίτυπός ἐστι τοῦ πνεύματος.³

¹ *Var. lect.* ἡμᾶς.
² E. KÜHL, *Die Briefe Petri*, p. 236, note 3, mentions older authors who wanted to read ὃ as referring to the whole of the previous sentence. He himself lets it refer to δι' ὕδατος. This, however, is not linguistically natural.
³ *Cf.* the *Sibylline Books* i. 33, the *Apostolic Constitutions* v. 14. 7, vi. 30. 2,

INVESTIGATION OF VERSES 20 AND 21 A

The only way of solving these difficulties is, we consider, to explain βάπτισμα as an apposition to the previous sentence drawn into the relative clause, and to understand ἀντίτυπον as an adjectival attribute to βάπτισμα. Seeing that an apposition in Greek[1] as in Latin[2] and also in English &c. can be drawn into a relative clause, the simple translation can thus be: »Which 'antitypical' baptism now saves you».[3] In this way the sentence is in fact clearly formed and gets a really satisfactory meaning.[4]

Here then βάπτισμα should not only be understood as concerning the Christian baptism, but that Noah underwent a baptism and that the same baptism now saves also the Christians. This baptism of Noah was »antitypical», it was a baptism in a metaphorical form, like all related in the Law, a figure of what was to come. The word ἀντίτυπος has thus exactly the same meaning as in Hebr. ix. 24 or 2 Clem. xiv. 3,[5] it means »being an image of the real Baptism», or more definitely stated, »prefigured». Compare τὰ ὑποδείγματα τῶν ἐν τοῖς οὐρανοῖς, Hebr. ix. 23.[6] It is, however, essentially the same Baptism which is now the Christians' means of salvation. Typological reasoning always presumes a certain »identity» between the actual item of the Law and the corresponding Christian phenomenon — if this were not so no demonstration could be given typologically. The Christian baptism, however, is not termed

---

Porphyr. De antro nymph. 9, where ἀντίτυπος throughout denotes the secondary counterpart, the copy.

[1] Cf. our excursus below.
[2] Cf. below, pp. 151 f.
[3] A similar suggestion was earlier put forth by G. W. BLENKIN, *The First Epistle General of St. Peter*, 1914, who takes ἀντίτυπον closely with ὅ, »which antitype» (E. G. SELWYN, *The First Epistle*, p. 299).
[4] One might perhaps think that there is a previous relative clause, which has the words οὐ σαρκὸς ἀπόθεσις ῥύπου [ἐστί] &c. as a following main sentence; but this is impossible because of the words δι' ἀναστάσεως which must probably refer to νῦν σώζει.
[5] P. LUNDBERG, *La typologie baptismale*, pp. 110f., wishes to separate 1 Pet. iii. 21 from Hebr. ix. 24 and 2 Clem. xiv. 3 in regard to the typological relation. We have no real reason for that, and it is also quite unnecessary, if our suggested interpretation is followed.
[6] Hebr. viii. 5 or ix. 9f. &c. are also illuminating passages.

»antitypical» although it looks so from the form of the sentence. We must think that the sentence ὃ καὶ ὑμᾶς ἀντίτυπον νῦν σώζει βάπτισμα, in combination with the indrawing of the apposition forms a somewhat illogical abridgement of a thought which really ought to have the following form: »an Ark in which some few were saved by water — an antitypical baptism, which now also saves you». Here strictly speaking the attribute »antitypical» refers only to Noah's baptism, but through the indrawing of the correlate into the relative sentence a confusion arises so that the Christian baptism also seems to be termed antitypical.

Concerning the καί in ὃ καὶ ὑμᾶς &c. we want to suggest that it should be understood in accordance with an observation made by H. J. CADBURY[1] that ὅς καί &c. appears to be used in Hellenistic Greek in much the same way as ὅστις, ὅσπερ, ὃς δή, without giving to the succeeding word the emphasis which καί is expected to convey, as in Acts xi. 30: ὃ καὶ ἐποίησαν. An example of that we have in 1 Pet. ii. 8: εἰς ὃ καὶ ἐτέθησαν, »(just) what they were appointed to». In that way we get a less considerable emphasis on the καί in verse iii. 21, and ὃ καί can be interpreted as almost equal to ὅπερ or ὃ δή.

Further on in a digression[2] we shall try to show that the phenomenon of an apposition being drawn into the relative clause so that there is a sentence like e.g. the Latin school example *Roma quæ urbs est in Italia*, often occurs in Greek and can also be found in several places in the N.T.[3] Here it will only be noted that in 1 Pet. 1. 10 we probably have a similar case. περὶ ἧς σωτηρίας, »a salvation, of which». When the indrawn antecedent is a noun,

---

[1] H. J. CADBURY, The Relative Pronouns in Acts and Elsewhere, *Journ. of Bibl. Lit.* xlii, 1923, pp. 157. *Cf.* below, p. 169.

[2] Below, pp. 149—172.

[3] E. G. SELWYN, *The First Epistle*, p. 299, discussing the suggestion by G. W. BLENKIN, to connect ὅ with ἀντίτυπον (*cf.* above, p. 145 note 3), declares that this construction of a relative pronoun with an epexegetic substantive introducing a new idea although legitimate in English does not appear to occur in Greek. Certainly it is not a very well-known peculiarity, but yet it is really to be found in Greek writers. In order to show that and to support our theory of 1 Pet. iii. 21 we have been obliged to make the extensive linguistic digression below.

as in 1 Pet. i. 10 and iii. 21 if our interpretation is correct, the relative pronoun has the function of an adjectival pronoun (we have a relative pronoun of adjectival character for instance in Mark vi. 11, ὃς ἂν τόπος μὴ δέξηται ὑμᾶς). That the noun βάπτισμα in iii. 21 is at the end of the sentence must be ascribed to the emphasis the word shall have.[1] Compare also the rule which holds good quite generally in the N.T., that a noun which is an antecedent and indrawn into the relative clause is not placed directly after the relative[2] — but an exception to this is clearly περὶ ἧς σωτηρίας in 1 Pet. i. 10, as also in general[3] it is written ἄχρι ἧς ἡμέρας &c.[4]

As we explain the relative clause in iii. 21 and also περὶ ἧς σωτηρίας in i. 10 as examples of the antecedent's indrawing if it is an apposition we can, of course, equally well explain these changes as cases of the so-called »relative connection», viz. that the relative pronoun shall really have a demonstrative meaning. Both phenomena are really in practice identical if the noun in the latter case is inserted so that the relative pronoun is adjectival.[5] The noun is in this case, too, inserted for epexegetic reasons.

In the Latin version of iii. 21 we probably have a case of such »relative connection»: *quod et vos nunc similis formæ salvos facit baptisma*. There *similis formæ* (genitive of quality) is certainly no adequate translation of ἀντίτυπον, but the expression clearly reveals that *quod* and *baptisma* belong to each other. Therefore this version in its way confirms that our interpretation of the Greek original is in the right direction. For the Latin translator has clearly conceived of the Greek text in the same way.[6]

Another textual fact which in its way confirms our interpretation is the variant reading without ὅ in the manuscript א. In this

---

[1] *Cf.* A. DEBRUNNER, *F. Blass' Grammatik*, 1943, § 473, p. 218.
[2] DEBRUNNER, *op. cit.* § 294. 5, p. 133.
[3] DEBRUNNER, *ibid.*
[4] See further discussions in our linguistic digression below.
[5] *Cf.* below, pp. 161 ff.
[6] Also other old Latin versions, given in the Fathers, have throughout this or similar forms. See P. SABATIER, *Bibliorum sacrorum latinæ versiones antiquæ*, iii, 1751, p. 952.

reading βάπτισμα is also considered as the subject of the sentence and ἀντίτυπον as its attribute.

A good support of our theory of the intimate relation between Noah's baptism and the Christian baptism as also of the linguistic circumstances is further to be found in Cyprian's *Epistola* lxxiv, *ad Pomp.*: ... *quod et vos similiter salvos facit baptisma: Quam breviter et spiritali compendio unitatis sacramentum manifestavit! Nam ut in illo mundi baptismo, quo iniquitas antiqua purgata est, qui in arca Noe non fuit, non potuit per aquam salvus fieri, ita nec nunc potest per baptismum salvus videri qui baptizatus in ecclesia non est.*[1]

With reference to the theological content it is here in any case clear that the diluvial »baptism» and the Christian baptism are thought to be complete counterparts of each other as means of salvation. And this view will naturally serve as comfort and trust in the Christians.

[1] J. D. MANSI, *Sacrorum conciliorum collectio*, i, 1759, col. 932; *cf. S. Th. Caec. Cypriani opera*, ed. Gv. HARTEL, ii, p. 809.

CHAPTER VI.

AN APPOSITIONAL ANTECEDENT INCORPORATED IN A RELATIVE CLAUSE.

RELATIVE INCORPORATION IN GENERAL.

In Greek a noun qualified by a relative clause is often incorporated in the latter, sometimes including the attributes. Such a noun with or without qualifiers often lacks the article and is often assimilated in case with the pronoun or *vice versa*, but then the syntactical elements thus connected usually get distinct places in the relative clause — *i.e.* the so-called *hyperbaton*.[1] This can be illustrated by the following general examples:

Xen. Mem. i. 1. 1: ἡ μὲν γὰρ γραφὴ κατ' αὐτοῦ τοιάδε τις ἦν· ἀδικεῖ Σωκράτης, οὓς μὲν ἡ πόλις νομίζει θεοὺς οὐ νομίζων.

---

[1] Selected literature: G. BERNHARDY, *Wissenschaftliche Syntax der griechischen Sprache*, 1829, p. 299ff. (a very rich collection of examples); V. C. F. ROST, *Griechische Grammatik*, 6. Ausg. 1841, § 99: 8—11, pp. 464ff., K. W. KRÜGER, *Griechische Sprachlehre*, § 51: 11—12; R. KÜHNER, *Ausf. Gramm.*, ii, Satzlehre, 3. Aufl. von B. GERTH, ii, 1904, pp. 416ff.; A. T. ROBERTSON, *A Grammar of the Greek N.T.*, 1919, pp. 718f., 731; R. MAYSER, *Grammatik der griechischen Papyri*, ii. 3, 1934, p. 98. For assimilation consult R. FÖRSTER, *Quæstiones de attractione enuntiationum relativarum*, 1868, and a series of later writings on this subject, generally by FÖRSTER's disciples. Bibliography of this literature in P. ROESLER, *De assimilationis pronominis relativi usu qualis fuerit apud Theophrastum* ..., 1906. Later FR. SCHÖN, *De assimilationis pronominis relativi extra dialectum Atticum usu*, 1909; H. SCHINDLER, *De Diod. Sic. et Strabonis enuntiationum relativarum attractione*, i. These works also treat sporadically cases of the incorporation of the antecedent. No special study of this incorporation by itself without reference to the case assimilation has been available for us, but we have had to content ourselves with the indications in the ordinary grammatical descriptions.

AN APPOSITIONAL ANTECEDENT INCORPORATED

Dem. xx. 142 (500): μὴ ... τῆς πόλεως ἀφέλησθε καὶ ὑμῶν αὐτῶν, ἣν διὰ παντὸς ἀεὶ τοῦ χρόνου δόξαν κέκτησθε καλήν.
Gen. ii. 4: ... ᾗ ἡμέρᾳ ἐποίησεν ὁ θεὸς τὸν οὐρανὸν καὶ τὴν γῆν.
Dion. Hal. Ant. viii. 29. 4f.: ἔπειθ' ὅσας ἄλλας ἱππικὰς καὶ πεζικὰς ἠγωνισάμην μάχας, ἐπιφανὴς ἐν ἁπάσαις ἐγενόμην.
Jos. Ant. iii. 13f. (296): ἀντὶ δ' ἧς ὑπέσχετο παρέξειν εὐδαιμονίας.
Luke xxiv. 1: ἦλθον φέρουσαι ἃ ἡτοίμασαν ἀρώματα.

The reason for such an arrangement is probably a need to express a more intimate relation between the antecedent and the relative clause and in that way to avoid interruptions in the phrase. The circumstance is very well characterized by E. MAYSER in the following words: »Enthält der Relativsatz lediglich eine attributive Bestimmung, die sich *ohne Pause*[1] and ein Nomen oder Pronomen anschliesst, so hat die griechische Sprache von jeher das Bestreben, den engen Zusammenhang zwischen dem Relativsatz und seinem Beziehungswort auch äusserlich zum Ausdruck zu bringen und beide Glieder zu einer begrifflichen Einheit zu verschmelzen. Dies kann auf doppelte Weise geschehen: entweder ohne Kasuswandel durch Hereinziehung des demonstrativen Substantivs in den Relativsatz oder durch Kasusassimilation oder -Attraktion des Relativs an sein Beziehungswort, das ebenfalls in dem Relativsatz herübergenommen werden kann.»[2]

INCORPORATION OF AN APPOSITION.

A special case of this indrawing into the relative clause of a noun which in general is true of an ordinary demonstrative correlation is the incorporation into the relative clause of an apposition to the actual antecedent. This apposition can be thought to have originally stood before or after the relative clause or from the first to have been within it.

In the great syntax of R. KÜHNER and B. GERTH this phenomenon is characterized by the following words: »Die Apposition zu dem

---
[1] Our italics.
[2] E. MAYSER, *Grammatik der griechischen Papyri*, ii. 3, 1934, p. 98.

vi.] AN APPOSITIONAL ANTECEDENT INCORPORATED 151

Substantive, auf welches sich der Adjektivsatz bezieht, wird bisweilen in diesen gezogen, wenn sie hier eine geeignetere oder nachdrücklichere Stellung einnimmt.»[1] This agrees with the observations made in the same work regarding the incorporation of a noun into the relative clause in general: »Aus allen [diesen] Beispielen erhellt, dass der Begriff, auf dem der eigentliche Nachdruck liegt, dem Adjektivsatze einverleibt ist.»[2]

In J. N. Madvig's Attic syntax the following rule for this peculiarity is given: »Besonders wird das Substantiv in den relativen Satz hineingezogen, wenn es ein neuer Begriff ist, der zum Vorhergehenden hinzugefügt wird: ὁ πατήρ, ὃν μόνον εἴχομεν βοηθόν, ἀπῆν.»[3] The meaning of this school example must be: »The father, the only helper we had, was absent.» Here the apposition »the only helper» which originally should be thought as placed before the relative clause has been drawn into it. Hereby the article has disappeared and we have, as to the word-order, a case of *hyperbaton*.

This gives us a special phenomenon in Greek construction fairly well-known from Latin[4] and also modern European languages. It is true that it has been described by the large grammatical text-books for classic Greek and Homer, and it has also been sporadically observed by some commentators of the classics, but otherwise it has not hitherto been, so far as we can see, a subject for special study, except for some observations on Homer in one or two earlier statements.[5] And it seems to have had no attention at all in so far as it appears in later Greek.

Our object here is to present, for the study of this phenomenon, a somewhat larger number of examples chosen from different epochs of the history of Greek, with the design to support our theory that the sentence ὃ καὶ ὑμᾶς ἀντίτυπον νῦν σῴζει βάπτισμα in 1 Pet.

---

[1] R. Kühner & B. Gerth, *op. cit.*, § 556: 4, p. 419.
[2] *Op. cit.*, § 556: 3, p. 419.
[3] J. N. Madvig, *Syntax der griechischen Sprache*, 1884, § 101b, p. 106.
[4] M. Leumann & J. B. Hofmann, *Stolz-Schmalz, Lateinische Grammatik*, 1928, p. 711 (»seit Cicero ...»; »die Regel bei Cæs., Nep. ...»).
[5] Works by Jos. Frenzel and Ed. Hermann, quoted below, p. 152, note 1, p. 153, note 4.

iii. 21 is a case of such indrawing of an apposition into the relative clause.

Here, of course, we must only take such constructions where there is undoubtedly a real incorporation of the apposition into the relative clause itself. Sentences which will not be considered are such as have an apposition placed closely after the relative clause in such a way that this apposition can certainly be assimilated in case with the relative clause but must not be assumed as belonging to the complex of that clause but as an epexegetic addition preceded by a necessary pause. Thus such sentences as the following will not be considered: καὶ τότε, ὡς ἔοικεν, ἡμῖν ἔσται, οὗ ἐπιθυμοῦμέν τε καί φαμεν ἐρασταὶ εἶναι· φρονήσεως, Plat. Phæd. xi (66 E), or καταστάντες δὲ ἐτείχισαν τὴν πόλιν ἐκ καινῆς, ἡ νῦν Ἡράκλεια καλεῖται, ἀπέχουσα Θερμοπυλῶν σταδίους ..., Thuc. iii. 92. 6, or 1 John ii. 25: αὕτη ἐστιν ἡ ἐπαγγελία ἣν αὐτὸς ἐπηγγείλατο ἡμῖν· τὴν ζωὴν τὴν αἰώνιον, for there the different epexegetical appositions ought clearly, as is indicated by the interpunction, not to be considered as part of the relative clauses although they are assimilated with them in case. What we shall seek will only be phrases where the apposition, thanks to the incorporation with the relative clause, is in such intimate connection with the relative pronoun that the latter has got the character of an adjectival pronoun,[1] as in the Latin school example *Roma, quæ urbs est in Italia,* »Rome, which town lies in Italy».[2]

HOMER.

In Homer we already find examples of this phenomenon. Certainly they are sometimes ambiguous boundary cases where it cannot be said definitely whether the relative pronoun is adjectival or not.

---

[1] For the problem of the adjectival use of the Greek relative pronoun see E. HERMANN, *Die Nebensätze,* 1912, p. 223; *id., Das Pronomen *ios als Adjectivum* (Gymn. Progr. Coburg), 1897 (not available).

[2] Compare for instance *Cic. Att.* v. 20. 3: *Amanus ... qui mons erat hostium plenus.*

vi.] AN APPOSITIONAL ANTECEDENT INCORPORATED 153

Thus it is very difficult to determine whether the apposition in a sentence like α. 69f.:

... Κύκλωπος κεχόλωται, ὃν ὀφθαλμοῦ ἀλάωσεν(,) ἀντίθεον Πολύφημον,

should really be conceived as some kind of independent insertion in the sentence, preceded, or possibly followed by some pause, and not as such an organically incorporated part of the relative clause that the relative pronoun is adjectival.[1]

Similarly in some cases it is difficult to determine whether a noun, possibly with adjuncts, which seems to be indrawn into the relative clause and as a principal word united with the relative pronoun, ought not rather to be considered a predicative expression. This is the case with the sentence Z. 314f.:

... ἔτευξε σὺν ἀνδράσιν, οἳ τότ' ἄριστοι ἦσαν ἐνὶ Τροίῃ ἐριβώλακι τέκτονες ἄνδρες.[2]

However, it is quite clear from these examples how easy it is to consider such a relative pronoun as adjectival.[3] On the one hand the case assimilation must be noticed, and on the other the absence of the article. Under no circumstances can one in any of these sentences from Homer allow the words in question to be separated from the rest by such a long pause as in the previously quoted examples from Plato and Thucydides. It seems to us most natural that the pause which was probably once here has gradually been allowed to disappear in reading the poems. It is also on the basis of this clear ambivalence that E. HERMANN founded his thesis that just clauses of this type form the starting-point for the development of phrases with a real adjectival use of the relative pronoun.[4]

For this reason we shall also quote some ambiguous examples from Homer, trusting that these phrases, from the point of view

---

[1] *Cf.* E. HERMANN, *Die Nebensätze, ibid.* We are however not so convinced as Hermann that the apposition in a verse like I. 131f.: τὰς μέν οἱ δώσω, μετὰ δ' ἔσσεται, ἣν τότ' ἀπηύρων / κούρην Βρισῆος, has with certainty not been taken as organically belonging to the relative pronoun. It is probable that we are here just at the boundary of an adjectival use of the pronoun.

[2] HERMANN, *ibid.*

[3] There are also many constructions of just this type in both older and newer grammatical text books used as examples of the indrawing of a noun into the relative clause. As a rule the philologists will not think of making a pause between such a noun and the relative clause. See *e.g.* G. BERNHARDY, *Wissenschaftliche Syntax*, 1829, p. 302, KÜHNER & GERTH, *op. cit.*, § 556: 4, pp. 419f.

[4] E. HERMANN, *op. cit.*, p. 223f., against Jos. FRENZEL, *Die Entstehung des relativen Satzbaues im Griechischen*, Gymn.-Progr. Wrongrowitz, 1889 (not available). HERMANN's theory is accepted by K. BRUGMANN & A. THUMB, *Griechische Grammatik*, 1913, p. 642.

of historical development, belong to the same category as the later, more certain instances of the adjectival use of the relative pronoun. The following are some more constructions from Homer which can be considered.[1] The simplest are sentences in which we can assume a more or less complete indrawing into the relative clause of an apposition which originally seems to have stood independently after it:

Γ. 122ff.:
Ἶρις δ' αὖθ' Ἑλένῃ λευκωλένῳ ἄγγελος ἦλθεν,
εἰδομένη γαλόῳ, Ἀντηνορίδαο δάμαρτι,
τὴν Ἀντηνορίδης εἶχε κρείων Ἑλικάων
Λαοδίκην Πριάμοιο θυγατρῶν εἶδος ἀρίστην.

Η. 186f.:
ἀλλ' ὅτε δὴ τὸν ἵκανε φέρων ἀν' ὅμιλον ἀπάντῃ,
ὅς μιν ἐπιγράψας κυνέῃ βάλε φαίδιμος Αἴας.

Ι. 131 f.:
... μετὰ δ' ἔσσεται, ἢν τότ' ἀπηύρων / κούρην Βρισῆος ...

Λ. 624ff.:
τοῖσι δὲ τεῦχε κυκειῶ ἐυπλόκαμος Ἑκαμήδη,
τὴν ἄρετ' ἐκ Τενέδοιο γέρων, ὅτε πέρσεν Ἀχιλλεύς,
θυγατέρ' Ἀρσινόου μεγαλήτορος, ἥν οἱ Ἀχαιοὶ / ἔξελον.

Τ. 326f.:
ἠὲ τὸν ὅς Σκύρῳ μοι ἔνι τρέφεται φίλος υἱός —
εἴ που ἔτι ζώει γε Νεοπτόλεμος θεοειδής.

β. 118ff.:
κέρδεά θ', οἷ' οὔ πώ τιν' ἀκούομεν οὐδὲ παλαιῶν,
τάων, αἳ πάρος ἦσαν ἐυπλοκαμῖδες Ἀχαιαί,
Τυρώ τ' Ἀλκμήνη τε ἐυστέφανός τε Μυκήνη.

In addition we can observe a few cases where from the beginning the apposition probably constituted a pause in the middle of the relative clause, though the pauses even there have gradually diminished so that the relative pronoun came to have an adjectival function:

[1] Many of them are quoted as examples of a noun's indrawing into the relative sentence in works such as G. BERNHARDY, *Wissenschaftliche Syntax*, 1829, pp. 299ff., B. DELBRÜCK, *Vergleichende Syntax*, iii, 1900, p. 299, R. KÜHNER & B. GERTH, *op. cit.*, ii, § 556: 4, pp. 419f., &c.

vi.] AN APPOSITIONAL ANTECEDENT INCORPORATED 155

E. 623f.:
δεῖσε δ', ὃ γ' ἀμφίβασιν κρατερὴν Τρώων ἀγερώχων,
οἳ πολλοί τε καὶ ἐσθλοὶ ἐφέστασαν ἔγχε' ἔχοντες.

Z. 452f.:
οὔτε κασιγνήτων, οἵ κεν πολέεις τε καὶ ἐσθλοὶ
ἐν κονίῃσι πέσοιεν ὑπ' ἀνδράσι δυσμενέεσσιν.

In the following examples the relative pronoun has undoubtedly come to be clearly adjectival:

λ. 122f. = ψ. 269f.:
εἰς ὅ κε τοὺς ἀφίκηαι (ἀφίκωμαι), οἳ οὐκ ἴσασι θάλασσαν
ἀνέρες οὐδέ θ' ἅλεσσι μεμιγμένον εἶδαρ ἔδουσιν.

Cf. δ. 10ff.:
υἱέι δὲ Σπάρτηθεν Ἀλέκτορος ἤγετο κούρην,
ὅς οἱ τηλύγετος γένετο κρατερὸς Μεγαπένθης / ἐκ δούλης.

Here the apposition seems also to be properly incorporated in the relative clause: notice the word-order.

In the following example we can probably think that a predicative expression has become the principal word to what has thereby become an adjectival relative pronoun:

δ. 112:
Τηλέμαχός θ', ὃν ἔλειπε νέον γεγαῶτ' ἐνὶ οἴκῳ.

In A. 271f.:
... κείνοισι δ' ἂν οὔ τις
τῶν, οἳ νῦν βροτοί εἰσιν ἐπιχθόνιοι, μαχέοιτο,

it seems on the other hand that εἰσίν means »to exist»: The adjectives βροτοί and ἐπιχθόνιοι stand out thus as the antecedents to the relative pronoun, and this will be adnominal.

We shall now see what the classical dramatists have to give us for a study of the attraction and incorporation of the apposition.

THE GREAT DRAMATISTS.

Æschylus in Sept., 553ff., shows a form of incorporation still but little developed:
ἔστιν δὲ καὶ τῷδ, ὃν λέγεις(,) τὸν Ἀρκάδα,
ἀνὴρ ἄκομπος ...

Here the definite article still appears before the apposition. But both the case assimilation and the rhythm of the verse reveal the fact that there is some intimate connection between the relative pronoun and this apposition. That is why the editors of the text and the grammars as a rule have refrained from putting a comma in front of τὸν Ἀρκάδα. Yet the relative pronoun cannot be considered quite adjectival. A shorter pause must, in spite of the attraction, be considered necessary in front of τὸν Ἀρκάδα. On the other hand the article is lacking in *Æsch. Suppl.* 1039ff.:

μετάκοινοι δὲ φίλᾳ ματρὶ πάρεισιν
Πόθος <ᾇ> τ' οὐδὲν ἄπαρνον
τελέθει θέλεκτορι Πειθοῖ.

Thus here we find the same tendency to incorporation as in Homer.

With the later tragedians, however, we find the phenomenon we seek more clearly developed.

Soph. Ant., 404f. is a case similar to the first example from Æschylus:

ταύτην γ'ἰδὼν θάπτουσαν, ὃν σὺ τὸν νεκρὸν
ἀπεῖπας,

as we have the article there too, but the noun is now quite closely incorporated in the clause.

But another passage in Sophocles has the noun incorporated without the article and is a very illuminating example of the same indrawing into a relative clause of an apposition consisting of a noun with qualifiers as we consider is to be found in 1 Pet. iii. 21, *Soph. Phil.* 1326ff.:

σὺ γὰρ νοσεῖς τόδ' ἄλγος ἐκ θείας τύχης,
Χρύσης πελασθεὶς φύλακος, ὃς τὸν ἀκαλυφῆ
σηκὸν φυλάσσει κρύφιος οἰκουρῶν ὄφις.

Here it seems that in reading aloud there should be no pause before κρύφιος &c. Thus we find an organic indrawing of the apposition into the relative clause with an omission of the article, an assimilation of the case, the adjectival function of the relative pronoun and *hyperbaton* as a consequence,[1] exactly as in the school

---

[1] V. C. F. ROST also states that this construction is a substitute for:

vi.]   AN APPOSITIONAL ANTECEDENT INCORPORATED   157

example from MADVIG's syntax quoted above: ὁ πατήρ, ὃν μόνον εἴχομεν βοηθόν, ἀπῆν, and as in 1 Pet. iii. 21, if we have rightly understood this passage; and here in Sophocles as in that passage we have the nominative case.

Another illustration of the same nature is *Soph. El.* 160ff.:

ὄλβιος, ὃν ἁ κλεινὰ
γᾶ ποτε Μυκηναίων
δέξεται εὐπατρίδαν Διὸς εὔφρονι
βήματι μολόντα τάνδε γᾶν Ὀρέσταν.

Here in our opinion both ὅν and εὐπατρίδαν should be combined with Ὀρέσταν as adjectival qualifications of it, while μολόντα on the other hand is a predicative attribute to Ὀρέσταν.[1]

The last two sentences constitute interesting examples of extensive *hyperbaton*. That the snake, or Orestes, are mentioned so far towards the end may probably be explained by the need to maintain the interest and thus bring about greater emphasis.[2] In this respect, too, we believe we can find an analogy in 1 Pet. iii. 21, where βάπτισμα is kept to the last as if to maintain the expectation in the long deduction chain.

Compare *Soph. El.* 203ff.:

ὦ νύξ, ὦ δείπνων ἀρρήτων
ἔκπαγλ' ἄχθη,
τοὺς ἐμὸς ἴδε πατὴρ
θανάτους αἰκεῖς διδύμαιν χειροῖν.

Here both νύξ and δείπνων ἀρρήτων should be explained by θάνατοι αἰκεῖς, »dann aber ist θάνατοι αἰκεῖς in den Relativsatz τοὺς ἐμὸς ἴδε πατήρ hineingezogen».[3] This incorporation, which also includes an adjectival attribute, is also here very close.

... φύλακος, κρυφίου οἰκουροῦντος ὄφεως, ὃς φυλάσσει, *Griechische Grammatik*, 1841, § 99, pp. 464f.

[1] Several grammarians, commentators and translators also accept the sentence in this way. ROST *e.g.* considers this construction has arisen instead of: εὐπατρίδης τ' Ὀρέστης ... ὅν ποτε δέξεται, *op. cit.* p. 465.

[2] Compare the rule in KÜHNER & GERTHS' syntax, quoted above, pp. 150 f., and E. BRUHN, *Sophokles, Anhang*, 1899, § 174, p. 99.

[3] E. BRUHN, *Elektra*, 1912, p. 74.

Euripides, too, offers some good examples of the construction under discussion.

First must be mentioned one in which we find a completely clear instance of the total incorporation of the apposition in the relative clause of just the kind we have found in Homer, *Eur. Fragm.* 14:

Ἕλλην γάρ, ὡς λέγουσι, γίγνεται Διός,
τοῦ δ' Αἴολος παῖς, Αἰόλου δὲ Σίσυφος
Ἀθάμας τε Κρηθεύς θ' ὅς τ' ἐπ' Ἀλφειοῦ ῥοαῖς
θεοῦ μανεὶς ἔρριψε Σαλμωνεὺς φλόγα.

Here it must be noticed, however, that Σαλμωνεύς is within the sentence, before φλόγα. To separate this apposition from the rest by a pause is absolutely impossible. The relative pronoun is thus necessarily adjectival.

In this way the use in the above of the verses from Homer is justified, which show almost the same structure as the sentence just quoted, but where the independence of the apposition could have been maintained, if necessary, because it comes last in the sentence. Thus here we find clear similarities in form, only a certain difference in the degree of attraction.

Compare further *Eur. Hec.* 771:

πρὸς ἄνδρ', ὃς ἄρχει τῆσδε Πολυμήστωρ χθονός,

and *ibid.*, 986ff.:

πρῶτον μὲν εἰπὲ παῖδ', ὃν ἐξ ἐμῆς χερὸς
Πολύδωρον ἔκ τε πατρὸς ἐν δόμοις ἔχεις,
εἰ ζῇ,

where the appositions are also clearly organically inserted in the relative clause.

Other examples from Euripides are the following:
Bacch. 860ff.:

... γνώσεται δὲ τὸν Διὸς
Διόνυσον, ὃς πέφυκεν ἐν τέλει θεὸς,
δεινότατος, ἀνθρώποισι δ'ἠπιώτατος.

Here ὅς ought possibly to be combined with θεός.

Hipp. 101:

τήνδ' ἢ πύλαισι σαῖς ἐφέστηκεν Κύπρις.

vi.] AN APPOSITIONAL ANTECEDENT INCORPORATED 159

Iph. T., 147f.:
αἰαῖ, κηδείοις οἴκτοις,
αἵ μοι συμβαίνουσ' ἄται.

Iph. T. 63f.:
σὺν προσπόλοισιν, ἃς ἔδωχ' ἡμῖν ἄναξ
Ἑλληνίδας γυναῖκας.

Herc. f. 1163f.:
Ἥκω σὺν ἄλλοις, οἳ παρ' Ἀσωποῦ ῥοὰς
μένουσ' ἔνοπλοι γῆς Ἀθηναίων κόροι.

In these last two examples the appositions have adjectival attributes.

Sometimes an adjective of appositional quality can alone be indrawn into the relative clause, while the governing noun remains as antecedent in the principal sentence:[1]

Eur. Or. 853f.:
... λόγους
ἄκουσον, οὕς σοι δυστυχεῖς ἥκω φέρων,

i.e. »words, difficult, which I ...».

An interesting example of the indrawing of an apposition is also given by Aristophanes in *Thesm.* 503f.:

ἑτέραν δ' ἐγᾦδ', ἣ 'φασκεν ὠδίνειν γυνὴ
δέχ' ἡμέρας, ἕως ἐπρίατο παιδίον,

»however I know another, a woman, who ...».

THE ATTIC PROSAISTS.

In Attic prose, however, the indrawing of the apposition is clearly something rather unusual. It seems as if this construction was not always considered quite decent by the strict Attic rhetoricians and prosaists. Only a few examples of the construction in question, yet in themselves very interesting, are known to us from classic prose.

Thucydides has incorporated a number in a relative clause in iv. 113: οἱ δὲ ἐς τὰς ναῦς, αἳ ἐφρούρουν δύο, καταφυγόντες διασῴζονται.

Xenophon shows an incorporation of the adjective in *Anab.* iii. 5. 17: τούτους γὰρ διελθόντας ἔφασαν εἰς Ἀρμενίαν ἥξειν, ἧς Ὀρόντας ἦρχε πολλῆς καὶ εὐδαίμονος (*scil.* χώρας).[2]

---
[1] A. Matthiä, *Ausführliche Griechische Grammatik*, ii, 1835, § 474, p. 1056; J. N. Madvig, *Syntax*, § 101b, p. 106.
[2] Rost, *Beispielsammlung zu den Griechischen Grammatiken von Buttmann und Rost*, ii, 1856, § xxi. 3, p. 66.

Plato has made use of the possibility of incorporating an apposition into a relative clause in one passage in The State, vii. 11 (p. 529 C—D): ταῦτα ... κάλλιστα μὲν ἡγεῖσθαι καὶ ἀκριβέστατα τῶν τοιούτων ἔχειν, τῶν δὲ ἀληθινῶν πολύ ἐνδεῖν, ἃς τὸ ὂν τάχος καὶ ἡ οὖσα βραδυτὴς ἐν τῷ ἀληθινῷ ἀριθμῷ καὶ πᾶσι τοῖς ἀληθέσι σχήμασι φοράς τε πρὸς ἄλληλα φέρεται καὶ τὰ ἐνόντα φέρει, where the relative clause must mean: »namely the movements with which the absolute rapidity and the absolute slowness move» & c. Otherwise Plato does not often incorporate an apposition in the relative clause but is content in general with case assimilation and retains the article, as in *Resp.* iii. 12 (p. 402 C): οὕς φαμεν ἡμῖν παιδευτέον εἶναι, τοὺς φύλακας, where it seems that a pause in front of the apposition must be assumed. If the apposition is really sometimes incorporated Plato seems to prefer retaining the article, as in *Leg.* i. 14 (p. 646 E—647 A): φοβούμεθα δέ γε πολλάκις δόξαν, ἡγούμενοι δοξάζεσθαι κακοὶ πράττοντες ἢ λέγοντές τι τῶν μὴ καλῶν· ὃν δὴ καὶ καλοῦμεν τὸν φόβον ἡμεῖς γε, οἶμαι δὲ καὶ πάντες, αἰσχύνην, »just the fear, which»[1] — or »just this fear», if one here thinks of a so-called »relative connection» (*cf.* below) —, and in *Theaet.* 167 B: ἕτερα τοιαῦτα, ἃ δή τινες τὰ φαντάσματα ὑπὸ ἀπειρίας ἀληθῆ καλοῦσιν. Here the appositions with the retained article are placed in the middle of the relative clauses and assimilated with them in case, and in spite of the article this must be considered an example of real incorporation, for no pauses around the appositional insertion are thinkable.

Demosthenes has a passage where there is first a personal name without the article, clearly incorporated in the relative clause, and then another with the article clearly only assimilated with the relative clause: δοθέντος τοίνυν τοῦ ἀργυρίου, ἐγράψατο μὲν ὀφείλοντα τὸν κελεύσαντα χρῆσαι Τιμόθεον, ὑπόμνημα δ' ἐγράψατο, ᾧ τε οὗτος ἐκέλευσε δοῦναι Ἀντιμάχῳ καὶ ὃν ὁ Ἀντίμαχος συνέπεμψεν ἐπὶ τὴν τράπεζαν ληψόμενον τὸ ἀργύριον, τὸν Αὐτόνομον, *Dem.* xlix. 8 (p. 1186). That Ἀντιμάχῳ, on the one hand, is incorporated in the relative clause appears from the absence of the article here, com-

---

[1] F. Passow, V. C. F. Rost, *e.a.*, *Handwörterbuch*, ii. 1, 1852, col. 550 b.

pared with the expression ὁ 'Αντίμαχος directly following; that τὸν Αὐτόνομον, on the other hand, is an independent apposition or epexegesis appears from the fact that the article is there. The difference is probably due to the many words between ὅν and τὸν Αὐτόνομον. But otherwise Attic prose is distinctly temperate with such constructions. The great orators seem to have avoided them.

EXAMPLES FROM EARLIER HELLENISTIC WRITERS.

The great Attic prosaists were important as models long after their own time. For this reason it seems that the special construction we are here seeking has been avoided by many later writers who are subservient to Atticism.

Yet we think we can trace in many other later writers a tendency, first careful, then somewhat bolder, to use something like the same incorporation of an apposition such as we have found in Homer, the tragedians &c. Certainly only sporadic examples can be given of this, as in studying the question without having preparatory work at hand we had to be content with examples taken at random from different authors. It is true that the material represented could be considerably extended with a more fundamental examination of different texts. Yet we hope that what will be presented here are sufficient evidence to show that an apposition can be indrawn into the relative clause also in later Greek language.

Among the examples which can now be quoted there are some where a relative clause is used instead of a demonstrative one, i.e. where there is a case of so-called »relative connection». This phenomenon, which seems more usual in later Greek, implies that a sentence has the same form as a relative subordinate clause but the same meaning as a demonstrative principal sentence.

If the relative pronoun in such a sentence is combined with a noun and is thus adjectival, the meaning of the sentence will be the same as if there was a demonstrative pronoun in conjoint position.

Thus if after a colon or a full stop there stands in the text: δι' ἥν αἰτίαν, the adequate translation of it will be: »for this reason». The nominal principal word has, however, not even in such a case any determinative function. Therefore such constructions will in form wholly coincide with the case of the indrawing of the apposition we have previously discussed, and it will be absolutely impossible to distinguish strictly between the two kinds of construction. It will often be quite arbitrary whether one considers a caesura before such a sentence to be so important that the translation should be according to the principle of »relative connection» or »the indrawing of the apposition into the relative sentence». As an example of such an ambiguous construction the passage just quoted from Plato, *Leg.* i. 14, may be mentioned.[1]

1 Pet. iii. 21 also contains a relative clause with such a Janus face.

Because of these circumstances we shall also place such clauses with an adjectival relative pronoun plus the governing noun which really has a demonstrative significance, on the same level as the usual relative clauses with an indrawn apposition.

When we now consider the examples we have collected from the post-classical Greek writers, it will first be stated that some stereotyped phrases containing certain ordinary words occur rather often. In this way we meet alternately real relative clauses and relative phrases with a demonstrative significance.

Typical examples to illustrate this kind of conventional idioms are found in Polybius:[2]

Hist. i. 47. 2: δι' οὗ τρόπου μόνως ἐστὶ δυνατὸν ... εὐστοχεῖν,
    i. 84. 5: ἐν οἷς καιροῖς,
    ii. 19. 6: ἐν ᾧ καιρῷ,
    ii. 39. 1: καθ' οὓς γὰρ καιρούς,
    ibid. 4: ἐν οἷς καιροῖς,
and similar phrases very often.

Compare Philo, *De opif. mund.* 84: παρ' ἥν αἰτίαν, or *ibid.*, 100: δι' ἥν αἰτίαν (»for this reason»).

---

[1] See above, p. 160.
[2] Polybius has clearly a preference for »relative connection».

vi.] AN APPOSITIONAL ANTECEDENT INCORPORATED 163

One word which certain writers very often combine with the relative pronoun in such clauses is the adjective πᾶς or ἅπας, also converted into a noun in neuter plural, e.g. in Philo: *De opif. mund.* 48: οὓς ἅπαντας ἡ τετρὰς ἔχει περιλαβοῦσα, *ibid.*, 117: ἃ δὴ πάντα καθάπερ ... νευροσπαστούμενα τότε μὲν ἠρεμεῖ τότε δὲ κινεῖται, *De Abr.* 242: οἷς ἅπασιν ἐφεδρεύων ὁ ἀστεῖος ..., *De Jos.* 216: οἷς ἅπασιν ἔνοχος ὤν ..., *ibid.*, 236: ἐξ ὧν ἁπάντων ἤδη συνεπείθετο, *De vita Mos.* 12: ἅ μοι δοκεῖ πάντα συμβῆναι. Compare μόνος in *Phil. De decal.* 67: τυφλώττοντες περὶ τὸ θέας ἄξιον, πρὸς ὃ μόνον ὀξυδορκεῖν ἀναγκαῖον ἦν. The adjective μόνος which often occurs in such sentences has certainly usually a clearly predicative function, but in this example it is the appositional character which is most outstanding.

Respecting the examples with πᾶς and ἅπας, it is true that the appositional character must be regarded with more attention than the predicative, which is here less naturally logical. See also e.g.: *Julian. Or.* i. 15 D: πλείστας ἂν κηλῖδας ἐναπόθοιτο τῇ ψυχῇ, ὧν πασῶν καθαρὸν εἶναι χρή, where πασῶν must be appositional. The sentence ἃ δὴ πάντα ἀθρόα συλλήβδην ἓν ὄνομα τὸ αἰνέσεως ἔλαχε, *Phil. De spec. leg.* i. 224, is clearly of another type, as also to some extent ἃ οὐκ ὀκνήσω σοι πάντα, ὦ καλὲ Τιμόκλεις, διεξελθεῖν, *Lucian. De merc. cond.* ii (654) where πάντα is indeed not so certainly appositional but possibly constitutes a new accusative to the infinitive.

Non-stereotyped constructions can, however, also be quoted in which a relative pronoun is used adjectivally with a governing noun of appositional character.

Of this we have an illustration from *Ps. Long. De sublim.* xv. 7 (p. 188 v.): ἄκρως δὲ καὶ ὁ Σοφοκλῆς ἐπὶ τοῦ θνῄσκοντος Οἰδίπου καὶ ἑαυτὸν μετὰ διοσημείας τινὸς θάπτοντος πεφάντασται, καὶ κατὰ τὸν ἀπόπλουν τῶν Ἑλλήνων ἐπὶ τἀχιλλέως προφαινομένου τοῖς ἀναγομένοις ὑπὲρ τοῦ τάφου, ἣν οὐκ οἶδ᾽ εἴ τις ὄψιν ἐναργέστερον εἰδωλοποίησε Σιμωνίδου,» a vision which ...». Notice how the whole previous graphic description is included in the appositional idea ὄψις, which has here been intimately incorporated in the relative clause but then definitely separated from the relative pronoun.

Hero of Alexandria can write in the following way, *Pneum.* ii. 36 (p. 326, ll. 13 ff.[1]): καταβὰν δὲ ἐπιβήσεται τῇ ἐξεχούσῃ κεραίᾳ

---

[1] *Herons von Alexandria Druckwerke und Automatentheater*, hrsg. von W. SCHMIDT, 1899.

τοῦ Κ μέρους τοῦ τυμπάνου, ὅπερ μέρος καταγόμενον ἐναρμόσει ... Here the apposition μέρος is valuable as a complement to the relative pronoun for the sake of clarity. In such technical texts explicitness is also clearly necessary. In Hellenistic poetry we find such constructions *i.a.* in *Callim. Hymn.* iv, *In Delum*, 2ff.:

... ἢ μὲν ἅπασαι
Κυκλάδες, αἳ νήσων ἱερώταται εἰν ἁλὶ κεῖνται,
εὔυμνοι ... (incorporation of an adjective including its genitive attribute),
or *ibid.*, 323 f.:

... ἃ Δηλιὰς εὕρετο νύμφη
παίγνια κουρίζοντι καὶ 'Απόλλωνι γελαστύν.

From the LXX a few sporadic cases can be noted:
Gen. xlix. 30: ἐν τῷ σπηλαίῳ τῷ διπλῷ τῷ ἀπέναντι Μαμβρὴ ἐν τῇ γῇ Χανάαν, ὃ ἐκτήσατο 'Αβραὰμ τὸ σπήλαιον παρὰ 'Εφρών ... Compare an almost similar phrase in Gen. l. 13. Here the definite article is used but the incorporation is quite clear. The Hebrew version of this phrase is as follows: במערה אשר בשדה המכפלה ... אשר קנה אברהם את השדה מאת עפרן. Here too the relative pronoun is supplemented by an appositional expression, השדה, incorporated in the relative clause. From this it appears that the Greek translation has faithfully preserved the syntactic construction of the Hebrew sentence, so that even the definite article is included. However it is astonishing that the Greek translation does not allow the relative pronoun to refer to the idea »field« in the previous phrase, supplementing the relative pronoun with this idea as the Masoretic text does, but to the idea »the cave«, which must then act as a complement to the relative pronoun.

Am. v. 1: 'Ακούσατε τὸν λόγον κυρίου τοῦτον, / ὃν ἐγὼ λαμβάνω ἐφ' ὑμᾶς θρῆνον, οἶκος 'Ισραήλ. In this case too the Hebrew text shows a formal analogy: ... אשר אנכי נשא עליכם קינה ...

Ps. xlv (xlvi). 9: δεῦτε ἴδετε τὰ ἔργα κυρίου, / ἃ ἔθετο τέρατα ἐπὶ τῆς γῆς. In the Hebrew text the relative clause runs: ... אשר שם שמות, *i.e.* here also there is a syntactical congruity.

vi.] AN APPOSITIONAL ANTECEDENT INCORPORATED 165

In the last two examples it may be that the relative pronoun appears to be substituted for an interrogative pronoun. We do not, however, think this is really the case, as the parallelism of the sentences here probably indicates that the noun in the second half of the verse should be thought to repeat the conception expressed by the noun in the first half in another variation. For this reason the noun in the second half appears rather as an apposition to the former noun and the pronoun then becomes an adjectival relative pronoun. At least in the example from Am. this should be quite clear.

In Hebrew this supplementing of אשר by the addition of a following noun as its principal word is not unique. See further Gen. xlv. 4 (אשר אתי, »me whom»), Judg. ix. 17 (אשר אבי, »my father, who»), 1 Sam. ii. 23.[1] It often happens, as is well known, that אשר is supplemented by a pronoun or a personal suffix. The latter has also had great influence on the Greek of the Bible.

THE NEW TESTAMENT.

In the N.T. there are also some clear cases of the incorporation of the apposition into the relative clause.[2]

First, a few examples with a proper noun in apposition, a special type well-known from Homer:

Mark vi. 16: ὃν ἐγὼ ἀπεκεφάλισα Ἰωάννην, οὗτος ἠγέρθη. The proleptic adjectival clause is here explained through the apposition Ἰωάννην.

John xvii. 3: ἵνα γιγνώσκωσιν σὲ τὸν μόνον ἀληθινὸν θεὸν καὶ ὃν ἀπέστειλας Ἰησοῦν Χριστὸν [εἰς τοῦτον τὸν κόσμον]. The apposition Ἰησοῦν Χριστόν stands out as completely incorporated in the relative clause especially by means of the bracketed words found in codex D.

---

[1] Cf. J. PEDERSEN, Hebræisk Grammatik, 1933, § 129. 1, p. 273.

[2] The peculiarity in the special phenomenon that an apposition is incorporated in a relative clause seems to have escaped the authors of N.T. grammars. The incorporation of a noun in the relative clause generally has of course been duly pointed out (in our opinion specially well in A. T. ROBERTSON, A Grammar of the Greek N.T., 1919, pp. 718f., 731).

Acts xxi. 16: συνῆλθον δὲ καὶ τῶν μαθητῶν ἀπὸ Καισαρείας σὺν ἡμῖν, ἄγοντες παρ' ᾧ ξενισθῶμεν Μνάσωνί τινι Κυπρίῳ, ἀρχαίῳ μαθητῇ. Here the structure of the relative clause is quite complicated, yet the position of the apposition within the clause is quite clear.

Philem. 10 ff.: παρακαλῶ σε περὶ τοῦ ἐμοῦ τέκνου, ὃν ἐγέννησα ἐν τοῖς δεσμοῖς μου Ὀνήσιμον, τόν ποτέ σοι ἄχρηστον νυνὶ δὲ ... ἐμοὶ εὔχρηστον, ὃν ἀνέπεμψά σοι αὐτόν, τοῦτ' ἔστιν τὰ ἐμὰ σπλάγχνα· ὃν ἐγὼ ἐβουλόμην πρὸς ἐμαυτὸν κατέχειν ... In this series of relative subordinate sentences there are two cases of the incorporation of the apposition. It is easily perceived that Ὀνήσιμον is incorporated in the relative sentence, because of the many analogies we have already met.[1] That, on the other hand, αὐτόν is incorporated seems probable by reason of the awkward construction obtained if a pause is made in front of this word, as many authors prefer. A demonstrative or a personal pronoun in the relative clause as a pleonasm to the relative pronoun is quite usual in the N.T. especially because of its Semitic basis (cf. above).

The following are further examples:

John xvi. 18, according to the codices B, L et al.: τί ἐστιν τοῦτο ὃ λέγει »μικρόν», = »what is that which he says, a little while?»

Acts xv. 11: καθ' ὃν τρόπον κἀκεῖνοι. The word τρόπον is here clearly in apposition. The literal meaning is »in which way».

Rom. iv. 17 contains the following relative clause: (πατὴρ πάντων ἡμῶν) ... κατέναντι οὗ ἐπίστευσεν θεοῦ τοῦ ζωοποιοῦντος τοὺς νεκρούς. This is in our view quite misconceived through the usual translation with the determinative pronoun, while the observation of incorporating an apposition in the relative clause gives a quite sensible meaning. If the translation runs: »before the god in whom he believed», it is necessary to assume a polytheistic belief and this is unreasonable. If God is written with a capital letter and the translation is: »before the God, in whom he believed»,[2] perhaps the

---

[1] Noted also e.g. by A. T. ROBERTSON, op. cit., p. 718.
[2] Thus e.g. W. BAUER, Griechisch-Deutsches Wörterbuch, 1937, col. 700; A. DEBRUNNER, Friedrich Blass' Grammatik des neutest. Griechisch, 7. Aufl. 1943, i, § 294: 2, p. 133.

polytheistic theory will not be such an obvious assumption, but it can only be wholly avoided if something adjectival is thought of in the idea »God», thus perhaps »the divine power which» or something similar, and this will be peculiarly forced, when God everywhere else in the context (iv. 2, 3, 6 &c.) is a personal noun. It is therefore considerably simpler and more natural to translate as follows: »before the one he believed in, (namely) God who» &c., which gives us yet another example of the indrawing of the apposition into a relative clause.

Rom. vii. 19: οὐ γὰρ ὃ θέλω ποιῶ ἀγαθόν, ἀλλὰ ὃ οὐ θέλω[1] κακὸν τοῦτο πράσσω. Here the first relative clause shows a peculiar structure in that the apposition is kept until after the — certainly very short — principal sentence but at the same time deprived of the definite article just as if it was in the same intimate connection with the relative clause as if incorporated. This is also really the fact. In considering the second relative clause which is parallel to the first it is found that here there has been a real incorporation of the apposition. The translation will then be: »For it is not what I will that I do, (namely) the good, but what I will not, the evil, that I do.»

2 Cor. x. 13: κατὰ τὸ μέτρον τοῦ κανόνος οὗ ἐμέρισεν ἡμῖν ὁ θεὸς μέτρου. The construction of this peculiar passage cannot be termed grammatically correct. Of that F. BLASS & A. DEBRUNNER's grammar says: »es ist wohl οὗ aus ὃ (auf μέτρον bezogen) an κανόνος attrahiert und dann μέτρου wiederholt, damit οὗ nicht auf κανόνος bezogen werde.»[2] This seems also to be a reasonable explanation.[3] Thus μέτρου is used here as an apposition incorporated in the relative sentence.

Hebr. vii. 14: πρόδηλον γὰρ ὅτι ἐξ Ἰούδα ἀνατέταλκεν ὁ κύριος ἡμῶν, εἰς ἣν φυλὴν περὶ ἱερέων οὐδὲν Μωϋσῆς ἐλάλησεν.

---
[1] ὃ μισῶ according to the MSS F, 1831, and Origenes.
[2] A. DEBRUNNER, op. cit., ii, § 294: 5, p. 50.
[3] Cf. A. T. ROBERTSON, A Grammar of the Greek N.T., p. 719: »In 2. Cor. x. 13 we have in the same sentence the substantive repeated (once incorporated and attracted to the case of the relative, but the relative itself attracted to the case of κανόνος)».

Some cases can also be quoted where the relative clause has really a demonstrative meaning, the so-called »relative connection», regarding which it has already been stated that complete formal analogy with the indrawing of the apposition can arise.

Acts vii. 20: Ἐν ᾧ καιρῷ ἐγεννήθη Μωϋσῆς (a common expression; similar cases have been previously treated).

2 Tim. i. 6, 12, Hebr. ii. 11: δι' ἥν αἰτίαν (cf. the previous remarks).

Acts xxvi. 6ff.: ... ἐπ' ἐλπίδι τῆς ... ἐπαγγελίας ... ἕστηκα κρινόμενος, εἰς ἥν τὸ δωδεκάφυλον ἡμῶν ... ἐλπίζει καταντῆσαι· περὶ ἧς ἐλπίδος ἐγκαλοῦμαι ὑπὸ Ἰουδαίων. Here the idea ἐλπίς which is expressed in the previous words, first in the verb ἐλπίζει, is again taken up through the appositional insertion in the latter relative clause. In this way the allusion is made clearer, and this is badly needed: notice that the pronoun in the previous relative clause refers to ἐπαγγελίας.

Hebr. x. 10: (ποιῆσαι τὸ θέλημά σου ...)· ἐν ᾧ θελήματι ἡγιασμένοι ἐσμέν.

1 Pet. i. 10: (τὸ τέλος τῆς πίστεως [ὑμῶν] σωτηρίαν ψυχῶν)· περὶ ἧς σωτηρίας ἐξεζήτησαν καὶ ἐξηρεύνησαν προφῆται. The last two examples are almost comparable with Acts xxvi. 6f., commented above.

It is also possible for a pronoun to be incorporated as an apposition in a relative clause. The following passages are such cases:

Rom. ix. 23ff.: ... σκεύη ἐλέους, ἅ προητοίμασεν εἰς δόξαν, οὕς καὶ ἐκάλησεν ἡμᾶς οὐ μόνον ἐξ Ἰουδαίων ἀλλὰ καὶ ἐξ ἐθνῶν. A predicative conception of the relative pronoun οὕς, which occurs in many translations of this passage,[1] is very debatable, partly because of the gender of the relative pronoun in comparison with the previous ἅ and partly because of the words ἐξ Ἰουδαίων &c. in the following. Only by taking ἡμᾶς as an incorporated apposition is a logical meaning obtained. We wish therefore to translate as follows: »— that is just us, whom He has called, not only from the

---

[1] Examples: »Ainsi nous a-t-il appelés», *La Sainte Bible* ... par L. SEGOND, 1892; »And to be such has He also called us», *Bibeln eller den Heliga Skrift*, 1917; »Zu denen er auch uns berufen hat», H. LIETZMANN, *An die Römer*, 1933, *ad loc.*

vi.] AN APPOSITIONAL ANTECEDENT INCORPORATED 169

Jews ...» &c.[1] In this translation οὓς καί is taken as being equal to οὕσπερ, as it incontrovertibly is many times in the N.T.[2] In this way it is possible to avoid a coordination of the relative clauses which just makes it difficult to explain the gender assimilation in οὕς. Thus the relative clauses will not be coordinated, but οὓς καί will be an attribute to ἡμᾶς, and in this way the gender assimilation in οὕς is satisfactorily explained.[3] The thought that »we» are called not only from the Jews' but also from the Gentiles' ranks is indeed quite natural in the context.

Gal. ii. 10: μόνον τῶν πτωχῶν ἵνα μνημονεύωμεν, ὃ καὶ ἐσπούδασα αὐτὸ τοῦτο ποιῆσαι, »just that, which» ... (comparable with *Herod*. iv. 44: Ἰνδὸν ποταμόν, ὃς κροκοδείλους δεύτερος οὗτος ποταμῶν πάντων παρέχεται, »this the second of all the rivers, which ...»; the incorporation here is quite clear although the relative pronoun is scarcely adjectival).

Notice an analogous complementing of the participle in Phil. i. 7:

... διὰ τὸ ἔχειν με ἐν τῇ καρδίᾳ ὑμᾶς, ἔν τε τοῖς δεσμοῖς μου καὶ ἐν τῇ ἀπολογίᾳ καὶ βεβαιώσει τοῦ εὐαγγελίου συγκοινωνούς μου τῆς χάριτος πάντας ὑμᾶς ὄντας, *i.e.* »in that you are all ...».

EXAMPLES FROM LATER GREEK TEXTS.

Now we shall proceed to some examples from the first centuries A.D. mostly found in common Greek texts.

In the Greek version of the *Res Gestæ Divi Augusti* there are several subordinate clauses with an adjectival relative pronoun

---

[1] *Cf. La Sainte Bible, version Synodale*, 1923, which translates in the following way: »je parle de nous, qu'il a appelés non seulement du milieu des Juifs», &c.

[2] H. J. CADBURY, The Relative Pronouns in Acts and Elsewhere, *Journ. of Bibl. Lit.* xlii, 1923, p. 157. *Cf.* above, p. 146.

[3] In *La Sainte Bible, version d'*OSTERWALD this gender assimilation is totally unexplained by the translation: »et qu'il a aussi appelées, (savoir) nous, non seulement ...» Here ἡμᾶς is certainly taken as an apposition but this relative clause is coordinated with the previous one, and it is just in that way that the difficulty mentioned arises. This is also true of W. J. RUTHERFORD's translation in *St. Paul's Epistles to the Romans*, 1914: »whom also he has called even us, not only from ...»

and a governing noun where the meaning is demonstrative (»relative connection»),[1] as *e.g.* ἐν ᾗ ἀποτειμήσει, = *quo lustro*, a stereotyped phrase, iv. 14, iv. 19, v. 1; [ᾗ]ν ἀρχιερατείαν ... ἀνείληφα, v. 22; ἥτις τειμὴ ... ἐψηφίσθη, vi. 18f.; αἵτινες ἐμαὶ ἐπιδόσεις ἦλθον, viii. 6; ἐν αἷς μονο[μαχίαις ἐμαχέσαντο], xii. 3; ἐξ ἧς αἰτίας, xvii. 22. This is of course sheer literal translations of the Latin phrases but it does show that the construction we are discussing was then possible even in Greek. And in one case the Greek translation uses this relative construction quite spontaneously without any direct correspondence in the Latin, for ἥτις ἀποτείμησις in iv. 12 has in the corresponding Latin only *lustrum*, introducing a principal sentence.[2]

The following examples we have noted from Philo's writings: *Quis rer. div.* 132: ἕκαστον οὖν τῶν τριῶν διεῖλε μέσον, τὴν μὲν ψυχὴν εἰς λογικὸν καὶ ἄλογον, τὸν δὲ λόγον εἰς ἀληθές τε καὶ ψεῦδος, τὴν δὲ αἴσθησιν εἰς καταληπτικὴν φαντασίαν καὶ ἀκατάληπτον· ἅπερ εὐθὺς τμήματα »ἀντιπρόσωπα τίθησιν ἀλλήλοις» (Gen. xv. 10) (»and just these sections ...»).

In Flacc. 75f.: ... προστάττει πάντας περιδυθέντας αἰκισθῆναι μάστιξιν ... ὡς ... εἰς ἀπόγνωσιν σωτηρίας ἐλθεῖν. ἧς ἐπιβουλῆς τὸ μέγεθος ἐξελήλεγκται μὲν καὶ δι' ἑτέρων ...

Lucianus can sometimes write constructions of a similar kind: *Muscæ laud.* v (94): τὴν μὲν γὰρ ἀνδρείαν καὶ τὴν ἀλκὴν αὐτῆς (*scil.* the fly's) οὐχ ἡμᾶς χρὴ λέγειν, ἀλλ' ὃς μεγαλοφωνότατος τῶν ποιητῶν Ὅμηρος. (This is a construction to which we have found analogies just in Homer.)

Epist. saturn. iii. 34 (414): ... ἐν μύθοις συμποτικοῖς καὶ σκώμμασιν ἀνεπαχθέσι καὶ φιλοφροσύναις ποικίλαις συνέσονται, οἷαι ἥδισται διατριβαί, φίλαι μὲν Διονύσῳ καὶ Ἀφροδίτῃ, φίλαι δὲ Χάρισιν.

Sextus Empiricus has an interesting example: *Adv. dogm.* iii. 24: εἰσὶ δὲ οἱ ἀπὸ τῶν γιγνομένων κατὰ τὸν κόσμον παραδόξων ὑπονοήσαντες εἰς ἔννοιαν ἡμᾶς ἐληλυθέναι θεῶν, ἀφ' ἧς φαίνεται εἶναι δόξης καὶ ὁ Δημόκριτος.

---

[1] A. P. M. MEUWEESE, *De rerum gest. D. Augusti vers. gr.*, 1920, p. 109f.
[2] *Op. cit.*, p. 110.

From *Herod. Ab exc. D. Marc.* viii. 1. 5 we have noted: ἐπὶ τὰς Ἄλπεις ... ἅπερ ὄρη ... ὑπερνεφῆ μὲν ... ἐπιμηκέστατα δέ ... Among later authors Porphyrius seems to be a good representative for this method of expression that we are discussing. We have noted the following examples: *De vita Plot.* vii (*Plotinus*, ed. R. VOLKMANN, p. 13, *ll.* 17ff.): εἰς τοσοῦτον ἀποστροφῆς τοῦ βίου τούτου προκεχωρήκει, ὡς πάσης μὲν κτήσεως ἀποστῆναι ... σιτεῖσθαι δὲ παρὰ μίαν· ἀφ' ἧς δὴ ἀποστάσεως καὶ ἀφροντιστίας τοῦ βίου ποδαγρῶντα μὲν οὕτως, ὣς καὶ δίφρῳ βαστάζεσθαι ἀναρρωσθῆναι ... — a case of »relative connection» in which the whole previous description of the man's ascetic moderation is recapitulated by inserting the appositions ἀπόστασις and ἀφροντιστία in the relative clause.

Ibid., xvii (VOLKMANN p. 21, *ll.* 18ff.):»Βασιλεὺς» δὲ τοὔνομα τῷ Πορφυρίῳ ἐμοὶ προσῆν, κατὰ μὲν πάτριον διάλεκτον Μάλχῳ κεκλημμένῳ, ὅπερ μοι καὶ ὁ πατὴρ ὄνομα κέκλητο. Note here the *hyperbaton*. *Cf.* also *Porph. De abstin.* i. 32: ἡ δ' ἀπόστασις γένοιτο μὲν ἂν καὶ μετὰ βίας, γένοιτο δ'ἂν καὶ πειθοῖ καὶ κατὰ λόγον διὰ μαράνσεως καὶ, ὡς ἄν τις εἴποι, λήθης αὐτῶν καὶ θανάτου, ἢ δὴ καὶ ἀρίστη [ἐτύγχανεν] οὖσα ἀπόστασις οὐχ ἧπται οὗ ἀπεσπάσθη. Whether or not the syntactically troublesome ἐτύγχανεν is here included,[1] the relative pronoun is adjectival and conjoint with ἀπόστασις which is an explanatory apposition. It is not impossible that just the predicative superlative has been the special reason for the insertion of the noun in the relative clause, as in the quite typical phrase ταύτην, ἥτις εἴη μεγίστη πίστις from *Dem. Or.* lii. 12 (p. 1239), or as in *Just. Ap.* I, xxx (63): ἥπερ μεγίστη καὶ ἀληθεστάτη ἐπίδειξις καὶ ὑμῖν ... φανήσεται.

From later poetry the following can be quoted:
Apollon. Arg. iv. 562ff.:

... τὰς δ'ἀπέλειπον, ὅσαι Κόλχοισι πάροιθεν
ἑξείης πλήθοντο Λιβυρνίδες εἰν ἁλὶ νῆσοι,
Ἴσσα τε Δυσκέλαδός τε καὶ ἱμερτὴ Πιτύεια.

---

[1] *Delendum*, explains A. NAUCK in his edition of the text.

CONCLUDING REMARKS.

The adjectival use of the relative pronoun already discussed has certainly been facilitated by the analogy which arises when a relative pronoun is used instead of an adnominal interrogative pronoun, which is not at all unusual.[1] The following are some examples:

Il. B. 38:
... οὐδὲ τὰ ᾔδη ἅ ῥα Ζεὺς μήδετο ἔργα.

Aristoph. Eq. 652 f.:
... εἰδὼς ἄρα
οἷς ᾔδεθ' ἡ βουλὴ μάλιστα ῥήμασιν.

Æschin. iii. 94: ... συνέδριον συνήγαγον· ὃν δὲ τρόπον καὶ δι' οἵων κακουργημάτων, ταῦτ' ἤδη ἄξιόν ἐστιν ἀκοῦσαι.

John vi. 14: ἰδόντες ὃ ἐποίησεν σημεῖον.

Julian. Or. i. 16 A: δείξω δὲ μόνον τῆς διατροφῆς τὸ διάφερον, ᾗ χρησάμενος κάλλει καὶ ῥώμῃ καὶ δικαιοσύνῃ καὶ σωφροσύνῃ διήνεγκας.

*

The incorporation of the apposition in the relative clause is thus a phenomenon which, although not perhaps specially usual in the Greek, can really be supported from many quarters and seems mostly to have been accepted as something legitimate and natural. This construction is found as early as in Homer and, in spite of a certain opposition from the Attic rhetoricians, has survived into late Hellenistic times.

By this means we consider that, from the history of language, we have good reason for the conception that 1 Pet. iii. 21 should be explained as a case of such appositional incorporation — *i.e.* the theory which was the starting-point of this syntactical investigation.

---

[1] See, for example, R. WAGNER, *Griechische Grammatik*, 1908, pp. 136 f.

CHAPTER VII.

HOW BAPTISM IS CHARACTERIZED IN 21 B—22.

TWO APPOSITIONS TO THE WORD βάπτισμα.

If we now return to the point in iii. 21 to which we had come before our digression into the Greek syntax we find two appositions to the idea βάπτισμα, which positively and negatively should indicate what, at least in this connection, is to be put forward as distinctive for Christian Baptism: οὐ σαρκὸς ἀπόθεσις ῥύπου, ἀλλὰ συνειδήσεως ἀγαθῆς ἐπερώτημα εἰς θεόν.

It is perhaps not so difficult to understand that Baptism is said not to be a putting away of the filth of the flesh — or possibly the flesh's putting away of its filth. But what Baptism positively is, that is really very difficult to understand. The usual translation [1] »prayer to God for a good conscience» is of course impossible, seeing that Baptism cannot be a prayer and also that »a good conscience» in our usual meaning is not something that one can reasonably pray for — rather this spiritual habit itself should be a prerequisite for undergoing Baptism. The problem is very actively discussed but should not be impossible to solve, if one only begins at the right end and does not bring in irrelevant modern ideas.[2]

---

[1] *E. g.* J. MOFFAT, *The General Epistles*, 1928, pp. 140, 143; J. FELTEN, *Die zwei Briefe*, pp. 112 f.
[2] E. HUTHER, *Kritisch exegetisches Handbuch*, pp. 190 ff., gives indications of the older debate. — In the following we partly agree with such presentations as *e. g.* in J. W. C. WAND, *The General Epistles*, 1934, pp. 101 f., or E. G. SELWYN, *The First Epistle*, pp. 205 f., but try to find a better solution of the problem by directing attention to the term συνείδησις.

As the emphasis lies on the expression συνείδησις ἀγαθή, we should take this as a starting point of the investigation. By means of that we may hope afterwards to solve the other problems.

THE SPECIAL MEANING OF συνείδησις ἀγαθή.

It should be quite clear that it is incorrect so lightly to translate συνείδησις ἀγαθή by »good conscience». In this way one thinks of modern psychological and moral conceptions which may be totally unsuitable in this textual connection.[1] There are certainly a few passages in the N.T. where it seems possible to translate συνείδησις by »conscience» in the meaning of »the voice of the heart», a feeling of blame or innocence, *conscientia consequens*, as possibly in Rom. ii. 15 and at least in John viii. 9 *var. lect.*, but in other passages the word seems to have quite other meanings. The term συνείδησίς in ancient Greek has a much more general content than our word »conscience», whose special significance has developed through the influence of preachers and moralists through many centuries. Here we can only present a few aspects of this Greek idea which are important in our problem and unfortunately has been too much neglected by modern inquirers. Doing so we shall keep more to popular texts than to those of professional philosophers, who may have special technical terminology.[2] The language of the N.T. has also often more affinity with the language of the people.

[1] In general the investigators of this conception in the N.T. have been eager to see indications of our psychological and moral idea »Conscience». This is really to a great extent uncritical wishful thinking. — The latest more important presentation of συνείδησις is that of C. SPICQ, La conscience dans le N.T., *Rev. Bibl.* xlvii, 1938, pp. 50ff. This author shows real feeling for the many variations in the meaning of this word, which we ought to notice. Yet he is not absolutely free from the usual keenness to find counterparts to our idea »conscience». *Cf.* also G. RUDBERG, Ur samvetets historia, *Studier och tankar, tillägn.* J. A. EKLUND, 1933, pp. 171 ff. — Earlier literature collected in W. BAUER, *Griechisch-Deutsches Wöterbuch, s. v.*

[2] A. BONHÖFFER, *Epiktet und das N.T.*, 1911, p. 156f., and after him H. OSBORNE, Συνείδησις, *The Journ. of Theol. Stud.* xxxii, 1931, pp. 168ff., have, among other scholars, shown that one ought not to seek the background of the N.T.'s συνείδησις idea in the Stoics, for the older authors of this school used the term very seldom.

vii.] HOW BAPTISM IS CHARACTERIZED IN 21 B—22 175

(1) Based upon the expression σύνοιδα έμαυτώ, συνείδησις has a fundamental meaning of »consciousness» in general. This idea contains much more than our »conscience». It is connected with the spiritual life in general. And it is certainly not always a question of the theoretical content of the consciousness, (a) a certain judgment for example, but often instead of (b) something voluntative, practical and final, so that we get a meaning something like »temper», »attitude of mind», »disposition», or »intention». Compare the following examples of the second aspect (b): Herodian, *Ab exc. D. Marc.* vii. 1. 3: μηδένα αὐτῷ παρεῖναι ἐκ συνειδήσεως εὐγενοῦς κρείττονα (»mind», »personality»); *Dion. Hal. Ant.* viii. 48. 5: ταῦτα ἥκω δεομένη σου ... πάσης ἀδίκου καὶ ἀνοσίου συνειδήσεως καθαρά (»intention»; »conscience» is impossible because of the attributes); *Ps. Lucian. Amor.* 49: οὐδεμιᾶς ἀπρεποῦς συνειδήσεως παροικούσης (similar); an inscription from Lydia, 2nd century A.D.:[1] ὡς ἱκανοποιοῦσα περὶ τοῦ πεφημίσθαι αὐτὴν ἐν συνειδήσει τοιαύτῃ (»intent»; or perhaps »plot», *cf.* below).

(2) We have, however, also the verbal expression σύνοιδά τινι.[2] On this, too, the term συνείδησις is partly based. In so far as this is the case we get the meaning *consensus* (note the etymological analogy), »consent», »agreement» (*cf.* expressions like to be *einverstanden* or consentient to something), »complicity» (*cf.* the Latin *consensio*, »plot»), »solidarity», »faith», »loyalty» and such words.[3] In this way we come near to expressions such as ὁμολογία, συμπάθεια, or πίστις. *Cf.* also the verb συγγιγνώσκω τινί which corresponds to σύνοιδά τινι (and observe here that συγγνώμη had already got the special meaning of »forgiveness»). In this way the perspective becomes more social than psychological. See the following examples: *Pap. Oxy.* i, no. 123 (3rd—4th cent. A.D.), *ll.* 12 ff.: ἤδη

---

[1] *Supplementum epigraphicum Græcum* iv, 1930, p. 124, no. 648, *ll.* 10f.
[2] *Cf.* R. Kühner, *Ausf. Gramm*, ii, Satzlehre von B. Gerth, ii, pp. 49f.; H. G. Liddell, R. Scott & H. Jones, *A Greek-English Lexicon*, *s.v.* σύνοιδα.
[3] Examples of σύνοιδά τινι in this meaning: *Xen. Mem.* ii. 7. 1: ἐρῶ δὲ καὶ ἐν τούτοις ἃ σύνοιδα αὐτῷ (»intimately know about him»); *Plut. Publ.* iv. 5 (99b): ἐλαυνόμενος τῷ συνειδότι τοῦ πράγματος (»complicity with»); *Acts* v. 2: συνειδυίης καὶ τῆς γυναικός (the wife was also involved in the affair).

γὰρ οἱ τῶν ἄλλων πόλεων (their representatives) συνείδησιν εἰσήνεγκαν τοῖς κολλήγαις αὐτῶν (»agreement»); *Pap. Par.* 21. 14 f.: ὁμολογοῦμεν γνώμῃ ἑκουσίᾳ καὶ αὐθαιρέτῳ βουλήσει καὶ ἀδόλῳ συνειδήσει ... (»guileless consensus»: notice here the intimate connection with the concept ὁμολογία); *Pap. Flor.* iii. 338 (3rd cent. A.D.). 17 f.: οἶδα γὰρ ὅτι συνειδήσι σπουδάζεις ἐμοί (»with solidarity»).

(3) One can also think of others' συνείδησις, in conformity with one's own personality and interests. See for instance *Pap. Par.* 18. 4[1] (2nd cent. A.D.). 7: ὅ]ταν ἰσελθῇς, καλῇ ὥρᾳ, εὑρήσις συνίδησιν, »consent» (*cf.* εὑρήσει πίστιν in Luke xviii. 8). When the word has this function it is not far to the meaning »(social) acknowledgement», »prestige», &c., where one thinks of the objective, of other people's συνείδησις regarding oneself. Here the idea is objectivised. We have the same shifting of the meaning *e.g.* in the English »good-will» which can be used both in a subjective and objective meaning. An example of this is *Demosth. ˙De coron.* (xviii), 110: τὸ γὰρ ὡς τὰ ἄριστά τ' ἔπραττον καὶ διὰ παντὸς εὔνους εἰμὶ καὶ πρόθυμος εὖ ποιεῖν ὑμᾶς, ἱκανῶς ... δεδηλῶσθαί μοι νομίζω ... ὑπολαμβάνων ... παρ' ὑμῶν ἑκάστῳ τὸ συνειδὸς [= συνείδησιν[2]] ὑπάρχειν μοι: »good-will».

We do not think these different meanings of συνείδησις should make it necessary to reckon with different words which accidentally have the same form. On the contrary συνείδησις is we consider throughout the same word, but with many varying aspects.

All these principal meanings in the word συνείδησις seem also to be reflected in the N.T. and similar literature. We have here no room to go through all the relevant passages, but must keep to those that are interesting in connection with the one we are trying to explain.

What must first be regarded in the question of 1 Pet. iii. 21 is of course the use of συνείδησις in other parts of the same Epistle. The word also appears in ii. 19 and iii. 16. It is very important to notice that in both these places συνείδησις is wholly surrounded by expressions which indicate that it must have the meaning of

---

[1] W. BRUNET DE PRESLE & E. EGGER, *Les papyrus grecs*, 1866, p. 422.
[2] See the lexica.

a certain practical direction of the will and attitude to society. This is especially clear in iii. 16. Here συνείδησις ἀγαθή must be considered as completing the exhortation to appear before the pagans with humility and respect; it must in some way harmonize with the words about good Christian habits which are thought to be an active reason for the pagans to change round to a more favourable conception of the Christians from a juridical and social point of view. One must also presume a certain agreement with ἀγαθοποιοῦντας in verse 17 (note the γάρ). Without such relations to the practically demonstrated character and the social attitude the idea συνείδησις ἀγαθή would here simply be left isolated. Compare the aspects of the word touched upon above in (1 b) and (2). To bring out the not theoretical but voluntative and social meaning which we must here presume, it would perhaps be best to say »good attitude» or »good-will». Here »good» has a special meaning of »blameless», »loyal». Cf. ἀγαθή ἀναστροφή in the same verse. The expression συνείδησις θεοῦ in ii. 19 must have something like the same import. The meaning cannot be »consciousness of God», because for the sake of such an internal fact (διά with the accusative must mean »for the sake of», it can scarcely indicate certain circumstances)[1] no one could really be punished. Here we must also consider the harmony with the following ἀγαθοποιοῦντες. The meaning should thus be something like »because of the attitude (of mind) which belongs to God».[2] The word θεοῦ is here taken as genitive of quality. Notice also the textual variants συνείδησιν ἀγαθήν with and without θεοῦ. Compare the above aspect of the term in question mentioned under (1 b).

For the rest both passages must, of course, be seen against the background of the great parenetic connection which begins with ii. 11 and goes on to iv. 19 and where one and the same thesis is stressed several times, namely: by blameless habits in loyal humility

---

[1] As is assumed if the expression is translated »with God before his eyes» or something similar. Cf. A. DEBRUNNER, F. Blass' Grammatik, § 222, p. 102.
[2] Cf. also the variant συνείδησις (τοῦ εἰδώλου) instead of συνήθεια in 1 Cor. viii. 7. These two words do not seem so heterogeneous to the reader who recognises our theory of συνείδησις.

and patience the Christian should frustrate all complaints from outsiders, ii. 12, 13ff., 18ff., iii. 1ff., 5ff., 14ff., iv. 14ff. Notice especially the passage ii. 13—17 corresponding to Rom. xiii which treats of a subjection to the state authorities and a positive political attitude. The extensive quotation from Ps. xxxiii (xxxiv) is evidently also intended to exhort the Christians to a blameless and humble behaviour in what concerns the community. In all the passages mentioned a general use of certain fundamental ideas can be observed, such as patience, freedom from fear, humility, ἀγαθοποιΐα, a striving after the good, a good way of life &c.: the συνείδησις in ii. 19 and iii. 16 must be interpreted in analogy with these ideas. The chief emphasis therefore lies not upon what the believers feel within themselves but on their honest and loyal attitude, so that their environment can have a good conception of the Christians' disposition and intention. This is what we mean when we suggest the translation »good-will» in iii. 16.

It is not at all unprecedented in the N.T. that συνείδησις should have this meaning. It is on the contrary a typical aspect of the N.T.'s συνείδησις idea which we have here found indicated.

Such cases, where it is mostly a question of the individual's character, disposition, intention, the direction of his will and feelings — cf. above under (1 b) — we probably find in the words about πονηρὰν συνείδησιν in Hebr. x. 22: ῥεραντισμένοι τὰς καρδίας ἀπὸ συνειδήσεως πονηρᾶς, and *Herm. Mand.* iii. 4: ἔδει ... πονηρὰν συνείδησιν μετὰ τοῦ πνεύματος τῆς ἀληθείας μὴ κατοικεῖν — in both cases the word seems to mean »evil disposition» or »tendency to evil», cf. the Hebrew יֵצֶר הָרַע. See further *Ign. Ad Smyrn.* xi. 1: οὐκ ἐκ συνειδότος ἀλλ' ἐκ χάριτος θεοῦ, »not by his own intention but by God's grace» (συνειδός = συνείδησις[1]).

The more social aspect of συνείδησις which we touched upon above under (2) is of still greater importance. Actually every time συνείδησις, with the attribute ἀγαθή or καλή, is found in the N.T. and in the earliest Church writings we have this idea συνείδησις with a meaning of good-will and solidarity. See Acts xxiii. 1:

---
[1] See above, p. 176.

πάση συνειδήσει ἀγαθῇ (»good-will», in a subjective meaning) πεπολίτευμαι τῷ θεῷ ἄχρι ταύτης τῆς ἡμέρας; *cf.* with this xxiv. 16: ἀσκῶ ἀπρόσκοπον συνείδησιν (»good-will», partly also in an objective meaning) ἔχειν πρὸς τὸν θεὸν καὶ τοὺς ἀνθρώπους διὰ παντός (these passages are from two of Paul's speeches). In Hebr. xiii. 18 we find precisely the same correspondence between συνείδησις and ἀναστροφή as in the passages of 1 Pet. under discussion. We suggest that here also καλὴν συνείδησιν should be translated by »good-will». Attention is directed towards the will to blameless behaviour: see the continuation καλῶς (*cf.* καλὴν) θέλοντες ἀναστρέφεσθαι (it would be nonsense to say πειθόμεθα ὅτι if it was a question of the inner voice). In 1 Tim. we also find συνείδησις ἀγαθή. There it is not so much a question of solidarity with the state, for this problem is discussed rather carefully in this Epistle, but of consensus with the teaching of the Church. See ch. i. 5, where συνείδησις ἀγαθή is clearly concerned with ἀγάπη as a means of concord, and with the genuine Church belief.[1] The best translation is probably »good consent» (to the creed of the Church). The relations are the same in i. 19. This Church solidarity and loyalty is reflected still more clearly in the Apostolic Fathers. We find a specially illuminating example of this in *Ign. Ad Magn.* iv where the word εὐσυνείδητος occurs, a word which must be termed equal to συνείδησιν ἀγαθὴν ἔχων: πρέπον ... μὴ μόνον καλεῖσθαι Χριστιανοὺς, ἀλλὰ καὶ εἶναι· ὥσπερ καί τινες ἐπίσκοπον μὲν καλοῦσιν, χωρὶς δὲ αὐτοῦ πάντα πράσσουσιν. οἱ τοιοῦτοι δὲ οὐκ εὐσυνείδητοί μοι εἶναι φαίνονται, διὰ τὸ μὴ βεβαίως κατ' ἐντολὴν συναθροίζεσθαι. A rather accurate translation seems to be: »quite loyal [to the Church]». Compare *Ign. Ad Trall.* vii. 2 where we have the same *motif*: ὁ χωρὶς ἐπισκόπου καὶ πρεσβυτερίου καὶ διακόνου πράσσων τι, οὗτος οὐ καθαρός ἐστιν τῇ συνειδήσει (quite irreproachable concerning his consent, *scil.* to the creed of the Church). See also 1 Clem. xxxiv. 7: ἐν ὁμονοίᾳ ἐπὶ τὸ αὐτὸ

---

[1] The relation between συνείδησις and faith seems to us clear from 1 Cor. viii, where Paul differentiates between those who have strong and weak συνείδησις, which in a certain connection must form a close parallel to Rom. xiv. 1ff. with its basic thesis ὃς μὲν πιστεύει, »has enough faith to».

συναχθέντες τῇ συνειδήσει, and xlv. 7: οἱ ἐν καθαρᾷ συνειδήσει λατρεύοντες. In respect of the positive and loyal attitude, laid down by God, towards superiors in community and family, συνείδησις ἀγαθή occurs in 1 Clem. i. 3: ἐν τοῖς νομίμοις τοῦ θεοῦ ἐπορεύεσθε, ὑποτασσόμενοι τοῖς ἡγουμένοις ὑμῶν ... γυναιξίν τε ἐν ἀμώμῳ καὶ σεμνῇ καὶ ἁγνῇ συνειδήσει πάντα ἐπιτελεῖν παρηγγέλετε, στεργούσας καθηκόντως τοὺς ἄνδρας ἑαυτῶν· ἔν τε τῷ κανόνι τῆς ὑποταγῆς ὑπαρχούσας ... οἰκουργεῖν. This is precisely the same idea as in the exhortation of the wives to a ἁγνὴ ἀναστροφή in 1 Pet. iii. 1—6 (thus the idea συνείδησις ἀγαθή could also have been used here). We have a similar parenetic *motif* in *Polyc*. v. 3: τὰς παρθένους ἐν ἀμώμῳ καὶ ἁγνῇ συνειδήσει περιπατεῖν (notice that it concerns their habits). In 1 Clem. xli. 1 it is a question of the general Christian life in different positions with »loyalty» or »good-will» towards God: ἕκαστος ... εὐαρεστείτω θεῷ ἐν ἀγαθῇ συνειδήσει ὑπάρχων, μὴ παρεκβαίνων τὸν ὡρισμένον τῆς λειτουργίας αὐτοῦ κανόνα, but in 1 Clem. ii. 4 συνείδησις probably implies interest for the religious well-being of the brother: ἀγὼν ἦν ὑμῖν ἡμέρας τε καὶ νυκτὸς ὑπὲρ πάσης τῆς ἀδελφότητος, εἰς τὸ σῴζεσθαι μετ' ἐλέους καὶ συνειδήσεως τὸν ἀριθμὸν τῶν ἐκλεκτῶν αὐτοῦ, with pity and »solidarity» or »sympathy» (*cf.* the above quotation from *Pap. Flor.* iii).

The idea of social συνείδησις in an objectivized sense, mentioned above under (3), is also found in the N.T. and in the Apostolic Fathers. So quite clearly in *Ign. Ad Philad.* vi. 3: εὐσυνείδητός εἰμι ἐν ὑμῖν, »I have a good will with you, »am well with you». This aspect should be suitable as regards Rom. xiii. 5: διὰ τὴν συνείδησιν, »with respect to [your] good-will with the authorities» (notice that ὀργή also has reference to the other component in the relation under discussion, the state), 2 Cor. i. 12: τὸ μαρτύριον τῆς συνειδήσεως ἡμῶν, »the testimony of our good-will» (refers to the fact just mentioned of intercession and thanksgiving on behalf of Paul), and 2 Cor. iv. 2: πρὸς πᾶσαν συνείδησιν ἀνθρώπων: »to obtain (πρός can scarcely mean »with», »in»: it should rather have a final meaning) all kinds of recognition from people». *Cf.* also Acts xxiv. 16 (see above).

HOW BAPTISM IS CHARACTERIZED IN 21 B—22

Now we have material for an interpretation of συνείδησις in 1 Pet. iii. 21. There is of course good reason here first to take up the voluntative and social meaning we found that συνείδησις has in ii. 19 and iii. 16: »attitude of mind» and »good-will». Above all it is valuable to place our passage in such correspondence with iii. 16 as must be peculiarly reasonable because of the similarity of the words, and the nearness, and the relations to the parenesis in 13—16 which we have otherwise observed. Besides that there is, as we have seen, a great amount of general material to exemplify these aspects of συνείδησις — see above under (1 b) and (2).

In this way there is a good linguistic analogy to the phrase so similar as to its content, ῥεραντισμένοι τὰς καρδίας ἀπὸ συνειδήσεως πονηρᾶς in Hebr. x. 22, where the allusion also is to Baptism. Just previous to that phrase we read προσερχώμεθα μετὰ ἀληθινῆς καρδίας ἐν πληροφορίᾳ πίστεως, and immediately afterwards the author says: κατέχωμεν τὴν ὁμολογίαν τῆς ἐλπίδος ἀκλινῆ, and speaks of ἀγάπη, καλὰ ἔργα and of solidarity with the Church community. Thus here too the idea συνείδησις is combined with way of living and it must also here be true of character, intention, the direction of the will. Similarly it is a question of loyalty, certainly not to the state but to the brothers.

We presume therefore the meaning »good or loyal attitude of mind» or »good-will» in 1 Pet. iii. 21. Here it is clear, however, that one must not only think of loyalty to the state authorities as in verse 16. Seeing that Christian Baptism is being discussed it should primarily be loyalty towards the commandments of God in the main that the author is considering. He recalls the duty to obey God and suffer patiently if that is necessary. Loyalty to authorities is, however, certainly also implied. We have just seen several examples from the writings of the Apostolic Fathers where συνείδησις can mean loyalty to God, the Church, the Creed and the fellow-creatures, partly in a religious meaning and partly in a profane, social meaning.[1] And it is clear from many passages in the N.T. that civil and political good behaviour shall be for God's

---
[1] *Cf.*, above, pp. 179 f.

own sake and to make possible undisturbed relationship with God, so that blamelessness before God or Christ and people are intimately connected and are two sides of the same thing: see for instance ὑποτάγητε πάσῃ ἀνθρωπίνῃ κτίσει διὰ τὸν κύριον in 1 Pet. ii. 13.[1] When the author speaks of συνείδησις in iii. 21 he refers to the willingness to fulfil loyally the whole of God's will, even as regards the duties towards the worldly authorities.

In this way, however, we have again confirmed that the author purposes in his different remarks to support the whole time his previous exhortation to an undaunted behaviour before the pagans.

WHAT THEN IS ἐπερώτημα?

Innumerably varying meanings to the word ἐπερώτημα in iii. 21 have been given by different authors. We will not repeat these in detail.[2] All earlier scientific theories seem to have issued from the psychologizing translation of συνείδησις by »good conscience». This must have been very misleading, especially as there is not elsewhere much linguistic material available for an explanation of this term. The word ἐπερώτημα is *hapax legomenon* in the N.T. although it appears in Dan. iv. 17 (14) according to Theodotion and in Ecclus. xxxvi (xxxiii). 3 *var. lect.*

It has often been assumed that ἐπερώτημα in 1 Pet. means »prayer» because ἐπερωτᾶν can have this meaning in Biblical language. But the verb has this meaning only in Ps. cxxxvi (cxxxvii). 3 *var. lect.* as a translation of שאל, »ask» or »pray», and possibly in Matt. xvi. 1.[3] But to reconstruct a meaning of »prayer» only on this ground is not advisable. The idea of »prayer» is actually quite unthinkable in this connection, where we are to obtain a definition of the essence of Baptism.

On the other hand the word often occurs in classical Greek in

---

[1] Further, Acts xxiii. 1, xxiv. 16, Rom. xiii. 1ff., xiv. 18, 1 Cor. viii. 11f., x. 31ff., 2 Cor. i. 12, viii. 21, Phil. i. 27, ii. 15f., Eph. vi. 5ff., Col. iii. 22ff., 1 Tim. ii. 2f., Tit. iii. 1ff., 1 Pet. ii. 15.

[2] See E. HUTHER, *Kritisch exegetisches Handbuch*, pp. 191ff.

[3] H. CREMER & J. KÖGEL, *Biblisch-theologisches Wörterbuch*, 1915, p. 454.

the meaning »question», e.g. in Thuc. iii. 53. 2, 68. 1. This seems also to be the fundamental meaning of the word.

Strangely enough, however, ἐπερώτημα can clearly also have the meaning »answer», »resolution» or »declaration». Perhaps it is the question put by an oracular institution to a god which has been transferred and so obtained such a meaning — (ἐπ)ερωτάω is a professional term for asking the gods for advice.[1] This meaning is found in certain official texts: W. DITTENBERGER, *Sylloge inscriptionum græcarum* no. 856 (2nd cent. A.D.), *l.* 6: κατὰ τὸ ἐπερώτημα τῶν κρατίστων Ἀρεοπαγειτῶν [Ἀθ.], »according to the resolution of»; *ibid.*, no. 977, *ll.* 1ff.: καθότι καὶ ὁ θεὸς ἔ[χρ]ησε[ν· τ]ᾶς δ' ἐπερωτάσεως (here, of course, = ἐπερώτημα) καὶ τοῦ χρησμοῦ ἀντιγραφά ἐστι τάδε, »just as the god declared: the record of the oracular response and the divine word is as follows»; *ibid.*, *ll.* 21ff. (a similar phrase); *ibid.*, no. 1008, *ll.* 2ff.: καθ' ὑπομνηματισμὸν τῆς ἐξ Ἀρείου πάγου βουλῆς καὶ ἐπερώτημα τῆς βουλῆς τῶν φ' καὶ τοῦ δήμου [Ἀθ.], »according to the decision of ... and the sanction of ...». This meaning of oracular response, »declaration» and similar words is probably found in the passages mentioned in the LXX, Dan. iv. 17 (14) according to Theodotion: διὰ συγκρίματος εἰρ (the »Watchers») ὁ λόγος, καὶ ῥῆμα ἁγίων τὸ ἐπερώτημα, »and a word from the Holy Ones is the (oracular) declaration»,[2] and Ecclus. xxxvi (xxxiii). 3 according to the MS א: ἄνθρωπος συνετὸς ἐνπιστεύσει νόμῳ, καὶ ὁ νόμος αὐτῷ πιστὸς ὡς ἐπερώτημα δήλων, »as reliable as a reply[3] from Urim and Thummim».

To a certain extent this official use of ἐπερώτημα agrees with the meaning *stipulatio*, »agreement», »undertaking», or »contract», of which we find some examples in juridical texts. The explanation of this meaning is that, according to ancient use, a contract was made by means of oral questioning or, as it is stated in E. FORCELLI-

---

[1] W. BAUER, *Griechisch-Deutsches Wörterbuch*, s.v., col. 473; H. GREEVEN, ἐρωτάω, G. KITTEL, *Theol. Wört.*, ii, pp. 683, 685.
[2] CREMER & KÖGEL, *loc. cit.*: *das Urteil*; H. GREEVEN, *loc. cit.*, p. 685: *Urteil, Entscheidung*.
[3] The Swedish Translation of the Apocrypha, 1921, has also understood the passage in this way.

NI's great Latin dictionary: *Stipulatio est contractus qui fit per interrogationem unius, v. gr.* »*decem dare spondes?*», *et alterius responsionem,* »*spondeo*» *vel* »*dabo*».[1] An instance of this meaning of ἐπερώτημα is found in *Pap. Cair. Preis.,*[2] no. 1 (2nd cent. A.D.), *l.* 16: ἐὰν γὰρ μηδὲν ἐπερώτημα ᾖ ἐνγεγρα[μμένον], »for if no undertaking[3] is written there»,[4] and in *Cod. Justin.* viii. 10. 12. 3 b: ἐκ τῶν συμφώνων ἤτοι ἐπερωτημάτων, »by agreements or undertakings». *Cf.* (ἐπ)ερώτησις in the same sense in *Cod. Justin., ibid.,* 1 a: ἐκ συμφώνου ἢ ἐπερωτήσεως; *Pap. Masp.* 158 (6th cent. A.D.), *l.* 29: ὥστε ταῦτα τῷ ἐμμένοντι μέρει ἐξ ἐπερωτήσεως, »so that this shall be paid to the party faithful to the agreement on the basis of the undertaking»; *ibid.*, no. 299, *l.* 56: ἐκ συμφώνου καὶ ἐπερωτήσεως; *Pap. Lond.* 1660 (6th cent. A.D.), *l.* 42: λόγῳ προστίμου ἐξ ἐρωτήσεως καὶ παραβάσεως: »on the basis of agreement and (later) transgression»: also *Pap. Oxy.* ix. 1205 (A.D. 291), *ll.* 9 f.: ἐπερωτήσεώς τε γενομένης [ὡμολογήσαμεν], »after agreement we declared». This last sentence shows clearly the connection with the standing formula ἐπερωτηθεὶς ὡμολόγησα constantly met with in papyrus texts containing contracts and similar things, meaning »I declared my consent to it» or »I undertook to do that».[5] See, for example, *Pap. Oxy.* vi, no. 905 (A.D. 170), *l.* 20; *Dura Pg.* 22 (A.D. 204):[6] ἐρωτηθεὶς ἔγραφα ... ὁμολογεῖ{ν} δὲ ὁ ὑπάνω;[7] *Pap. Tebt.* ii, no. 378 (A.D. 265), *ll.* 30, 34; *Pap. Osl.* no. 37 (295 A.D.), *ll.* 18 f., *Pap. Genev.* i, no. 42 (A.D. 224—225), *l.* 31.

---

[1] According to the edition of CORRADINI: J. FACCIOLATI, M. FORCELLINI ... & F. CORRADINI, *Lexicon totius latinitatis*, iv, 1887, p. 492.

[2] FR. PREISIGKE, *Griechische Urkunden des Ägyptischen Museums zu Kairo*, 1911, p. 1.

[3] The editor renders ἐπερώτημα by *stipulatio*, with the assent of U. WILCKEN.

[4] *Cf.* FR. PREISIGKE, *Fachwörter des öffentlichen Verwaltungsdienstes Ägyptens*, 1915, p. 82: »Wenn die Schuldurkunde keine Angelobung (ἐπερωτηθεὶς ὡμολόγησα) enthält.»

[5] *Cf.* M. MODICA, *Introduzione allo studio della papirologia giuridica*, 1913, p. 128.

[6] *The Excavations at Dura—Europos*, vi, 1936, p. 432.

[7] It is valuable to have now a record of this formula from another quarter than Egypt and from a rather early epoch.

The verb also occurs in an active construction: *Dura Pg.* 22 (A.D. 204):[1] πίστι ἐκπ>ερώτησαν ἀλλήλοις καὶ ὡμολόγησαν ἀλλήλοις; *Dura P.* 73 (A.D. 251):[2] πίστι ἐπηρώτησεν 'Α. καὶ πίστι ὡμολόγησεν Γ.; *Pap. Oxy.* x, no. 1273 (A.D. 260), *ll.* 40f.: περὶ δὲ τοῦ ταῦτα ὀρθῶς καλῶς γείνεσθαι ἀλλήλους ἐπερωτήσαντ[ε]ς ὡμολόγησαν.[3]

The word ἐπερώτημα as a professional term for the making of a contract probably arose from these questions. They have given their name to the whole proceeding.

From this meaning we have certainly the best possibilities for a really satisfactory understanding of 1 Pet. iii. 21.[4] If we now connect up our earlier observations regarding συνείδησις we obtain a quite natural and satisfactory translation, »an agreement about» or »an undertaking to a loyal attitude of mind» or »a good-will». The genitive of συνείδησις here becomes an objective genitive or a genitive of the content. The questioning party in this agreement is God, the Church, He who administers Baptism or some other similar authority. The answering party is the candidate for Baptism. Either the author is thinking of a special act in the ritual of Baptism, perhaps a statement of belief or something similar, or else he terms Baptism an agreement or an undertaking only in a general meaning. We shall see below some interesting features of Christian Baptism which can illustrate the case.[5]

To define the Christian act of initiation as an undertaking to be loyal towards God and men fits very well in this connection. It is quite natural that Baptism is defined as an undertaking in an ethical meaning. But it is not very natural to let Baptism be merely termed a question, which ἐπερώτημα literally signifies,

---

[1] *The Excavations at Dura—Europos, ibid.*

[2] *Op. cit.*, p. 437.

[3] See also J. H. Moulton & G. Milligan, *The Vocabulary of the New Testament illustrated from the Papyri*, iii, 1919, pp. 231f.; F. Preisigke, *Wörterbuch der griechischen Papyrusurkunden*, hrsg. von E. Kiessling, i, 1925, col. 538.

[4] *Cf.* M. L. Smith, 1 Peter III 21. Ἐπερώτημα, in *The Exp. Times* xxiv, 1912—13, p. 47; G. C. Richards, 1 Pet. iii 21, *The Journ. of Theol. Stud.* xxxii, 1931, p. 77. — *Cf.* also »Œcumenius» *ad loc.* (*P.G.* cxix, col. 560 B): ἐπερώτημα=ἀρραβών, ἐνέχυρον, ἀπόδειξις.

[5] See below, pp. 191 ff.

and it is also both practically and linguistically impossible to make it a »prayer». On the other hand, after stating that Baptism has the power to save, it is quite natural to insert this reservation, as a parenthesis, that it is not a removal of carnal impurity but a positive moral undertaking. Baptism does not save unconditionally but only on certain conditions, the author seems to say — naturally with a parenetic object to stress still further what he has already said in his exhortations. Baptism implies an acceptance of the divine demand for a positive habit of mind in loyalty to God and man. As to the latter it includes a humble, loyal and benevolent attitude to the pagans and their rulers. Yet this does not imply any association with heathen ways, but a complete preservation of the Christian peculiar hope of freedom, ii. 11, 16 &c. This contrast between a purification of the flesh and a positive, moral undertaking (οὐκ—ἀλλά) is really logically acceptable. But clearly this cannot be said of an antithesis which arises through other prevalent translations such as »prayer to God for a good conscience», »the prayer of a good conscience to God», or similar suggestions.[1]

In this way we also get an interesting analogy to a sentence in Rom. x. 10: στόματι ὁμολογεῖται εἰς σωτηρίαν — notice νῦν σῴζει in 1 Pet. The formal phrase ἐπερωτηθεὶς ὡμολόγησα can be combined not only with ἐπερώτημα but also with ὁμολογία which is a close equivalent.[2] As regards indicating Baptism as an obligation notice should also be directed to the expressions εἰς ὑπακοὴν καὶ ῥαντισμὸν αἵματος Ἰησοῦ Χριστοῦ in 1 Pet. i. 2 and τέκνα ὑπακοῆς in i. 14 which probably also refer to baptisees.

WHERE DOES εἰς θεόν BELONG?

The words εἰς θεόν can either be referred to ἐπερώτημα or to συνείδησις. Both conceptions are equally possible as regards the meanings of these terms which we have now found.

---

[1] P. LUNDBERG's proposal, *La typologie baptismale*, pp. 114 f., to interpret ἐπερώτημα as »demande d'une audience», »pour trouver accès de Dieu», gives a good practical continuity but lacks philological justification.

[2] M. L. SMITH, *op. cit.*, p. 47.

HOW BAPTISM IS CHARACTERIZED IN 21 B—22

Yet for linguistic reasons we prefer to refer εἰς θεόν to ἐπερώτημα as is also most natural considering the position of the words immediately after the latter. Certainly we may have an argument for the other theory in the sentence ἀπρόσκοπον συνείδησιν ἔχειν πρὸς τὸν θεὸν καὶ τοὺς ἀνθρώπους, Acts xxiv. 16, but there the word is πρός and not εἰς. A more convincing argument for the second theory is, however, found in a sentence like the following: ἐρωτῶ σε εἰς τὴν θεῶν εὐσέβειαν, *Pap. Giess.* 66 (beginning of the 2nd cent. A.D.). 8ff. *Cf.* ὀμνύναι εἴς τι, Matt. v. 35. This shows that εἰς can be used of the person or thing »by» or »before» whom or which an oath or other assurance is given. Such a meaning: »an agreement», »a pledge» or an »assurance before God of a loyal attitude of mind» gives a natural and good meaning to our passage.

PURPOSE OF THE NEGATIVE REMARKS ABOUT PHYSICAL UNCLEANNESS.

Whether σαρκός in iii. 21 is subjective or objective genitive does not matter as regards the content. Perhaps one should rather take it to be objective genitive because of the analogy with συνειδήσεως.[1]

Sometimes the first negative and then positive remarks concerning Baptism in 1 Pet. iii. 21 are combined with Hebr. x. 22. There is also a similarity in the use of the idea συνείδησις as we have already stated. On the other hand there is this difference that in 1 Pet. Baptism is said not to imply a physical purifying, while Hebr. x. 22 assumes that without reservation

Why then does the author in 1 Pet. especially state that Baptism is not merely a physical cleansing? Some will answer that he wishes to present the sacramental purification of Baptism as something superior and more valuable than a merely physical cleansing.[2] But this does not seem to be satisfactory, seeing that such a thesis would be merely a truism. So much ought to be quite clear to the candidates however new they are to Christianity, that Baptism is a sacrament with spiritual effects and not a mere physical washing.

---

[1] *Cf.* above, p. 185.
[2] So *e.g.* E. G. SELWYN, *The First Epistle*, p. 204.

This did not need to be stated. And οὐ as correlative of ἀλλά is not equivalent to οὐ μόνον, but it means an absolute denying, so that the antithesis is quite exclusive (cf. for instance οὐ φθαρτοῖς ... ἀλλά in 1 Pet. i. 18 or several similar expressions in Phil. ii. 3—7[1]). It is not an insufficient estimation of the sacramental energy of Baptism that is repudiated. No, the author appears to reject a positively erroneous baptismal theory and practice, namely a ritual purifying with a mere physical or material blamelessness as its aim. The object of his remark is not to give information, but to polemize against a faulty theory of the sacrament. What we here must think of is, of course, specially Judaism with its zeal for ceremonial cleansing — but possibly also corresponding pagan theories of observance.

The same contrast between the early Christian and especially the Jewish cleansing and the συνείδησις of the Christian faith is found in Hebr. ix. 13f. although there is no mention of Baptism in this text. These purifications are termed »dead works» in verse 14, that is valueless observances (see also vi. 1), from which the blood of Christ cleanses our συνείδησις to the worship of the Living God. Here too συνείδησις must on account of its connection with works and the worship of God mean »mind», »attitude», »will» (not »conscience», something that cannot be cleansed from »dead works»). The resemblance to 1 Pet. iii. 21 is very great. In both cases it is a question of denying purely ritual cleansing actions and a direction of »the will» towards a life in subjection to God. The thought of suffering is also there in Hebr. as is clear from the remark about »the blood». There is another analogy in Tit. i. 14f. The readers are here exhorted to repudiate the Jewish teaching and commandments which involve an impure συνείδησις. As we shall try to show later on,[2] the writer of the Epistle to Titus here directs himself against the tendency to negative isolationism in regard to the pagan

---

[1] On οὐκ—ἀλλά in Phil. ii. 6 see A. FRIDRICHSEN, »Icke akta för rov», *Nysvenska Studier*, 1945, pp. 67 ff., with further references.

[2] Below, ch. x.

world and the superiors, which is in conflict with τῇ ὑγιαινούσῃ διδασκαλίᾳ (ii. 1).

With these analogies we want to combine the remark in 1 Pet. iii. 21 that Baptism is not a removal of physical uncleanness. The meaning is probably that the ceremonial purification must not be over-emphasized so that it results in isolationism from the pagan world. Here we have again an opportunity to connect with the theme in the parenesis, that the Christians should appear before the pagans without fear.

The term ἀπόθεσις, however, also demands special attention. It indicates an active personal action and reveals clearly that the author is not only thinking of how the water of Baptism cleanses the body in a physical meaning, but how the candidates themselves in the sacramental action »deposit», »lay aside», »put off» uncleanness. This is also illustrated by 1 Pet. ii. 1: ἀποθέμενοι οὖν πᾶσαν κακίαν καὶ πάντα δόλον &c. Here, too, it is baptisees who are being addressed, as appears from the context. The same verb, always in the aorist ἀποθέσθαι, is used several times in the N.T. Epistles of removing the evil &c., Rom. xiii. 12, Eph. iv. 22, 25, Col. iii. 8, Hebr. xii. 1, James i. 21 (ῥυπαρίαν). Here is a technical term in the epistolary pareneses used in a certain connection. As a correlate to the exhortations to »put off» the old man there often arises immediately afterwards an appeal to »put on», ἐνδύσασθαι, the new man with righteousness, holiness &c., Rom. xiii. 12—14, Eph. iv. 24, Col. iii. 10, 12. Thus both these expressions are in a traditional correlation to each other.[1] To ἀπόθεσις in 1 Pet. iii. 21 we can also find such a correlate. In iv. 1 we find τὴν αὐτὴν ἔννοιαν ὁπλίσασθε, the latter verb being clearly analogous to ἐνδύσασθαι as *e.g.* in Rom. xiii. 12 with the accusative ὅπλα τοῦ φωτός &c. And ἔννοια is almost a double of συνείδησις as we have interpreted this word: »intention».[2] In this way we get an idea that the antithesis between

---

[1] PH. CARRINGTON, *The Primitive Christian Catechism*, 1940, pp. 47f.; E. G. SELWYN, *op. cit.*, pp. 393ff.

[2] Here the word ἔννοια cannot mean »thought», for then it would be nonsense to speak of »the same», τὴν αὐτήν. The »thought» of Christ at His suffering and death does not interest the Biblical authors. No, but the mind or inten-

ἀπόθεσις ῥύπου and ἀγαθῆς συνειδήσεως ἐπερώτημα is not only logical according to the idiomatic meanings of the terms but also can be placed in a traditional connection. It is certainly not difficult now to connect these terms »put off» and »put on» also with certain practical points of the Christian baptismal ceremonies, as we know them from the service of the Early Church. We ought here, of course, to think about the baptismal renunciations and the symbolic removal of the candidate's clothes on the one hand[1] and the investiture, the putting on of a white garment and other emblems on the other.[2] Thus the writers of the Epistles quoted above probably allude to the Christian baptismal rites when they use these expressions.[3] It is also not difficult to see that the writer of 1 Pet. probably did the same, as he specially mentions Baptism.

We can thus assume that in 1 Pet. iii. 21 the writer defines the essence of Christian Baptism by allusions to two points of its ritual. When he speaks of the removal of physical uncleanness, his expression is a reflex from the removal of the clothes in connection with the renunciations. And when he speaks of positive ethical duties in the words about a good συνείδησις, this, too, has its practical basis in the baptismal ritual. In part the idea συνείδησις is very near ἔννοια, i.e. what the Christians according to iv. 1 should »arm themselves with» so that here we have a certain analogy to the »putting on», the »investiture» in Baptism. In part also the religious and ethical undertakings are a characteristic part of Baptism in the Early Church: namely in the positive side of the

tion that Christ had should be a suitable pattern for the Christians. The word ἔννοια also means »intention» in Hebr. iv. 12, parallel with ἐνθύμησις. Cf. the sensible remarks on 1 Pet. iv. 1 in E. G. SELWYN, op. cit., pp. 208f., where »principle», »counsel», »mind» are suggested as translations of ἔννοια, besides which a number of parallel texts are quoted. See also below, pp. 202f.

[1] See e.g. P. DE PUNIET, Baptême, Dict. d'archéol. chrét. ii. 1, cols. 278, 291 ff.; cf. the text from Theodore of Mopsuestia, below, pp. 191 ff.

[2] According to the text from Theodore of Mopsuestia mentioned below, and other testimonies. — A combination with the renunciations &c. already in H. GROTIUS, Annotationes, ad loc.

[3] Regarding Eph. see N. A. DAHL, Dopet i Efesierbrevet, Svensk Teol. Kvartalskr. xxi. 2, 1945, pp. 93f., 96.

renunciations and the Creed. We shall illustrate this further by going through a few important baptismal texts of the Early Church which confirm the whole of the conception of 1 Pet. iii. 21 here put forward.

COMPARISON OF SOME IMPORTANT BAPTISMAL TEXTS OF THE EARLY CHURCH.

Among our most important sources of the liturgical and dogmatic history of Baptism in the Early Church is Theodore of Mopsuestia's *Commentary on the Lord's Prayer and on the Sacraments of Baptism and the Eucharist*, made accessible to scientific research by means of A. MINGANA's edition 1933.[1] This is rightly termed by the editor of outstanding importance for the historical and theological background of our Sacraments,[2] and Theodore's theories on Baptism seem to the editor even more archaic than those in the *Apostolic Constitutions*,[3] which otherwise play a very important part for all investigators in this sphere.

We shall now consider what this text says of the baptismal renunciation and the Creed. The synopsis of chapter iii is as follows:[4]

»You stand barefooted on sackcloth while your outer garment is taken off from you and your hands are stretched towards God in the posture of one who prays. First you genuflect while the rest of your body is erect, and then you say: 'I abjure Satan and all his angels, and all his works, and all his service, and all his deception, and all his worldly glamour; and I engage myself and believe, and am baptised in the name of the Father, and of the Son and of the Holy Spirit.' While you are genuflecting, and the rest of your body is erect, and your look is directed towards heaven, and your hands are outstretched in the posture of one who prays, the priest, clad in linen robes that are clean and shining, signs you on your forehead with the holy Chrism and says: 'So and so is signed in the name of the Father, and of the Son and of the Holy Spirit.' And your godfather who is standing behind you spreads an orarium of linen on the crown of your head, raises you and makes you stand up erect.»

---

[1] *Commentary of Theodore of Mopsuestia on the Lord's Prayer* ..., ed. by A. MINGANA, Woodbrooke Studies, vi, 1933.

[2] *Op. cit.*, p. x.

[3] *Op. cit.*, p. xvi.

[4] We follow the translation of MINGANA, *op. cit.*, pp. 34f.

Then, in the following detailed comments to the different items of the ritual, we read: »And thus you recite the words of the profession of faith and of prayer, and through them you make engagements and a contract with God (ܘܥܡܐ ܕܝܠܗ ,ܐܝܬܘ ܕܐܠܗܘܬܐ), before the Priests, that you will remain in the love of the Divine nature — concerning which, if you think the right things, it will be to you the source of great benefits ... — and that you will live in this world to the best of your ability in a way that is consonant with the life and citizenship of Heaven.»[1]

The engagements and promises are expressly formulated as follows: »I abjure Satan and all his angels, and all his service and all his deception, and all his worldly glamour: and I engage myself and believe, and I am baptised in the Name of the Father and the Son and the Holy Ghost.»[2] Notice the mention of the angels which are certainly then interpreted by Theodore in a demythologizing way as heretics and other human representatives of the evil power, but yet clearly considered the cause of idolatry and error[3] — as we have earlier found in the ideology of Enoch.

A little further on Theodore states what the service of Satan here implies, and what actions in the cult are to be given up by the Christians: partly everything dealing with paganism, partly also the washings, the knots, the hanging of yeast, the observances of the body, the fluttering or the voice of birds and any similar things: *i.e.* »service of Satan is to indulge in the observances of Judaism».[4] *Cf.* our assumption above regarding the polemic purpose of the words οὐ σαρκὸς ἀπόθεσις ῥύπου. By the words in the renunciation »I engage myself before God» — Theodore goes on — »you show that you will remain steadfastly with Him, that you will henceforth be unshakably with Him, that you will never separate yourself from Him, and that you will think it higher than anything else to be and to live with Him and to conduct yourself in a way

---

[1] *Cf. op. cit.*, p. 35.
[2] *Ibid.*, p. 37.
[3] *Ibid.*, pp. 39 ff.
[4] *Ibid.*, p. 41 f.

vii.] HOW BAPTISM IS CHARACTERIZED IN 21 B—22   193

that is in harmony with His commandments.»¹ This is very near our interpretation of συνειδήσεως ἀγαθῆς ἐπερώτημα.

Towards the end of the chapter Theodore mentions that the assisting godfather spreads an orarium of linen on the head of the candidate which denotes the freedom to which he has been called (cf. 1 Pet. ii. 16), that he by rising from his genuflexion shows that he has cast away (cf. ἀπόθεσις) his ancient fall, that he has been called to Heaven, and that he ought henceforth to direct his course to its life and citizenship while spurning all earthly things. Cf. again συνείδησις ἀγαθή in 1 Pet. iii. 21 according to our intérpretation, and ἔννοιαν ὁπλίσασθε and θελήματι θεοῦ ... βιῶσαι in iv. 1 f.² Thus the baptisee is singled out and stamped as a soldier of Christ the Lord and receives the remaining part of the Sacrament and is invested with the complete armour of the Spirit. Here we have an indication of the point of »putting on».³ When later the real action of Baptism is carried out, as Theodore describes in ch. iv, there is again a putting off of the clothes and a putting on, this time of a very radiant garment.⁴ These points have of course also symbolic meaning, but now attention is directed towards death and resurrection and not towards the ethics of the earthly life. The latter, however, was clearly enough underlined in the earlier speaking of putting off and on in connection with the renunciation. There we have a concrete commentary to what we have already said about ἀποθέσθαι and ἐνδύσασθαι.

Thus, what we have put forward from chapter iii should illustrate very well the remarks regarding Baptism in 1 Pet. iii. 21 as we have tried to understand them.

Some more details from Theodore may now be added to illustrate his general conception of Baptism which seems to agree fairly well with 1 Pet. In chapter ii Theodore quite clearly and very interestingly speaks of how the candidate for Baptism is first introduced

---

¹ *Op. cit.*, p. 44.
² *Op. cit.*, p. 47. — *Cf.* above, pp. 189 f., and below, pp. 202 f.
³ *Ibid.*
⁴ *Op. cit.*, pp. 54, 68.

into the circle of the Church. Such a person »comes» (possibly a *vox technica* for coming forward to Baptism)[1] to the Church of God and is there received by a registrar of Baptism, »who will question him about his mode of life in order to find out whether it possesses all the requisites of the citizenship of that great City». This moment of the baptismal office can possibly be associated with the N.T. formula τί κωλύει &c. found in baptismal connections in Acts viii. 36, x. 47 &c. and investigated by O. CULLMANN[2] who has drawn the following conclusion: »Dès le premier siècle, toute les fois qu'un converti a été présenté au baptême, on s'est renseigné pour savoir si aucun empêchement n'existait, c'est-a-dire si le candidat remplissait bien les conditions requises.»[3] We do not think that the question τί κωλύει and related ideas has given rise to the definition of Baptism as an ἐπερώτημα[4] but it has perhaps contributed to that terminology, and the emphasis on the personal blamelessness is in any case very illuminating in this connection. In a similar way Theodore then states that after the candidate has abjured all the evil found in this world and cast it completely out of his mind, he has to show that he is worthy of the citizenship of the City and of his enrolment in it.[5] There is also a godfather who is responsible for the blamelessness of the candidate and who bears witness to what the catechumen has done.[6] It is the latter's own task to think then of the duties which are attached to the citizenship of the heavenly City, »pay perpetual taxes to the King and live a life consonant with Baptism»[7] The whole of this introductory ceremony is, one can say, like applying for work to the

---

[1] *Cf.* προσέρχεσθαι, *e.g.* in Hebr. x. 1, xi. 6, 1 Pet. ii. 3; προσαγωγή, προσάγειν, Rom. v. 2, 1 Pet. iii. 18. *Cf.* below, pp. 217f.

[2] O. CULLMANN, Les traces d'une vieille formule baptismale dans le N.T., *Rev. d'hist. et de phil. rel.* xvii, 1937, pp. 424ff.

[3] *Op. cit.* p. 428.

[4] A. SCHLATTER, *Petrus und Paulus nach dem Ersten Petrusbrief*, 1937, pp. 144f.

[5] Theodore of Mopsuestia, *op. cit.*, p. 25.

[6] *Cf.* F. J. DÖLGER, Der Taufbürge nach Theodor von Mopsuestia, *Antike u. Christ.* iv, 1934, pp. 231f.

[7] Theodore of Mopsuestia, *loc. cit.*

owner of a house: »we approach the major-domo of this house (*i.e.* the Priest) and after we have recited our profession of faith for him, we make with God through him a contract and our engagements concerning the faith and we solemnly declare that we will be His servants, that we will work for Him and remain with Him to the end, and that we will keep His love always and without a change».[1] This can really in general be said to illustrate well how Baptism can have been conceived as »an agreement before God with regard to a loyal attitude of mind».

We may be allowed to supplement these references from Theodore of Mopsuestia with a few other quotations from the older Church literature which can illustrate 1 Pet. iii. 21 in the same way.

A few phrases in Justin the Martyr's *Apol.* I belong to the most ancient of the statements on Baptism made by the Fathers of the Church. In ch. lxi (68) those who wished to be baptized are spoken of as follows: ὅσοι ἂν πεισθῶσι καὶ πιστεύωσιν ἀληθῆ ταῦτα ... εἶναι, καὶ βιοῦν οὕτως δύνασθαι ὑπισχνῶνται.[2] Justin thinks of Baptism therefore as a promise to live in a certain way. Later Isa. i. 16 ff. is quoted as referring to Baptism: λούσασθε, καθαροὶ γένεσθε, ἀφέλετε τὰς πονηρίας ἀπὸ τῶν ψυχῶν ὑμῶν· μάθετε καλὸν ποιεῖν, &c.[3] Notice here the words about »good works». In ch. lxv (81) Justin speaks of the prayers of the relatives at the Baptism: ἡμεῖς δέ, μετὰ τὸ οὕτως λοῦσαι τὸν πεπεισμένον ... κοινὰς εὐχὰς ποιησόμενοι ... ὅπως καταξιωθῶμεν, τὰ ἀληθῆ μαθόντες, καὶ δι' ἔργων ἀγαθοὶ πολιτευταί, καὶ φύλακες τῶν ἐντεταλμένων εὑρεθῆναι, ὅπως τὴν αἰώνιον σωτηρίαν σωθῶμεν.[4] This is the same ideology in the main as in 1 Pet. and in Theodore of Mopsuestia, with the conceptions of citizenship, dignified behaviour, &c. The expression φωτιζομένων τὴν διάνοιαν in ch. lxi (72)[5] also leads the thought to συνείδησις or ἔννοια in 1 Pet.

A reflex of the »putting off» *motif* is also to be found in *Herm. Sim.* ix. 16. 2: not even the just of the O.T. would be able to enter

---

[1] *Op. cit.* p. 33f.
[2] *P.G.* vi, col. 420 B—C.
[3] *Ibid.*, cols. 420f.
[4] *Ibid.*, col. 428 A.
[5] *Ibid.*, col. 421 B.

the Kingdom of God, εἰ μὴ τὴν νέκρωσιν ἀπέθεντο τῆς ζωῆς αὐτῶν [τῆς προτέρας] (*scil.* at Baptism). Notice also that the picture of the souls as stones which shall be built into the Church's spiritual house appears in connection with Baptism both here in Hermas and in 1 Pet. ii. 5.

The viith book of the *Apostolic Constitutions*[1] states in ch. 44. 3 that if the priest does not carry out the Christian epiclesis over the baptismal water, then the baptisee actually goes down into merely ordinary water, ὡς οἱ Ἰουδαῖοι, καὶ ἀποτίθεται μόνον τὸν ῥύπον τοῦ σώματος, οὐ τὸν ῥύπον τῆς ψυχῆς. Here we have the same contrast which must be thought to lie in 1 Pet. iii. 21. Judaism is likewise included, as we have also seen in Theodore of Mopsuestia. But the contrast to the isolation of Judaism which we desire to assume in 1 Pet. because of the analogy with Titus, seems no longer to have been of current interest in the *Apostolic Constitutions*. Regarding the renunciations and the confession of faith as a pledge these Constitutions say that the catechumen shall before Baptism learn τὰ περὶ τῆς ἀποταγῆς τοῦ διαβόλου καὶ τὰ περὶ τῆς συνταγῆς τοῦ Χριστοῦ, vii. 40. 1; *cf.* ch. 41. 2ff., where the formula for˙ the confession to God and Christ runs asˊ follows: συντάσσομαι τῷ Χριστῷ καὶ πιστεύω καὶ βαπτίζομαι εἰς ἕνα ἀγέννητον ... &c. Thus here also Baptism is characterized by an accompanying promise.

The following examples can be quoted from Latin Christendom. Tertullian says in *De resurr. carn.* xlviii: *anima enim, non lavatione, sed responsione sancitur.*[2] These words are a fairly close analogy to 1 Pet. iii. 21 but seem not to be a quotation of this passage, as a dissimilarity appears in the negative part. But Tertullian thinks in any case as in 1 Pet. that it is the confession to Christ which gives Baptism its saving power and he calls it *responsio*, in some ways a counterpart to ἐπερώτημα in 1 Pet. Compare *Tert. Lib. ad mart.* iii. (4): *vocati sumus ad militiam Dei vivi jam tunc, cum in sacramenti verba respondimus*,[3] or *De pudic.* ix: (*christianus*)

---

[1] *Didascalia et Constitutiones Apostolorum*, ed. F. X. FUNK, i, 1905.
[2] *P.L.* ii, col. 865 A.
[3] *P.L.* i, col. 624 A.

vestem pristinam recipit; statum scilicet eum quem Adam transgressus amiserat; annulum quoque accipit tunc primum, quo fidei pactionem (N.B.) *interrogatus obsignat*.[1] Augustine often speaks of *interrogationes baptismi* referring to the renunciation and the confession of faith,[2] *e.g. Serm.* ccxciv.[3] The synod at Carthage A.D. 255 declared: *Ipse interrogatio quœ fit in baptismo testis est veritatis: nam cum dicimus »credis ...?» intelligimus ...*[4] In the same town a synod was held A.D. 348 which in canon no. 1 discussed the following question: *An descendentem in aquam et interrogatum in Trinitatem secundum evangelii fidem et apostolorum doctrinam et confessum bonam conscientiam in Deum de resurrectione Jesu Christi, liceat iterum interrogari in eandem fidem et in aqua iterum intingui?*[5] The constitutive importance of the *interrogatio*, the confession of faith, appears clearly in all these texts. In the last one quoted it is interesting to find a direct link with 1 Pet. iii. 21. There is *confessum bonam conscientiam* corresponding to συνειδήσεως ἀγαθῆς ἐπερώτημα very like the interpretation we desire to give the latter phrase. The meaning of *conscientia*, because of *confessum* and *in Deum*, must be: »attitude», or rather »faith». The words εἰς θεὸν and δι' ἀναστάσεως 'Ι. Χρ. in 1 Pet. have in the text from this synod been taken as depending on συνείδησις. This is perhaps not in agreement with the meaning of the basic text. But it does not hinder, it even contributes to the proof that συνείδησις, or *conscientia*, have been taken in about the same way as we have proposed, in a considerably wider conception than our »conscience».

The word ἐπερώτημα's close contact with the confession of faith also appears in the immediate continuation in 1 Pet., which clearly quotes certain items of a christological formula.

A very interesting support of our theory on ἀγαθὴ συνείδησις

---

[1] *P.L.* ii, col. 998 B. — *Cf.* H. Grotius, *Annotationes, ad* 1 Pet. iii. 21.
[2] P. de Puniet, Baptême, *Dict. d'arch, chrét.*, ii. 1, col. 316.
[3] *P.L.* xxxviii, col. 1342.
[4] *Cypr. Epist.* lxx. *S. Thasci Caec. Cypriani opera omnia*, rec. Gv. Hartel, ii, 1871, p. 768. *Cf.* p. 756.
[5] J. D. Mansi, *Sacrorum conciliorum collectio*, iii, 1759, col. 153; *cf.* 145.

and ἐπερώτημα is also available in Pliny's famous letter to the Emperor Trajan dealing with the Christians' life in his province at this time. What Pliny had found was that the Christians *stato die ante lucem convenire carmenque Christo quasi deo dicere secum invicem seque sacramento* (*cf.* ἐπερώτημα![1]) *non in scelus aliquod obstringere, sed ne furta, ne latrocinia, ne adulteria committerent ... ne fidem fallerent,* &c., *C. Plin. Sec. Epist.* x. 96. 7. The main acts of the ritual thus seem to have been a recitation of a *carmen* to Christ as God, which ought to be something in the way of a declaration of faith, as PH. CARRINGTON[2] states, and the taking of an oath to abstain from certain (social) sins, and to be true to the faith. We may ask with Carrington: »What should this be but baptism? or something connected with baptism?» Pliny seems to have come in contact with the Christians' baptismal service and especially noticed the same feature as we suppose to be a main point in 1 Pet. iii. 21, viz. the ethical obligations.

Finally we may also, concerning our interpretation of the terms συνείδησις and ἔννοια in 1 Pet., remind of the fundamental N.T. expression βάπτισμα μετανοίας.

THE AIM OF THE CHRISTOLOGICAL FORMULÆ IN VERSES 21 c—22.

It must be most natural to connect δι' ἀναστάσεως in 21 c with νῦν σώζει at the beginning of the same verse, not with συνείδησις. For the two appositions to βάπτισμα are clearly a parenthesis, and it is not nearly so logical to have »the good attitude» justified by Christ's resurrection as to have the saving power of Baptism justified by this fundamental fact.

Thus the passage 21 c—22 treats of what it is that gives Baptism its saving power: the resurrection of Christ and all connected with it. As we said the words seem to have been taken from some formula

---

[1] A comparison between ἐπερώτημα and the term *sacramentum* is also made in E. G. SELWYN, *The First Epistle,* p. 205. *Cf.* R. EISLER, The Sadoqite Book of the New Covenant, *Orient and Occident,* being Studies ... in Honour of M. GASTER, 1936, p. 130 (on the *Damascus Documents* xv).

[2] PH. CARRINGTON, *The Primitive Christian Catechism,* p. 91.

of confession. But they can never be correctly understood if they are considered only as a mechanical lesson or a doxological conclusion to the previous reasoning. No, these well-known primary Christian facts must also have been included to support the exhortation to boldness before the pagans, to serve as a proof with a parenetic purpose. We will group these sentences ideologically as follows:

δι' ἀναστάσεως Ἰησοῦ Χριστοῦ,
ὅς ἐστιν ἐν δεξιᾷ θεοῦ,
πορευθεὶς εἰς οὐρανόν,
ὑποταγέντων αὐτῷ ἀγγέλων καὶ ἐξουσιῶν καὶ δυνάμεων.

The resurrection of Christ gives Baptism power to rescue the Christian that he may have eternal life with God: for this reason the author thinks the believers have nothing to fear. To some extent this is also emphasized when it later says that Christ sits at God's right hand, according to Ps. cix (cx). 1. But in the main it is the supremacy of Christ in the spirit world which must be remembered, seeing that the position at God's right hand according to Ps. cix (cx) is a place for him who is enthroned and takes over the power and shall pronounce judgment.[1] The following expression, the 3rd,[2] πορευθεὶς εἰς οὐρανόν, harmonizes on the contrary with the words about the resurrection in the first phrase. On the other hand the 4th expression ὑποταγέντων αὐτῷ ἀγγέλων &c. has a completely different purpose from the first and third phrases but harmonizes very well with the second as it is also intended to emphasize the supremacy of Christ. Thus it can be seen that the four expressions contain two different notions: the one is Christ's

---

[1] See also *e.g.* the *Book of Enoch*, xlvi. 1ff., *Polyc. Ad Phil.* ii. 1. — *Cf.* L. DÜRR, Ps. 110, *Verz. der Vorles. zu Braunsberg* im Wintersem. 1929/30, 1929, pp. 12ff.; G. WIDENGREN, *Psalm 110*, 1941, pp. 4f.

[2] Here we do not consider the Latin addition in iii. 22: *deglutiens mortem ut vitæ æternæ heredes efficeremur.* See A. v. HARNACK, *Beiträge zur Einleitung in das N.T.*, vii, 1916, p. 83; *cf.* J. LEIPOLDT, review in *Theol. Lit.-bl.* xxxviii, 1917, col. 213. But if this sentence is an original part of the text, as Harnack presumes, and as is, perhaps, not quite impossible, it fits our theory very well.

resurrection and elevation, the other His complete power. It must especially be observed that the second and fourth expression are both connected with Ps. cix (cx).

Now the resurrection and the elevation are mentioned to confirm the fact that Baptism saves one for everlasting life, as we have said. Why then is the position at God's right hand and the power over Angels &c. mentioned? Undoubtedly in order to add to the conviction that the Christian, by means of Baptism, is released from any dependence on these Powers which are ruled by Christ from His throne by His Father's side. The Powers are called ἄγγελοι καὶ ἐξουσίαι καὶ δυνάμεις, thus using the typical formula which includes all the spiritual Powers of the world (cf. Eph. i. 21 and parallels). It is therefore the worldly Powers from which Baptism is here said to rescue the Christians. Compare Peter's words in Acts ii. 40: σώθητε ἀπὸ τῆς γενεᾶς τῆς σκολιᾶς ταύτης — also concerning Baptism — or the words about Lot's rescue from his evil environment in 2 Pet. ii. 2f. It is quite true that our author could also mean that Baptism rescues from sin, condemnation &c., but here his attention is directed to the ability of Baptism to rescue from the worldly Powers. Why is that? Well, if »the spirits in prison» can represent the disobedient and hardened pagan environment of the Christians, the spiritual Powers in general of which the fallen Angels of primeval times formed the principle, can of course play the same role. Compare 1 Cor. ii. 6ff., 2 Cor. vi. 15, Gal. iv. 1ff., Eph. ii. 2 about the Prince of the power of the air who works among the disobedient — and Col. ii. 8. This is just the case here. The spiritual Powers of this world are behind the aberration of the heathen. But the Christian cannot suffer any real harm from them, for by means of Baptism into Christ, the Lord of the Spirits, he has been set free in principle from any dependence on the pagan world.[1] In consideration of this

---

[1] Compare the words about Christ Himself in Col. ii. 15: ἀπεκδυσάμενος τὰς ἀρχὰς καὶ τὰς ἐξουσίας, where ἀπεκδύσασθαι is possibly also a reflection of the cultic terminology and can be connected with ἀποθέσθαι and its antithesis ἐνδύσασθαι — cf. above, pp. 189ff.

fact the believers should, without fear, allow the light of the Gospel to shine out on their pagan environment however unwilling it may be. Right up to and including verse 22 we have thus to deal with ideas which shall support the exhortation to a bold setting forth of the Gospel to outsiders. The author has retained the same theme all the time. One can even connect the last of these *motifs* ὑποταγέντων αὐτῷ ἀγγέλων καὶ ἐξουσιῶν καὶ δυνάμεων with the Isaiah quotation (Isa. viii. 12f.) in verse 14: τὸν δὲ φόβον αὐτῶν (obj. gen.) μὴ φοβηθῆτε μηδὲ ταραχθῆτε, κύριον δὲ τὸν Χριστὸν ἁγιάσατε ἐν ταῖς καρδίαις ὑμῶν, for here the word κύριος has clearly a pregnant meaning: by sanctifying in their heart the Lord of all beings viz. Christ (in the Hebrew text it is יהוה צבאת, but even if this had not been of current interest for the author, κύριος must be said here to have this emphatic meaning, judging from its position) the Christians place themselves outside the area of the pagans' power — that is the same thought as is expressed in the last part of iii. 22 only that there it is said of Baptism.

CHAPTER VIII.

COMPARATIVE EXAMINATION OF IV. 1—6.

In order 'to fulfil all righteousness' we must also try to examine more closely the passage iv. 6, which is so often related to iii. 19, although it is seldom quite clearly explained that this undoubtedly has some justification. And it may be convenient to do that now, simply continuing our examination of iii. 19—22.

In iv. 1—6 we have a new passage with somewhat new thoughts and new content. But we shall try to show, that the reasoning is logical all the time, without any digressions or interruption, and that the beginning of this passage contains natural links with what has just been said in iii. 17—22.

VERSES 1—5.

The connecting particle οὖν, »thus», at the beginning of iv. 1 reveals clearly and incontrovertibly that the author still has in his thought the previous exhortations of chapter iii when he now again puts forward some parenetic arguments. At first there must be a connection with iii. 17 and 18. Thus we here have support for the theory that the author in the presentation in 19—22 still keeps in mind the preceding parenetic *motifs*. But there is probably in this οὖν also a logical connection with the idea συνειδήσεως ἀγαθῆς ἐπερώτημα in iii. 21, by the exhortation to arm with a Christian ἔννοια. We have already touched upon this[1] but the observation may be added that it is still a question of a certain practical attitude

---

[1] *Cf.* above, pp. 189 f., 193.

and a practical way of life, for this ἔννοια is the same as to live θελήματι θεοῦ, verse 2, and no longer to practise τὸ θέλημα (or τὸ βούλημα¹) τῶν ἐθνῶν, verse 3.

However, through these exhortations the author is leading the thought no longer to frankness in the company of pagans but to the opposite side of the matter, the necessary limits which the newly baptized must draw as regards the pagans. Yet this is not repugnant to the former presentation. It is the same order in both cases as to positive and negative behaviour. The same exhortation followed by the same reservation and limitation we have also in ii. 16 when the author urges the Christians to be loyal to the pagan authorities while preserving their freedom without making it an excuse for evil, and in ii. 11f. when he urges them to understand their position as strangers in the world and refrain from »fleshly lusts», while observing blamelessness as citizens.

The author in this way urges the newly made Christian to refrain from the heathen lusts and debaucheries. He thinks that the pagans shall have reason to »be astonished» when they see how the Christians, who previously for a considerable time had taken part in dissipation, now will not join them, verse 4 — ἐν ᾧ is equal to »therefore» as we have already stated.² They wonder what use this abstinence is, and the author remarks that the pagans suspect and slander the Christians for their abstinence, *ibid*. Notice that here βλασφημοῦντες³ which ought to have ὑμᾶς as its object, can be compared with καταλαλοῦσιν and ἐπηρεάζοντες in ii. 12 and iii. 16, and ὀνειδίζεσθε in iv. 14.⁴ It states in the last passage that the Christians have been accused just as Christians, not as thieves &c., and according to iv. 17 a general legal action against the Christians is in progress. The whole reasoning agrees quite well with the exposition in Wisd. ii, where it is described how the arrogant are surprised at and suspect the just man for his

---

¹ Two variants.
² *Cf.* above, p. 111.
³ *Cf.* βλασφημέω in such passages as Rom. iii. 8 &c.
⁴ *Cf.* R. KNOPF, *Die Briefe Petri*, p. 166.

desire to be clean and free from the ordinary human sinfulness, dragging him before the court and punishing him for it. In both cases we have astonishment at the peculiar abstinence of the righteous which does not seem to serve any purpose, and suspicion and slandering with a legal punishment for it.

Then in iv. 5 the author calmly explains that the slanderers themselves will have to give an account at the coming judgment over the living and the dead. Here he is practising, it may be said in passing, the rule indicated in ii. 23 that a Christian may not abuse in revenge but leave his case in the hands of the Great Judge. At the same time he reveals that he is thinking of how the Christians must give account to the pagans, when he states that they themselves in their turn will have to give an account.[1] From this it is clear that he still thinks of the phenomenon touched upon in iii. 15 that the Christians will be required to give reason for their belief. In both cases the word λόγος is used for »account».

Then follows iv. 6, this verse so enormously discussed[2] and which is often related to iii. 19. How shall it be interpreted? And have we the right to relate it to iii. 19?

THE DIFFICULT VERSE IV. 6.

The immediate impression is that iv. 6 treats of a preaching of the Gospel among the Dead in the Realm of Shadows in general.

Beside the very ordinary scientific theory which agrees with this first impression[3] we have mainly two attempts to avoid this primary theory which must be mentioned: first the figurative or

---

[1] *Cf.* above, pp. 133 f.

[2] In his commentary on 1 Pet., J. LORINUS, 1609, already counts 12 different explanations, which is still not enough (*cf.* E. HUTHER, *Kritisch exegetisches Handbuch*, p. 206, note 1).

[3] Older literature on this theory in K. GSCHWIND, *Die Niederfahrt Christi*, pp. 23f., and in U. HOLZMEISTER, *Commentarius*, pp. 364f. Most of those who consider that iii. 19 treats of Descent, insert this theory here also. It is unnecessary to give more than a few examples: C. NORDBLAD, *Föreställningen om Kristi Hadesfärd*, 1912, pp. 11f.; K. BORNHÄUSER, Jesu Predigt für die Geister, *Allg. Ev.-Luth. Kirch.-Zeit.* liv, 1921, col. 340.

moral interpretation of the terms »living» and »dead» in verses 5 and 6,[1] secondly the interpretation of »the dead» in verse 6 as alluding to Christians now dead who heard the Gospel in their lifetime.[2] These two later interpretations make it impossible to link iv. 6 with iii. 19. Probably these avoiding theories must be repudiated. Spiritually dead people cannot here be meant, seeing that the word εὐηγγελίσθη is in the aorist, expressing a given fact (»complex» aorist). The preaching of the Gospel still continues, and there are still spiritually dead, so that if the author had wished to say something about non-Christians in general considered as spiritually dead he ought absolutely to have spoken in the present tense. In Acts x. 42, Rom. xiv. 9, 2 Tim. iv. 1 the words »the living and the dead» are also undoubtedly used in the physical meaning. And 1 Pet. iv. 5 clearly deals with the *parousia* and the Final Judgment. Thus these individuals are physically dead.[3]

The second attempt at evading the Descent theory, the interpretation of νεκροί in verse 6 as »now dead» who have heard the Gospel during their lifetime and received judgment already on earth, seems to be upset by the impossibility which then arises to maintain the clear philological analogies between verses 5 and 6. Against this theory one might state the following reasons. The word νεκροί ought to have the same meaning in both verses. When the dead in general are mentioned in verse 5 — ζῶντες καὶ νεκροί is evidently in the N.T. a designation of all who have ever lived[4] — the same should be the case in verse 6. And the verb κρίνειν, too, must in both places denote the same kind of judgment. When verse

---

[1] *E.g.* K. GSCHWIND, *op. cit.*, pp. 26ff.; U. HOLZMEISTER, *Commentarius*, pp. 366 f.

[2] *E.g.* F. W. BUGGE, *Apostlerne Peters og Judas' Breve*, 1885, pp. 145f.; G. WOHLENBERG, *Der erste und zweite Petrusbrief*, pp. 128ff.; E. G. SELWYN, *The First Epistle*, pp. 215f., 337ff.

[3] In spite of the large amount of material put forward by K. GSCHWIND in *Die Niederfahrt Christi*, pp. 26ff., one is not convinced of the possibility of moralizing these antithetical conceptions in this passage.

[4] See the passages mentioned above. *Cf.* further Barn. vii. 2, 2 Clem. i. 1, Polyc. *Ad Phil.* ii. 1, and the *Apostles' Creed*. See also, for instance, A. SEEBERG, *Der Katechismus der Urchristenheit*, 1903, p. 86.

5 states that God or Christ — which of the two is impossible to decide, but perhaps it does not matter — is ready for judgment, the judgment indicated in verse 6 ought also to be a future event. In both cases it must be the coming Great Judgment that is referred to. These analogies between verses 5 and 6 tell against the interpretation of νεκροί as »now dead».

Thus it seems to be a question of dead people, in a proper sense, who hear the Gospel in Hades, in order to be judged on the Last Day in the flesh, and to live in the Spirit.

One should not object that the dead in Hades, deprived of their bodies, can scarcely be said to be judged »in the flesh».[1] On the contrary it was even a characteristic of Judaism and Early Christianity that to a great extent they expected a resurrection of the body together with the soul for judgment or eternal life,[2] as in Tertullian's *De resurrectione carnis* or in the *Apostles' Creed*. Some especially concrete and interesting examples of this are found in the following texts:

Ezech. xxxvii, in so far as it has been interpreted by the Church as an indication of general Resurrection, as for instance in *Just. Apol.* I, lii,[3] *Iren. Contra hær.* v. 15. 1, 34. 1.[4]

The *Sibylline Books* ii. 221 ff.:

καὶ τότε[5] νερτερίοις ψυχὰς καὶ πνεῦμα καὶ αὐδὴν
δώσει ἐπουράνιος καί τ' ὀστέα ἁρμοσθέντα
ἁρμοῖς παντοίοις σαρξίν, σάρκας τ' ἰδὲ νεῦρα
καὶ φλέβας ἠδέ τε δέρμα περὶ χροῒ καὶ πρὶν ἐθείρας·
ἀμβροσίως πηχθέντα καὶ ἔμπνοα κινηθέντα
σώματ' ἐπιχθονίων ἐνὶ ἤματι ἀναστήσονται.
καὶ τότ' ἀμειλίκτοιο καὶ ἀρρήκτου ἀδάμαντος
κλεῖθρα πέλωρα πυλῶν παγχαλκεύτων Ἀΐδαο

---

[1] C. F. KEIL, *Commentar*, 1883, pp. 150ff.; G. WOHLENBERG, *Der erste und zweite Petrusbrief*, p. 129.
[2] A. NYGREN, *Agape and Eros*, i, 1932, pp. 176 f., ii. 1, 1938, pp. 64 ff. e. p.
[3] *P.G.* vi, col. 405 A.
[4] *P.G.* vii, cols. 1164 A, 1215 B.
[5] *Scil.* at the Last Day.

ῥηξάμενος Οὐριὴλ μέγας ἄγγελος εὐθὺ βαλεῖται,[1]
καὶ πάσας μορφὰς πολυπενθέας ἐς κρίσιν ἄξει ...

cf. later lines 245f.:

ἥξει καὶ Μωσῆς ὁ μέγας φίλος ὑψίστοιο
σάρκας δυσάμενος· Ἀβραὰμ δ' αὐτὸς μέγας ἥξει ...

Then the severe corporal punishments of the sinners are described. Probably we have here actually reflections of genuine Jewish eschatology[2] though the presentation is hellenized and christianized, and there are also many relations to Jewish apocalypses as the *Book of Enoch*[3] &c. *Cf.* also for instance *Gen. R.* xxviii. 3, *Lev. R.* xviii. 1 (on the necessity of the *lūz*, a bone of the spinal column, for the individual's resurrection).[4]

Epistola apostolorum xxii (xvi)ff. (according to the translation by C. SCHMIDT *e.a.*): ... »O, Herr, ist es wahr, dass das Fleisch mit der Seele und dem Geist zugleich gerichtet werden wird, (die eine Hälfte) in dem Himmelreich ruhen wird, die andere Hälfte aber lebendig ewiglich bestraft wird?« (Jesus answers:) »Wahrlich, ich sage euch, der Körper eines jeden Menschen wird [lebendig] mit einer Seele zugleich auferstehen und Geist.« ... (And later:) »Das Fleisch wird samt der Seele lebendig auferstehen, damit sie Geständnis ablegen und nach der Gerechtigkeit gerichtet werden ...«

3 Enoch xlvii. 1—2 (the bodies of failing Angels are burnt in the stream of fire, but their spirits and their souls return to the Shekina).[5]

The opinions disclosed in such passages may convince us that it was not unnatural for a N.T. writer to state that the Last Judgment would be performed »in the flesh». These texts may be considered to be good illustrations of the words ἵνα κριθῶσι σαρκί in 1 Pet. iv. 6, interpreted as concerning the Last Day. One can even

---

[1] N.B. Here we find a descent in the form of *Höllenstürmung* performed by the Angel Uriel.

[2] RZACH, Sibyllinische Orakel, *Paulys Real-Encycl.* Ser. II, iv, 1923, col. 2150, with references.

[3] RZACH, *loc. cit.*; *cf. ibid.*, col. 2147, and *Die Oracula Sibyllina*, hrsg. von J. GEFFCKEN, 1902, pp. 36ff.

[4] *Cf.* K. BORNHÄUSER, *Die Gebeine der Toten*, 1921.

[5] *Cf.* the commentary in *3 Enoch*, ed. by H. ODEBERG, 1928, ii, p. 152.

observe that the presentations of the treatment of the body and the soul in our quotations from the *Epistola apostolorum* and *3 Enoch* are very interesting analogies to the correlation between this phrase in iv. 6 and the other, (ἵνα) ζῶσι κατὰ θεὸν πνεύματι.

But really we must recognize a certain difficulty for the theory in question if we find it necessary to understand the expression κατὰ ἀνθρώπους in a strict analogy to κατὰ θεόν. The latter words are generally said to mean »according to God», »in God's likeness», that is »as God lives».[1] Possibly the meaning might also be: »according to God's disposition», *deo iubente*.[2] But in neither case do we get any possibility to give a quite analogous meaning to the κατά before ἀνθρώπους. At the most these words seem to mean »as (being) men» or »as it belongs to men».[3] Here we have no comparison of two factors but a relation of identity. Yet there is perhaps no possibility to avoid this discrepancy between the two κατά's.[4] And on the other hand the scholars in general have not at all even observed the difficulty of this point.

Thus we must prefer the theory that the allusion is to the judgment of all the dead at the Last Day. The evangelization mentioned in iv. 6 is consequently to be regarded as an action performed by Christ — perhaps by the Apostles, but probably not — in Hades, at His descent. Compare also the statement above concerning the Early Church's interpretation of iv. 6 as having reference to Christ's descent.[5] In this way the thesis in iv. 6 must have the purpose to give an argument for the preceding assertion of the approaching general judgment, by stating that also the dead have

---

[1] Lately stated by E. G. SELWYN, *The First Epistle*, p. 216. And he has many predecessors on this point, e. g. CH. BIGG, *A Critical and Exegetical Commentary*, p. 171, E. KÜHL, *Die Briefe Petri*, p. 257, J. MONNIER, *La première épître*, pp. 203f., U. HOLZMEISTER, *Commentarius*, p. 364.

[2] As, for instance, the meaning of the stereotyped phrase κατὰ θεόν is in *Plat. Euthyd.* ii (272 E), *Apol.* vii (22 A), *Soph.* xlix (265 D).

[3] E. G. SELWYN, *op. cit.*, pp. 216, 338. — Selwyn has suggested translating κατὰ ἀνθρώπους as »in men's eyes», but then the impropriety arises that the judgment will not be real in God's eyes, which can scarcely be right: this judgment must be real from God's point of view also, it must be determined by God to fall upon these people.

[4] SELWYN has also accepted the discrepancy as a fact, *op. cit.*, p. 216.

[5] Above, pp. 16 ff. — A very interesting indication of Christ's visiting the dead we seem to have also in John v. 25: ἔρχεται ὥρα καὶ νῦν ἐστιν ὅτε οἱ νεκροὶ ἀκούσουσιν τῆς φωνῆς τοῦ υἱοῦ τοῦ θεοῦ. See E. G. SELWYN, *The First Epistle*, pp. 346 ff., on John v. 19—29 as a parallel to 1 Pet. iv. 6.

had an opportunity to hear the Gospel, in Hades, so that they can be judged immediately.

Here, of course, the thought must be implied that the Gospel is to be communicated to all beings so that the Judgment can be performed on the basis of everybody's attitude to that Gospel. If this is acknowledged, we have good reason to direct the attention again to what we stated regarding iii. 19, that this verse implies the principle of a universal mission, a universal evangelization. Verse iv. 6 is thus a good illustration of iii. 19, as to this underlying principle.

Now it is not probable that the author has quite the same action in view in both cases, and quite the same objects of the preaching. »The dead» cannot possibly mean only the sinners from Noah's day; it must denote all dead beings in general. But on the other hand it is not quite impossible to include the disobedient »spirits» among the dead. We have earlier tried to show that there were not such fixed boundaries between Angels and men in the generation before the Flood.[1] This is confirmed by the description of the Last Judgment in the *Sibylline Books*. It is said there in verses ii. 230 ff., in immediate connection with the passage just quoted above:

καὶ πάσας μορφὰς πολυπενθέας ἐς κρίσιν ἄξει·
εἰδώλων ῥα μάλιστα παλαιγενέων Τιτήνων
ἠδέ τε Γιγάντων καὶ ὅσας εἷλεν κατακλυσμός,
ὅσσας δ' ἐν πελάγεσσιν ἀπώλεσε κῦμα θαλάσσης
ἠδ' ὁπόσας θῆρες τε καὶ ἑρπετὰ καὶ πετεηνὰ
θοινήσανθ', ἁλέας ταύτας ἐπὶ βῆμα καλέσσει.

Here we find that the Titans, or the Giants are the first beings to suffer judgment (notice also the μάλιστα), but that they otherwise are quite equal to ordinary men in this respect. Similarly the text from *3 Enoch* referred to above[2] states that the failing Angels are punished in their bodies at the same time as their souls are allowed to live before God. These examples make it more natural to combine

---

[1] See above, pp. 57 ff.
[2] P. 207.

1 Pet. iii. 19 and iv. 6. It is not advisable to identify the two *motifs* completely, but a certain connection may be legitimate.

The preaching to the sinners from Noah's time may be considered as a special form of the general preaching to the dead. This general preaching to the dead was possibly a fact well-known to all Christians. We have above seen examples of the rather general acquaintance with these ideas in Early Christianity.[1] The author could allude to this conception without giving any special arguments. But when in iii. 19 he mentions the special form of this preaching, directed to the sinners from the Flood, he is obliged to speak somewhat more explicitly, and on this ground, too, he especially emphasizes: »also to these spirits». In such a way we can understand the relations between iii. 19 and iv. 6 rather satisfactorily.

CONCLUSION.

As regards the first verses of ch. iv. we have been able to observe several logical connections with iii. 17—22. This gives further support to our conception of the continuous reasoning in the context of verse 19.

It may also be that there is a certain connection between iii. 19 and iv. 6, so that the author has in the latter place linked the thought again to the preaching at the Descent. This is important for us in our enquiry because we see that the author keeps in mind the same *motif* for a long time. The most important is the fact that he does not only allude to certain mythological specialities but in both cases projects the evangelization. In iv. 6, too, the peculiar putting forward of this as an argument may be connected with his desire to urge the Christians to communicate the Gospel in their paganish environment — for »also to the dead has the Gospel been preached», with regard to the coming Judgment. This strengthens our attempt to include iii. 19 in the parenetic connection while rejecting the digression theory.

---

[1] Above, pp. 16 ff., 20 ff.

CHAPTER IX.

BACKWARD GLANCE AT III. 17—18.

In addition to earlier sporadic observations on verses 17—18 we shall now pay attention more closely to the main thoughts in these verses and their purpose in the context. Thus we can get still more illustration of what we have already found concerning verses 19ff.

THE SPECIAL IMPORT OF THE THESIS IN VERSE 17.

The rule in iii. 17 that it is better to suffer while doing or for[1] the doing of good deeds than evil is, as we have seen, the first of the different arguments for the parenesis in verses 13—16. What is the intention of the author here?[2]

We get the best answer to this question while observing the special values which the verbs ἀγαθοποιεῖν and κακοποιεῖν must have in this connection. Every passage where these verbs occur in our Epistle refers to a juridical and civic blamelessness and to the fulfilment of social duties.[3] In ch. ii. 14 the punishment by the state and other authorities of κακοποιοί is mentioned, which means »criminals»,[4] cf. ii. 12, iii. 16 var. lect., iv. 15, where the word cor-

---

[1] *Causaliter*, states U. HOLZMEISTER, *Commentarius*, p. 294.

[2] There is a special study of 1 Pet. iii. 17 by J. RAWSON LUMBY, with that title, in *The Exp.* iv. 1, 1890, pp. 142ff. We interpret here »do good» &c. otherwise than he, but agree with him in stressing the author's intention to strengthen the Christians' courage.

[3] We miss a stressing of this in W. GRUNDMANN, ἀγαθοποιέω, in G. KITTEL, *Theol. Wört.*, i, 1933, p. 17.

[4] W. GRUNDMANN, κακοποιέω, *op. cit.*, iii, 1938, p. 486.

responds to φονεύς &c.¹ — and the rewarding of ἀγαθοποιοί, which must thus mean »loyal citizens». And when the Christians are then urged to ἀγαθοποιοῦντας φιμοῦν τὴν ... ἀγνωσίαν, ii. 15, the meaning clearly must be: »by being ἀγαθοποιοί, viz. good citizens», »by behaving loyally». In the same way the verb ἀγαθοποιεῖν occurs in ii. 20 of the slaves' blameless behaviour towards their masters, and in iii. 6 of the wives' fulfilling of all their marriage duties. Cf. καλοποιέω, »to live a proper life», in 2 Thess. iii. 13. Probably ἀγαθοποιέω has this meaning in contrast to κακοποιέω, and this verb in its turn has its meaning because of the noun κακοποιός, »criminal». In this connection it can also be pointed out that the expression »good deeds», ἀγαθά or καλά ἔργα, or »the good», τὸ ἀγαθόν, in the Pastoral and the General Epistles do not always indicate morally meritorious actions in the nature of »actions according to the law», benevolence, and similar things, but often instead blameless behaviour from the point of view of society:[2] see e.g. 1 Tim. ii. 10, 2 Tim. iii. 17, Tit. i. 16, iii. 1, 1 Pet. iii. 11 (cf. ποιοῦντας κακά in verse 12), iii. 13.[3] In one passage of Paul, which agrees in many respects with this Epistle's exhortations to a positive attitude to the state in ii. 13ff., namely Rom. xiii, we have also a clear expression of the social and political nuances in both ἀγαθοποιεῖν and κακοποιεῖν: »οἱ ἄρχοντες οὐκ εἰσὶν φόβος τῷ ἀγαθῷ ἔργῳ ἀλλὰ τῷ κακῷ. If you wish to avoid fearing authority, do what is right, τὸ ἀγαθόν, so you will be praised by it. For it is God's servant for τὸ ἀγαθόν. But if you do τὸ κακόν, then

---

[1] See also John xviii. 30. — Cf. κακοῦργος, »criminal», Luke xxiii. 32f., 2 Tim. ii. 9.

[2] In this way »good works» in these N.T. passages is something quite different from what Judaism meant by its term מעשים טובים, i.e. the study of the Torah, works of mercy, visiting the sick, hospitality, alms and other such acts (H. STRACK & P. BILLERBECK, Kommentar zum N.T., iv. 1, 1928, pp. 536f., 559ff.). One must therefore be careful in saying that there has been a relapse into the righteousness of good works of Judaism, e.g. in the Pastoral and General Epistles.

[3] We have also ἀγαθοποιεῖν with its opposite πονηρεύειν in Herm. Sim. ix. 18. 1ff. of acting righteously in general, not to be benevolent, charitable and such things.

fear. For ... it is an avenger for wrath to him who does τὸ κακόν», verses 3f. We thus find that these verbs in 1 Pet. iii. 17 must for several reasons have the meaning of »to be a good citizen», and »to be a criminal». Notice also that immediately before we find ἀγαθὴ ἀναστροφή as a synonym to ἀγαθοποιεῖν.

From this it appears that the purport of the thesis here expressed must be definitely social, juridical and political: »It is better to suffer as a good citizen, if the will of God so demands, than as a criminal.» The purpose of the expression »it is better» is probably a very general one: that it is more righteous in God's eyes and makes more impression on people if a martyr is politically and socially blameless. Compare ii. 12, 19ff., especially κλέος in verse 20, further iii. 13f., 16, and our earlier remarks on the characteristic basic thought that the heathen will bow when they see the blamelessness of the Christians.[1]

Thus our previous observations regarding verses 19ff. are confirmed. Here too, the political perspective proves to be important. In the expression ἀγαθοποιεῖν we have an analogy to συνείδησις ἀγαθή, as we interpret this idea. Verse 17 is clearly an argument which shall support the exhortation to »a loyal attitude» in verse 16. Here too it is a question of blamelessness in the community.

A consequence of this is that we see still more clearly how the following verse 18 with its introductory ὅτι does not in the first place appear as an argument for the thesis in verse 17, for this is unsuitable from our observations as regards the contents. It must on still more certain grounds be considered as a co-ordinated reasoning to verse 17 for the parenesis in 13—16.[2]

WHAT IS THE TERTIUM COMPARATIONIS IN VERSE 18?

There are two main variants of iii. 18, the one running περὶ ἁμαρτιῶν ὑπὲρ ἡμῶν (or ὑμῶν) ἀπέθανεν and the other only περὶ ἁμαρτιῶν ἔπαθεν. If one prefers the previous type one must not, as

---

[1] See above, pp. 132 f., 177 f.
[2] *Cf.* above, pp. 128 ff.

has been done in C. von Tischendorf's and E. Nestle's text editions,[1] omit ὑπὲρ ἡμῶν (ὑμῶν), for it is codex B, the Koine recension and certain other texts which lack these words, but they have ἔπαθεν as the predicate, and all the others of the most important manuscripts which have ἀπέθανεν have at the same time included the words ὑπὲρ ἡμῶν. Through this mechanical, atomistic text reconstruction a form is obtained which, seen as a whole, does not correspond to a single tradition of the text. In H. von Soden's edition[2] on the other hand, we find a consistent maintenance of the first text form, the one represented by all the central evidence except B: ὑπὲρ ἡμῶν ἀπέθανεν. It is now scarcely possible to decide critically which reading was the original,[3] for both can be explained as later changes in connection with other expressions in the text (θανατωθείς in iii. 18; ἔπαθεν in ii. 21, Χριστοῦ παθόντος in iv. 1). As a matter of fact it is also of less importance which reading is followed, seeing that the meaning is about the same in both cases.[4] The expression ἔπαθεν must also refer to the Death on the Cross just as the verb παθεῖν also appears in other parts of the N.T. as a paraphrase for »to die» or »to be crucified»,[5] e.g. in Luke xxiv. 46: γέγραπται παθεῖν τὸν Χριστὸν καὶ ἀναστῆναι, or in 1 Pet. ii. 21,[6] also e.g. in Ignatius,[7] &c.[8] And ὑπὲρ ἡμῶν is to a great extent replaced later first by ὑπὲρ ἀδίκων and then by ἵνα ἡμᾶς προσαγάγῃ τῷ θεῷ so that its absence from the text is of no great importance.

---

[1] *Novum Testamentum Grœce,* rec. C. Tischendorf, ed. octava critica maior, ii, 1872, p. 290; *Novum Testamentum Grœce,* ed. E. Nestle, 1937, p. 588.

[2] *Die Schriften des Neuen Testaments,* hergestellt von H. von Soden, ii, 1913, p. 631.

[3] E. Kühl, *Die Briefe Petri,* p. 209, absolutely prefers ἔπαθεν. Most scholars, however, seem to keep to ἀπέθανεν.

[4] E. G. Selwyn, *The First Epistle,* p. 196.

[5] H. von Campenhausen, *Die Idee des Martyriums in der alten Kirche,* 1936, pp. 62 f.

[6] See also Matt. xvii. 12, Luke xxii. 15, Acts i. 3, iii. 18, xvii. 3, xxvi. 23, Hebr. ix. 26, xiii. 12.

[7] *Ad Smyrn.* ii.

[8] *Cf.* Campenhausen, *loc. cit.,* and E. G. Selwyn, *The First Epistle,* p. 196.

What then is the meaning of iii. 18? Above all where have we the *tertium comparationis* when here it says »Christ also»? It is clear that it is the Saviour and the believers who are compared, but what is common to both of them?

It may be doubted whether all the expressions in verse 18 should indicate what is common to the Saviour and the saved.[1] At least the word ἅπαξ perhaps has not so pregnant a meaning that it shall also be applied to the Christians: on account of the comparison which seems to lie in καί we believe that the meaning is quite simply »once upon a time», neutrally, like ποτέ.[2] But even if ἅπαξ has the meaning »once for all» as in Hebr. ix. 28[3] and as ἐφάπαξ in Rom. vi. 10 — from which passages the occurrence of the word could perhaps be explained — the meaning is less intelligible if the Christians are really also said to die once for all περὶ ἁμαρτιῶν.[4] In this case ἅπαξ should only refer to Christ.

It is however, on the other hand, impossible to see the means of comparison only in that the Christians shall also die or suffer generally speaking.[5] In that case περὶ ἁμαρτιῶν and the other qualifiers of the predicate would be meaningless. Now, περὶ ἁμαρτιῶν ἀπέθανεν must certainly be translated according to the terminology of the LXX with »He died as a sin-offering». We have namely a current phrase περὶ or ὑπὲρ ἁμαρτίας or ἁμαρτιῶν[6] with or without

---

[1] A fine review of the older discussions of this question is found in E. KÜHL, *Die Briefe Petri*, pp. 210ff.

[2] *Cf.* also below, p. 223.

[3] *Cf.* E. G. SELWYN, *The First Epistle*, p. 195.

[4] *Contra* FR. C. A. SIEFFERT, Die Heilsbedeutung des Leidens und Sterbens Christi nach dem ersten Briefe des Petrus, *Jahrb. f. deutsch. Theol.* xx, 1875, p. 406. He understands περὶ ἁμαρτιῶν as »in Bezug auf Sünden», and then the Christians can also be said to die »once for all». But if the words have the meaning we suppose below, the latter is unnatural.

[5] *Cf.* E. SCHWEIZER, *Der erste Petrusbrief*, 1942, p. 58: »Das (»getötet— lebendig gemacht», iii. 18) gilt darum wie für den Christus selber so von ihm her und durch ihn auch für seinen Leib, für seine verfolgte, unterdrückte und doch lebendige Gemeinde.»

[6] Because of the changes from singular to plural in the standard terminology E. G. SELWYN is scarcely correct in saying in *The First Epistle*, p. 196, that the plural in 1 Pet. makes the phrase less technical. In any case the difference is merely unimportant.

a noun as προσφορά which is a translation of the Hebrew חטאת, »sin-offering», e.g.: Lev. vi. 30 (23), xiv. 19; xvi. 3: εἰσελεύσεται ... ἐν μόσχῳ ... περὶ ἁμαρτίας, »with a goat as a sin-offering»; 5: δύο χιμάρους ... περὶ ἁμαρτίας, »as a sin-offering», &c.; Numb. viii. 8; Ps. xxxix (xl). 7: περὶ ἁμαρτίας οὐκ ᾔτησας; Hebr. v. 1: θυσίας ὑπὲρ ἁμαρτιῶν, 3: προσφέρειν περὶ ἁμαρτιῶν, »to present sin-offerings»; x. 6, 8 (= Ps. xxxix. 7), x. 12, 18 (similar expressions); 26: θυσία περὶ ἁμαρτιῶν; xiii. 11: τὸ αἷμα περὶ ἁμαρτίας (= Lev. xvi. 27), »the sin-offering blood». See also Rom. viii. 3 where this translation gives a good meaning: »Sending His Son in the likeness of the flesh of Sin and[1] as a sin-offering,[2] God condemned Sin in the flesh.» As regards 1 Pet. iii. 18 it is important to observe that the description here is connected with the conception of the Suffering Servant in Isa. liii, as is clear from the parallel passage ii. 21—25. Now we also find περὶ ἁμαρτίας just in Isa. liii. 10 clearly in the meaning »sin-offering». Notice too that Hebr. v. 3: περὶ τοῦ λαοῦ ... καὶ περὶ ἑαυτοῦ προσφέρειν περὶ ἁμαρτιῶν, forms a very good analogy to the double attributes of ἀπέθανεν in 1 Pet. iii. 18, both with περὶ ἁμαρτιῶν and ὑπὲρ ἡμῶν. In consequence of all this there is peculiarly good reason to translate περὶ ἁμαρτιῶν in 1 Pet. iii. 18 by »as a sin-offering». But because of the καί before Χριστός we must presume that even the believers can be thought to die as a sin-offering. And this conception necessarily implies that death takes place for the sake of others. Therefore we must also include the expression ὑπὲρ ἡμῶν &c. with the common points in this comparison.

The *tertium comparationis* must thus be death as a sin-offering for others. The emphasis lies on ὑπὲρ ἡμῶν if these words originally belong here, but still more on their synonyms ὑπὲρ ἀδίκων and ἵνα ἡμᾶς προσαγάγῃ. It is indeed clear that this expression

---

[1] Notice that καί co-ordinates the two adverbials to the participle πέμψας: περὶ ἁμαρτίας can therefore not be combined with κατέκρινεν.

[2] The preposition περί with genitive can scarcely have the meaning »for the sake of» in this connection, as alleged, for example, in H. LIETZMANN, *Der Römerbrief*, ad. loc., p. 78 (»um—willen»).

is a repetition of one and the same thought in different wordings. It must therefore have special importance in the context.

In this way verse 18 has a really clear and intelligible meaning. The Christians shall not be afraid to try to win the pagans by their good way of living in Christ in spite of the risk of suffering: that is the content of the parenesis in verses 13—16. And then after verse 17 comes verse 18 with another argument for this: Christ also as is known died as a sin-offering for us, unrighteous as we were, namely to bring us to God. The conclusion must be: thus we likewise must be prepared if necessary to die as a sin-offering for the sake of other pagans, namely to lead them also to God.

Some comments to this are necessary. It must be observed that ὑπέρ is not the same as ἀντί. It means only »for the sake of». The intended analogy between Christ and the believers is not that the latter shall die a substitute, reconciling death as Christ once did. This would perhaps be theologically unreasonable. But what the parallelism implies is clear from the following detailed explanation: ἵνα ἡμᾶς προσαγάγῃ τῷ θεῷ. This is the most important thing in the context. Here and especially on ἡμᾶς is the real emphasis. The expression ὑπὲρ ἡμῶν and ὑπὲρ ἀδίκων are proleptic synonyms to it, which later are more defined by this ἵνα-clause. And in that way the reasoning is that the Christians also by their patient suffering in innocence shall make such an impression on the pagans just as Christ once did on themselves, that these pagans will be won for God, for the Gospel and for Baptism. Compare ὑμᾶς ... δι' αὐτοῦ πιστοὺς εἰς θεόν in i. 21. The expression προσάγειν τῷ θεῷ[1] indicates not so much a mystical act in heaven with a long pedigree in the history of pagan religion, as one has been inclined to assume,[2] but much more the winning of souls for the Church. This appears also from δι' οὗ ... προσαγωγὴν ἐσχήκαμεν [τῇ πίστει] εἰς τὴν χάριν ταύτην (the Gospel) in Rom. v. 2 and similar turns of phrase in

---

[1] Different theories of this are reported by E. G. SELWYN, *The First Epistle*, p. 196.

[2] H. GUNKEL, Der erste Brief des Petrus, *Die Schriften des N.T:s*, ii, 1908, p. 528; R. PERDELWITZ, *Die Mysterienreligionen und das Problem des I. Petrusbriefes*, 1911, p. 86; R. KNOPF, *Die Briefe Petri*, p. 145.

Eph. ii. 18 and iii. 12. One can also recall προσερχόμενοι in 1 Pet. ii. 3 and the general term προσήλυτος as a name for converted pagans. The passages in 1 Pet. ii. 21 and 25 are similarly instructive for this question. Presumably that investigator is quite right who has recently tried, starting from 1 Pet. i. 18f. to assume an allusion to the Jewish sacrifice for converts in iii. 18.[1] Christ's sacrifice is here considered in a special meaning: through His sacrificial Death He has prepared for us, formerly pagans, the way to belief and Baptism — cf. especially Eph. ii. 16—18. This must be meant both objectively and subjectively. See the clear parallel in ii. 21. On this basis a comparison between the self-sacrifice of Christ and the possible suffering of the Christians for the sake of the pagans is really possible.[2] By their patient suffering after the pattern of Christ the latter would in their turn influence the pagans so that they would be won for Christianity.[3]

Now, by observing this parallelism between Christ and the Christians, new light falls over the two appositions to Christ in verse 18, θανατωθείς &c. Here too, the Christians seem to be in the background. They also should be prepared to be treated so that they died in the flesh and at the same time were made living in the spirit.[4] For we have a clear martyr ideology in the whole context. It is probably just with respect to this applicability to the Christians that the author has here specially remarked that Christ was put to death in the flesh but made living again in the spirit. Certainly this is said in an allusion to some catechistical formula. But its

---

[1] W. C. VAN UNNIK, *De verlossing 1 Petrus 1: 18—19 en het problem van den eersten Petrusbrief*, 1942, pp. 69ff.

[2] Reservations have often been made regarding a too wide comparison between Christ and t. e Christians in verse 18, *e.g.* TH. SCHOTT, *Der erste Brief Petri*, 1861, p. 213 (»nur in entfernter Analogie»). By our special conception of the problem there will not arise so great dogmatic doubts of such parallelism.

[3] *Cf.* E. KÜHL, *Die Briefe Petri*, p. 213; U. HOLZMEISTER, *Commentarius*, p. 353.

[4] *Cf.* G. WOHLENBERG, *Der erste und zweite Petrusbrief*, p. 106: »Derselben Verklärung dürfen die Christen entgegenharren und sich dadurch ... trösten.»

special stress is probably not mechanical but has surely a certain practical intention.

In this way we have again a possibility to confirm the thesis that the *motif* in iii. 19 shall serve as an argument for the exhortation in the parenesis to fearless behaviour before the pagans, and that all which is stated in this verse and the following has really a practical and parenetic task. For in the whole connection the rule evidently prevails that the Christians shall follow the pattern of Christ — *cf.* ὑπογραμμόν in ii. 21 — so that what is said of Christ has an urging power as regards the Christians' way of life.[1] And in verse 18, too, it is the winning of the pagans for the Gospel which is really intended. Verse 19 then follows with a new argument for the same parenesis quite logically and naturally if both the verses are understood according to the lines here drawn. Thus we find that there is good reason to consider verses 17, 18 and 19ff. as three co-ordinated arguments for the previous parenesis in verses 13—16, as previously assumed.[2]

*

After this detailed investigation of iii. 19 and its context we will now study some outside texts containing illustrating analogies which can, at least to some extent, form the basis of formal and substantial explanations to our whole passage. In so doing we shall also have the opportunity to confirm several of our assumptions both of principle and of detail.

---

[1] *Cf.* the exposition of Christ as the Pattern which the Christian congregations were under an obligation to follow in Tʜ. Spörri, *Der Gemeindegedanke im ersten Petrusbrief*, 1925, p. 256.
[2] See above, pp. 128 ff., *cf.* 213.

CHAPTER X.

PARALLELS TO THE WHOLE PERICOPE.

Fairly often, as has been stated several times, 1 Pet. iii. 17—22 has been regarded as a specially unique phenomenon. We shall here try to show that there are some quite close analogies to it, not only in the neighbouring passage ii. 19—25 but also in other parts, analogies from which a quite instructive light falls upon what we have now stated with regard to the whole passage.

THE CLOSE PARALLEL IN 1 PET. II. 19—25.

It is quite easy to see, at least now that we have had the opportunity to study the verses 17 and 18 a little more closely, that the pericope iii. 17—22 has to a certain extent a counterpart in ii. 19—25. In verse ii. 18 an exhortation is addressed to the slaves, rather closely corresponding to the general exhortations in iii. 13—16, to submit themselves to their masters and live humbly and patiently. This is to happen, the author clearly means, just as in iii. 13ff., to make a good impression on them and get them converted, for this principle has just been clearly stated in ii. 12.[1] Then follow the arguments for the exhortation in a way very similar to iii. 17ff. (1) The first justification for this patience, as we found in iii. 17, namely that an innocent suffering is something better, has a direct

---

[1] CH. BIGG, too, in his *Commentary*, p. 159, has seen the central importance of the principle in ii. 12.

analogy in ii. 19 and 20 where it is stated that innocent suffering is a merit with God and involves κλέος, honour, evidently said also with regard to fellowmen. (2) The second justification which is in iii. 18, that quite as Christ the Righteous offered Himself for the previously unrighteous Christians in order to lead them to belief and the grace of Baptism, so the Christians in their turn should sacrifice themselves for the unrighteous pagans in order to lead them to belief, can be clearly recognized in ii. 21.[1] There it says: »Thereto have ye been called», namely to this patient suffering. »Even Christ suffered as ye know once for you» — notice ὑπὲρ ὑμῶν with emphasis, like the corresponding word and ὑπὲρ ἀδίκων in iii. 18 — »leaving you an ensample that ye should follow in His foot-steps.» Here the reasoning is exactly the same as in the phrase »even Christ»[2] &c. in iii. 18,[3] only perhaps still more clearly formulated. In verse 25 there is also a special commentary to this: »Ye were like sheep who had gone astray but have now returned» &c. (3) Now we have left a third argument to the parenesis which we consider we have found in iii. 19ff. It has no direct counterpart in ch. ii, if we only think of the peculiar *motif* with the spirits in prison. Yet certainly so much in common can be discovered that the author in ii. 22—25 continues the argument for the previous parenesis by mentioning certain instructive facts from the story of Christ. But in the main the two texts divide at this point. It may, however, in spite of this, be fairly clear that ch. ii. 19ff. contains an interesting analogy to our passage in ch. iii, because the justifications for the parenesis at first correspond almost exactly.

---

[1] Many investigators have of course compared ii. 21 and iii. 18, but they go no farther than to indicate the general resemblance that in both cases Christ is put forward as the example, as for instance R. Knopf, *Die Briefe Petri*, p. 143. We are inclined to go deeper by concentrating on the relation between Christ and the believers on the one side and the believers and the pagans on the other.

[2] Rom. xv. 3 can be compared with this phrase »Christ also» &c.: καὶ γὰρ ὁ Χριστὸς οὐκ ἑαυτῷ ἤρεσεν. It there concerns also Christ as the binding pattern.

[3] Admitted also by G. Wohlenberg, *Der erste und der zweite Petrusbrief*, p. 104 — although he explains ὑπὲρ ἡμῶν in iii. 18 as a false addition, p. 105, note 50.

AN ANALOGY PERHAPS STILL MORE STRIKING IN TIT. III.

It does not seem to have been noticed before that in Tit. also there is a text which contains many presentations comparable with our passage in 1 Pet., indeed which perhaps are in form even nearer to our passage than the parallel text recently mentioned. This is Tit. iii. 1—8. Here too we have first a parenesis concerning loyalty, humility and good-will towards the pagan authorities, iii. 1—2, corresponding to 1 Pet. iii. 13—16. Verse 8 in Tit. belongs also to 1 and 2, for the same exhortations are here repeated in a concentrated form after the arguments put forward in 3—7.[1] We have not precisely the same thoughts in Tit. iii. 1—2 as in 1 Pet. iii. 13—17, for the question of suffering which sets its seal upon the passage in 1 Pet. is not current in Tit. The Pastoral Epistles are very careful regarding the problem of the Christians' suffering from the state authorities and only preach loyalty and mutual understanding.[2] Yet the first two verses in Tit. iii and verse 8 are characterized by the same kind of thought that distinguishes 1 Pet. both in and beside iii. 13—17. Verse 1 contains the verb ὑποτάσσεσθαι (which is supplemented here with the unusual πειθαρχεῖν). This verb is used in exhorting to submission in a political or familiar *milieu* not only in Rom. xiii. 1, 5, in Eph. v. 22 and Col. ii. 18, but also in Tit. three times, ii. 5, 9 and iii. 1, and in 1 Pet. four times, ii. 13, 18, iii. 1 and 5 The expression ἕτοιμος εἶναι πρός, be ready for, used of relations

---

[1] J. JEREMIAS, Der Brief an Titus, *Das Neue Testament Deutsch*, pp. 54, 56, takes »good works» in Tit. iii. 8 as »Werke der Liebe». This is not so easily justifiable. The meaning of καλὰ ἔργα in this verse should be the same as that of πᾶν ἔργον ἀγαθόν in verse 1, where it is clearly social and juridical; in both cases loyal behaviour is meant.

[2] *Cf.* the digression about »Das Ideal christlicher Bürgerlichkeit», in M. DIBELIUS, *Die Pastoralbriefe*, 1931, pp. 24f. — Here it seems there is too much emphasis on the need for calm and rest. It must not be forgotten that a good impression was to be made on the pagans in order to win them for the Gospel. An honest good-will and desire to win them is clear, especially in Tit. iii — *cf.* the presentation below but also, *e.g.*, πάντας ἀνθρώπους in 1 Tim. ii. 4 and πᾶσιν ἀνθρώποις in Tit. ii. 11.

with the pagan authorities we recognize from 1 Pet. iii. 15, and willingness to πᾶν ἔργον ἀγαθόν[1] agrees with τὸ ἀγαθοποεῖν in 1 Pet. iii. 17, and the counterparts in ii. 14, 15, 20, iii. 6 and iv. 19. Notice also καλῶν ἔργων προΐστασθαι in Tit. iii. 8. This clearly does not refer to deeds of love and charity &c., but to the fulfilling of civic duties, seeing that the context speaks of obedience and submission in political matters. In verse 2 we find several expressions for the accommodating temper the Christians ought to show towards the pagans. As a summary it speaks of πᾶσαν πραΰτητα πρὸς πάντας ἀνθρώπους. Similarly the believers are recommended in 1 Pet. iii. 16 to behave μετὰ πραΰτητος καὶ φόβου before the pagans. Here we have come to the justification given by Tit. and 1 Pet. for their exhortations to a positive attitude towards the pagan world. Tit. offers in iii. 3—8 striking parallels to 1 Pet. iii. 18. We too, were once, ποτέ, — *cf.* ἅπαξ in 1 Pet. iii. 18, which thus seems to have only this vague meaning — foolish &c., among other things ἀπειθεῖς (*cf.* ἀπειθήσασιν in 1 Pet. iii. 20), πλανώμενοι, verse 3 (*cf.* 1 Pet. ii. 25). But thanks to the revelation of the goodness of our God, 4, we are saved by Baptism and by the Spirit, 5, which was poured out by our Saviour Jesus Christ. For this reason we should strive after a life of »good deeds», *i.e.* of submission to society, for that is profitable for men, 8. Here we have counterparts both to 1 Pet. iii. 17, 18 and partly to 19—22.

(1) It is better to suffer if one behaves as a loyal citizen (ἀγαθοποιοῦντας) than the opposite, asserts 1 Pet. iii. 17. This corresponds to verse 8 in Tit. If we consider that the words about the advantageous effect of a loyal behaviour, even if it leads to suffering, here in verse 17 actually refer to better possibilities to get the pagans converted,[2] that here it is not only a question of what is profitable for the individual Christian but what is useful for the cause of the Gospel and then also for the pagans themselves, we have here a good

---

[1] W. Lock, *A Critical and Exegetical Commentary on the Pastoral Epistles*, 1924, p. 152, clearly also thinks that the words here about good works mainly include civic, municipal duties.
[2] *Cf.* above, pp. 132 f., 177 f., 213, 218.

analogy to Tit. iii. 8: ταύτά (*i.e.* to strive after »the good» or »loyal deeds») εστίν καλά και ωφέλιμα τοις άνθρώποις, *i.e.* the outsiders. (2) The next argument for the parenesis in 1 Pet., viz. iii. 18, has a close counterpart in Tit. iii. 3ff. As is easily seen, ότι και Χριστός άπαξ ... υπέρ ημών απέθανεν, δίκαιος υπέρ αδίκων (N.B.), corresponds in its intention quite well with ήμεν γάρ ποτε και ημείς ανόητοι, άπειθείς (N.B.; *cf.* 1 Pet. iii. 20), πλανώμενοι &c. in Tit. iii. 3. The analogy is also strengthened by the sentence ήτε γάρ ως πρόβατα πλανώμενοι in 1 Pet. ii. 25 which is very much like the sentence in Tit. and which clearly seen in connection with ii. 21 has the same logical function as iii. 18 in its place. In both cases the argument implies that the Christians must have a positive attitude towards the pagans in spite of the latter's unrighteousness, for once they themselves were no better, when Christ converted them.[1] In 1 Pet. iii. 18 the earlier sinfulness of the Christians is expressed by the short phrase υπέρ αδίκων, while in Tit. iii. 3 we have a whole catalogue of vices, but there is no essential difference. God's goodness and love to mankind manifested in Christ towards the earlier unrighteous Christians obliges them according to Tit. iii. 4 and 6—7 to corresponding kindness towards others. We have the same thought in 1 Pet. iii. 18, if we there let the sacrificial Death of Christ be mentioned as a motive to the corresponding sacrifice in order to win others — as we have earlier attempted to interpret this verse.

(3) The preaching to the spirits in prison has no counterpart in Tit. On the other hand we find here, too, Baptism mentioned as a reason for the positive attitude towards the pagans, verses 4—5, just as in 1 Pet. iii. 20f. In both cases God's saving grace in this the Christians' sacrament of consecration, is emphasized: τού σωτήρος ημών θεού, and έσωσεν ημάς in Tit., όκτώ ψυχαι διεσώθησαν, and ημάς (or υμάς) νύν σώζει in 1 Pet.; and likewise the gift of new life which accompanies it: παλιγγενεσία in Tit. iii. 5, κληρονόμοι ... κατ' έλπίδα ζωής αιωνίου, in verse 7, and the symbolism

---

[1] Regarding the passage in Tit. see also J. JEREMIAS, Der Brief an Titus, p. 55.

with Noah and the reference to the resurrection of Jesus in 1 Pet. iii. 20 and 22. In 1 Pet. Baptism is declared not to be a physical cleansing but an agreement about a good attitude. Previously we wished to assume that the negative section here refers to Jewish observances.[1] Similarly Tit. iii. 5 contains a polemic pungency against the deeds of self-righteousness.

OTHER POINTS OF COMPARISON IN TITUS.

If we consider Tit. ii. 11 ff. we discover a duplicate to the passage we have just mentioned, iii. 4 ff., just as 1 Pet. iii. 17—22 has a duplicate in ii. 19—25; in both Epistles these previous duplicates are inserted after the exhortations to the slaves. In this duplicate in Tit. Baptism is not directly mentioned as in iii. 5 but is probably in the thought of the author partly because of the similarity with iii. 4 ff. and partly because of turns of speech like ἀρνησάμενοι τὴν ἀσέβειαν and καταρίσῃ (cf. Ezech. xxxvii. 23, 1 Cor. vi. 11, Hebr. ix. 14, x. 22) ἑαυτῷ λαὸν περιούσιον (cf. 1 Pet. ii. 9). Here we find an analogy to the positive definition of Baptism as an »agreement about a good attitude», as we prefer to interpret this phrase in 1 Pet. iii. 21. In verses 12—14 it is stated that after we have abjured godlessness and worldly lusts we should live sensibly, righteously (N.B.), and justly in this present world waiting for the epiphany of Jesus Christ, He who gave Himself for us to save us from all lawlessness (N.B.; cf. Ps. cxxix [cxxx]. 8) and purify to Himself a peculiar people (cf. 1 Pet. ii. 9), who should be zealous for good works (1 Pet. iii. 13). All this is like a detailed commentary to συνειδήσεως ἀγαθῆς ἐπερώτημα in our view. The stress is laid upon civic blamelessness.

The whole of this passage ii. 11—14 appears as a summarizing conclusion to a series of shorter pareneses in ch. ii, addressed to different groups of Christians, and all the time mostly concerned with this civic blamelessness. In this connection the term συνείδησις itself plays a certain part.

---

[1] Above, pp. 188 f.

In i. 14—16 it is said that the false prophets' συνείδησις like their νοῦς are defiled because they have fallen a victim to false Jewish zeal for purification and appear as disobedient (N.B.) and useless for any »good deed» (N.B.). In contrast to this distorted attitude to life the older Christian men are exhorted quite neutrally, but then the older Christian women are urged to bring up the younger to love their husbands and their children, to be good housewives and subject to their husbands so that God's word should not be blasphemed, ii. 4f. (cf. 1 Pet. iii. 1f.). In the same way Titus himself is urged to be a pattern for the younger men in »good deeds» &c., in order that ὁ ἐξ ἐναντίας (N.B.) shall be ashamed and not have anything discreditable to say, verses 7f. (corresponding to 1 Pet. ii. 12, 15, iii. 16). Finally the slaves are urged to have good relations with their masters in order to be in everything an ornament of God's word, verses 9f. (κοσμέω also in 1 Pet. iii. 5). They are also urged not to isolate themselves (νοσφίζεσθαι) but to show all kinds of »good faith», ἀγαθὴ πίστις. This last idea is, in this connection, a fairly close counterpart to συνείδησις according to our interpretation, and we have already stated that συνείδησις and πίστις are sometimes close to each other.[1] In this way we have a certain reflex of the antithesis we wished to prove between σαρκὸς ἀπόθεσις ῥύπου and συνειδήσεως ἀγαθῆς ἐπερώτημα: not negative isolation but positive loyalty. After these exhortations to different categories of people, this *Haustafel* in ii. 1—10, the passage ii. 11—14 earlier mentioned comes as a summary. Against the background here examined it is clear how interested the writer is that the Christians shall give evidence of social good conduct as we have just observed in this passage also. The remarks above are confirmed by this.

On the other hand the *Haustafel* appears in ii. 1—10 in its turn as a direct continuation of the warnings at the end of ch. i, against false prophets who do not follow »sound learning», i. 13, but have given themselves over unto »Jewish myths and the commandments of men», so that their συνείδησις is defiled. The polemic against these Judaisers comes again in ch. iii. 9. If we wish to know in what

---

[1] *Cf.* above, p. 179.

the distortion of these false teachers and their impure συνείδησις consisted, more closely considered, we must in reason take our information just from the exhortations in ch. ii recently touched upon, which are expressly introduced with the antithetic »but preach thou what is necessary of sound learning». Because of the emphatic tendency of these exhortations to a positive attitude against pagan or at least partly pagan surroundings we consider it clear that the συνείδησις of the false prophets leaning towards Judaism is defiled because they isolate themselves in some kind of zeal for ceremonial purity — see ἐντολαῖς ἀνθρώπων and καθαρὰ τοῖς καθαροῖς, verses 14f. — and are ἀνυπότακτοι, verse 10 (cf. the exhortation to ὑπόταξις under the state authority in iii. 1) and ἀπειθεῖς (N.B.) καὶ πρὸς πᾶν ἔργον ἀγαθὸν (N.B.) ἀδόκιμοι, verse 16, to a great extent in a social, political meaning. It is because of such a Jewish ceremonially justified isolation and opposition to authority that they lack a συνείδησις ἀγαθή.[1] In this way we have found a certain confirmation of the theory developed above[2] concerning the συνείδησις-passage in 1 Pet. iii. 21.[3]

CONCLUSION.

In general there is much in the peculiarities of Tit. which agree with 1 Pet., if we think of the interest for social and political blamelessness and positive fulfilment of duty which we have chosen to consider as a characteristic in the pericope of 1 Pet. here investigated.

[1] Cf. our theory of the the words οὐ σαρκὸς ἀπόθεσις ῥύπου in 1 Pet. iii. 21, above, pp. 188f.
[2] Cf. above, pp. 176ff.
[3] We believe that the Epistle to Titus requires a more thorough analysis than those in the available literature on the subject, and above all that such an analysis should bear in mind not only what Tit.'s theology has in common with the other Pastoral Epistles, but also what is peculiar to it. If one studies what is said in the fine commentaries of LOCK and DIBELIUS, for example, the latter aspect seems to be ignored. Our observations regarding the great stress on social good conduct in Tit. places this Epistle in surprisingly close relation to 1 Pet. Other peculiarities can certainly also be noticed.

What we have here observed is, besides a series of detailed similarities between 1 Pet. and Tit., a more systematic correspondence in form and content between certain portions of these Epistles, namely 1 Pet. ii. 19—25 and iii. 17—22 on the one side and Tit. ii. 11—14 and iii. 1—8 on the other. It is noticeable here that the earlier passages of each Epistle also resemble each other as regards their place in the context: they are both inserted after the exhortations to the slaves. The latter parts in each Epistle are alike in that they both follow summarized exhortations to believers in general.

It is probable that these similarities are not at all due to any direct effect from one Epistle upon the other.[1] The dissimilarities which appear at the same time are also evidence against it. It is more probable that both Epistles were affected by a current type of preaching regarding the mission of the Church and Baptism. We can thus assume a definite parenetic figure, a literary τόπος, as a basic explanation of the many similarities.[2]

Such a theory agrees very well with the idea of resemblance in the N.T. epistolary literature which has recently been put forward especially by two important Anglo-Saxon researchers in this sphere, PH. CARRINGTON[3] and E. G. SELWYN.[4] They oppose the idea of many older investigators that there is a direct literary influence of one Epistle on the other, *e.g.* of the Pauline Epistles on 1 Pet.[5] Instead they consider that we ought to assume common traditions, a general linguistic usage and current *motifs* and figures as a foundation to the different Epistles.[6] It appears also from a deeper

---

[1] W. LOCK, *Commentary on the Pastoral Epistles*, pp. xxxiv, states there are certain points of resemblance between Tit. and 1 Pet. but thinks after all that in no case is there proof of literary dependence; »they may all be independent treatment of similar subjects», he assumes.

[2] *Cf.* M. DIBELIUS' assumption in *Die Pastoralbriefe*, pp. 91 ff., that Tit. iii. 1—8 rests on the basis of older traditions.

[3] PH. CARRINGTON, *The Primitive Christian Catechism*, 1940.

[4] E. G. SELWYN, *The First Epistle*, 1946.

[5] SELWYN, *op. cit.*, Essay ii, On the Inter-relation of Peter and other N.T. Epistles, pp. 365 ff.

[6] CARRINGTON, *op. cit.*, pp. 31 ff.

study of all the interrelations of the epistolary literature that the similarities are far too many and too involved to infer a direct influence of the one writing upon another. Thus 1 Pet. can be placed in intimate contact with every possible N.T. Epistle. Wherever one turns one finds striking similarities. It is not enough to bring out the likeness to the primary Pauline Epistles, which is really very clear. Even the secondary Pauline Epistles, the Epistle to the Hebrews, and partly also 2 Pet. offer very significant parallels.[1] One is frankly bewildered if, in the face of this overwhelming amount of material, one must choose some special writing and say: »here is the source», *e.g.* of a passage in 1 Pet. The presentation of the extraordinary wealth of parallels have made the conception less natural which was expressed for example in A. JÜLICHER's[2] definition of 1 Pet. as »ein Abklatsch paulinischer Arbeiten».[3] We are led instead to a common parenetic and catechistic, oral basis by fixed writing, probably rooted in the practical traditions of the Christian public worship.[4]

As far as these promptings to a partly new view of the non-pauline epistolary literature in the N.T. can contribute to a better general and individual understanding of the problems connected therewith it may be of value that we have here come up against certain connections between 1 Pet. and Tit. which can quite well be said to be best interpreted according to the lines mentioned, by assuming a common traditional basis in the Christian cult, parenesis, and catechism. The τόπος we wish to presume would in this case have come into use in such a connection when it was a question of the general Christian missionary duty, carried out

---

[1] See the fine reviews and references in U. HOLZMEISTER, *Commentarius*, pp. 105 ff., PH. CARRINGTON, *op. cit.*, pp. 22 ff. and E. G. SELWYN, *op. cit.*, pp. 369 ff. (with many illustrating tables).

[2] A. JÜLICHER, *Einleitung in das Neue Testament*, 5—6. Aufl. 1931, hrsg. von E. FASCHER, p. 196.

[3] See also the observations by D. DAUBE in his investigation of the Participle and Imperative in 1 Peter, supplement to E. G. SELWYN, *The First Epistle*, on p. 488.

[4] A far-sighted presentation of these catechetical foundations is A. SEEBERG's suggestive work *Der Katechismus der Urchristenheit*, 1903.

by, among other things, a faultless behaviour among the pagans in their environment and a positive attitude to them. It is not impossible that this parenetic figure is inherited from earlier Jewish pareneses. Notice, for example, the anxiety that the pagans shall not blaspheme on account of the believers' behaviour in the *Damascus Documents* xii. 7f.[1]

*

As we have not found in these parallel texts any direct analogy to the reasoning in iii. 19, we must ask ourselves where the author has obtained the *motif* worked into the traditional argumentation we appear to find here. We shall now pass over to this question.

---

[1] *Cf.* 1 Tim. vi. 1. — S. SCHECHTER, *Fragments of a Zadokite Work*, p. l.

CHAPTER XI.

PARALLELS TO THE APPEARANCE BEFORE »THE SPIRITS».

In the middle of the τόπος we have tried to find, the author of 1 Pet. has inserted a special *motif*, the preaching to the spirits and certain accompanying circumstances. The intention of this observation we have already considered it possible to determine with fairly good evidence. Now the task is to find traces of an ideological back-ground to the strange *motif* of a preaching to the spirits in prison — for which we clearly must turn to quite other quarters than Tit. &c.

THE DESCENT A CONSTITUENT PART OF THE MESSIANIC DRAMA.

The idea of a descent is probably to be found in nearly all religions, especially, of course, in connection with the dying and rising again of gods. Unfortunately we cannot go more deeply into the whole of the enormous amount of this comparative material; several valuable reviews of it are available.[1] In the Near East regions there are also good examples of such ideas. Among examples of later years, which should supplement earlier available materials, may be specially mentioned newly edited and commented texts to the Tammuz cultus of the Sumerians and the Babylonians,[2]

---

[1] Above all M. LANDAU, *Hölle und Fegfeuer*, 1909, R. GANSCHINIETZ, Katabasis, *Pauly's Real-Encycl.* x. 2, 1919, cols. 2359ff., J. A. MACCULLOCH, *The Harrowing of Hell*, 1930, and J. KROLL, *Gott und Hölle*, 1932.

[2] M. WITZEL, *Tammuz-Liturgien und Verwandtes*, 1935.

texts of Ishtar's descent,[1] and the important 'Al'iyān Ba'al texts from Ras Shamra or Ugarit in Phœnicia.[2] Here there are good possibilities for a deepened study of the Descent ideology. It is quite clear that the going down into the underworld has often been a part of the plan of action, the drama, which belonged to the worship of several gods and even divine kings.[3] The O.T. also contains certain traces of Descent ideas, as appears from such passages as Gen. xxxvii. 35 (which, as is known, has some close analogies in the Phœnician texts about 'Al'iyān Ba'al),[4] Ps. xvi. 10, lxxxvi. 13, lxxxviii. 5ff.,[5] Isa. liii. 8ff. The O.T. material might well be subjected to a new general examination in the light of modern opinions. In later Judaism the Descent *motif* occurs quite often. We need only think e.g. of the *Book of Enoch* which has played an important role in the proofs already given. Besides, reference can be made to 4 Ezra ch. xiii,[6] *Ma'aseh de R. Yehoshua' ben Lewi*,[7] *Erubin* xix a, *Jalqut chadash* xxxv.[8] Also in the N.T.

---

[1] New literature: G. CONTENAU, *Le déluge babylonien, suivi de: Ishtar aux enfers, La Tour de Babel*, 1941; S. N. KRAMER, Inanna's Descent to the Nether World. The Sumerian Version of »Ištar's Descent», *Revue d'assyr.* xxxiv. 3, 1937, pp. 93ff.; M. WITZEL, Zur sumerischen Recension der Höllenfahrt Ischtars, *Orientalia* xiv. 1—2, 1945, pp. 27ff.

[2] Material and literature on the Ugaritic AB-texts in I. ENGNELL, *Studies in Divine Kingship*, 1943, pp. 110ff., R. DE LANGHE, *Les Textes de Ras-Shamra-Ugarit*, i, 1945, pp. 153ff.

[3] In the large amount of material collected by J. KROLL in his *Gott und Hölle*, there are good starting-points for a deeper study of these questions. In our opinion this material should, however, be considered more in connection with an actual ritual basis than is done by Kroll, and not merely as mythology and literary expression of passionate feelings (*Pathosformel*). — On reflections in the N.T. of the ideas of a king's descent see T. ARVEDSON, *Das Mysterium Christi*, 1937, pp. 125f.

[4] R. DUSSAUD, Le mythe de Ba'al, *Rev. de l'hist. des rel.* cxi, 1935, pp. 47f.; *id., Les découvertes de Ras Shamra et l'A.T.*, 1941, p. 134. — This refers to a few phrases in I* AB vi. 25b, I AB i. 7* g—8* a.

[5] G. WIDENGREN, Konungens vistelse i dödsriket. En studie till Psalm 88, *Svensk Exeget. Årsb.* x, 1945, pp. 66ff.

[6] H. GRESSMANN, *Der Messias*, 1929, p. 348.

[7] A. JELLINEK, *Beth ha-Midrasch*, ii, 1853, p. 50; A. WÜNSCHE, *Aus Israels Lehrhallen*, iii, 1909, pp. 101f.

[8] F. WEBER, *Jüdische Theologie*, 1897, p. 343.

THE APPEARANCE BEFORE »THE SPIRITS» 233

several passages indicate such Descent ideas, besides that in 1 Pet. iii. 19, as *e.g.* Matt. xii. 40, Acts ii. 23ff., Rom. x. 7, Eph. iv. 9.[1] Similarly several passages from the O.T. can be quoted which clearly were interpreted within Christendom as referring to Christ's Descent, especially Ps. xv (xvi). 10. We need not go more deeply into these Biblical passages but content ourselves with listing those which are put forward as examples of patristic quotations in connection with the Descent in P. J. JENSEN's *Læren om Kristi Nedfart*: Ps. xxiv. 7, lxxxvi. 13, cvii. 14ff., cxix. 153ff., Isa. xxvi. 19, xlv. 2, Dan. iii, Hos. xiii. 14, Zech. ix. 11; Matt. xii. 29, 40, xvi. 18, xxvii. 52f., Luke xxiii. 43, Acts ii. 24, 27, Rom. xiv. 9, Eph. iv. 8f., Rev. i. 18.[2]

If 1 Pet. iii. 19 really is a Descent *motif*, we have already here a part explanation of how the author could put forward the statement that Christ went to »the Prison» and preached to the spirits there. The *descensus ad inferos* was presumably a special point of the Christ drama at the very beginning of the history of Christianity, although its occurrence in the *Apostles' Creed* cannot be noticed before the 4th Century.[3] The words about »the sign of Jonah» alone in Matt. xii. 39f. and Luke xi. 29f. should show that, but other passages in the N.T. can be mentioned, several references to the Descent in the Messianic texts of the O.T. and a large amount of analogous material from the surrounding pagan world. This going to the beings in »the Prison» is probably a rather natural point here directly after the mention of Christ's Death.

There are, however, two special circumstances in this procedure which make it peculiar and difficult to understand from the history

---

[1] Good review and a thorough analysis especially in K. GSCHWIND, *Die Niederfahrt Christi*, pp. 157ff.

[2] P. J. JENSEN, *Læren om Kristi Nedfart*, p. 32.

[3] *Cf.* above p. 32. — As some representative works from the discussion on this subject may be mentioned: P. KING, *The History of the Apostles' Creed*, 1702; G. H. WAAGE, *De ætate articuli, quo ... traditur ... descensus*, 1836; C. P. CASPARI, *Quellen zur Geschichte des Taufsymbols und der Glaubensregel*, i—iii, 1866—75; P. J. JENSEN, *Læren om Kristi Nedfart*, excursus pp. 246ff.; HJ. LINDROTH, *Den apostoliska trosbekännelsen*, 1933.

of ideas aspect. The one is that this descent is connected with a preaching, and the other that the preaching is just for the disobedient spirits from the days of Noah.

We shall now try to put forward some material which will make these circumstances less peculiar and special than one usually imagines them.

A PREACHING BY THE SAVIOUR AT HIS DEATH.

It is not a unique occurrence in early Christianity that the Saviour Himself, following a well-known pattern, e.g. in Isa. l. 4—11, undertakes a proclamation to the spirit world, an announcement of His righteousness and triumph. In 1 Tim. iii. 16 we have an allusion to a self-revelation of Jesus to the Angels, ὤφθη ἀγγέλοις, which though it certainly does not indicate a *praedicatio verbalis*, only *realis*, yet may be considered as very closely approaching a verbal announcement. The whole hymn in 1 Tim. iii. 16 has also great similarity to 1 Pet. iii. 18—22.[1] From this it is fairly clear that the appearance to the Angel world is a *motif* organically embodied in the Salvation drama.[2] It is a short step from ὤφθη ἀγγέλοις in 1 Tim. iii. 16 to the idea of an oral proclamation. Col.

---

[1] E. G. SELWYN, *The First Epistle*, p. 325, has arranged a comparison between these texts in the following excellent manner:

1 Tim. iii. 16.	1 Pet.
ἐφανερώθη ἐν σαρκί	iii. 18. θανατωθεὶς μὲν σαρκί
	[iv. 6. ἵνα κριθῶσι μὲν κατὰ ἀνθρώπους σαρκί]
ἐδικαιώθη ἐν πνεύματι	ζωοποιηθεὶς δὲ πνεύματι
	[iv. 6. ζῶσι δὲ κατὰ θεὸν πνεύματι]
ὤφθη ἀγγέλοις	⎰19. τοῖς ἐν φυλακῇ πνεύμασι πορευθεὶς ἐκήρυξεν ⎱22. ὑποταγέντων αὐτῷ ἀγγέλων καὶ ἐξουσιῶν καὶ δυνάμεων
ἐκηρύχθη ἐν ἔθνεσιν ⎫ ἐπιστεύθη ἐν κόσμῳ ⎬ ἀνελήμφθη ἐν δόξῃ	iii. 21. ὑμᾶς νῦν σῴζει βάπτισμα... συνειδήσεως ἀγαθῆς ἐπερώτημα εἰς θεόν iii. 22. ὅς ἐστιν ἐν δεξιᾷ θεοῦ πορευθεὶς εἰς οὐρανόν

[2] *Cf.* above, pp. 121 f.

ii. 15, ἐδειγμάτισεν ἐν παρρησίᾳ (τὰς ἀρχάς &c.),[1] may also possibly refer to an oral reproval of the enemy spiritual powers, immediately at the Death or the Resurrection.

An interesting example of an announcement by the Saviour Himself of His righteousness and supremacy can be quoted from Melito's *Homily on the Passion*,[2] recently found in Greek, §§ 101 ff.: ἀνέστη ἐκ νεκρῶν καὶ ταύτην [βοᾷ ὑμῖν] τὴν φωνήν· τίς ὁ καταρκρινόμε- [νος πρὸς] ἐμέ; ... τίς <ὁ> ἀντιλέγων μοι; There, too, the Descent is clearly mentioned in the context. Later there is an invitation from Christ directed to all generations of men who are sullied with sins to come and receive forgiveness of their sins, 103. This also seems to be a fairly close counterpart to 1 Pet. iii. 19.

The Odes of Solomon have other passages containing such a proclamation or *auto-louange*, e. g. xvii and xxxi.

Thus a proclamation by the Saviour Himself in connection with His Death and Resurrection can quite well be taken as forming a natural part of the Messianic drama.

THE TRANSGRESSORS FROM THE FLOOD.

It has already been stated that the generation of the Flood were of great importance for the N.T. world, also that they were suitable to be used as types of contemporary disobedient people who should be judged at the approaching Great Judgment.[3]

The most significant thing in this connection is, however, that the *Book of Enoch* chs. i—xxxvi or corresponding texts as we have tried to show were an extraordinarily important source for the author at this point. As a matter of fact we have probably here the weightiest material basis for the explanation of the reasoning in 1 Pet. iii. 19. We may have in this book the main source from which the author has taken his material for this verse.

When this is stated, however, the question arises: How has the author been led to use this text at this point of his presentation?

---
[1] *Cf* also above, p. 200, note 1.
[2] Melito, *The Homily on the Passion*, ed. by C. BONNER, 1940, pp. 161 ff.
[3] *Cf.* above, pp. 70 ff.

Why does he here appeal to the Enoch ideology? And how could this be interpreted with a Christological tendency as has been done here?

One answer to these questions is that the *Book of Enoch* in those quarters has been taken as Holy Scripture and placed on a level with the prophets' writings in the O.T. as is clear from Jude 14 and the other passages mentioned above.[1] In that way it also became the subject of the typological interpretation which the whole of the O.T. experienced in Early Christendom, in that everything in the Old Covenant was taken as prophesying about Christ and as counterparts to Him.[2] In this way there was already a good possibility for the connections to the Enoch ideology which we consider can be proved. Another explanation of the importance of the *Book of Enoch* for our author is that it deals so much with the problem of the just versus the pagans with their Kings and the Mighty on the earth (see *e.g.* chs. xlv ff.). Here our author found good matter for his argument just of that problem which, according to our presentation, is fundamental to the whole context: the relation between the Christians and their pagan environment.

These explanations are, however, perhaps not sufficient. It may, therefore, be of value to try to find support for the connection with the *Book of Enoch* by pointing out some other texts which may have contributed to the rise or the maintenance of the conception of an appearance by Christ to the sinners from the Flood similar to Enoch's appearance to the imprisoned spirits. These texts also facilitate our understanding in general of how the spirits from the days of the Flood can have appeared in this connection.

There is a text in Isa. xxiv which may have been taken in Early Christianity as a prophecy of how Christ, after a long time, goes to the beings who perished in the Flood and manifested Himself to them in some way. In verses 18—23 it is said:

---

[1] Pp. 66 ff.

[2] A short discussion of the Church's typological interpretation of the O.T. from modern points of view is to be found in N. A. DAHL, *Das Volk Gottes*, 1942, pp. 273 ff.

THE APPEARANCE BEFORE »THE SPIRITS»

»(18) For the windows are opened from the height, and the foundations of the earth quake. (19) The earth breaks asunder, the earth utterly splits, the earth utterly shakes. (20) The earth staggers like a drunkard, and sways like a night-refuge. And its rebellion weighs heavily on it, and it falls, and arises no more. (21) And it passes in that day, Yahweh punishes the host of the height in the height and the kings of the earth on the earth. (22) And they are gathered as prisoners are gathered into the pit, and imprisoned in the prison. And after many days they are visited (וְיִפָּקֵדוּ). (23) And the moon is abashed, and the sun is ashamed, for Yahweh is King in the mount of Zion and in Jerusalem, and before His elders is glory.» In the LXX the conclusion runs: (22b) διὰ πολλῶν γενεῶν ἐπισκοπὴ ἔσται αὐτῶν. (23a) καὶ τακήσεται ἡ πλίνθος, καὶ πεσεῖται τὸ τεῖχος ... These phrases can quite well have been considered as alluding to the Flood. Such expressions as the windows of Heaven, verse 18 — cf. Gen. vii. 11 and viii. 2 — the rebellion of the earth, 20, the host of the height and the kings of the earth, the thrusting into the pit or the prison, 22, and the transgressors so punished, taken in about the same way as in the *Book of Enoch*, easily causes one to think of the Flood. Then one has in the allusion to a »visitation» after »many days» in verse 22, according to the current Christological interpretation, a prophecy of how Christ in the fullness of time visits the imprisoned creatures from the time of the Flood.

Now in all ages it has been much discussed whether this visitation shall be accepted in a good or a bad meaning.[1] The Hebrew verb פקד in verse 22 can have both the meaning of »to afflict» and »to visit» and the Greek ἐπισκοπή which occurs in the LXX has the same double meaning. It seems to us very probable that the favourable meaning of the visitation is the primary, from the viewpoint of religious traditions, because of the interesting analogy in the Babylonian Epic of Creation, *Enūma elish*, iv. 106—114, com-

---

[1] »Gnädige Heimsuchung»: Origenes, CALVIN, EWALD, DILLMANN; »strafende Heimsuchung»: Raschi, VITRINGA, BREDENKAMP, DUHM, BUHL, according to O. PROCKSCH, *Jesaja I*, 1930, p. 314.

pared with vii. 27 f. There it is described in the passage first mentioned how the sea monster Tiāmat's host is scattered and bound in prison. These beings are elsewhere called »the captured gods» or »the bound gods». In the latter passage in *Enūma elish* Marduk is called »He who had mercy on the bound gods», and it says: »the yoke imposed upon the gods his enemies he caused to be removed».[1] This epithet of Marduk is also illumined by a text published and commented upon by TH. G. PINCHES in his paper The Legend of Merodach.[2] There it says of Marduk according to Pinches' rendering (A. 1—8): »He strengthened his bonds. He goes down to the prison. He rises (?) and approaches the prison. He opened the gate of the prison, he comforts them. He looked upon them then, all of them; he rejoices. Then the captive gods looked upon him. — Kindly the whole of them regarded (him).» From this it seems that Marduk appears and »visits» — in a good meaning — these beings bound after the struggle in primitive time, who probably may in some way correspond to the fallen Angels in the Biblical tradition of the Flood.[3] Another illuminating analogy to the visitation in Isa. xxiv. 22, if taken in a good meaning, occurs in the *Aramaic Incantation Texts from Nippur*, published by J. A. MONTGOMERY, no. iv, *ll.* 4 f.:[4] »I charm you with the seal with which were charmed the Seven Stars and the Twelve Signs of the Zodiac unto the great day of judgment, and to the great hour of the redemption of your heads.» Here it is the same kind of evil spirits as in Isaiah and the

---

[1] As regards the quoted passages from *Enūma elish* see *The Babylonian Epic of Creation*, ed. by S. LANGDON, 1923, p. 142 note 9, where the expression »the bound gods» is also discussed.

[2] TH. G. PINCHES, The Legend of Merodach, *Proceed. of the Soc. of Bibl. Arch.* xxx, 1908, pp. 60 ff.

[3] E. J. KISSANE, *The Book of Isaiah*, i, 1941, p. 283, also makes a comparison between Isa. xxiv. 22 and the passage quoted from *Enūma elish* iv, but does not compare it with the other passages mentioned above and therefore only leads the thought to a definite condemnation.

[4] J. A. MONTGOMERY, *Aramaic Incantation Texts*, 1913, pp. 135 ff. It is Montgomery's merit to have combined 1 Pet. iii. 19 with Isa. xxiv. 22, and also set forth in that connection *Enūma elish* and certain of the other texts referred to above, *op. cit., ibid.* But Montgomery's suggestions were not observed in the exegetical literature.

THE APPEARANCE BEFORE »THE SPIRITS»

Book of Enoch that are referred to, and it is presumed that in the fulness of time they will be released from imprisonment. However, the original meaning of Isaiah's text is of less importance. The main question is how it was accepted in the N.T. time and whether it can be used as an analogy to such ideas as we should assume behind 1 Pet. iii. 19.

Now, the *Targum of Jonathan* has the following exposition of the expression in Isa. xxiv. 22: וּמִסְגֵי יוֹמִין יְעוּל דכרניהון, »and after many days shall come their remembrance». It appears that the Targum here, too, as in other places, can have a Messianic implication,[1] and that this »remembrance» is favourably meant must certainly be the most probable assumption. He who read this Targum text or a similar version of Isa. xxiv and assumed that Christ was the Person referred to in all the prophecies, could thereby receive a direct impulse to a theory of how Christ visited the imprisoned spirits of the Flood. As regards the other old versions of the Isaiah text, some of them can be mentioned as support for the same theory. Like the Targum, Saadia Gaon has the expression يذكرون, »they will be remembered».[2] The LXX text implies that the rare Hebrew expressions לְבִנָה and חַמָּה have been taken by the translators as לְבֵנָה and חוֹמָה, so that the whole has been made to treat of a breaking down of »the bricks» and »the wall»; but in that way the thought is led direct to the descent conception which we have called *Höllenstürmung*. In the Peshito it is still clearer: ܘܡܢ ܒܬܪ ܝܘܡܬܐ ܣܓܝܐܐ, »and after many days they will be redeemed». Thus there are several signs that Isa. xxiv. 22 in early traditions was accepted as the description of a visitation in a good meaning. And this can well have been interpreted as a prophecy of how Christ would go to the beings of the Flood in prison.

The resemblances between the passage in Isaiah and the *Book*

---

[1] »There is a strong inclination on the part of the targumist (Jonathan) to shift the predicted reality to the Messianic age whenever the contents admit of such a presentation», states P. CHURGIN, *Targum Jonathan*, 1922, p. 79. Among the passages interpreted as bearing upon the Messiah he also mentions Isa. xxiv. 16—18, xxv. 4—5, *op. cit.*, p. 80.

[2] W. GESENIUS, *Der Prophet Jesaia*, ii. 2, 1821, p. 773.

of *Enoch* are also quite clear.¹ By means of this analogy we obtain further help in explaining the background in the history of ideas to 1 Pet. iii. 19.

Another interesting passage is Job xxvi. 2—6 according to the LXX, some verses which, like the whole context, can easily be interpreted as treating of Christ: »(2) Whom are You favourable to or whom will You help? Is it not Him who has much power and whose arm is strong? (3) With whom have You consulted? Is it not Him who has all wisdom ...? (5) μὴ γίγαντες μαιωθήσονται ὑποκάτωθεν ὕδατος καὶ τῶν γειτόνων αὐτοῦ; (6) γυμνὸς ὁ ᾅδης ἐνώπιον αὐτοῦ, καὶ οὐκ ἔστιν περιβόλαιον τῇ ἀπωλείᾳ.» Here verses 5 and 6 can easily be made to refer to the descent of the Messiah into Hades when he overthrows the house of perdition, and when »the Giants» of Gen. vi. 4 »are in the throes of agony» — this is probably how μαιωθήσονται should be interpreted in analogy to the יחוללו lying behind it.

A passage from the *Book of Baruch* can also be read as an allusion to how Christ reveals Himself to beings of the same kind as the fallen Angels in the *Book of Enoch*. Here we must remember that the transgressors, in the angelological part of the later writing, are in some places described as stars which have been cast down into the Abyss. In the *Book of Baruch* iii. 24—38 it runs as follows: (24) ὦ Ἰσραήλ, ὡς μέγας ὁ οἶκος τοῦ θεοῦ ... (26) ἐκεῖ ἐγεννήθησαν οἱ γίγαντες οἱ ὀνομαστοὶ ἀπ' ἀρχῆς γενόμενοι, εὐμεγέθεις, ἐπιστάμενοι πόλεμον. (27) οὐ τούτους ἐξελέξατο ὁ θεός, οὐδὲ ὁδὸν ἐπιστήμης ἔδωκεν αὐτοῖς· (28) καὶ ἀπώλοντο παρὰ τὸ μὴ ἔχειν φρόνησιν, ἀπώλοντο διὰ τὴν ἀβουλίαν αὐτῶν.

(29) τίς ἀνέβη εἰς τὸν οὐρανὸν καὶ ἔλαβεν αὐτήν (the Wisdom), καὶ κατεβίβασεν αὐτὴν ἐκ τῶν νεφελῶν; (30) τίς διέβη πέραν τῆς θαλάσσης καὶ εὗρεν αὐτὴν καὶ οἴσει αὐτὴν χρυσίου ἐκλεκτοῦ; (31) οὐκ ἔστιν ὁ γινώσκων τὴν ὁδὸν αὐτῆς, οὐδὲ ὁ ἐνθυμούμενος τὴν τρίβον αὐτῆς; (32) ἀλλὰ ὁ εἰδὼς τὰ πάντα γινώσκει αὐτήν, ἐξεῦρεν αὐτὴν τῇ συνέσει αὐτοῦ· ὁ κατασκευάσας τὴν γῆν εἰς τὸν αἰῶνα χρόνον ἐνέπλησεν αὐτὴν κτηνῶν

---

¹ W. Gesenius, *op. cit.*, pp. 773f.; B. Duhm, *Das Buch Jesaja*, [1892] 1922, pp. 177f.; G. B. Gray, *The Book of Isaiah*, i, 1912, pp. 421ff.; J. Lindblom, *Die Jesaja-Apokalypse*, 1938, pp. 27f.

τετραπόδων· (33) ὁ ἀποστέλλων τὸ φῶς καὶ πορεύεται, ἐκάλεσεν αὐτό, καὶ ὑπήκουσεν αὐτῷ τρόμῳ· (34) οἱ δὲ ἀστέρες ἔλαμψαν ἐν ταῖς φυλακαῖς αὐτῶν καὶ εὐφράνθησαν· (35) ἐκάλεσεν αὐτούς, καὶ εἶπον Πάρεσμεν· ἔλαμψαν μετ᾽ εὐφροσύνης τῷ ποιήσαντι αὐτούς. (36) οὗτος ὁ θεὸς ἡμῶν, οὐ λογισθήσεται ἕτερος πρὸς αὐτόν. (37) ἐξεῦρεν πᾶσαν ὁδὸν ἐπιστήμης, καὶ ἔδωκεν αὐτὴν Ἰακὼβ τῷ παιδὶ αὐτοῦ καὶ Ἰσραὴλ τῷ ἠγαπημένῳ ὑπ᾽ αὐτοῦ. (38) μετὰ τοῦτο ἐπὶ τῆς γῆς ὤφθη, καὶ ἐν τοῖς ἀνθρώποις συνανεστράφη.

It is first important to note that the Giants are mentioned in this connection. If we then read the text in a consistently christological manner, as the Early Christians read the O.T. writings, a revelation of Christ is obtained to those transgressors thought of as stars in different »prisons» (φυλακαί). Some few special details in this passage, which can easily be taken as alluding to Christ, are the words τίς ἀνέβη εἰς τὸν οὐρανόν in verse 21 (Rom. x. 6f.), ὁ παῖς and ὁ ἠγαπημένος in verse 37 and the words about a later appearance among men on earth in verse 38, after this descent-like journey right through the sea and an appearance to the stars — imagined as persons. We must also recall that such a cosmic journey to fetch the fruits of Wisdom to which the whole passage seems to allude, is a Descent *motif* known both in the Biblical and other religions,[1] as is shown for instance by the *Gilgamesh Epos*, or the Song of the Pearl in the *Acts of Thomas*.[2] Above all it is important to notice that this passage, at least in the last part, was often quoted by some of the Early Fathers[3] as a Messianic text instructive from the aspect of Christological dogma.[4]

---

[1] *Cf.* the chapter »Descent to obtain a Boon» in J. A. MacCulloch, *The Harrowing of Hell*, pp. 21 ff.
[2] On the Pearl see C. M. Edsman, *Le baptême de feu*, 1940, pp. 190 ff.
[3] *E.g.* Athenagoras, Origenes (*passim*), Hippolytus, Tertullian, Cyprian, Commodianus, &c. See the references in P. Sabatier, *Bibliorum sacrorum latinæ versiones antiquæ*, ii, 1751, pp. 744f.; F. H. Reusch, *Erklärung des Buchs Baruch*, 1853, pp. 3ff., 268ff.; and J. Knabenbauer, *Commentarius in Dan., Lament. et Baruch*, 1891, pp. 488f. The passage is mentioned in the *Apostolic Constitutions*, v. 20. 3, as quoted by the Jews.
[4] *Cf.* also the exposition in some commentaries as for instance H. Wace, *Apocrypha*, ii, 1888, pp. 277ff.

16

This presentation of a revelation to the stars followed by their hymn of praise which may be interpreted from verses 34f. of the Baruch text quoted has, to some extent, a counterpart in the *Book of the Secrets of Enoch* ch. xviii: »(1) The men took me on to the fifth heaven, and there I saw many and countless soldiers, called Grigori (»Watchers») ... (3) who had rejected the Lord of Light ... (8) And I said: 'Wherefore do you wait, brethren, and do not serve before the Lord's face' ... (9) And they listened to my admonition, and spoke to the four ranks in heaven ... And the Grigori broke into song with one voice, and their voice went up before the Lord pitifully and affectingly.» Here we have what is probably a close parallel to 1 Pet. iii. 19. An important difference is that the prison in the Enoch text has been sublimated to one of the heavenly spheres, which probably has no direct analogy in 1 Pet. But this is only a difference of degree. In any case this Slavonic Enoch Book shows that the Enoch traditions also contained tendencies to state a more positive result of the meeting with the imprisoned transgressors of the Flood than does the Ethiopic *Book of Enoch*. This confirms our theory of an intimate interdependence of the Enoch ideology. The latter Book is one of the sources for 1 Pet. iii. 19 from a formal aspect, but as regards the contents, the tradition here is formulated more positively than the preserved text of the *Book of Enoch* can show, just as this tradition has also a more positive character in the *Book of the Secrets of Enoch*.

Our desire to direct attention to the O.T. passages as contributory sources of inspiration for 1 Pet. iii. 19 may be justified by the following fact. When studying the oldest Descent traditions of the Church, it appears generally that there is often an intimate relation to O.T. passages. This is especially clear in the most famous of the Descent texts of the Early Church, the *Gospel of Nicodemus*. Here all the time, we find ourselves in the section *Descensus Christi ad inferos* with reflections from texts from the Psalms, Isaiah, &c. suitably interpreted so that they deal the whole time with Christ and the underworld.[1] All these connections with

---

[1] C. SCHMIDT, Der Descensus ad inferos, pp. 575 f.

the O.T. in the literature of the Church reveal the fact that the writings of the Old Covenant have fairly generally been interpreted as containing evidence of the Descent which should belong to the Christ drama.[1] For this reason it is not impossible that the author of 1 Pet. in iii. 19 also found support in similar evidence obtained by a certain interpretation of the Holy Scriptures. Notice how the context is quite filled with allusions to facts from those writings.

On the other hand it can also be thought that the appearance of the Saviour to the transgressors of the Flood belongs in some way to the inherited scheme for the drama of salvation, if we are sure that the Christ *mysterion* has older counterparts in form. In that way these passages from the *Book of Enoch*, Isaiah xxiv &c. would not themselves have given the impulse to that *motif* in iii. 19 but they could easily have helped to keep alive thoughts which had earlier been expressed.

On the basis of the *Ode of Solomon* no. xxiv, it seems possible to assume that the Messianic scheme can really have involved a point where the Saviour at the Descent comes into contact with the transgressors from the days of the Flood, without any special written passage originating such a theory. The passage from the Ode also clearly treats of Baptism:

»The Dove flew over the head of our Lord the Messiah (denoting a connection with Christ's baptism) ... (3) And the inhabitants were afraid, and the sojourners were frightened. (4) The birds lifted their wings and fled, and the creepers died in their holes. (5) And the abysses were opened and closed, and they were seeking for the Lord, like (women) who are in travail. (6) But He was not given to them for food, because He did not belong to them. (7) And the abysses were indeed sealed[2] by the seal of the Lord.

---

[1] *Cf.* ὅτι Χριστὸς ἀπέθανεν ... κατὰ τὰς γραφάς, καὶ ὅτι ἐτάφη, καὶ ὅτι ἐγήγερται ... κατὰ τὰς γραφάς, 1 Cor. xv. 3 f.

[2] On the basis of the analogies in a Coptic baptismal office and a Syrian Jacobite office, quoted by J. H. BERNHARD, *The Odes of Solomon*, 1912, p. 106, it is perhaps best to render ܚܬܡ here as »seal», and not as »submerge», as is also possible.

244 THE APPEARANCE BEFORE »THE SPIRITS» [CH.

ܘܐܒܕܘ ܒܗ̇, ܒܚܘܫܒܐ And they perished in this thought
ܕܐܝܬܝܗܘܢ ܗܘܘ those who were[1]
ܡܢ ܩܕܝܡ. from the beginning.

(8) For they became corrupt[2] in the beginning, but the end of their corruption was life. (9) And every one of them that was defective perished, because it was not permitted to them to make a defence for themselves that they might remain. (10) But the Lord destroyed the imaginations of all them that had not the truth with them. (11) For they were defective in wisdom, those who were lifted up in their hearts. (12) And they were rejected, because the truth was not with them. (13) For the Lord disclosed His way, and spread about His grace. (14) And those who understood it know His holiness. Hallelujah.»

If our interpretation of the expression in verse 7b: »those who had existed from the beginning» is correct, it is easy to think that the reference is to the primeval sinners who now are in the abysses of the underworld.[3] As to the expression »those who were from the beginning» in verse 7 we can compare it with the words ἀπ' ἀρχῆς γενόμενοι in the text from the *Book of Baruch* just quoted, verse 27,[4] and likewise »they perished in the thought» may possibly be

---

[1] This is about the same rendering as in J. R. HARRIS, *The Odes and Psalms of Solomon*, 1909, p. 121, and in H. GRESSMANN, Die Oden Salomos, in E. HENNECKE, *Neutestamentliche Apokryphen*, p. 459. R. HARRIS & A. MINGANA, *The Odes and Psalms of Solomon*, ii, 1920, have: »They perished in the thought which they had existed in from the beginning.» Yet such a construction of ܕ seems less natural especially as we have no supplement to the relative pronoun by a preposition with a suffix. Certainly ܕ often can be used in a more free way with a local or temporal meaning, but this is mostly the case with such nouns as are of especially local or temporal character (TH. NÖLDEKE, *Syrische Grammatik*, 1898, pp. 271 ff.). — But even with Harris & Mingana's rendering we get a qualification of these beings as belonging to primeval times.

[2] The Pa'el of ܚܒܠ does not so often mean »to be in pains of childbirth» as »to corrupt» or »to become corrupt». The latter meaning must also be most natural here.

[3] J.H. BERNHARD, *The Odes of Solomon*, pp. 105 f., also considers that here we have to distinguish between the Abyss and the »evil demons» who dwell there. Yet he has not related the latter to the Flood in any way.

[4] *Cf.* οἱ ἀπ' αἰώνων in John of Damascus, *De fide orthod.* iv. 29 (see above, p. 33).

connected with ἀπώλοντο διὰ τὴν ἀβουλίαν αὐτῶν in the same text, verse 28. These evil beings are also said to be corrupt from the very beginning, and it is specially stated that they lacked wisdom (*cf.* the *Book of Baruch* iii. 27f.) and were over-bold (*cf.* Wisd. xiv. 6 &c.). To these the Lord has revealed Himself, verse 13, so that they were put to shame. And this clearly happened in connection with His Baptism, as indicated by the dove, verse 1.[1] The Flood may also be under consideration because of the dove and the terror that her message arouses in the Abyss and among its inhabitants.[2]

In this way an analogy to the spirits of the Flood in 1 Pet. iii. 19 is obtained from a tradition which possibly also is partly independent of the Biblical foundations and which is of very great interest especially on account of the intimate relation to the Descent, Baptism[3] and the Flood. The two texts can of course only be considered parallel with a reservation concerning the language difficulties which all the *Odes of Solomon* present.

THE TRANSITION FROM VERSE 18 TO 19 F.
AND THENCE TO 21 F.

Verse iii. 18 mentions Jesus dying as the suffering Messiah. According to the view inherited from the O.T. and Judaism, the Messiah's suffering could be imagined as a struggle in the waters of Death, which heave and surge around the Chosen of God. In accordance with this, Jesus in Mark x. 38 and Luke xii. 50 calls His coming Death by suffering a Baptism. Thinking of these

---

[1] H. GRESSMANN, Die Sage von der Taufe Jesu und die vorderorientalische Taubengöttin, *Arch. f. Rel.-wiss.* xx, 1920/21, pp. 27 ff.

[2] J. R. HARRIS, Two Flood-Hymns of the Early Church, *The Exp.* viii. 2, 1911, pp. 410 ff.; P. LUNDBERG, *La typologie baptismale*, pp. 89 f.

[3] A specially emphatic stress on the relation between the Descent and Baptism has been made, as is well known, by J. H. BERNHARD just in connection with the *Odes of Solomon* and 1 Pet. iii. 19, in his book *The Odes of Solomon*, pp. 32 ff., and his essay The Descent into Hades and Christian Baptism, *The Exp.* viii. 11, 1916, pp. 241 ff. See also P. LUNDBERG, *La typologie baptismale*, pp. 87 ff., and, earlier, B. SCHMIDT, Die Feier des heiligen Feuers in der Grabeskirche, *Palästinajahrbuch* xi, 1915, pp. 85 ff.

ideas it is possible to make the transition from Christ's Death in verse 18 to the spirits of the Flood in 19f. less sudden and similarly the transition to Baptism in verse 21f.

The Christians could read, especially in certain of the Psalms, of the suffering and agony of the Messiah when the waters of Death forced their way in, e.g. xvii. 5—8, 17, xli. 8, lxviii. 2—4, 14—16, lxxxvii. 4—10, 18f., cxxix. 1, cxliii. 7 (according to the LXX). All these passages describe the suffering as a death struggle in the waters' depth.[1] In the synoptic accounts of the Passion, there are quotations from two of these Psalms: xli. 6 and 12 in Matt. xxvi. 38 with parallels, Ps. lxviii. 22 in Matt. xxvii. 34 and 46 with parallels, and in two others there are certain expressions which could easily be understood as referring to the suffering Christ — the words about the relatives' flight in lxxxvii. 9 and 19 and υἱὸς ἀνθρώπου in cxliii. 3. Two other Psalms which, without resembling the suffering with a distress in waters, yet put forward precisely the same complaint as the others quoted, are xxi and xxx (LXX), and they, as is well known, play an important part in the Passion Stories. »The sign of Jonah» in Matt. xii. 40 and xvi. 4 with the parallel in Luke xi. 32 points in the same direction — cf. Jonah ii. 3—10.[2] Otherwise also the Sea seems to be identified with Hades in Rev. xx. 13.

From such instances it appears that, in the stories of His suffering, Christ is in many respects accepted as the Messiah who appears as struggling in the Waters of Death in these Psalms of Lamentation.

By means of this reasoning we have the possibility of finding the transition from 1 Pet. iii. 18 to 19 in a very simple way. If the author regarded the Death of Christ as such a »baptism» so that he did not so much think of the scene on Golgatha as of the waters

---

[1] We have probably in late Judaism a trace of this idea that the Messiah has to undergo Baptism, in *4 Ezra* xiii, which treats of the Son of Man arising from the sea.

[2] One can also think of the ancient Christian symbol with Christ as a fish. *Cf.* F. J. DÖLGER, IXΘΥΣ, 1910ff., and R. EISLER, *Orpheus — the Fisher*, 1921.

THE APPEARANCE BEFORE »THE SPIRITS» 247

of Death and their terrible surging, then it was not a big step to the spirits from the Flood who were probably regarded as surviving as prisoners beneath just these waters which were their punishment (notice also ὑποκάτωθεν ὕδατος in the Job text quoted above). In this way we have a smooth and logically intelligible transition between the Death of Christ in verse 18 and the preaching to the spirits in verse 19.

The thought passes then easily from the spirits of the Flood to Noah. But how does the author pass thence to Christian Baptism? To this the easy reply is that the Flood was a suitable prototype for Baptism. Yet there is probably something deeper in this connection than a simple association of ideas. In as far as Christian Baptism, as Paul says in Rom. vi, is conceived as an image of Christ's death, it is easy for the thought to pass to the cosmic masses of water considered as distressing the suffering Messiah, and thence it is not far to the waters of the Flood. And the intimate resemblance between ch. iv. 1—2 and Rom. vi[1] makes it very probable that 1 Pet. shares the Pauline view of a baptism to the Death of Christ.[2] There are also many other connections between the Flood and Baptism: God's gracious intervention to rescue from destruction, the thought of a Covenant, the dove, *i.e.* the symbol of the Spirit which brought the first greeting from the new earth, and many others, most of which have been mentioned in our detailed investigation of these verses above.[3]

*

---

[1] As noticed in many commentatory presentations.
[2] P. LUNDBERG, *La typologie baptismale*, pp. 98ff., who, however, puts forward other arguments in this matter than those mentioned above. — On these intricate relations of ideas see also the interesting references in T. ARVEDSON, *Das Mysterium Christi*, pp. 125f.
[3] It is also very interesting to observe that the *Missale Gregorianum* and *Gallicanum* have the story of the Flood among the lessons on the Easter *vigilia* before the great Day of Baptism. Here we have a practical connection of this pericope and Baptism which can very well be based on early traditions. *Cf.* K. SCHMALTZ, Das heilige Feuer in der Grabeskirche im Zusammenhang mit der kirchlichen Liturgie ..., *Palästinajahrbuch* xiii, 1917, pp. 66 ff.

If an enquiry is made in this way into the ideas which our author may have had in connection with the different *motifs* in this passage the reasoning appears more connected than it does at first sight to a modern reader, and verses 19f. fit quite naturally and logically into the rest of the context.

BIBLIOGRAPHY.

ALTANER, BERTHOLD: Patrologie. Freiburg im Breisgau 1938.
ARVEDSON, TOMAS: Das Mysterium Christi. Eine Studie zu Mt. 11: 25—30. (Arbeiten und Mitteilungen aus dem neutestamentlichen Seminar zu Uppsala hrsg. v. A. Fridrichsen. vii.) Uppsala 1937.
ATZBERGER, LEONHARD: Die christliche Eschatologie in den Stadien ihrer Offenbarung im Alten und Neuen Testament. Mit besond. Berücksichtigung der jüdischen Eschatologie im Zeitalter Jesu Christi. Freiburg i. Br. 1890.
— Geschichte der christlichen Eschatologie innerhalb der vornicänischen Zeit. Freiburg im Breisgau 1896.
BACHER, WILHELM: Die älteste Terminologie der jüdischen Schriftauslegung. Ein Wörterbuch der bibelexegetischen Kunstsprache der Tannaiten. Leipzig 1899.
BALDENSPERGER, W.: Das Selbstbewusstsein Jesu im Lichte der messianischen Hoffnungen seiner Zeit. Erste Hälfte. Die messianisch-apokalyptischen Hoffnungen des Judentums. 3. Aufl. Strassburg 1903.
BALJON, J. M. S., Bijdragen op het gebied der conjecturalkritiek. De eerste Brief van Petrus: Theol. Studiën 1892, pp. 425—433.[1]
BARDENHEWER, OTTO: Geschichte der altkirchlichen Literatur. ii. Freiburg i. Br. 1903.
BAUER, WALTER: Griechisch-Deutsches Wörterbuch zu den Schriften des Neuen Testaments und der übrigen urchristlichen Literatur [begründet von E. PREUSCHEN]. 3. Aufl. Berlin 1937.
— Das Leben Jesu im Zeitalter der neutestamentlichen Apokryphen. Tübingen 1909.
BAUR, FERD. CHR., Der erste petrinische Brief, mit besonderer Beziehung auf das Werk: Der petrinische Lehrbegriff ... von B. WEISS, 1855: Theol. Jahrbücher xv, 1856.[1]
BECK, J. T.: Erklärung der Briefe Petri. Hrsg. von J. LINDENMEYER. Gütersloh 1896.
BELLARMINO, ROBERTO: Disputationes Roberti Bellarmini de controversiis christianæ fidei, adversus huius temporis hæreticos. i—iii. Ingolstadii 1586—93.

---

[1] Not available.

BERNHARD, J. H. [Dublin], The Descent into Hades and Christian Baptism. (A Study of I Peter III. 19ff.): The Expositor viii. 11, 1916, pp. 241—274.

BERNHARDY, G.: Wissenschaftliche Syntax der griechischen Sprache. Berlin 1829.

BERTHOLDT, LEONHARD: Christologia Iudæorum Jesu apostolorumque ætate in compendium redacta observationibusque illustrata. Erlangæ 1811.

BESSER, W. F.: Die Briefe St. Petri in Bibelstunden für die Gemeinde ausgelegt. (Bibelstunden. viii.) Halle 1854.[1]

BEYSCHLAG, WILLIBALD: Neutestamentliche Theologie oder Geschichtliche Darstellung der Lehren Jesu und des Urchristentums nach den neutestamentl. Quellen. 2. Aufl. Halle a.S. 1896.

Bibeln eller Den Heliga Skrift. Gamla och Nya Testamentet. De kanoniska böckerna. Översättning ... stadfäst av Konungen år 1917. Stockholm 1917 &c.

BIGG, CHARLES: A Critical and Exegetical Commentary on the Epistles of St. Peter and St. Jude. (The International Critical Commentary.) 2nd ed. Edinburgh 1902.

BISPING, AUG.: Erklärung der sieben katholischen Briefe. (Exeget. Handbuch. viii.) 2. Aufl. Münster 1871.[1]

BLASS, FRIEDRICH, see DEBRUNNER, ALBERT.

BLENKIN, G. W.: The First Epistle General of Peter. (Cambridge Greek Testament for Schools and Colleges.) Cambridge 1914.[1]

BONHÖFFER, ADOLF: Epiktet und das N.T. (Religionsgeschichtl. Versuche und Vorarbeiten. x.) Giessen 1911.

BONNER, CAMPBELL: The Last Chapters of Enoch in Greek. (Studies and Documents. viii.) London 1937.

BORNEMANN, W., Der erste Petrusbrief — eine Taufrede des Silvanus?: Zeitschr. für die neutest. Wiss. xix, 1919/20, pp. 143—165.

BORNHÄUSER, KARL: Die Gebeine der Toten. Ein Beitrag zum Verständnis der Anschauung von der Totenauferstehung zur Zeit des Neuen Testamentes. (Beitr. zur Förd. christl. Theologie. xxvi. 3.) Gütersloh 1921.

— Jesu Predigt für die Geister. (Nach 1. Petri 3, 19. 20.): Allg. Evangel.-Luth. Kirchen-Zeitung. liv, 1921, cols. 322—324.

BOUSSET, WILHELM: Hauptprobleme der Gnosis. (Forsch. zur Rel. und Lit. des A. und N.T:s. x.) Göttingen 1907.

— Kyrios Christos. Geschichte des Christusglaubens von den Anfängen des Christentums bis Irenäus. 2. umgearb. Aufl. Göttingen 1921.

— Die Religion des Judentums im späthellenistischen Zeitalter. 3. verb. Aufl. hrsg. v. H. Gressmann. (Handbuch zum N.T. xxi.) Tübingen 1926.

— Zur Hadesfahrt Christi: Zeitschr. für die neutest. Wiss. xix, 1919/20, pp. 50—66.

---

[1] Not available.

BIBLIOGRAPHY 251

Bowyer, William: Critical conjectures and observations on the New Testament collected from various authors, as well in regard to words as pointing, with the reasons on which both are founded. 3rd ed. enlarged ed. by J. Nichols. London 1782.[1]

Brockelmann, Carl: Lexikon Syriacum. Editio secunda. Halis Saxonum 1928.

Brugmann, Karl: Griechische Grammatik. Lautlehre, Stammbildungs- und Flexionslehre, Syntax. 4. Aufl. von A. Thumb. Mit Anhang über Griechische Lexikographie von L. Cohn. (Handbuch der klass. Altertumswiss., hrsg. von I. von Müller. ii. 1.) 4. Aufl. München 1913.

Bruhn, Ewald: Sophokles, erklärt von F. W. Schneidewin & A. Nauck. viii. Anhang. Berlin 1899.

Brun, Lyder, »Um der Engel willen» 1 Kor. 11. 10: Zeitschr. für die neutest. Wiss. xiv, 1913, pp. 298—308.

Brunet de Presle, W., & Egger, W.: Les papyrus grecs du Musée du Louvre et de la Bibliothèque Impériale. (Notices des manuscripts de la Bibliothèque Impériale. xviii. 2.) Paris 1866.

Bruston, C.: La descente du Christ aux enfers, d'après les apôtres et d'après l'église. Paris 1897.[1]

Budge, E. A. Wallis: Coptic Apocrypha in the Dialect of Upper Egypt, ed. with English Translations. London 1913.

Bugge, F. W.: Apostlerne Peters og Judas' Breve. Indledede, oversatte og forklarede. Christiania 1885.

Cabrol, Fernand, Descente du Christ aux enfers d'après la liturgie: Dictionnaire d'archéologie chrétienne et de liturgie, iv. 1, Paris 1920, cols. 682—693.

Cadbury, Henry J., The Relative Pronouns in Acts and Elsewhere: Journ. of Bibl. Lit. xlii, 1923, pp. 150—157.

Calov, Abraham: Biblia Novi Testamenti illustrata. ii. Francofurti ad Mœnum 1676.

Campenhausen, Hans von: Die Idee des Martyriums in der alten Kirche. Göttingen 1936.

Carrington, Philip: The Primitive Christian Catechism. A study in the Epistles. Cambridge 1940.

Caspari, C. P.: Ungedruckte, unbeachtete und wenig beachtete Quellen zur Geschichte des Taufsymbols und der Glaubensregel, hrsg. und in Abhandlungen erkl. i—iii. (Univ.-Program.) Christiania 1866—75.

Chaine, J., Descente du Christ aux enfers: Dictionnaire de la Bible, Supplément, ii, Paris 1934, cols. 395—431.

Charles, R. H.: The Apocrypha and Pseudepigrapha of the Old Testament in English. i—ii. Oxford 1913.

— A Critical and Exegetical Commentary on the Revelation of St. John. (The International Critical Commentary.) i—ii. Edinburgh 1920.

---

[1] Not available.

CHURGIN, PINKHOS: Targum Jonathan to the Prophets. (Yale Oriental Series. Researches. xiv.) [1907; ought to be:] 1922.
CLEMEN, CARL, Die Einheitlichkeit des 1. Petrusbriefes verteidigt: Theol. Stud. u. Krit. lxxviii, 1905, pp. 619—628.
— »Niedergefahren zu den Toten.» Ein Beitrag zur Würdigung des Apostolikums. Giessen 1900.
Constitutiones Apostolorum, see Didascalia.
CONTENAU, G.: Le déluge babylonien, suivi de: Ischtar aux enfers, La Tour de Babel. (Bibliothèque historique.) Paris 1941.
CRAMER, DANIEL: De descensu Jesu Christi ad inferos exegema. Stetini 1615.
CRAMER, J. A.: Catenæ græcorum patrum in Novum Testamentum. viii. Oxonii 1844.
CRAMER, JAKOB, Exegetica et critica. ii. Het glossematisch karakter van 1. Petr. 3, 19—21 en 4, 6: Nieuwe Bijdragen vii. 4, 1891, pp. 73—149.[1]
CREMER, HERM., Über den Zustand nach dem Tode. Nebst einigen Andeutungen über das Kindersterben und über den Spiritismus. Gütersloh 1883.
CREMER, HERMANN, & KÖGEL, JULIUS: Biblisch-theologisches Wörterbuch der Neutestamentlichen Gräzität. 10. Aufl. Gotha 1915.
CULLMANN, OSCAR: Königsherrschaft Christi und Kirche im Neuen Testament. (Theologische Studien. x.) Zürich 1941.
— Les traces d'une vieille formule baptismale dans le Nouveau Testament: Revue d'hist. et de philos. relig. xvii, 1937, pp. 424—434.
Cyprian. S. Thasci Cæcilii Cypriani opera omnia, rec. Gv. HARTEL. (Corpus scriptorum ecclesiasticorum latinorum. iii. 1—3.) Vindobonæ 1868—71.
DAHL, NILS ALSTRUP, Dopet i Efesierbrevet: Svensk Teol. Kvartalskrift xxi. 2, 1945, pp. 85—103.
— Das Volk Gottes. Eine Untersuchung zum Kirchenbewusstsein des Urchristentums. (Skrifter utg. av Det Norske Videnskaps-Akademi. Hist.-filos. Kl. 1941. ii.) Oslo 1941.
DAUBE, DAVID, Participle and Imperative in 1 Peter: Appended note to E. G. SELWYN, The First Epistle of Peter, 1946, pp. 467—488.
— Two Haggadic Principles and the Gospels: The Journ. of Theol. Stud. xliv, 1943, pp. 149—155.
DEBRUNNER, ALBERT: Friedrich Blass' Grammatik des neutestamentlichen Griechisch bearbeitet. 7. Aufl. i—ii. Göttingen 1943.
DEHN, G., Engel und Obrigkeit: Theologische Aufsätze Karl Barth zum 50. Geburtstag, München 1936, pp. 90—109.
DELBRÜCK, B[ERTHOLD]: Vergleichende Syntax der indogermanischen Sprachen. i—iii. (Grundriss der vergleichenden Grammatik der indogermanischen Sprachen ... von K. BRUGMANN & B. DELBRÜCK. iii—v.) Strassburg 1893—1900.
DELITZSCH, FRANZ, & HOFMANN, JOHANN CHR. K. VON: Theologische Briefe. Hrsg. von W. VOLCK. Leipzig 1891.
DENNISTON, J. D.: The Greek Particles. Oxford 1934.

---

[1] Not available.

BIBLIOGRAPHY 253

Dibelius, Martin: Die Pastoralbriefe. (Handbuch zum N.T., hrsg. von H. Lietzmann. xiii.) Tübingen 1931.
Didascalia et Constitutiones Apostolorum, ed. F. X. Funk. i—ii. Paderbornæ 1905.
Dietelmaier, Joh. Augustinus: Historia dogmatis de descensu Christi ad inferos litteraria. Norimbergæ 1741. [Ed. secunda, Altdorf 1762.]
Dittenberger, Guilhelmus: Sylloge inscriptionum græcarum. Ed. tertia. i—iv. Lipsiæ 1915—21.
Dölger, Franz Joseph: ΙΧΘΥΣ. i—v. Freiburg 1910, Münster 1922—43.
— Der Taufbürge nach Theodor von Mopsuestia: Antike und Christentum iv, 1933—34, pp. 231—32.
— Zum Oktogon des altchristlichen Taufhauses: Antike und Christentum iv, 1933—34, p. 288.
— Zur Symbolik des altchristlichen Taufhauses: Antike und Christentum iv, 1933—34, pp. 153—187.
Dorner, I. A.: System der christlichen Glaubenslehre. i—ii. Berlin 1880—81.
— A System of Christian Doctrine. Transl. by A. Cave & J. S. Banks. i—iv. London 1881—82.[1]
Dublin, see Bernhard, J. H.
Duhm, Bernhard: Das Buch Jesaja. (Göttinger Handkommentar zum A.T. iii. 1.) [1892] 4. Aufl. Göttingen 1922.
Duhm, H.: Die bösen Geister im Alten Testament. Tübingen 1904.[1]
Dürr, Lorenz, Psalm 110 im Lichte der neueren altorientalischen Forschung: Verzeichnis der Vorlesungen an der Staatl. Akademie zu Braunsberg im Wintersemester 1929/30, Kirchhain N.-L. 1929, pp. 3—26.
Dussaud, René: Les découvertes de Ras Shamra et l'Ancien Testament. 2ème éd. Paris 1941.
— Le mythe de Ba'al et d'Aliyan d'après des documents nouveaux: Revue de l'hist. des religions, cxi, 1935, pp. 5—65.
Eckhard, Henricus, Tractatus de descensu Christi ad inferos et aliis ... quæstionibus. Lipsiæ 1623.
Edsman, Carl Martin: Le Baptême de feu. (Acta semin. neotest. Upsal. ix.) Diss. Uppsala 1940.
— Gezelii bibelverk och en återklang av kristen kronologi och antik världs-ålderslära. (Uppsala Univ. årsskrift 1941. vii. 7.) Uppsala 1941.
Eisentraut, E., Evangelien: Lexikon für Theologie und Kirche, iii, 2. Aufl. Freiburg i. Br. 1931, cols. 878—882.
Eisler, Robert: Orpheus — the Fisher. Comparative Studies in Orphic and Early Christian Cult Symbolism. London 1921.
— The Sadoqite Book of the New Covenant. Its Date and Origin: Orient and Occident, being Studies ... in Honour of M. Gaster's 80th Birthday, London 1936, pp. 110—143.
Eliezer. Pirke de Rabbi Eliezer, translated and annotated by G. Friedlander. London 1916.

---

[1] Not available.

254 BIBLIOGRAPHY

ENGNELL, IVAN: Studies in Divine Kingship in the Ancient Near East. Diss. Uppsala 1943.

Enoch. The Ethiopic Version of the Book of Enoch ed. by R. H. CHARLES. (Anecdota Oxoniensia.) Oxford 1906.

— The Book of Enoch or 1 Enoch. Translated from the Editor's Ethiopic Text ... by R. H. CHARLES. Oxford 1912.

— Das Buch Henoch übersetzt und erklärt von A. DILLMANN. Leipzig 1853.

— Le livre d'Hénoch traduit ... par F. MARTIN ... (Documents pour l'étude de la Bible. Les Apocryphes de l'A.T.) Paris 1906.

— 3 Enoch or The Hebrew Book of Enoch, edited and translated by HUGO ODEBERG. Cambridge 1928.

Ephræm. S. Ephraemi Syri Carmina Nisibena, additis prolegomenis ... edidit ... G. BICKELL. Lipsiæ 1866.

ESTIUS, GUILH.: Commentarius in omnes D. Pauli epistolas, item et catholicas. ii. Duaci 1616.[1]

EWALD, HEINRICH, Übersicht der 1855—1856 erschienenen Schriften zur Biblischen Wissenschaft: Jahrbücher der Bibl. Wiss. viii, 1856, pp. 118—273.

The Excavations at Dura-Europos conducted by Yale University and the French Academy of Inscriptions and Letters. Preliminary Report. vi. Ed. by M. I. ROSTOVTZEFF ... New Haven ... 1936.

FACCIOLATI, J., FORCELLINI, ÆG., ... CORRADINI, F.: Lexicon totius latinitatis. iv. Patavii 1887.

FARRAR, F. W.: Mercy and Judgment. London 1881.[2]

FELTEN, JOSEPH, Zur Predigt Jesu an »die Geister im Gefängnis», 1. Petr. 3, 19s. und 4, 6: Festschrift der Vereinigung katholischer Theologen »Aurelia», Bonn 1926, pp. 28—31.

— Die zwei Briefe des Heiligen Petrus und der Judasbrief übersetzt und erklärt. Regensburg 1929.

FOERSTER, WERNER, ἐξουσία: G. KITTEL, Theol. Wörterb., ii, 1935, pp. 559—571.

FÖRSTER, RICHARD: Quæstiones de attractione enuntationum relativarum, qualis quum in aliis tum in Græca lingua potissimumque apud Græcos poetas fuerit. Berolini 1868.

FRENZEL, JOS.: Die Entstehung des relativen Satzbaues im Griechischen. (Gymn.-Progr.) Wrongrowitz 1889.[1]

FREY, J. G., Apocryphes de l'Ancien Testament: Dictionnaire de la Bible, Supplément, i, 1928, cols. 354—460.

FRIDRICHSEN, ANTON, The Conflict of Jesus with the Unclean Spirits: Theology xxii, 1931, pp. 122—135.

— Exegetisches zum N.T., Symbolæ Osloënses xiii, 1934, pp. 38—46.

— »Icke akta för rov»: Nysvenska studier xxv, 1945, pp. 67—72.

---

[1] Not available.
[2] Available in Swedish translation (1882).

FRIDRICHSEN, ANTON, Zur Auslegung von Röm 1, 19f.: Zeitschr. für die neutest. Wiss. xvii, 1916, pp. 159—168.

FRIEDRICH, G., κῆρυξ, κηρύσσω &c.: G. KITTEL, Theol. Wörterb., iii, 1938, pp. 682—717.

FRINGS, JOS., Zu 1 Petr. 3, 19 und 4, 6: Bibl. Zeitschr. xvii, 1925/26, pp. 75—88.

FRONMÜLLER, G. F. C.: Die Briefe Petri und der Brief Judä. (Theologischhomiletisches Bibelwerk ... hrsg. von J. P. LANGE. N.T. xiv.) 2. Ausg. Bielefeld 1862.

GANSCHINIETZ[, R.], Katabasis: Paulys Real-Encyclopädie der classischen Altertumswiss., Neue Bearb. von G. WISSOWA & W. KROLL, x. 2, 1919, cols. 2359—2449.

GEIGER, ABRAHAM, Einige Worte über das Buch Henoch: Jüdische Zeitschr. für Wiss. und Leben iii, 1864/65, pp. 196—204.

GERHARDUS, JOHANNES: Commentarius super Priorem D. Petri epistolam. Jenæ 1641.

GESENIUS, WILHELM: Der Prophet Jesaia. i—iii. Leipzig 1820/21.

GOODSPEED, EDGAR J.: Problems of New Testament Translation. Chicago 1945.

GONTARD, L.: Essai critique et historique sur la première épître de Saint Pierre. [Thèse.] Lyon 1905.[1]

GOPPELT, LEONHARD: Typos. Die typologische Deutung des Alten Testaments im Neuen. (Beitr. zur Förd. christl. Theol. R. II, xliii.) Gütersloh 1939.

GRAY, GEORGE BUCHANAN: A Critical and Exegetical Commentary on the Book of Isaiah i—xxxix. i. i—xxvii. (The International Critical Commentary.) Edinburgh 1912.

GREEVEN, HEINRICH, ἐρωτάω, ἐπερωτάω, ἐπερώτημα: G. KITTEL, Theol. Wörterb., ii, 1935, pp. 682—686.

GRESSMANN, HUGO: Der Messias. (Forsch. zur Rel. und Lit. des A. und N.T:s. N.F. xxvi.) Göttingen 1929.

— Die Oden Salomos: E. HENNECKE: Neutestamentliche Apokryphen, 1924, pp. 437—472.

— Die Sage von der Taufe Jesu und die vorderorientalische Taubengöttin: Archiv für Religionswiss. xx, 1920/21, pp. 1—40.

— Vom reichen Mann und armen Lazarus. Eine literaturgeschichtliche Studie. Mit ägyptologischen Beiträgen von G. MÜLLER. (Abhandl. der Kgl. Preuss. Akad. der Wiss. Jg. 1918. Philos.-hist. Kl. vii.) Berlin 1918.

GROTIUS, HUGO, Annotationes in Epistolam Petri priorem: Annotationum in Novum Testamentum pars tertia, Parisiis 1650, pp. 3—37.

GRÜNBAUM, M., Beiträge zur vergleichenden Mythologie aus der Hagada: Zeitschr. der Deutsch. Morgenländ. Gesellsch. xxxi, 1877, pp. 183—359.

GRUNDMANN, W., ἀγαθοποιέω: G. KITTEL, Theol. Wörterb., i, 1933, p. 17.

— κακοποιέω: G. KITTEL, Theol. Wörterb., iii, 1938, pp. 486f.

---

[1] Not available.

GSCHWIND, KARL: Die Niederfahrt Christi in die Unterwelt. Ein Beitrag zur Exegese des Neuen Testamentes und zur Geschichte des Taufsymbols. (Neutestamentl. Abhandl. hrsg. von M. MEINERTZ. ii. 3/5.) Münster i. W. 1911.

GÜDER, EDUARD: Die Lehre von der Erscheinung Jesu Christi unter den Todten. In ihrem Zusammenhange mit der Lehre von den letzten Dingen. Bern 1853.

GUNKEL, HERMANN, Der erste Brief des Petrus: Die Schriften des N.T:s, 2. Aufl., ii, 1908, pp. 529—571; 3. Aufl., iii, 1917, pp. 248—292.

HAHN, AUGUST: Bibliothek der Symbole und Glaubensregeln der Alten Kirche. 3. Aufl. Breslau 1897.

HARNACK, ADOLF VON: Beiträge zur Einleitung in das Neue Testament. vii. Leipzig 1916.

— Des heiligen Irenäus Schrift zum Erweise der apostolischen Verkündigung ... Nachwort und Anmerkungen: Texte und Untersuch. xxxi. 1, 1907 pp. 53—68.

HARRIS, J. RENDEL, A Further Note on the Use of Enoch in 1 Peter: The Expositor vi. 4, 1901, pp. 346—349.

— On a Recent Emendation in the Text of St. Peter: The Expositor vi. 5, 1902, pp. 317—320.

— Two Flood-Hymns of the Early Church: The Expositor viii. 2, 1911, pp. 405—417.

HART, J. H. A., Scribes of the Nazarenes. ii. The Gospel according to St. Luke and the Descent into Hades: The Expositor vii. 3, 1907, pp. 53—71.

HATCH, E., & REDPATH, H. A.: A Concordance to the Septuagint and other Greek Versions of the Old Testament. i—ii. Suppl. Oxford 1897—1906.

HAUCK, FRIEDRICH, Der erste Brief des Petrus: Das Neue Testament Deutsch. Neues Göttinger Bibelwerk, hrsg. von P. ALTHAUS & J. BEHM, iii, Göttingen 1935, pp. 162—206.

HENNECKE, EDGAR; Handbuch zu den neutestamentlichen Apokryphen. Tübingen 1904.

— Neutestamentliche Apokryphen. In Verbindung mit Fachgelehrten in deutscher Übersetzung und mit Einleitung hrsg. 2. Aufl. Tübingen 1924.

HERMANN, EDUARD: Griechische Forschungen. I. Die Nebensätze in den griechischen Dialektinschriften in Vergleich mit den Nebensätzen in der griechischen Literatur und der Gebildetensprache im Griechischen und Deutschen. Leipzig & Berlin 1912.

— Das Pronomen *ios als Adjectivum. (Gymn.-Progr.) Coburg 1897.[1]

Hero. Herons von Alexandria Druckwerke und Automatentheater, hrsg. von W. SCHMIDT. (Bibliotheca ... Teubneriana.) Leipzig 1899.

HILGENFELD, A., Die jüdische Apokalyptik und die neuesten Forschungen: Zeitschr. für wiss. Theol., iii, 1860, pp. 300—362.

---

[1] Not available.

BIBLIOGRAPHY 257

Hippolytus. Hippolytus Werke. i. Exegetische und homiletische Schriften. Hrsg. von G. BONWETSCH & H. ACHELIS. i. 1. Die Kommentare zu Daniel und zum Hohenliede. i. 2. Kleinere exegetische und homiletische Schriften. Leipzig 1897.
HOFMANN, J. CHR. K. VON: Die heilige Schrift des neuen Testaments. vii. 1. Der erste Brief Petri. Nördlingen 1875.
— Der Schriftbeweis. Ein theologischer Versuch. i—ii. 2. Aufl. Nördlingen 1857—60.
— see also DELITZSCH, FRANZ.
HOLTZMANN, H., Höllenfahrt im Neuen Testament: Archiv für Religionswiss. xi, 1908, pp. 285—297.
— Literatur zum Neuen Testament: Theol. Jahresber. xi (1891), 1892, pp. 93—132.
HOLZMEISTER, URBANUS: Commentarius in Epistulas SS. Petri et Iudæ Apostolorum. i. Epistula Prima S. Petri Apostoli (cum vita ipsius Apostoli). (Cursus Scripturæ Sacræ. iii. 13.) Parisiis 1937.
— Review of J. CHAINE, Les Épîtres catholiques, 1939: Biblica xxii, 1941, pp. 71—77.
HUIDEKOPER, FRED.: The Belief of the First Three Centuries concerning Christ's Mission to the Underworld. Boston 1854. 7th ed. 1887.[1]
HUTHER, JOH. ED.: Kritisch exegetisches Handbuch über den 1. Brief des Petrus, den Brief des Judas und den 2. Brief des Petrus. (Kritisch exegetischer Kommentar über das N.T. von H. A. W. MEYER. xii.) 4. Aufl. Göttingen 1877.
Irenæus. S. Irenæus: Εἰς ἐπίδειξιν τοῦ ἀποστολικοῦ κηρύγματος. The Proof of the Apostolic Preaching. With Seven Fragments. Armenian Version, ed. and transl. by KARAPET TER MĚKĚRTTSCHIAN & S. G. WILSON with the co-operation of H. R. H. Prince MAXE OF SAXONY. (Patrologia Orientalis. xii. 5.) Paris 1919.
— Des Heiligen Irenäus Schrift zum Erweise der apostolischen Verkündigung, Εἰς ἐπίδειξιν τοῦ ἀποστολικοῦ κηρύγματος. In armenischer Version entdeckt. Hrsg. und ins Deutsche übers. von KARAPET TER-MĚKĚRTTSCHIAN und ERWAND TER-MINASSIANTZ. (Texte und Untersuch. xxxi. 1.) Leipzig 1907.
JAMES, M. R.: Apocrypha anecdota. (Texts and Studies. v. 1.) Cambridge 1897.
— see also Ps. Philo.
JANNARIS, A. N.: An Historical Greek Grammar chiefly of the Attic Dialect. London 1897.
JANSEN, H. LUDIN: Die Henochgestalt. Eine vergleichende religionsgeschichtliche Untersuchung. (Skrifter utg. av Det Norske Videnskaps-Akademi i Oslo. ii. Hist.-filos. Kl. 1939. 1.) Oslo 1939.
JANSSENS, LAURENT.: Summa theologica ad modum commentarii in Aquin. v. 2. Freiburg 1902.[1]

---

[1] Not available.

JELLINEK, ADOLPH: Beth ha-Midrasch. Sammlung kleiner Midraschim und vermischter Abhandlungen aus der älteren jüdischen Literatur. ii. Leipzig 1853.
JENSEN, P. JOHS.: Læren om Kristi Nedfart til de döde. En Fremstilling af Lærepunktets Historie tilligemed et Indlæg i dette. København 1903.
JEREMIAS, JOACHIM, Der Brief an Titus: Das Neue Testament Deutsch. Neues Göttinger Bibelwerk, hrsg. von P. ALTHAUS & J. BEHM, iii, Göttingen 1935, pp. 49—56.
JOSEPHSON, H., Niedergefahren zur Hölle: Der Beweis des Glaubens, xxxiii, 1897, pp. 400—418.
JUNG, LEO: Fallen Angels in Jewish, Christian and Mohammedan Literature. Philadelphia 1926.
JÜLICHER, ADOLF: Einleitung in das Neue Testament. (Grundriss der theologischen Wissenschaften iii. 1.) 7. Aufl. hrsg. von E. FASCHER. Tübingen 1931.
KARMIRIS, J.: Ἡ εἰς "Ἀδου κάθοδος τοῦ Χριστοῦ ἐξ ἐπόψεως ὀρθοδόξου. Athens 1939.[1]
KAUTZSCH, E.: Die Apokryphen und Pseudepigraphen des Alten Testaments. i—ii. Freiburg i. B. & Tübingen 1898—1900.
KEIL, CARL FRIEDRICH: Commentar über die Briefe des Petrus und Judas. Leipzig 1883.
KELLY, W.: Preaching to the Spirits in Prison. London 1900.[1]
KENYON, FREDERIC: The Bible and Archæology. London 1940.
— The Palæography of Greek Papyri. Oxford 1899.
KING, PETER: The History of the Apostles' Creed with Critical Observations on its Several Articles. London 1702.[1]
KISSANE, EDWARD J.: The Book of Isaiah. Translated from a Critically Revised Hebrew Text with Commentary. i—ii. Dublin 1941—43.
KITTEL, GERHARD: Theologisches Wörterbuch zum N.T. i—iv. Stuttgart 1933—40.
— ἄγγελος: G. KITTEL, Theol. Wörterb., i, 1933/34, pp. 72—87.
KLIEFOTH, TH.: Christliche Eschatologie. Leipzig 1886.
KNABENBAUER, Ios.: Commentarius in Danielem prophetam, Lamentationes et Baruch. (Cursus Scripturæ Sacræ Commentariorum in V.T. III. iv.) Parisiis 1891.
KNAPP, PAUL, 1 Petri 3, 17 ff. und die Höllenfahrt Jesu Christi: Jahrbücher für Deutsche Theol. xxiii, 1878, pp. 177—228.
KNOPF, RUD.: Die Briefe Petri und Judä, völlig neu bearbeitet. (Kritischexegetischer Kommentar über das N.T. begr. von H. A. W. MEYER. Abt. xii. 7. Aufl.) Göttingen 1912.
KÖNIG, J. L.: Die Lehre von Christi Höllenfahrt nach der heiligen Schrift, der ältesten Kirche, den christlichen Symbolen und nach ihrer vielumfassenden Bedeutung dargestellt. Frankfurt am Main 1842.[1]

---

[1] Not available.

KÖRBER, JOH.: Die katholische Lehre von der Höllenfahrt Jesu Christi. Landshut 1860.¹

KOWALSKI, SEWERYN: Zstąpienie do piekieł Chrystusa Pana wedle nauki św. Piotra Apostoła (Razbiór krytyczny Dz. II, 27, 31 i 1 Piotr. III, 19, 20; IV, 6). (Studia Gnesnensia.) Poznán 1938.¹

KRAMER, S. N., Inanna's Descent to the Nether World. The Sumerian Version of »Ištar's Descent«: Revue d'assyriologie xxxiv. 3, 1937, pp. 93—134.

KROLL, JOSEPH, Beiträge zum Descensus ad inferos: Verzeichnis der Vorlesungen an der Akademie zu Braunsberg im Winter 1922/23, Königsberg 1922, pp. 2—56.

— Gott und Hölle. Der Mythos vom Descensuskampfe. (Studien der Bibliothek Warburg hrsg. von FRITZ SAXL. xx.) Berlin 1932.

KRÜGER, K. W.: Griechische Sprachlehre für Schulen. i—ii. 5. Aufl., besorgt von W. PÖKEL. Leipzig 1875—79.

KTONIECKI, F., Review of S. KOWALSKI, Zstąpienie ...: Biblica xxi, 1940, pp. 96—99.

KÜHL, ERNST: Die Briefe Petri und Judæ. (Kritisch-exegetischer Kommentar über das N.T. begr. von H. A. W. MEYER. xii. 16. Aufl.) Göttingen 1897.

KÜHNER, RAPHAEL: Ausführliche Grammatik der griechischen Sprache. Zweiter Teil: Satzlehre. 3. Aufl. in zwei Bänden. In neuer Bearbeitung besorgt von B. GERTH. 1—2. Hannover & Leipzig 1898—1904.

LACAU, P., SCHMIDT, C., & WAJNBERG, I.: Gespräche Jesu mit seinen Jüngern nach der Auferstehung. (Texte und Untersuch. iii. 13.) Leipzig 1919.

LAGARDE, P. DE: Analecta syriaca. Lipsiæ 1858.¹

LANDAU, MARCUS: Hölle und Fegfeuer in Volksglaube, Dichtung und Kirchenlehre. Heidelberg 1909.

LANGDON, S.: The Babylonian Epic of Creation. Restored from the recently recovered Tablets of Aššur. Transcription, translation and commentary. Oxford 1923.

LANGHE, ROBERT DE: Les textes de Ras Shamra-Ugarit et leurs rapports avec le milieu biblique de l'Ancien Testament. i—ii. (Universitas Catholica Lovaniensis. Dissertationes. ii. 35.) Gembloux & Paris 1945.

LAUTERBURG, M., Höllenfahrt Christi: Realencyclopädie für protestantische Theologie und Kirche, 3. Aufl., vii, Leipzig 1900, pp. 199—206.

LAWLOR, H. J., Early Citations from the Book of Enoch: The Journ. of Philology xxv, 1897, pp. 164—225.

LEBON, J., Review of J. KARMIRIS, Ἡ εἰς ῞Αδου κάθοδος, 1939: Revue d'hist. ecclésiastique xxxv, 1939, pp. 929f.

LECLERQ, H., Arche: Dictionnaire d'archéologie chrétienne et de liturgie, i. 2, 1907, cols. 2709—2732.

---

¹ Not available.

LEIGHTON, ROBERT: A Practical Commentary upon the First Epistle General of Saint Peter. i—ii. (New ed.) London, The Religious Tract Society, *s.a.*

LEIPOLDT, [J.], Review of A. HARNACK, Beiträge zur Einleitung in das Neue Testament, vii: Theol. Lit.-blatt xxxviii, 1917, cols. 211—213.

LEUMANN, MANU, & HOFMANN, JOH. BAPT.: STOLZ-SCHMALZ, Lateinische Grammatik. (Handbuch der klass. Altertumswiss., hrsg. von I. VON MÜLLER. ii.2. 5. Aufl.) München 1928.

LIDDELL, H. G., & SCOTT, R.: A Greek-English Lexicon. A New Ed. rev. by H. S. JONES. i—ii. Oxford 1925—40.

LIETZMANN, HANS: An die Römer erklärt. Nebst Einführung in die Textgeschichte der Paulusbriefe. (Handbuch zum N.T. viii.) 4. Aufl. Tübingen 1933.

LINDBLOM, JOHANNES: Die Jesaja-Apokalypse, Jes. 24—27. (Lunds Univ. Årsskrift. N.F. Avd. I. xxxiv. 3.) Lund 1938.

LINDROTH, HJALMAR: Den apostoliska trosbekännelsen. Till frågan om dess upprinnelse, dess ursprungliga innebörd och dess bestående betydelse. Stockholm 1933.

LOCK, WALTER: A Critical and Exegetical Commentary on the Pastoral Epistles. (The International Critical Commentary.) Edinburgh 1924.

LODS, ADOLPHE, La chute des anges. Origines et portée de cette spéculation: Revue d'hist. et de philos. relig. vii, 1927, pp. 295—315.

— Le livre d'Hénoch. Fragments grecs découverts à Akhmim (Egypte) publiés avec les variantes du texte éthiopien. Paris 1892.

LOHMEYER, ERNST: Die Offenbarung des Johannes erklärt. (Handbuch zum N.T. xvi.) Tübingen 1926.

LOOFS, FRIEDRICH, Christ's Descent into Hell: Transactions of the Third Internat. Congress for the Hist. of Religions, Oxford, 1908, ii, pp. 254—301.

— Descent to Hades (Christ's): Encyclopaedia of Religion and Ethics, iv, 1911, pp. 654—663.

LORINUS, JOHANNES: In catholicas tres B. Joannis et duas B. Petri Epistolas commentarii. Lugduni 1609.[1]

LUMBY, J. RAWSON, 1 Peter III 17: The Expositor iv. 1, 1890, pp. 142—147.

LUNDBERG, PER: La typologie baptismale dans l'ancienne Eglise. (Acta semin. neotest. Upsal. x.) Diss. Uppsala 1942.

LUTHER. D. Martin Luthers Werke. Kritische Gesamtausgabe. (»Weimar-Ausgabe».) Weimar 1883 ff.

MACCULLOCH, J. A., Descent to Hades (Ethnic): Encyclopædia of Religion and Ethics, iv, 1911, pp. 648—654.

— The Harrowing of Hell. A Comparative Study of an Early Christian Doctrine. Edinburgh 1930.

MADVIG, J. N.: Syntax der griechischen Sprache, besonders der attischen Sprachform, für Schulen und für jüngere Philologen. 2. verb. Aufl. Braunschweig 1884.

---

[1] Not available.

BIBLIOGRAPHY 261

MANSI, J. D.: Sacrorum conciliorum nova et amplissima collectio ... i—iii. Florentiæ 1759.

MATTHIÄ, AUGUST: Ausführliche Griechische Grammatik. 3. Aufl. i—iii. Leipzig 1835.

MAYSER, EDWIN: Grammatik der griechischen Papyri aus der Ptolemäerzeit. ii. 3. Leipzig 1934.

MEESTER, A. DE, Descente du Christ aux enfers dans les liturgies orientales: Dictionnaire d'archéologie chrétienne et de liturgie, iv. 1, Paris 1920, cols. 693—696.

Melito. The Homily on the Passion by Melito Bishop of Sardis ... ed. by C. BONNER. (Studies and Documents. xii.) London & Philadelphia 1940.

MEUWEESE, ALPHONSUS PETRUS MARIA: De rerum gestarum Divi Augusti versione græca. Specimen litterarium inaugurale. Boscoduci 1920.

MEYER, ARNOLD: Die moderne Forschung über die Geschichte des Urchristentums. Vortrag, gehalten auf dem ersten religionswissenschaftlichen Kongresse in Stockholm am 1. September 1897. (Sammlung gemeinverständlicher Vorträge und Schriften aus dem Gebiet der Theologie und Religionsgeschichte.) Freiburg i.B. 1898.

Midrash Rabbah, translated into English ... under the editorship of H. FREEDMAN & M. SIMON. i. London 1939.

MODICA, MARCO: Introduzione allo studio della papirologia giuridica. (Biblioteca giuridica contemporanea.) Milano 1914.[1]

MOFFAT, JAMES: The General Epistles. James, Peter and Judas. (The Moffatt New Testament Commentary.) London 1928.

— A New Translation of the Bible. Containing the Old and New Testaments. London [1925] 1928.

MONNIER, JEAN: La descente aux enfers. Etude de pensée religieuse d'art et de littérature. (Thèse.) Paris 1904.

— La première Epître de l'apôtre Pierre. Commentaire. (Thèse ... pour le grade de Licencié en Théologie. Paris.) Macon 1900.

MONTGOMERY, JAMES A.: Aramaic Incantation Texts from Nippur. (Univ. of Pennsylvania. The Museum. Publications of the Babylonian Section. iii.) Philadelphia 1913.

MOULTON, J. H., & MILLIGAN, G.: The Vocabulary of the Greek Testament illustrated from the Papyri and other Non-Literary Sources. i—viii. London 1915—1929.

NESTLE, EB., Review of J. FLEMING & L. RADERMACHER, Das Buch Henoch, 1901: Theol. Lit.-blatt xxxiii, 1902, cols. 164—166.

NEUSS, WILHELM: Das Buch Ezechiel in Theologie und Kunst bis zum Ende des xii. Jahrhunderts. (Beiträge zur Geschichte des alten Mönchtums. 1/2.) Münster in Westf. 1912.

NEWBOLD, WILLIAM ROMAINE, The Descent of Christ in the Odes of Solomon: Journ. of Bibl. Lit. xxxi, 1912, pp. 168—209.

---
[1] Not available.

NÖLDEKE, THEODOR: Kurzgefasste syrische Grammatik. 2. Aufl. Leipzig 1898.
NORDBLAD, CARL: Föreställningen om Kristi hadesfärd undersökt till sitt ursprung. En religionshistorisk studie. Uppsala 1912.
Novum Testamentum Græcum, ad fidem Græcorum solum codicum MSS. nunc primum expressum ... Accessere in altero volumine Emendationes conjecturales virorum doctorum undecumque collectæ. [Ed. by W. BOWYER.] 1—2 + Suppl. Londini 1763.[1]
Novum Testamentum Græce. Rec. C. TISCHENDORF. Ed. octava critica maior. ii. Lipsiæ 1872.
Novum Testamentum Græce cum apparatu critico curavit EBERH. NESTLE novis curis elaboravit ERW. NESTLE. Ed. sexta decima. Stuttgart 1936 [1937].
NYGREN, ANDERS: Agape and Eros. i—ii. 1—2. Transl. London 1932—39.
ODEBERG, HUGO, 'Ενώχ: G. KITTEL, Theol. Wörterb. ii, 1935, pp. 553—557.
— »Nederstigen till dödsriket»: Bibliskt Månadshäfte xviii. 12, 1944, pp. 357—359.
— see also Enoch.
The Odes of Solomon ed. by J. H. BERNARD. (Texts and Studies. viii. 3.) Cambridge 1912.
The Odes and Psalms of Solomon, publ. by J. R. HARRIS. Cambridge 1909.
The Odes and Psalms of Solomon, reedited by R. HARRIS & A. MINGANA. i—ii. Manchester 1916—20.
ODLAND, S., Kristi prædiken for »aanderne i forvaring» (1 Petr. 3, 19): Norsk teol. tidsskrift ii, 1901, pp. 116—144, 185—229.
OEPKE, A., ἀποκαθίστημι, ἀποκατάστασις: G. KITTEL, Theol. Wörterb. i, pp. 386—392.
OERTEL, J. R.: Hades. Exegetisch-dogmatische Abhandlung über den Zustand der abgeschiedenen Seelen. Leipzig 1863.[1]
OESTERLEY, W. O. E., The Belief in Angels and Demons: Judaism and Christianity, 1, The Age of Transition, London 1937, pp. 191—209.
ÖPPENRIEDER, AD., 1 Petr. 3, 19. Von der Predigt, welche Christus nach Petri Wort den im Gefängnis befindlichen Geistern gehalten hat: Der Beweis des Glaubens, xxix, 1893, pp. 230—246.
Origenes. Origenes Werke. iv. Der Johanneskommentar. Hrsg. von E. PREUSCHEN. (Die griechischen christlichen Schriftsteller der ersten drei Jahrhunderte.) Leipzig 1903.
OSBORNE, H., Συνείδησις: The Journ. of Theol. Stud. xxxii, 1931, pp. 167—179.
OTTO, J. C. TH. DE: Corpus apologetarum christianorum sæculi secundi. ix. Ienæ 1872.
OTTO, RUDOLF: Reich Gottes und Menschensohn. Ein religionsgeschichtlicher Versuch. 2. verb. Aufl. München 1940.

---
[1] Not available.

The Oxyrhynchus Papyri. Ed. by B. P. GRENFELL, A. S. HUNT ... i—xvii. (Egypt Exploration Fund. Græco-Roman Branch.) London 1898—1927.
PASSOW, FRANZ: Handwörterbuch der griechischen Sprache. Neu bearb. von V. CHR. F. ROST, F. PALM ... i—iv. Leipzig 1841—57.
PEDERSEN, JOHANNES: Hebræisk Grammatik. Andet Oplag. København 1933.
PERDELWITZ, RICHARD: Die Mysterienreligionen und das Problem des I. Petrusbriefes. Ein literarischer und religionsgeschichtlicher Versuch. (Religionsgeschichtl. Versuche und Vorarbeiten. xi. 3.) Giessen 1911.
PESCH, CHRISTIAN: Prælectiones dogmaticæ. iv. De verbo incarnato. Freiburg i.B. 1900.[1]
Ps. Philo. The Biblical Antiquities of Philo now first translated from the Old Latin Version by M. R. JAMES. London 1917.
PINCHES, THEOPHILUS G., The Legend of Merodach: Proceed. of the Soc. of Bibl. Archæology xxx, 1908, pp. 53—62, 77—85.
PITRA, JOANNES BAPTISTA card.: Analecta sacra Spicilegio Solesmensi parata. iv. Patres antenicæni. Parisiis 1883.
PLOOIJ, D., Der Descensus ad inferos in Aphrahat und den Oden Salomos: Zeitschr. für die neutest. Wiss. xiv, 1913, pp. 222—231.
— De descensus in I Petrus 3^{19} en 4^6: Theol. Tijdschrift xlvii, 1913, pp. 145—162.
Plotinus. Plotini Enneades præmisso Porphyrii de vita Plotini deque ordine librorum eius libello, ed. R. VOLKMANN. i—ii. (Bibliotheca ... Teubneriana.) Lipsiæ 1883—84.
PLUMPTRE, EDWARD HAYES: Spirits in Prison and other Studies on Life after Death. London 1884.[1]
Porphyrius. Porphyrii philosophi platonici opuscula selecta, iterum recognovit A. NAUCK. (Bibliotheca ... Teubneriana.) Lipsiæ 1886.
— see also Plotinus.
POTT, DAV. JUL.: Epistolæ catholicæ græcæ perpetua annotatione illustratæ. i—ii. 1786—90.[1]
PREISIGKE, FRIEDRICH: Fachwörter des öffentlichen Verwaltungsdienstes Ägyptens in den griechischen Papyrusurkunden der ptolemäisch-römischen Zeit. Göttingen 1915.
— Griechische Urkunden des Ägyptischen Museums zu Kairo. (Schriften der Wissenschaftl. Gesellschaft in Strassburg. 1911. viii.) Strassburg 1911.
— Wörterbuch der griechischen Papyrusurkunden, hrsg. von E. KIESSLING. i—iii. Berlin 1925—31.
PREUSCHEN, ERWIN, Die Echtheit von Justins Dialog gegen Trypho: Zeitschr. für die neutest. Wiss. xix, 1919/20, pp. 102—127.
— Vollständiges griechisch-deutsches Handwörterbuch zu den Schriften des Neuen Testaments. Giessen 1910 (cf. BAUER, W.).
PROCKSCH, OTTO: Jesaja I. (Kommentar zum A.T. hrsg. von E. SELLIN. ix. 1.) Leipzig 1930.

---
[1] Not available.

PRÜMM, KARL: Der christliche Glaube und die altheidnische Welt. i—ii. Leipzig 1935.
PUNIET, P. DE, Baptême: Dictionnaire d'archéologie chrétienne et de liturgie, ii. 1, Paris 1910, cols. 251—346.
QUENSTEDT, JOH. ANDREAS: Theologia didactico-polemica sive systema theologicum. i—ii. Vittebergæ 1685.
QUILLIET, H., Descente de Jésus aux enfers: Dictionnaire de théologie catholique, iv, Paris 1911, cols. 565—619.
RADERMACHER, L., Der erste Petrusbrief und Silvanus: Zeitschr. für die neutest. Wiss. xxv, 1926, pp. 287—295.
RESCH, ALFRED: Agrapha. Ausserkanonische Schriftfragmente. 2. Aufl. Leipzig 1906.
REUSCH, FR. HEINRICH: Erklärung des Buchs Baruch. Freiburg im Breisgau 1853.
RICHARDS, G. C., 1 Pet. iii. 21: The Journ. of Theol. Stud. xxxii, 1931, p. 77.
ROBERTSON, A. T.: A Grammar of the Greek New Testament in the Light of Historical Research. 3rd ed. New York 1919.
ROESLER, PAULUS: De assimilationis pronominis relativi usu qualis fuerit apud Theophrastum, Polybium, Dionysium Halicarnaseum. Dissertatio inauguralis. Vratislaviæ 1906.
ROHDE, ERWIN: Psyche. Seelencult und Unsterblichkeitsglaube der Griechen. 1893. [7. u. 8. Aufl. Tübingen 1921.]
ROST[, V. C. F.]: Beispielsammlung zu den Griechischen Grammatiken von BUTTMANN und ROST. i—ii. 2. Ausg. Göttingen 1856.
ROST, VAL. CHRIST. FRIEDR.: Griechische Grammatik. 6. Ausg. Göttingen 1841.
RUDBERG, GUNNAR, Ur samvetets historia: Studier och tankar tillägnade J. A. EKLUND på 70-årsdagen den 7 jan. 1933, Stockholm 1932, pp. 165—188.
RUTHERFORD, W. G.: St. Paul's Epistle to the Romans. A New Translation with a Brief Analysis. London 1914.
RYDBERG, VIKTOR: Bibelns lära om Kristus. 4. uppl., genomsedd och tillökad med en afhandling »Till läran om de yttersta tingen». Stockholm 1880.
SA, EMMANUELE: Notationes in totam scripturam sacram. Antverpiæ 1598.
SABATIER, PETRUS: Bibliorum sacrorum latinæ versiones antiquæ seu Vetus Italica. i—iii. Parisiis 1751.
La Sainte Bible ou l'Ancien et le Nouveau Testament. Version Synodale. Paris 1923.
La Sainte Bible, qui comprend l'Ancien et le Nouveau Testament, traduits sur les textes originaux, Hébreu et Grec, par LOUIS SEGOND. London 1892.
La Sainte Bible, qui contient L'Ancien et Le Nouveau Testament. Version d'OSTERVALD. Paris 1903.

---

[1] Not available.

BIBLIOGRAPHY 265

Salmeron, Alph.: Commentarii in epistolas canonicas. Opera omnia xvi. Colonæ Agr. 1615.[1]

Schechter, S.: Fragments of a Zadokite Work. (Documents of Jewish Sectaries. i.) Cambridge 1910.

Scheftelowitz, I.: Die altpersische Religion und das Judentum. Unterschiede, Übereinstimmungen und gegenseitige Beeinflussungen. Giessen 1920.

Schindler, Heinrich: De Diodori Siculi et Strabonis enuntiationum relativarum attractione. I. De admissa attractione. [Schul-Progr.] Frankenstein i. Schl. s.a.

Schlatter, Adolf: Petrus und Paulus nach dem Ersten Petrusbrief. Stuttgart 1937.

Schlier, Heinrich: Christus und die Kirche im Ephesierbrief. (Beitr. zur hist. Theol. vi.) Tübingen 1930.

— Religionsgeschichtliche Untersuchungen. (Beihefte zur Zeitschr. für die neutest. Wiss. viii.) Giessen 1929.

Schmaltz, Karl, Das heilige Feuer in der Grabeskirche im Zusammenhang mit der kirchlichen Liturgie und den antiken Lichtriten: Palästinajahrbuch xiii, 1917, pp. 53—99.

Schmidt, Bernhardt, Die Feier des heiligen Feuers in der Grabeskirche: Palästinajahrbuch xi, 1915, pp. 85—118.

— Die Vorstellungen von der Höllenfahrt Christi in der alten Kirche: 16. Bericht des Verbandes ehem. Mitglieder des Klosters Naumburg a. Queis, Wintersemester 1906/07.[1]

Schmidt, Carl, Der Descensus ad inferos in der alten Kirche: P. Lacau, C. Schmidt & I. Wajnberg, Gespräche Jesu mit seinen Jüngern nach der Auferstehung, Excurs ii, pp. 453—576.

Schmidt, Karl W. Ch.: Die Darstellung von Christi Höllenfahrt in den deutschen und den ihnen verwandten Spielen des Mittelalters. Inaugural-Dissertation. Marburg 1915.

Schmidt, Paul, Zwei Fragen zum ersten Petrusbrief: Zeitschr. für wiss. Theol. l. 1, 1908, pp. 24—52.

Schneider, K., Achteck: Reallexikon für Antike und Christentum, i, 1940, cols. 78ff.

Schoeps, Hans Joachim, Mythologisches bei Symmachus: Biblica xxvi, 1945, pp. 100—111.

Schön, Franciscus: De assimilationis pronominis relativi extra dialectum Atticam usu. Dissertatio inauguralis philologica. Vratislaviæ 1909.

Schott, Theodor: Der erste Brief Petri. Erlangen 1861.

Schrader, Eberhard: Die Keilinschriften und das Alte Testament. 3. Aufl. von H. Zimmern & H. Winckler. Berlin 1903.

Schrenk, Gottlob, ἐκλεκτός: G. Kittel, Theol. Wörterb., iv, 1940, pp. 186—197.

---

[1] Not available.

SCHÜRER, EMIL: Geschichte des jüdischen Volkes im Zeitalter Jesu Christi. i—iii; Register. 3.—4. Aufl. Leipzig 1901—11.

SCHWAB, MOÏSE, Vocabulaire de l'angélologie d'après les manuscrits hébreux de la Bibliothèque Nationale: Mémoires présentées par divers savants à l'Académie des Inscriptions et Belles-Lettres de l'Institut de France, sér. I, tome x. 2, Paris 1897, pp. 113—430.

SCHWEIZER, ALEX.: Hinabgefahren zur Hölle, als Mythus ohne biblische Begründung durch Auslegung der Stelle 1. Petr. 3. 17—22 nachgewiesen. Zürich 1868.[1]

SCHWEIZER, EDUARD: Der erste Petrusbrief ausgelegt. (Prophezei. Schweizerisches Bibelwerk für die Gemeinde.) Zürich 1942.

SCOTT, C. A., »The Sufferings of Christ». A Note on 1 Peter I. 11: The Expositor vi. 12, 1905, pp. 234—240.

SEEBERG, ALFRED: Der Katechismus der Urchristenheit. Leipzig 1903.

SELWYN, EDWARD GORDON: The First Epistle of St. Peter. London 1946.

Septuagint. The Old Testament in Greek according to the Septuagint. Edited by HENRY BARCLAY SWETE. i, 4th ed., ii, 3rd ed., iii, 4th ed. Cambridge 1909—1922.

SIEFFERT, FR. E. A., Die Heilsbedeutung des Leidens und Sterbens Christi nach dem ersten Briefe des Petrus: Jahrbücher für Deutsche Theol. xx, 1875, pp. 371—440.

SMITH, M. LINTON, 1 Peter iii. 21. Ἐπερώτημα: Expository Times xxiv, 1912/13, pp. 46f.

SODEN, H. VON: Die Schriften des Neuen Testaments in ihrer ältesten erreichbaren Textgestalt. i—ii. Berlin & Göttingen 1902—1913.

— Hebräerbrief, Briefe des Petrus, Jakobus, Judas. (Hand-Commentar zum N.T. iii. 2.) Freiburg i.B. 1890.

SOLTAU, WILHELM, Die Einheitlichkeit des 1. Petrusbriefes: Theol. Stud. und Krit. lxxviii, 1905, pp. 302—315.

— Nochmals die Einheitlichkeit des 1. Petrusbriefes: Theol. Stud. und Krit. lxxix, 1906, pp. 456—460.

Sophokles. Sophokles erklärt von F. W. SCHNEIDEWIN & A. NAUCK. v. 10. Aufl. von E. BRUHN. Berlin 1912.

SPENER, PH. JAC.: Einfache Erklärung der christlichen Lehre nach der Ordnung des kleinen Katechismus Luther's in Fragen und Antworten verfasst ... [1677.] Neudruck hrsg. von DETZER. 2. Aufl. Erlangen 1833.

SPICQ, C., La conscience dans le N.T.: Revue Biblique xlvii, 1938, pp. 50—80.

SPITTA, FRIEDRICH: Christi Predigt an die Geister (1 Petr. 3, 19ff.). Ein Beitrag zur neutestamentlichen Theologie. Göttingen 1890.

SPÖRRI, THEOPHIL: Der Gemeindegedanke im ersten Petrusbrief. Ein Beitrag zur Struktur des urchristlichen Kirchenbegriffs. (Neutestamentl. Forschungen hrsg. von O. SCHMITZ. ii. 2.) Gütersloh 1925.

STÄHLIN, OTTO: Clemens und die Septuaginta. (Gymn.-Progr.) Nürnberg 1901.

---

[1] Not available.

BIBLIOGRAPHY

STEIGER, WILHELM: Der erste Brief Petri mit Berücksichtigung des ganzen biblischen Lehrbegriffs. Berlin 1832.

STEIN, EDMUND: Philo und der Midrasch. Philos Schilderung der Gestalten des Pentateuch verglichen mit der des Midrasch. (Beihefte zur Zeitschr. für die alttest. Wiss. lvii.) Giessen 1931.

STIER, R., & THEILE, K. G. W.: Polyglotten-Bibel zum praktischen Handgebrauch. iv. Neues Testament. 2. Aufl. Bielefeld 1849.

STRACK, H., & BILLERBECK, P.: Kommentar zum Neuen Testament aus Talmud und Midrasch. i—iv. München 1922—1928.

STRÖM, ÅKE V.: Vetekornet. Studier över individ och kollektiv i Nya Testamentet med särskild hänsyn till Johannesevangeliets teologi. Joh. 12: 20—33. (Acta semin. neotest. Upsal. xi.) Diss. Uppsala 1944.

Supplementum epigraphicum Græcum. iv. Lugduni Batavorum 1930.

SVAREZ, FRANCISCUS: Commentariorum ac disputationum in Tertiam partem Divi Thomæ. ii. Venetiis 1598.

Theodore of Mopsuestia. Commentary of Theodore of Mopsuestia on the Lord's Prayer and on the Sacraments of Baptism and the Eucharist. (Woodbrooke Studies. Christian Documents edited and translated with a critical apparatus by A. MINGANA. vi.) Cambridge 1933.

Thomas ab Aquino. Divi Thomæ Aquinatis Summa Theologica. i—vi. Romæ 1886—87.

THORNTON, L. S.: The Common Life in the Body of Christ. Westminster [1940] 1944.

TURMEL, JOSEPH: La descente du Christ aux Enfers. Paris 1903.[1]

The Twentieth Century New Testament. A Translation into Modern English made from the Original Greek (WESTCOTT and HORT's Text). Tentative edition 1903; final edition 1904.[1]

UNNIK, W. C. VAN: De verlossing 1 Petrus 1: 18—19 en het probleem van den eersten Petrusbrief. (Mededeelingen der nederlandsche Akad. van Wetensch. Afd. Letterk. N.R. v. 1.) Amsterdam 1942.

USTERI, JOH. MARTIN: »Hinabgefahren zur Hölle.» Eine Wiedererwägung der Schriftstellen: 1 Petr. 3: 18—22 und Kap. 4, Vers 6. Zürich 1886.[1]

VIGERUS, FRANCISCUS: De præcipuis græcæ dictionis idiotismis liber. Ed. 4a. Lipsiæ 1834.

VITEAU, J.: Etude sur le grec du Nouveau Testament. i—ii. Paris 1893—96.

VOGELSANG, ERICH, Weltbild und Kreuzestheologie in den Höllenfahrtsstreitigkeiten der Reformationszeit: Archiv für Reformationsgesch. xxxviii, 1941, pp. 90—132.

VOLKMAR, GUSTAV, Einige Bemerkungen über Apokalyptik. ii. Das Buch Henoch: Zeitschr. für wiss. Theol. iv, 1861, pp. 111—136.

— Über die katholischen Briefe und Henoch: Zeitschr. für wiss. Theol. iv, 1861, pp. 422—436.

VÖLTER, D.: Der erste Petrusbrief, seine Entstehung und Stellung in der Geschichte des Urchristentums. Strassburg 1906.[1]

---

[1] Not available.

VOLZ, PAUL: Die Eschatologie der jüdischen Gemeinde im neutestamentlichen Zeitalter nach den Quellen der rabbinischen, apokalyptischen und apokryphen Literatur dargestellt. Tübingen 1934.

VREDE, WILHELM, Judas-, Petrus- und Johannesbriefe: Die heilige Schrift des Neuen Testaments, iv, Berlin 1915, pp. 89—210.

WAAGE, GEORGIUS HOLGER: De ætate articuli, quo in Symbolo apostolico traditur Jesu Christi ad inferos descensus, commentatio. (Diss.) Hauniæ 1836.

WACE, HENRY: Apocrypha. i—ii. (The Holy Bible ... by Clergy of the Anglican Church.) London 1888.

WAGNER, REINHOLD: Griechische Grammatik. (Grundzüge der klassischen Philologie von B. MAUREMBRECHER & R. WAGNER. ii. 1.) Stuttgart 1908.

WAND, J. W. C.: The General Epistles of St. Peter and St. Jude. (Westminster Commentaries.) London 1934.

WEBER, FERDINAND: Jüdische Theologie auf Grund des Talmud und verwandter Schriften. 2. Aufl. hrsg. von F. DELITZSCH & G. SCHNEDERMANN. Leipzig 1897.

WEISS, BERHARD: Lehrbuch der biblischen Theologie des Neuen Testaments. 6. Aufl. Berlin 1895.

— Der Petrinische Lehrbegriff. Beiträge zur biblischen Theologie sowie zur Kritik und Exegese des ersten Briefes Petri und der petrinischen Reden. Berlin 1855.

WELLHAUSEN, J.: Reste arabischen Heidentums. 2. Ausg. Neudruck. Berlin & Leipzig [1897] 1927.

WETTE, WILHELM MARTIN LEBERECHT DE: Lehrbuch der christlichen Dogmatik in ihrer historischen Entwicklung dargestellt. i—ii. Berlin 1813—16.

WEXELS, W. A.: Aaben Erklæring til mine Medkristne om min Anskuelse og Bekjendelse angaaende Christi Nedfart till Helvede og Muligheden af en Omvendelse efter Döden. Christiania 1845.

WIDENGREN, GEO, Konungens vistelse i dödsriket. En studie till Psalm 88: Svensk exeget. årsbok x, 1945, pp. 66—81.

— Psalm 110 och det sakrala kungadömet i Israel. (Uppsala Univ. årsskrift 1941. vii. 1.) Uppsala 1941.

WINCKELMANNUS, JOHAN., Commentarius in Epistolas Petrinas ... revisus ... a J. H. FEUSTKINGIO: Ægidius Hunnius, Thesaurus Apostolicus complectens commentarios in omnes Novi Testamenti epistolas et Apoc. Johannis ... ed. a J. H. FEUSTKINGIO, Wittenbergiæ 1705, pp. 1011—1068.

WINDISCH, HANS: Die katholischen Briefe. (Handbuch zum N.T. xv.) Tübingen 1930.

WITZEL, MAURUS: Tammuz-Liturgien und Verwandtes. (Analecta Orientalia. x.) Roma 1935.

— Zur sumerischen Recension der Höllenfahrt Ischtars: Orientalia xiv. 1/2, 1945, pp. 24—69.

WOHLENBERG, G.: Der erste und zweite Petrusbrief und der Judasbrief. (Kommentar zum N.T. hrsg. von TH. ZAHN. xv.) Leipzig 1915.

WÜNSCHE, AUG.: Aus Israels Lehrhallen. Kleine Midraschim zur jüdischen Eschatologie und Apokalyptik. iii. Leipzig 1909.

ZAHN, THEODOR: Einleitung in das Neue Testament. 3. Aufl. i—ii. Leipzig 1906—07.

— Forschungen zur Geschichte des neutestamentlichen Kanons und der altkirchlichen Literatur. iii. Supplementum Clementinum. Erlangen 1884.

— Geschichte des Neutestamentlichen Kanons. i—ii. Erlangen 1888—92.

ZEZSCHWITZ, CARL ADOLPH GERH. VON: Petri Apostoli de Christi ad inferos descensu sententia ex loco nobilissimo I ep. III, 19 eruta, exacta ad epistolæ argumentum. Dissertatio exegetica dogmatica. Lipsiæ 1857.

ZIMMERMANN, FRANZ, Verkannte Papyri: Archiv für Papyrusforsch. xi, 1935, pp. 165—188.

INDEX OF SUBJECTS

Acts of Thomas 141, 241
Akhmim-fragments 55, 58f., 62ff.
»Ambrosiaster» 21, 32
Ambrosius 32
Angels 52—91, 123f., 134, 200, 209f., 234
Aphraates 35
Apostles Creed 1, 32, 44, 206, 233
Apostolic Fathers 15
Ark 138f.
Athanasius 31f.
Augustine 22, 37—39, 53
Baptism (cf. βάπτισμα) 245ff.
Beda Venerabilis 39
Bellarmine 42f.
Beza 40
Book of Enoch 52f., 57—91, 235f., 245f.
Carthage 197
Descent 1, 7—49, 116ff., 231—234, 242ff.
Dornerism 48
Earthly Powers 131ff., 200
emendation 41, 93f.
Enoch 95, 97ff., 100ff.
Enūma elish 237ff.
3 Enoch 207ff.
Epistola apostolorum 207ff.
Ephræm 21f., 35
Epiphanius 20
Eulogius 22
Euodius 22, 37
Fall of the Angels 76f.
Flood 52, 71ff., 246ff
Flood beings, generation 56ff., 70ff., 124f., 235ff., 246
Giants 52—83, 123, 209, 240f.
Gilgamesh Epos 241
Gospel of Nicodemus 17ff., 21, 242
Gospel of Peter 17ff.
Gregory of Nazianzen 21
Hermas 15, 18, 19, 28
Hieronymus 21, 39

Hilarius 36, 39, 42
Hippolytus 14, 21, 23—28, 32, 35, 42, 51
Höllenstürmung 9, 21, 26f., 35, 207, 239
idolatry 77, 89f.
Ignatius 15
interpolation 49f., 95
Irenæus 15f., 19f.
Jeremiah-logion 16ff., 19
Joannes Zonaras 33
John of Damascus 32f., 244
Judgment 72, 75, 85, 87, 137
Justin 16, 18f.
kings 85f.
Luther 1, 12f., 36, 40
lūz 207
Marcion 20f.
Melito 20, 235
Noah 95f., 140ff., 145, 148, 225
Odes of Solomon 35, 235, 243ff.
Origenes 14, 30f.
Peshito 27, 34
Preaching 1, 93ff., 115ff., 118ff., 234f.
prototype 74ff.
relative incorporation 149—172
renunciation 191ff.
Sibylline Books 206ff.
spirits in prison 1, 11, 52—92, 136, 200, 231ff.
Syncellus 59, 63
Targum 239
Tertullian 16, 68, 196, 206
Theodore of Mopsuestia 191—195
Theophylactus 33
Thomas Aquinas 39f.
Vulgate 27, 36, 42
Walafrid Strabo 39
Watchers 57—89, 123ff.
Waters of Death 245ff.
Zwingli 40

INDEX OF SUBJECTS

ἀγαθοποιέω 177, 211ff., 223
ἄγγελοι 199ff.
ἀντίτυπον 144ff.
ἅπαξ 215, 223
ἀπειθήσασιν 26, 99, 137f., 223f.
ἀπόθεσις 173, 189f., 192ff., 226f.
βάπτισμα 144ff., 173—201
γάρ 128f.
δι' ἀναστάσεως 198ff.
διασώξειν 139f.
εἰς 140
ἐν ἡμέραις Νῶε 137
ἐν ᾧ 34, 60, 93f., 97, 99, 103ff., 203
ἐνδύσασθαι 189, 193
ἔννοια 189f., 193, 195, 202.
ἐπερώτημα 182—187, 190—198, 225
ξωοποιηθείς 117f., 218f.
θανατωθείς 218f.
κακοποιέω 211ff.
κηρύσσω 119ff.
κρεῖττον 127, 213, 223f.
κύριος 201
μακροθυμία 137f.
ὁ καί 144ff.
ὀκτώ 140f.
ὅτι καὶ Χριστός 129f., 221ff.
περὶ ἁμαρτιῶν 129, 213ff.
πνεῦμα(τα) 35, 53—59, 60f., 64, 79, 104ff.
πορευθείς 26, 64ff., 199
προσάγειν 217f.
ῥύπος 187—190, 192, 226f.
συνείδησις 173—198, 202, 225ff.
ὑπὲρ ἡμῶν, ἀδίκων 213ff., 221, 224
ὑποταγέντων 199ff·
ὑποτάσσεσθαι 222
φυλακή 26, 35, 53, 66f., 96, 116ff., 241
ψυχή 54f., 107

INDEX OF BIBLICAL QUOTATIONS

Gen. ii. 4	150	xlv (xlvi). 9	164	vii. 16f.		85
iv. 20—22	75	lxi. 8	86	Jonah ii. 3—10		246
v. 24	102	lxviii (LXX). 2—4,		Zech. ix. 11		233
29	141	14—16, 22	246	Isa. i. 16ff.		195
vi—ix	50	lxxii. 10ff.	85	viii. 21f.		201
vi. 1—4	52, 56, 57,	lxxxi (lxxxii)	134	xiii. 21		83
	82, 121	lxxxvi. 13	232f.	xiv. 9		83
3	138	lxxxvii (lxxxviii). 4		12—21		84
4	78, 83	—10	246	xxiv. 18—22	84, 88
5	77	11	84	18—23	
6	57	18f.	246		236—240
vii.7	142	19	246	22		96
11	88	lxxxviii. 5ff.	232	xxvi. 14		84
23	76	cvii. 14ff.	233	19		233
viii. 21	77	cix (cx). 1	199	xxxiv. 13, xliii. 20 83
xxxvii. 35	232	cxviii. 82	39	xlv. 2		233
xlv. 4	165	cxix. 153ff.	233	l. 4—11		234
xlix. 30, l. 13	164	cxxix (LXX). 1	246	liii. 8ff.		232
Ex. xviii. 14	86	cxxix (cxxx). 8	225	10		216
Lev. vi. 30 (23),		cxxxvi (cxxxvii). 3		Jer. l. 39		83
xiv. 19	216		182	Book of Baruch
xvi	83, 88	cxliii (LXX). 3, 7	246	iii. 24—38		240f.
xvi. 3, 5, 27	216	Prov. iii. 25	133	27f,		244
Numb. viii. 8	216	ix. 18, xxi, 16	01	Ezech. i, x		72
Deut. i. 28	84	Job xxvi. 2—6	240	xxxvii	103, 206
iv. 10	28	5	83f.	xxxvii. 23		225
Jos. xiii. 12	83	xxviii. 2	28	Dan. iii		233
Judg. ix. 17	165	xxx. 29	83	iv. 10, 14		72
1 Sam. ii. 23	165	Wisd. ii	203	17 (14)		182f.
Ps. ii. 4	84	iii. 1	55	20		72
xv (xvi). 10	10, 31,	x. 1f.	38	vii. 14		85
	38, 55, 107	4	139	2 Macc. iv. 30	107
xvi. 10	232	4ff.	71			
xvii (LXX). 5—8,		xiv. 5	139, 142	Matt. iv. 23		120
17	246	Ecclus. xvi. 6ff. 71, 244		v. 16		133
xxi (LXX)	246	7	61	vii. 13f.		129
xxiv. 7	233	xxiv. 45	18	14		140
xxx (LXX)	246	xxxvi (xxxiii). 3 182f.		viii. 29		82
xxx (xxxi). 6	107	xliv. 16, xlix. 14		xi. 9ff.		102
xxxiii (xxxiv)	178	(16)	102	29f.		129
xxxix (xl). 7	216	Hos. xiii. 14	20, 233	xii. 29	20, 233
xli (LXX). 6,		Am. v. 1	164	39ff.	103, 233
8, 12	246	Mic. i. 8	83	40	10, 116, 233,

INDEX OF BIBLICAL QUOTATIONS

xii.	246	iii. 18	214	x. 1		142
43	61	v. 2	175	4		97
xiv. 36	142	vii. 20	168	31 ff.		182
xvi. 1	182	viii. 36	194	xi. 10		82
4	246	x. 42	205	xv. 3 f.		243
🝆 8	233	47	194	45		106
🝆 25—27	129	xi. 30	146	54		20
xvii	214	xv. 11	166	2 Cor. i. 12	180,	182
xxiv. 37 ff.	58, 69, 70	xv. 21	120	iii. 6		106
xxvi. 38	246	xvii. 3	214	iv. 2		180
xxvii. 34, 46	246	xxi. 16	166	vi. 15		200
51 ff.	20, 233	xxiii. 1	178 f., 182	viii. 21		182
Mark i. 7	31	xxiii. 8 f.	54, 61	x. 13		167
23, 26	61	24	142	xi. 12, 21		105
ii. 19	108	xxiv. 16	179 f., 182,	Gal. ii. 10		169
vi. 11	147		187	iv. 1 ff.		200
16	165	18	109	iv. 22 ff.		74
x. 38	245	xxvi. 6 ff.	168	v. 11		120
xiii. 9 ff.	134	12	109	Eph. i. 10		122
Luke iv. 44	120	23	214	21		200
vii. 3	142	Rom. i. 19 f.	89	ii. 2		200
viii. 31	82	ii. 1	108	16—18		218
xi. 29 f.	233	15	174	17		65
32	246	21	120	18		218
xii. 1	109	iv. 4	107	iii. 12		218
50	245	11 ff.	74	iv. 8 ff.	10, 116,	233
xvi. 26	38	17	166	9		233
xvii. 26 f.	69, 70	v. 2	194, 217	10		45
xviii. 8	176	vi	247	22, 24, 25		189
xix. 13	108	vi. 10	215	v. 22		222
xx. 38	75	vii. 19	167	vi. 5 ff.		182
xxii. 15	214	viii. 3	110, 216	Phil. i. 7		169
xxiii. 32 f.	212	10, 11	106	27		182
43	233	ix. 6 ff.	74	ii. 3—7		188
46	107	23 ff.	168 f.	10		33
xxiv. 37—39	54	x. 7	10, 233	15 f.		182
46	214	10	186	iii. 13		114
47	120	xiii	134, 178, 212	Col. ii. 8		200
John i. 15 f.	129	xiii. 1	222	14		121
v. 7	108	1 ff.	182	15	200,	234 f.
19, 19—29, 25	208	5	180, 222	18		222
vi. 14	172	12, 12—14	189	iii. 8, 10, 12		189
63	103	xiv. 1 ff.	179	22 ff.		182
viii. 9	174	9 116, 122, 205,		2 Thess. iii. 13		212
39 ff.	74		233	1 Tim. i. 5, 19		179
xi. 16	31	18	182	ii. 2 f.		182
xiv. 30	134	xv. 3	221	4		222
xvi. 18	166	1 Cor. i. 23	120	ii. 10		212
xvii. 3	165	ii. 6	134	iii. 16	45, 120,	122,
xviii. 30	212	6 ff.	200		126,	234
Acts i. 3	214	7	107	2 Tim. i. 6, 12		168
ii. 23 ff.	10, 223	7 ff.	121	ii. 9, iii. 17		212
24	38, 116, 233	iii. 15	142	iv. 1		205
36	38	v. 5	54	Tit. i. 10		227
27	55, 107, 116,	vi. 11	225	13		226
	233	viii	179	14 f.	188 f.,	227
40	143, 200	viii. 11 f.	182	16		212

274 INDEX OF BIBLICAL QUOTATIONS

Tit. ii. 1—10	226	3	194, 218	17—22	1—6,210,	
ii. 5, 9, 11	222	5	139, 196		220, 225, 228	
11—14	225—228	8	104, 138	18	28, 34, 54,	
iii. 1	212	9	225		94f., 99, 103—	
iii. 1 ff.	182	10	104		107, 117f.,	
1—8	222—224,	11	186, 203		127ff., 194,	
	228	11—iv. 19	177f.		213—219, 221,	
iii. 5	225	12	110, 133, 178,		223f., 245f.	
9	226		203, 211, 213,	18—20	31	
10	227		220, 226	18—21	30	
Philem. 10ff.	166	13	182	18—22	3, 5, 46,	
Hebr. i. 14	61	13ff.	178, 212		126, 234	
ii. 11	168	14	211, 223	19	1—4, 6, 7—51,	
18	110	15	133, 182, 212,		52—56, 59—61,	
iv. 12	190		223, 226		64—70, 90—92,	
v. 1, 3	216	16	186, 193		93—125, 126—	
vi. 17	110	18	129, 220, 222		136, 205, 209,	
vii. 14	167	18ff.	178		219, 231—247	
viii. 5	145	19	176ff., 181	19f.	33, 36, 213,	
ix. 9f.	145	19ff.	213, 221		221	
13f.	188	19—21	129	19—20a	34	
14	225	19—25	220—221,	19—22	2, 5, 94,	
23	145		225, 228		202	
24	144f.	20	212, 221, 223	19—iv. 6	14	
26	214	21	214, 218ff.,	20	70, 98f., 137	
28	215		224		—143, 224f.	
x. 1	194	21—25	94, 216	20—22	6, 136	
6, 8	216	22—25	221	21	6, 135, 137,	
10	168	23	204		142—148, 151f.,	
12, 18	216	25	218, 221, 224		156f., 162,	
22	178, 181, 187,	iii. 1	132f., 138, 222		172ff., 176,	
	225	1ff.	111, 178, 226		181—198, 202,	
26	216	1—6	180		225, 227, 245ff.	
xi. 5	102	5	222, 226	21c—22	198—	
6	194	5ff.	133, 178		201	
7	138	6	74, 133, 212,	22	53, 65, 91,	
xii. 1	189		223		121, 199ff., 225	
23	54	11	212	iv. 1	190, 193, 202,	
xiii. 11	216	13	130, 222, 225		214	
12	214	13ff.	133f., 213,	1ff.	95, 247	
18	179		220	1—5	202—204	
James i. 4	105	13—16	127—130,	1—6	202—210	
21	189		136, 211, 213,	4	110f., 133, 203	
1 Pet. i. 2	186		217, 219f.	5f.	70, 204—206	
6	110f.	14	130, 201	6	11f., 16, 18f.,	
10	104, 146f.,	14ff.	178		23, 29, 38, 45,	
	168	15	130f., 133,		49f., 54, 56,	
11f.	121		135, 204, 223		106, 119, 132,	
12	68, 104,	16	110f., 113,		204—210.	
	122		133, 176ff., 181,	7	70, 132, 138	
13	70		203, 211, 213,	14	203	
14	186		223, 226.	14ff.	178	
18	188	17	6, 127ff., 211	15	211	
18f.	218		—213, 217, 220,	17	70, 138, 203	
21	217		223	19	107, 223	
ii. 1	189	17—18	130f.,	v. 12	140	
2	134		202, 211—213	2 Pet. ii. 2	67	

INDEX OF BIBLICAL QUOTATIONS

ii 2f.	200	1 John ii. 25	152	xiv. 6	86
4	52, 54, 61, 67, 116, 122	Jude 6	52, 54, 58, 61, 67, 116, 122	xvi. 13	61
5	70, 96, 140, 143	7	58	xvii. 2	86
5f.	71	13	82, 84	xviii. 2	53, 61, 66
7	143	14	62, 101	xx. 3	67, 116
8	146	14f.	61, 64, 66f., 82	xx. 4	55
9f.	61	Rev. i. 18	20, 233	7	53, 66, 116
iii. 6f.	73	vi. 9	55	10	67
8	114	10	86	13	246